I Catch Killers

I Catch Killers

GARY JUBELIN

with Dan Box

HarperCollins*Publishers*

All dialogue and other direct speech in this book are taken from publicly available records tendered during the relevant court proceedings or, in some instances, from the memories of those involved. In particular, the dialogue with Gordon Wood is taken from records tendered during his 2008 trial. The material described as having been captured on both authorised and unauthorised listening devices used to record Paul is taken from records tendered in the local court proceedings involving Gary Jubelin during February 2020.

Dan Box is a Walkley Award–winning journalist who has worked for *The Australian*, as well as London's *The Sunday Times* and the BBC.

HarperCollins*Publishers*
Australia • Brazil • Canada • France • Germany • Holland • Hungary
India • Italy • Japan • Mexico • New Zealand • Poland • Spain • Sweden
Switzerland • United Kingdom • United States of America

First published in Australia in 2020
This edition published in 2021
by HarperCollins*Publishers* Australia Pty Limited
Level 13, 201 Elizabeth Street, Sydney NSW 2000
ABN 36 009 913 517
harpercollins.com.au

HarperCollins Publishers
Macken House, 39/40 Mayor Street Upper
Dublin 1, D01 C9W8, Ireland

A catalogue record for this book is available from the National Library of Australia.

ISBN 978 1 4607 5892 2 (paperback)
ISBN 978 1 4607 1264 1 (ebook)
ISBN 978 1 4607 8447 1 (audiobook)

Cover design by Darren Holt, HarperCollins Design Studio
Cover images: Gary Jubelin by Lindsay Moller / Newspix; all other images by shutterstock.com
Typeset in Bembo Std by Kirby Jones
Printed and bound in Australia by McPherson's Printing Group

MIX
Paper | Supporting responsible forestry
FSC® C001695

Dedicated to the memory of:

James Kelly
Eileen Cantlay
Martin Davidson
Bernadette Matthews
Colleen Walker-Craig
Evelyn Greenup
Clinton Speedy-Duroux
Barbara Saunders
Jayden March
Caroline Byrne
Terry Falconer
Michael Davies
Michelle Pogmore
Bob Ljubic
Ian Draper
Ryan Pringle
Matthew Leveson
William Tyrrell
Tori Johnson
Katrina Dawson
Courtney Topic
Mengmei Leng
Theresa Binge
Clint Starkey

and to all the other victims, their families and the cops who try to solve these cases.

The trauma ripples out.

Compassion leads to courage.
– Lao Tzu

Contents

Prologue
1

Round One
3

Round Two
111

Round Three
249

Postscript
390

Acknowledgments
391

PROLOGUE

This is Not Going to be Simple

'Fuck you, policeman!'

The voice comes through the closed front door beside which I am sheltering. 'We've got a warrant,' I shout back.

'Fuck off!' The man's voice gets louder and more violent.

'We're not going anywhere. Open the door.' *You're trapped in the fucking unit, stupid*, I think. *If you don't open the door, we're going to knock it down.*

'Fuck youse. Go on, get fucked!' he shouts.

I look across the doorway at the other detective who, like me, has his pistol drawn and his back flat against the wall. A tough unit who played reserve-grade footy and goes by the nickname Strongboy, his eyes tell me he's thinking the same as I am: *This is not going to be simple.*

Two other cops standing in the shadows of the stairwell are also waiting for my decision on how to play this. If only this fucking idiot would unlock the door, then I could turn, reach out and force it open. Then we'd be through it and inside his place in a few seconds.

Except, we don't know who is in there with him. And we don't know if he is armed.

'Just open up and talk to us,' I shout.

'Get fucked!' he shouts again from inside the unit.

'Drop the knife!' Another voice.

What's going on?

The quick sound of a gunshot.

Silence.

A woman screams.

We start kicking the door – only it doesn't buckle.

With Strongboy, I shoulder-charge the door, one at a time at first, then both of us together until it breaks off its hinges and falls down flat, sending the two of us crashing into the apartment.

Inside, a man's body is lying on the floor in front of us, with a long-bladed knife beside him.

The woman is on my left, bent over, still screaming.

In front of me is a policeman, still holding his gun.

Round One

Not Giving Up

Late 1960s

My father stands above me, forcing one of my arms back and up until it hurts, then forcing it further.

The easy thing would be to cry out.

Like every time he does this, it started off as a wrestle, the two of us grappling on the floor of our little house in North Epping, me in my pyjamas, a kid of five or six. Then he started twisting my arm behind my back until it feels as if the shoulder will pop free of its socket.

The pain makes me gasp.

'Do you give up?' he asks. It is a test.

'No,' I tell him.

Another twist.

I could beg him to stop, but Dad's trying to teach me something. Something he doesn't seem to need to teach his other children. I am his first son, and he wants me to be tough, like he is. He's teaching me to be a man because he knows that life is hard.

'Give up?'

'Not giving up.'

However much he hurts me, I won't cry out. I am as much a part of this as he is. I am not going to fail him.

He laughs and lets me go. I've passed the test. The pain subsides.

I look at him.

My dad, Kevin, can hold a room's attention. Sometimes it seems as if he's too large for any room to hold him. A tradie, Dad is working his way up and will one day retire as General Manager of the New South Wales Building Services Corporation, one of the last people to get to the top of the public service without formal qualifications. I want to be like him myself when I am older.

When he's at work, I know that Dad is smart, decent, a leader. When he's at home, he's different. If he's cranky then the house is full of tension, but if he's happy the whole house relaxes. During the summer evenings, he sits outside by the barbecue with men from work or with our neighbours late into the evening, playing cards and laughing. As kids, we don't understand what getting drunk is, but they seem to be happy and we like it when he smiles.

There are fun times, when Dad leads the athletics competitions at our birthday parties, leaping over lounges and hitting the walls, or when he pours so much petrol on the bonfire at Cracker Night that we all run, screaming, at the explosion.

Other times I think I shouldn't have to take this.

My father is a bully. You can dress it up, say that he's a hard man or whatever, or that it's just the way men are. But I've seen him control his temper when he wants to. He chooses to let it control him at home.

At home, I am often in trouble. I'm the kid who's crying in the corner, unable to get what he wants but too proud to back down. 'Men don't cry,' Dad says, leaning down and holding my shoulders with his big hands, his face close to mine. The way I understand it, he's telling me: *You don't show weakness*.

Sometimes, he also hits me. I think it's more out of temper than chastisement. There is never a closed fist, he never knocks my teeth out. It is a slap, or he'll grab me and throw me around.

Sometimes, he takes the feather duster to me, whipping me with the hard, wooden handle. One day, when I'm six or seven, we're having lunch in the backyard and I think about that feather duster. I decide to throw it on the barbecue.

My dad sees what I'm doing and warns me, 'I dare you.' I throw it right into the flames and watch it burn with satisfaction. It is gone.

He stands above me, suddenly enormous. He's angry, but to my surprise I realise he's also proud of my rebellion. Dad laughs. It's confusing.

I think my father is a decent person, despite all his anger.

Born in 1936, so long ago I can't imagine what the world was like then, and the youngest of four, he was called 'Tiny' by the rest of his family. His lost his mum when he was eight, not much older than I am when I destroy the feather duster. His elder sister married and started her own family when he was in his early teens, leaving Dad with just his brothers and his father. The three boys stole the few clean clothes that they had from each other.

My only memory of Dad's father is from the hospital before he died. Dad was a young man then himself. He told me about how hard his father found it, bringing up four children on his own.

One time, his father refused to let him in the house. Another, his father shot at him through the closed front door but missed.

Maybe Dad wants to make sure I'm better able to deal with what life is going to throw at me than he was. He didn't have a mother to teach him how to deal with his emotions, and so I like to think that when he grew up and thought, *What can I give my son?*, the only answer he came up with was to teach me toughness.

I know that he loves me, but neither of us ever says 'I love you' to the other. Instead, I learn my lessons. Don't show weakness. Swallow your anger and resentment. Let them burn inside you.

So when he asks me: 'Do you give up?' I reply, 'Not giving up.'

Not giving up, no matter how much it hurts.

That Looks Good

Early 1984

Two policemen run past as I'm having lunch with my girlfriend Debbie on the grass in Ryde Park, in Sydney's northwest suburbs. They're chasing someone down the main road towards the local shopping centre.

'That looks good,' I say to Debbie. She looks at me and frowns, but can't see what I'm thinking.

I'm five years out of high school and working as an electrician. It's all right. I go to work from Monday to Friday, then great, the week is over. On the weekends I surf, taking wild trips along the coast with mates, partying beside a fire on the beach at night, then camping out or sleeping on a mattress in the back of my Mitsubishi L300 Express van. I'm tall and thin, my skin is tanned and my unruly hair, which curls around my head on each side in a tumble, has grown long, with streaks of blond in it from the sun and saltwater.

I live my own life and tell myself that I do exactly what I want to. If I'm looking forward at all, then it's only to imagine a succession of other surf weekends stretching out in front of me. Debbie is my first steady girlfriend, she and I have been together since the end of school and we are going good. She is a little wild, like I am.

One day, maybe, we'll probably get married.

Only, something pulls at me like an underwater current. Sometimes, when I'm paddling back towards the shore after a surf, it feels like life onshore is just a little empty. I'm free of responsibilities, but still my happiness is dictated too often by the ocean: I ride high when the waves are good, then crash into depression when the conditions are not right.

I guess I'm looking for some deeper meaning. Something to fill those days between the weekends. Except, at 22, I don't know what that looks like.

Watching those two cops chasing that crook, I feel that pull again, but stronger. I don't want to come to terms with a life spent in the building game. I don't want to do the same thing, day in, day out for 20 years. I can do it if I have to but nothing about the prospect excites me. I like the thought of catching bad guys, just like I grew up hating bullies. Staring down the empty road, where the two cops have turned a corner and run out of sight, I find I like the thought of having purpose.

After lunch, back at work, I tell one of the other blokes about seeing the foot chase.

He grins. 'Mate, I'm just about to join the cops myself.'

He has all the application papers on him. He gets them out and starts showing me what I need to fill in where. It is exciting. We are feeding off each other. Being a cop beats sitting amid the dust of the construction site getting ready to go back into the ceiling cavity and start crawling around in the dust and dirt fixing the wiring in place.

Both of us want more from life, we tell each other.

The next day I go to the local police station at Eastwood and get my own application forms. Suddenly I'm leaving Debbie in Sydney and driving my surf van down the Hume Highway, heading inland, away from the beaches where I've spent all my weekends, to the New South Wales Police Academy in Goulburn.

I fight a battle with my feelings the whole way there.

Have I sold out? I've been enjoying freedom, I think. I surf, I drink, I get into a few fights. My nose is slightly crooked from where it got busted during a brawl on the Gold Coast one New Year's Eve. The cops are not my favourite people. For starters, I don't like authority – I ask too many questions. The people I look up to do not wear uniforms, they're surfers, who've made a life out of doing what they want to do.

I can't be a cop.

I drive on, staring out at the low scrub on either side of the empty highway. But then, I've always liked the idea of being tough and having discipline. Maybe it's growing up with a strict father, but I crave it. When I was younger, I thought about joining up and becoming a soldier, although I never did it. I like the thought of being part of something bigger than I am.

I have these two parts to my character. The surf bum and the kid who refuses to show weakness. They're both a part of me, I'm not one or the other, like how some of the older hippies I've hung out with on surfing trips talked about yin and yang. The light and dark. I don't really understand it, but it seems to make sense.

I think about turning the van around, then hear my father's voice, or something like it. I remember how he used to look at my school reports and tell me they weren't good enough. How I felt like I could never do enough to please him.

Running a hand through my hair, which is now cut short, ready for the academy, I tell myself, *If I'm going to go through with this, then I'm going to give it everything.*

I remember what Dad taught me.

Do you give up?

Never.

I drive on down the highway.

***

The squat accommodation blocks at the academy in Goulburn are as bleak as the bushland that surrounds them. It's January 1985 and the summer sun seems to have bleached the life out of everything.

The little window in my bedroom faces the boiler tower. From outside, I can hear the sound of marching feet as new recruits are drilled on the parade ground.

When my turn comes, I line up for inspection and the instructors walk along the line of wannabe police officers, stopping only to shout at us. My collar isn't straight. My spit-polished boots aren't shiny enough. My hair is still not short enough, so they send me to the barbers, who cut it even shorter. As the days pass, these inspections are a regular routine. 'Jubelin, what are you doing?' becomes a familiar cry.

This treatment breaks you down. Makes you conform. I learn that, at first, you ask yourself: *Why am I marching round this oval in the middle of the day?* Later, you learn the answer is: *Because it's an order.* Eventually you stop asking the question.

In our first week we have a gym session, working in pairs. My partner, Bill, is doing the leg press, lifting a stack of weights, and starts to shake with exhaustion. An instructor puts his hand into the weight stack and says to Bill, 'Drop it and you'll crush my fingers.' I'm impressed. That is hardcore. Bill manages another repetition.

Nearby, another of the recruits collapses and starts throwing up. The instructors make him do press-ups over his own vomit.

Fucking fantastic, I think. It's weird, I've given up my freedom, and found this is exactly what I wanted. It's yin and yang. The physicality of the endless drills seems real, while being an electrician who went surfing when he wanted feels like a dream from which I have awakened. It is as if the cops know who I really am, better than I did myself.

The instructors watch as I take my turn on the leg press, pushing myself to my limits. Each exercise they give us, I aim to finish first or, at worst, second among my recruit intake.

If you want someone who will not give up, then I'm that person, I tell them silently, straining at the gym equipment.

'OK, Jubelin, maybe you can ease up now,' they tell me.

***

As much as I am loving my new life, it's difficult being apart from Debbie.

She's a year younger than me, slight and slender, with long dark hair and a smile that makes you want to smile along with her. We went to the same primary school, then separate high schools, then became friends again after school was over. I liked the fact she was a little bit rebellious. During a surfing holiday with mates around Byron Bay, we drank and partied, slept in cars or on beaches, and realised the two of us had another shared history from when we were kids; both of us had gone bushwalking separately with our fathers when each family got lost. The two groups found each other in the bush and worked together to find our way home, making it back well after dark had fallen.

After that surf trip to Byron, Debbie and I went on another one with friends near Palm Beach, in the north of Sydney. We lit a huge fire and fell asleep around it, and by the morning she and I were sharing a blanket.

When we started going out, I realised just how smart Debbie was.

She'd done a lot better in her HSC than I had, but seemed to settle into working as a PA for an insurance company. Her parents were older than mine, they'd grown up in the Great Depression and were farmers, so I got the feeling they didn't want her taking risks. Better to get a secure job, they said. Stay living in the suburbs. Better that than chase your dreams.

Still, Debbie was all for it when I talked about joining the cops. She could tell something wasn't right with me working in the building trade and we talked about how Goulburn was only a few hours away from Sydney, where she has an apartment with a friend, and that I wouldn't be at the academy forever. It's only a few months, I told her. I'd drive up and see her at weekends.

Lying alone at night, I wake up and I miss her. I've told her that I love her, though we're still young, and looking out the window at the shadow of the water tower, I often think about exactly what love means. When morning comes, I wonder what she's doing at the same time as we are marching around the parade ground and later sitting in the lecture hall or practising arrests in the mocked-up shops and houses. I hope that she is happy. It feels as if I care more about her happiness than my own. *Maybe that is love*, I think.

Being away from home makes me realise how contained our life was. In Epping, I could throw a net over Debbie, my friends, my work and everything I knew before joining the police force. At the academy, we spend hours being trained by veterans who've seen the worst the world can offer. I change, in little ways that I barely notice.

Debbie notices, though. Towards the end of my training, I drive to Sydney for a weekend and she tells me she's met someone else, a surfer, during a holiday in Bali.

'A surfer?' I ask her. 'I'm a surfer.' She says she wants to break up. The two of us should have some time apart, she tells me.

I feel adrift, as if I'm starting a new life and just beginning to realise what the world has out there, but Debbie is my lifeline back to my old self. I don't want to break the tie between us, I say, but she doesn't agree. We argue. I have to drive back to Goulburn on the Sunday without any resolution.

Along the way, I try to understand what happened.

Over the past year, Debbie spent months in hospital for an operation on her back, then months longer in a plaster cast after she was discharged. For a while we weren't sure if she would walk again. After she did, I guess the world had opened up for her just like it had for me in Goulburn.

I worry about whether it was me leaving that made her start to look for something else.

In my accommodation block, there is only one phone, in the foyer. I use it to call her, every evening, trying to win her back, while all the other recruits are listening.

I tell Debbie I understand why she fell for this surfer, but that I haven't changed. I'm still the same free spirit who she first fell in love with. 'I could be the surfer you met in Bali,' I tell her. I'm just as carefree as he was, only our circumstances right now are different. Just because I've given myself to the cops, doesn't mean I'm a different person, I argue.

Eventually, it works.

***

On 24 April 1985 – my 23rd birthday – my parents and Debbie drive down to watch us march in step across the academy parade ground in our uniforms, then throw our black police caps into the air. We've graduated.

Mum hugs me. I get a kiss from Debbie, which comes as a relief because I'm still not completely sure where she and I are and was uncertain even if she would make the journey. The two of us have our photo taken holding hands. I'm grinning.

Dad's not the type to grin in photographs or make speeches, but I can see he's proud of me also.

As we stand beside each other for the camera, I notice that, particularly in my new policeman's hat, I tower over him.

I Look Like a Policeman

26 April 1985: first day in

The blue uniform feels hot, made of a thick, scratchy material, and I know I will sweat inside it. Beneath the jacket is a stiff blue shirt with metal buttons. A blue tie that clips in place, so nobody can use it to strangle me. Blue trousers. Black leather boots. A black leather trouser belt and then a gun belt over it.

My handcuffs sit inside a pouch on my left side, next to a baton ring, from which will hang the 22-inch forged-steel club I'll be given when I arrive at the police station for the first time this morning. My gun holster is on my right. I pick up the .38 Smith and Wesson revolver I was issued with on my last day at the police academy and load it with six bullets, each in its individual chamber. I carry six more spare, in case – in case of what? I have no real idea of what the uniform will ask of me.

The peaked policeman's cap sits on the bed, waiting for me to pick it up. It seems ridiculous and foreign, here in the spare bedroom of my parents' house, where I am staying.

I put it on. Wanting to see how I look, I walk into the tiled bathroom, where there is a big recessed mirror across the full width of the basin.

Yeah, I look the part, I tell myself, staring at my reflection. The punishing gym sessions they put us through at the academy mean I'm broader than I was before my time there, and fitter. My face still has some of that young man's softness to it, not like the faces of the instructors there, all veterans who taught us how to make arrests, shoot and drive at speed, and whose faces were hard and lined with everything they'd seen. But that will change.

I look like a policeman.

I see the pistol sitting in its holster at my hip and wonder how quickly I can draw it. In the mirror, I'm a real detective: I'm Dirty Harry, 'Sonny' Crockett in *Miami Vice* or 'Mac' MacKay in *Homicide*. I grab the pistol, bring my right hand up and clip the bathroom basin, knocking the weapon from my grip. It clatters onto the floor tiles.

Shit!

Panic.

Silence. No one in the house has noticed.

It's OK.

I take a breath. I haven't shot myself or put a bullet through the mirror. How would I explain if it had gone off, before I'd even arrived at work on my first morning?

I bend down to pick up the gun, more carefully this time, then straighten up to take another look at my reflection.

I am not yet a policeman.

16-1

April 1985: first week in

I'm sent to work as a probationary constable in 16 Division, based at the police station in Hornsby and covering a long slice of northern Sydney between Cowan and the Hawkesbury River, reaching down to Pennant Hills, Dural to the west and Turramurra on its eastern side. On my first day, I realise how the uniform changes the way others look at me when I step out to cross the road and the traffic stops. Soon, I get used to kids staring at me in the street, and adults either looking to me for help or with suspicion.

After leaving the academy, I'm paired with a 'buddy', Tony, who's about five or six years ahead of me, so has already experienced everything that I'm about to and can help me understand it. I'm lucky he's a good teacher and I try to learn.

On the night shifts, bringing in some local thug who's shirtless, spitting, screaming and twisting in his handcuffs, I watch the reactions of the cops around me. Sometimes, if the right station sergeant is on duty, I'm inspired. These guys can talk the man in the handcuffs down with a few words. They're battle-scarred but they still have compassion.

You're the cop I want to be, I tell these sergeants silently.

After six weeks, I start working with whoever is on the roster, which sometimes means I'm one of two probationary constables sent out together in the police truck, both of us hoping that the other has had longer on the job, so will have a better understanding of how to handle anything that happens.

In a few months, I am the senior officer inside the truck, with another nervous newbie fresh out of the academy sitting beside me and staring through the windscreen at the darkness as we drive out to start another night shift.

***

The veterans who taught us at the academy said there is really no way to prepare you for what you'll see and do when you put on the blue uniform. Instead, you have to live it.

During 1985, I live it. That means I see a lot of dying.

***

One rainy afternoon, we get a call over the police radio about a traffic accident where petrol is still leaking from the damaged car, meaning it might catch fire at any moment. When we arrive, we see the driver's gone through traffic lights and crashed. His feet are trapped inside the wreckage. We go to help him but the car explodes. There's nothing we can do to stop the fire or get him out and so we're forced to watch the poor man burn to death. We wait there in the rain for hours before his body is recovered. We drive back and I shower, trying to wash away the smell of cooking flesh. At dinner time, an older cop fries up a steak. I cannot eat.

***

One Saturday, I'm looking forward to finishing a night shift when we're called to another traffic accident and race towards it, siren wailing. This driver, too, is trapped inside his car. He looks to be about the same age I am. The paramedics ask if I can climb inside the wreckage to hold some of their equipment while they work to save him. I am centimetres from his broken body, thinking how only a few minutes ago my greatest concern was looking forward to getting some sleep. The ambos can't stop the blood. He dies. I stare at him, realising just how fragile life is.

***

Another Saturday, and this time all I'm focusing on is finishing my shift in time to play soccer later. A sports car crashes and rolls at nearby Pennant Hills, and I'm told to go to the morgue and sign in the driver's body, which means making sure his personal belongings are collected and recorded, including any jewellery and clothing. We roll him over and I recognise his face. We were mates. He was in the year below me at school. We played water polo together.

***

A telex arrives at the police station, saying an Australian has been killed overseas and I am told to drive out and knock on the family's door and deliver the news. A woman answers. I'm so caught up in worrying about the process I'm supposed to follow that I don't think about its impact. Instead, I stand there and say bluntly: 'I'm sorry to inform you that your son is dead.' She collapses and lies there, crumpled, screaming. I stare at her. I've never been this close to grief before, and it is overwhelming.

***

My first arrest is for 'avail railway fare' – someone fails to pay for their train ticket, then runs away when challenged. By luck, a witness happens to know the offender. I go to his house and, thinking I am following my training, caution him, make the arrest then call it in over the radio from the police truck, giving our callsign: '16-1.'

'16-1,' the operator answers.

'16-1. Returning to Hornsby Police Station with someone on board.' I feel proud.

Only, I haven't realised such a minor offence doesn't actually require an arrest and should be dealt with more simply instead by issuing a written summons to attend court. The first I sense that I've done something wrong is when we get back to the station and the charge room officer looks at me strangely. By luck, before I can make a goose of myself, a knockabout senior constable walks past and says, 'Well played, that bloke is a shithead. Gutsy call locking him up.'

It turns out he's a local hoodlum, who's caused us no end of problems. My ignorance turns out to be a positive because, as the story grows, people start to look at me like I'm a serious policeman.

Soon after, I see my first murder. I work the tape, meaning it's my job to stand in the driveway just outside the blue and white plastic ribbon strung around the crime scene and check who enters and leaves it. I stand there for hours, sweating inside my uniform, watching the detectives walk in and out in their sharp suits and sports jackets.

They have a swagger to them. *There's an idea*, I think. They're older, and to a rookie seem to inhabit a different world – loud-mouthed, tough guys who make their own decisions. I'm still a probationary constable, the lowest rank in the police force, meaning I do what I'm told each day when I turn up at work. For me, being a cop is simple. We chase crooks. We run towards danger. It gives me a sense of purpose when I wake up in the morning but I do not overthink it.

As part of my year-long probation, I get to spend a week with the detectives. Unlike the bare muster room we uniformed police file into at the start of every shift, the detectives' office is crowded with typewriters and stacks of paper. They seem to come and go when they want to. On the few times I've been in there before, to talk about a job, they're always sitting around, playing cards and smoking. Then someone would look at me and make some smartarse comment, and I'd stand there mute, feeling inadequate.

This morning, two detectives, Mick and Glen, ask me if I want to go for a drive. Glen is a solid, muscular unit with a bald head and a face that's been busted up from boxing. He's just arrived at Hornsby on a transfer and Mick wants to show him around.

We're driving near Berowra, where the Pacific Highway leaves the city, when a call comes over the radio about a stolen car full of known offenders. These are bad guys, heading our way, and it's obvious even to me, listening wide-eyed from the back seat, that we're going to get caught up in what's about to happen.

We see the car come gunning it towards us. Mick, who used to be a highway patrol officer and knows how to drive, swings our car through a handbrake turn and comes up right behind them.

It's the type of chase you see on television. We race south through Mount Colah, Asquith and Hornsby, as I try not to flinch at the near-misses with other cars.

At Waitara, a highway patrol car pulls out in front of the stolen car. The bad guys try to swerve but do not make it, the two cars collide and our car smashes into the back of both.

Police arrive from everywhere with guns. One cop uses his baton to break the stolen car's window and drag out the driver.

The men inside are arrested, at gunpoint. They're driven off. Standing amid the chaos, feeling the fear and excitement wash out of my stomach, leaving only an empty, sickened feeling, I think about how we chased that car for 13 kilometres and risked our lives and got a result.

If this is what detectives do at work, then I want to be part of it.

***

But there are other things I want to be sure of first. If breaking up with Debbie during my time at the police academy changed the way I looked at her, then the months since have only brought us closer.

Some of our friends have got engaged. It feels like this is how life is lived in Sydney's suburbs; you find a girl, go out, get engaged, then get married. I don't think to ask if there are any other options. Debbie and I have been together almost five years now.

As 1985 draws to an end, I ask her to marry me. She says yes.

I love her. I'm so happy.

Debbie's parents throw us an engagement party at their house in Epping, on the night a freak storm hits the suburb. Her family have lived there for 20 years and the house has never flooded before but now it's raining so hard the ceiling fills up with water. Dad, along with some of my tradie mates, say it might bring the roof down, so we set about making holes in the Gyprock to drain out the rainwater.

It's fun. We laugh. We're in our early twenties, too young to care that it might be an omen.

Too young to know anything about the responsibility I'll need for married life.

On my buck's night, there's around 30 of us drinking in a pub in the city centre, who walk outside and find ourselves facing the Sydney headquarters of the Church of Scientology. A close mate joined the Church six months before and disappeared. *He should be here on my buck's night*, I think, so we stand there, spilling across the footpath, chanting for the Church to free him.

Other people join in and the shouting gets louder. I think it's a good idea to use some of my police training and form the crowd into an arrowhead formation, then lead them as we burst through the front doors of the building.

I'm standing inside, directing traffic with a schooner in my hand when I first hear the sirens. Then I'm in a wrist lock, then in the back of a paddy wagon.

This isn't good.

I see a sergeant and say, 'Hi mate, this is my buck's night,' thinking that will be enough for him to let us go.

He doesn't answer.

I try again. 'Sorry, mate, I'm in the job.' *I'm a policeman.*

'I'm not your mate,' he says, pointing to the stripes on his uniform. 'And you're a fucking idiot.' He looks at me in silence for a moment, while I realise he is right. I'd treated this like harmless fun, the kind of wild times I used to have in my old life.

The sergeant says, 'If I let you out of here, you and your idiot mates better be gone within five minutes or you're all getting locked up.'

'Perfect,' I say, scrambling out of the truck.

I could have lost my career for this, I think, sobering up. As Debbie and I plan our wedding over the following months, I realise that old life is gone. I'm not a young man any longer.

Afraid That I Will Fail Her

Late 1960s

We live in one of the new red-brick housing estates being built in North Epping, on the northern edge of Sydney. It's 1960s suburban white Australia. The little lady stays at home while the man is out working. On Saturdays the men go to the pub and on Sundays the church bells ring to call the kids to Sunday school. I have no interest in the lessons, though I do like the Bible illustrations with their vivid colours. Adam and Eve. How they both ate the apple, gaining the knowledge of good and evil, and then fell. Their children, Cain and Abel. How Cain committed the first murder when he killed his brother.

One day at home when I am six or seven, I find a black and white photograph from before I was born, of Mum wearing a winner's sash at a heat of the Miss Gold Coast competition. She tells me she was on holiday with a friend at the time. She didn't expect to win, but when she did, the beauty pageant organisers drove her around the Gold Coast in a convertible. When she got home, Dad refused to let her go back and compete in the final.

It is almost impossible to imagine Mum had a life before she had us kids. She's the person who gives us breakfast, dresses us, takes us to school, and then is there to greet us when we burst into the house again in the afternoon. She makes our dinner, sits with us to do our homework and puts us to bed. In the evenings, she works at the knitting machine in our crowded living room, making us clothes. But because she's always there, we take those things for granted.

Mum's softer than Dad is. She's the one we cuddle up to when he's away on work trips. When he's at home, he sometimes dominates her, which upsets me. There are some things that I don't like to think about, like when I'm 10 or 11 and we go on holidays to the New South Wales South Coast. Afterwards, when we get home, something inside Dad explodes.

My sister Karen and I cower behind the heavy bifold doors that separate the dining room from the kitchen, peering around them at where Dad is getting angry and smashing plates. Mum is crying, she pushes him away, only that doesn't stop him. Outside, it's a peaceful summer afternoon. The sun is shining. But in the kitchen it is dark, with heavy, timber cupboard doors and furniture.

The argument continues. It's getting worse. I know I have to do something, so I walk into the kitchen and stand there, silent, staring ahead of me. I want to step between them, thinking that I should be the big man who stands up to my father, but I'm frozen with fear. So I watch him, feeling helpless.

Afterwards, I tell myself that I was a coward. That I needed to protect Mum. That what Dad did was bad, but he's not a bad person. It's confusing. He's my dad and I love him.

I'm not sure who makes the call, but Mum's dad, Charles, turns up and takes us away for a week to live with him. I look up to him without question. He boxed when he was younger and has a fighter's busted nose. We play together, with him kneeling on the floor and teaching me how to throw my punches.

During that week, he tells my mum, 'Don't worry', and points at me. 'He won't be able to do that shortly with him there,' he says.

He means that I am growing up. That I will be able to protect her. He shows me how to stand with my right foot behind the left one and how to lift my heel and twist my hips to put some power behind my fist.

I Want to Become a Detective

21 November 1986: one year in

Debbie and I marry in a church service in Beecroft, near where we both grew up in Sydney. She wears white, I wear a suit with a bow tie and my groomsmen are my brother, Jason, a schoolmate called David and Mark, my elder sister Karen's ex who used to take me surfing growing up. When Debbie and I walk out of the church, I look up and see a group of drunken mates who've climbed up to sit on the awning of a nearby bottle shop. I laugh as they start cheering.

Debbie's still doing secretarial work and, after my year on probation, I've recently been back to the police academy for six weeks' secondary training to become a full constable. This time, being apart was easier. The relationship feels solid. Neither of us doubt that we are meant to spend our lives together.

We're renting an apartment behind a pub, and when we're not at work we do a lot of partying. We honeymoon at Noosa Heads, on Queensland's Sunshine Coast and then, in 1988, we follow Sydney's suburban expansion and buy a house further out, in Dural, where my parents have also moved.

Nobody's talking about children yet, but we know they will happen.

On the weekends I turn up at my parents' house with one of my mates, wearing boardshorts and usually hungover after a night on the drink, to play doubles against Dad and his partner, who wear proper tennis whites, as if they've just stepped off the courts at Wimbledon. The four of us have some epic battles; the older men are better players and my mate and I are often playing not to lose, but I like that feeling. It brings out something deep inside me. A determination. I find I'm often at my best when the match is going against me.

Facing Dad across the net also marks a change in our relationship. We are men now, I'm married and starting out in a career, just like he did. I've started to appreciate the responsibilities he carried as a husband and to leave my own childhood behind me when, too often back then, I hated him. Instead, I now remember how he was always there when I needed him.

He is my mate. I have his name – Gary Kevin Jubelin.

One weekend, walking past the Dural squash courts, I see a sign advertising a kickboxing class. *That looks cool*, I think. I did judo briefly as a kid but lost interest, though I've watched countless Bruce Lee and other martial arts movies over the years since. I also remember the boxing moves my grandfather Charles taught me and follow the sport so keenly even Debbie's started to get into it – on the first day of our honeymoon, we watched Mike Tyson win his first world title on the TV in our motel room.

I go inside. A woman's leading the kickboxing class, and judging by size, my first thought is that I could knock her out. But there's a confidence about her that catches my interest. I sign up and quickly learn she could knock me out any time she wants to. At first, watching her fight, it's like watching Bruce Lee, as if she has superpowers. But the classes focus on drills, not one on one combat. We line up and practise how to kick and punch. I realise the secret. It's not a superpower. Anyone can do it if they're prepared to put in the work. It's simply repetition, repetition, repetition.

A class a week turns into four or five. I love the discipline and the physical exertion. I learn to love the feeling of fear and excitement when you do face your opponent. In those moments, nothing matters, not what is going on at work or home. You can live a thousand lives in each sparring session and, afterwards, I learn to love the feeling that you have survived, when you are soaked in sweat, your breath feels hot and your mind races in wild exhilaration.

The classes become more advanced and the instructors start to talk about the mental side of the martial arts. We line up on the mats in horse stance, legs bent at the knees, thighs at 90 degrees to the floor, until our thigh muscles are screaming. The instructors tell us to not fight the pain. Let your mind wander, they say. Let the pain pass out of your body with your breathing.

I feel myself becoming stronger. My uniform is growing tighter round the shoulders. I like the confidence that comes with knowing I can handle myself when someone comes at me during an arrest, or on a Friday night when everyone's been drinking. Knowing how to fight helps you deal with some of the fear that comes with being a policeman.

***

The uniform itself does not protect you, especially in some of the isolated semi-rural areas we cover, like Dural, Arcadia and

Wisemans Ferry, where there's no radio contact. During night shifts, I wonder what is hiding in the shadows. Fear is a familiar feeling now, a mix of adrenaline and excitement, which leaves your stomach churning afterwards.

Even in daylight, that feeling can be on you in a moment, like when you're surfing and a wave crashes down and tumbles you beneath the water. That's how it feels on the morning of 4 August 1987, when the car radio crackles '16-1' and then: 'Armed hold-up in progress.'

Armed robberies are a serious problem for the cops. They seem to happen all the time. People get shot. Three months ago, in May, a man was shot and killed during the robbery of his jewellery store in Cabramatta, southwest Sydney. Right now, Australia's most wanted man, Russell 'Mad Dog' Cox, is an armed robber and on the run after escaping prison. The radio tells us to head to the nearby Hornsby branch of the National Australia Bank and my first thought is, *Mad Dog might be there ahead of us.*

Pulling up, we see a red Toyota Hilux has driven straight through the bank's plate-glass window.

We watch as a policeman seems to fly out of the building and land in the shattered glass on the sidewalk. Has he been shot? I think: *It's on here.*

I draw my gun and run into the building.

Inside, whoever's robbed the bank is gone. A young teller is bleeding badly from a head wound and I'm not sure he will make it. Witnesses tell us how the Hilux hit him when it smashed its way in, driven by two men, both armed with guns, who must have been sitting outside, waiting for somebody to open up the night safe.

A photographer arrives. The robbery will make the morning paper. Mad Dog has not been seen, it seems, although that doesn't stop the journalists from saying he might have been involved somehow. It turns out nobody got shot either. That policeman I saw had tripped and fallen through what was left of the window.

With no one to arrest, I put out a description of the two men and the car they were seen driving away in over the police radio, then stand guard on the scene until the detectives get here. It's only after, as the fear drains away, that I get that familiar sick sensation in my stomach.

***

There are other arrests. One night shift, we discover a firearms store's been set alight. A witness gives me a description of who lit it and, remembering somebody I pulled up just the day before who looked like that, we talk our way into a house and find an Aladdin's cave of stolen jewellery and electronics.

Soon after this, Glen asks me if I've considered coming over to join the detectives.

'Yeah, I've considered it,' I say, almost too shy to admit it's what I want. Being a detective means more of the excitement I'd seen with Glen during that car chase. It means more responsibility for solving crimes, not just dealing with whatever trouble comes your way on the night shift. The detectives are the elite, I think, and I would never have the front to knock on their office door and say, 'Hey, I want to join you.'

I'm also uncertain because Glen recently chewed me out in public for making a sloppy entry in the occurrence pad, where we record what's happened on each shift and which hangs by the front counter of the police station. It is a pain to fill it in, you have to put the sheet of paper into the typewriter with another carbon sheet behind it to make a copy and start the whole thing again to correct a mistake. But I misspelt a word and Glen picked up on it.

'The occurrence pad is what you're judged by. This is the first report of a crime. Take some pride in your work,' he told me. I knew he was right, and said it. So I'm surprised to now receive an invitation to step up and work beside him.

But, even though I want it, I'm conflicted. The detectives wear plain clothes and part of me wants to stay loyal to the mates I have in uniform.

We've been through so much together in the two years since I joined up – faced life and death and grief and triumph, sat in police cars at night talking shit until the sun came up, rolled around with crooks in the streets and gone into houses together without knowing what was waiting for us. Every time, I knew I could rely on the guy in blue beside me.

Leaving all that and putting on a suit will feel like a betrayal.

I seek advice from an older cop, Russell, who used to work as a Homicide detective and who manages my soccer team. I've loved the game since I was a kid, and it suits me. I play defence and, while I'm not the most skilful player on the pitch, I make sure you have to work to beat me.

'Go for it,' he tells me. 'It's a good thing.'

With his blessing, I allow myself to be excited and can't stop thinking about a move to the detectives' office. Next time we play a soccer match, I slide into a tackle, mis-time it and my opponent comes down hard with his knee on the back of my head. It knocks me out.

I came round, stunned, but feeling euphoric. As my head clears, I realise why.

That's it, I think. *I'm going to be a detective.*

I'll Fight You

1973

Not long after we spend the week with my grandfather Charles, Dad and I are blueing in the driveway, in full view of all the surrounding houses. Dad wants me to register for the upcoming soccer season, I love the game but don't fancy the commitment. I just want to spend my weekends with my mates.

'I don't want to play soccer this year,' I say to him.

'You gotta play,' he tells me.

'I've got other stuff I want to do. I'm not playing.'

'You're bloody playing.'

'No I'm not.'

He screams at me.

'I'm not playing,' I say again.

He lashes out, but I square up and tell him that I'm ready to fight him.

He looks at me and something shifts between us.

***

I still want to be like Dad when I am older – he works so hard, and can put his hand to anything. But nothing I do is good enough, no matter how hard I try to impress him.

When he watches me play soccer, he never says that I played well. Instead it is: 'You shouldn't have let in that goal.' If I bring home a school report, he'll find the one subject where I've done badly.

One night, he comes into my room while I'm sitting at my desk and asks, 'What are you doing?'

'Doing my homework.'

He leans over to look and doesn't think it's good enough. I say something and he grabs my hair, smashing my face into the desk.

I tell myself it doesn't hurt.

***

I have my first organised fight, with a kid from school called Trevor. He and I play soccer together and have a disagreement over something.

Trevor's not the type you'd want to fight – he's one of those kids who look like they're carved from granite – but neither of us will back down, and so it is decided we will settle this in person when the school day is over.

We agree to meet at North Epping Oval, near Trevor's house. It's out of my way, so if I wanted, it would be easy for me not to show up. I could just make my way home and go nowhere near the oval. Only my pride will not allow it.

I'm frightened, walking there alone, still in my school uniform, but am not about to show it. Instead, I accept I am going to get my lumps. When I get there, Trevor's waiting.

A group of other kids is crowded near the roller on the pitch to watch us, but there's not much we can show them. There is no skill or science to our fighting. A few punches are thrown. We wrestle each other to the ground and grapple in the dirt. I'm in a headlock when Trevor hits me in the face. His punches hurt.

In that moment, every sense is stronger, the red blood on our hands and faces brighter, our classmates' shouts are clearer, the smell of earth and grass being ground into our skin more powerful than I have ever sensed them.

We punch each other out, then something breaks us up and we each look at the other. My shirt is torn, my eye swollen and my nose is bleeding. I don't think I'm the winner, but I've held my own. I'm proud of myself.

Afterwards, I think our differences are settled, particularly as we play soccer together the following weekend. But I'm wrong.

I never tell anyone about this, but a year later, after school is finished for the summer, I walk out of the shops in North Epping and see Trevor on his bike across the road. He calls me out: 'Come on, come on, I'll fight you!'

This time his aggression scares me. I say nothing and don't move. I am frozen.

He throws some more abuse, then turns his back on me and rides away.

I watch him go. I feel relieved but also shameful. His family are moving north, to Newcastle, a couple of hours away, so this will be the last time I see him. Maybe if there had been a crowd watching us, I would have acted differently, I would have fought him. But I didn't.

It makes me doubt myself. Am I a tough guy, or do I only care about my reputation? Am I actually a coward? Have I let myself down? Have I let my dad down, even though he didn't see me?

Trevor is gone. I look around. No one has seen us.

I decide never to talk about it, ever. It is my secret.

I'll think about that moment constantly. It drives me. It dictates how I live my life from that day forward.

If a Killer Offers Me His Hand

1987: two years in

I start working as an A, meaning I'm wearing plain clothes and have a desk in the Hornsby detectives' office but haven't yet qualified as a designated detective. My first partner is Jim Williams.

A decade older than me, Jim's in his mid-30s but looks younger and is a dead-set charmer. If Jim wants people to like him, then they like him, whether it's crooks or women or whoever. He knows his law and makes sure he's across every detail of our cases. He pushes me hard, so hard that it's exhausting, and I like that. It's like when I play soccer, what I lack in skills I can make up for in commitment.

Best of all, Jim teaches me to interview a suspect.

'You need to be good at this,' Jim tells me, 'because we rarely have much in the way of forensic evidence.' This is the late 1980s; fingerprints are manually checked, there are hardly any CCTV cameras, and a bloodstain might tell us a victim's blood type but little else. Instead, Jim says, the measure of a true detective is how he or she can talk to victims and witnesses, and how they get confessions.

As the months pass, the different people that we interview start to blur in the memory, but each one starts the same. Jim and I stand together outside the door of the small, dark interview room at Hornsby. Inside, our suspect will be sitting at a bare table with two more empty chairs. They might be a man or a woman. They might be a hardarse or a softhead – someone who thinks that they're a hardarse when they're not. Depending on the crime, they might be handcuffed to the table beside the overflowing ashtray.

Hopefully, they are already uncomfortable. The room has no windows. They don't know what is coming next.

'How are we going to carry ourselves this time?' I'll ask Jim.

Every time, our approach to the interview is different. Sometimes we'll walk into the room in suits and other times in shirtsleeves. A proper crook might call for something different from a first-time offender, or someone who was driven by anger or who did something that was simply stupid. One person might need gentleness, another flattery. Sometimes Jim and I are good cop–bad cop, sometimes we're good cop–good cop and at others we are bad cop–bad cop together.

'I think I'll wear my shoulder holster in on this one,' Jim might say. Weapons on or weapons off is a conscious decision. If we have a softhead, a shoulder holster might just be enough to impress them. After all, it is what detectives wear in the cop shows on television. As Jim explains it, during an interview, we are not allowed to threaten a suspect, but wearing a pistol might be just enough to make them sit up and think, *Shit, these are real policemen.*

Time and again, we walk out with a confession.

Jim starts encouraging me to lead the interviews, which helps to build my confidence. He teaches me to trust my instincts, including what I learned from those veteran custody sergeants during my first weeks on the job – that empathy's important. You don't really have to feel compassion for your suspect but don't act like you're above it.

Sure, you can intimidate a suspect if you want to. A lot of cops will go into the interview room and not try to hide their disgust, like even talking to a crook's beneath them. Jim says, 'If a killer offers me his hand, I shake it.' I might not want to shake his hand, I might want to spit on him, but what I want is not important. What matters is to solve the case, however much it costs us.

When somebody's carried out a crime they're isolated. They often want you to reach out. Sometimes a crook just needs a chance to unburden themselves of guilt.

Over the years, the rules around how cops conduct their interviews will tighten, but right now, they're still pretty relaxed. We can take a suspect to the station, interview them formally or informally, and the courts will accept our notes of what was said as evidence, regardless of whether the suspect has signed our notebook entry.

But Jim teaches me to be proud of what we do as detectives, not to abuse the system. We don't need to fake a confession or, worse, beat one out of somebody. There's an old line about cops using phone books during interviews, because they don't leave bruises. Under Jim's guidance, I learn instead to love the contest between detective and suspect. My senses become heightened. It's one on one and, like a boxing match, why would you cheat? Win by cheating and you will always know it's not a real victory. Phone books would be the dumb approach.

***

I'm learning. While working in Hornsby, I'm also accepted into the Tactical Response Group (TRG), the police unit made up of heavily armed and armoured cops trained to deal with crowd control or violent offenders, which often involves dealing out violence in return. We dress in black and get sent in to deal with those situations thought too dangerous for normal cops to handle. It's one way I've found to keep the promise I made to myself aged 11 when Trevor called me out, that I would never again back down.

Australia Day, 26 January 1988, marks the bicentenary of the First Fleet's arrival in Australia and we've been told the Aborigines are going to riot. On days like these, being in the TRG means I get called away from working as a detective, kitted out with shield, baton and helmet and sent out to wait for the fighting.

When our bosses tell us there'll be riots, we don't ask them any questions. Today, rattling around in the truck during our deployment, I don't think too much about what the date means. Australia Day is just a national celebration.

As the sun rises over Sydney Harbour, we all jog down to the Opera House in step, chanting 'Hut, hut, hut, hut, hut', then line up and stand there in position, facing outwards.

Only, nobody turns up to fight us. It's hot. There are thick crowds around the harbour and boats out racing on the water. Everyone seems happy, walking arm and arm, carrying flags and drinking. We listen to the car horns, cheering and loud music as the sun crawls across the sky, casting sharp, black shadows on the white sails of the Opera House behind us. The temperature rises. But no one seems to want a confrontation.

We are stood down, so I go for a beer. At the bar, I see an old mate, Peter, whom we all call Ekker, drinking on his own.

Ekker has a reputation as a street fighter. Some of the people he's said to hang out with I know from work as being among Sydney's worst, including Graham 'Abo' Henry, who's mates with Arthur 'Neddy' Smith, a violent crook who has himself been linked to several murders. But I know Ekker through a childhood friend. Sue and him had a baby together. Ekker and I also played touch footy together for a couple of years.

Ekker is Aboriginal and, inside the pub, he's really low. It's like he's drinking to forget something. When I ask if I can join him, he tells me to get lost. He says he doesn't want to talk.

I'm happy just having a cold beer after a hot day in uniform, so sit and wait. Finally, Ekker opens up.

'What's gone on today is really bad,' he says. To him, today is not for celebration. To Aboriginal Australians, he says, the First

Fleet was an invasion. The settlers were an occupying army. The anniversary I've just stood ready to protect, with violence if required, marks the day his people had their country stolen.

I've never heard anyone describe it like that before. They never taught us anything like that in school.

Ekker and I drink together into the night, unpacking our hearts onto the bar counter. He makes me look at who I am; a white cop who lives in a white suburb, works in a mostly white police force and plays soccer at the weekends, which I call 'wog ball'.

I tell him that I'm grateful, that he has opened my eyes for me. I tell him that it isn't right that I needed the lesson.

Looking back, there were other people who could have taught me all these things in my own childhood. I blame myself for never having learned.

Diving into Cool Blue Water

Late 1960s

Mum and Dad move us into our new family house in North Epping, which has one bathroom, three bedrooms and a yellow clay road leading to the front door. Heavy work trucks rumble along it every morning as the rest of the suburb is still being built. Two more kids, Michelle and Jason, come along to follow Karen and me, and Dad builds a series of extensions on our home to keep up with the expanding family.

Our house overlooks a thickly forested valley and what feels like wilderness beyond that all the way to the horizon. To me it's a paradise. The bush gives me a sense of being part of something bigger than myself and bigger than my family.

Karen, my elder sister by two years, is Miss Perfect. She does nothing wrong. It's good, because it means when I spend hours staring out the window when I should be doing homework, she ends up doing the work for me. It also means that, as the second eldest, I'm the first of the four children to get caught smoking and stealing. Retribution follows, hard and fast.

As children, we live only in the moment. Michelle is five years younger and we clash furiously at times. Her bedroom is next to the one I share with Jason and I complain to Mum and Dad that she plays her radio too loud. It's like she is trying to annoy me.

Jason, who's two years younger than Michelle, also tests my patience. When he's a baby, I lie in bed with my hands over my ears, trying to shut out his crying. He gets better as we grow up, and even share a bunk bed, though I have the top bunk, which is right because I am the older brother.

Getting older, our family is always close. My mum has five sisters and one brother, while Dad has two brothers and a sister, so we have 30 or 40 cousins all together and most of them live near us. Either the four of us kids are at one of our cousins' places, or they're at ours. We have a pool in the backyard, and spend our summers sitting round it with our aunties, uncles, cousins and neighbours, diving into the cool blue water then drying out in the sunlight.

Starting high school, I'm lucky that an older cousin on my dad's side, Russell, has a reputation as a tough guy. He runs with a gang of kids who carry knives and wear mullets, which look like crewcuts at the front but with the hair left long at the back. The different gangs, like the Epping Sharpies and the Town Hall Sharpies, aren't afraid to fight each other and there's talk of Russell causing trouble, maybe even bashing people. When people at school ask if Russell is my cousin, I say yes and they leave me alone.

But, even with that protection, my first fight with Trevor ends up being one of many. I tell myself that I get picked on because I'm shy. That I end up getting into all these fights because I don't like bullies, so will always stand up to them. The truth is that I'm always angry, deep inside. At school, someone will say something and I'll take offence, which backs me into a corner, then I don't have the wit to talk my way out of it and so my pride kicks in and soon I'm throwing punches.

Russell lives with us for short stints when he's causing trouble at home, so he and I grow closer. I want to be just as tough as he is. Sadly, he later dies young, of a heroin overdose. I am a teenager by then and we've drifted further apart. I'm caught up in my own life. But I see the effect it has on other people and the sadness running through the family.

Growing up, my best mate in the truest sense is Anthony. He just turns up one day at home, adopted by the family who live opposite. He's different: Indigenous, when all the other kids are white. When Anthony laughs, you can't help but laugh with him, so we are often happy. He means I always have someone to escape from home with. Because Anthony is wild.

Each morning I wake up and hang around outside until Anthony gets up too. Or he comes over and knocks on my window. Then the two of us sneak off and set out on an adventure.

The suburb is still expanding, pushing back the bushland, so there are building sites everywhere for the two of us to break into. I'm smaller, so Anthony helps me climb up onto the roofs, where I can lift the tiles, climb down into the building and open the door. Then the half-finished home becomes a free-for-all in which the two of us will run around, play hide and seek or smoke cigarettes we've stolen from our parents. We walk down the unfinished roads, throwing rocks and shattering the windows, getting chased by angry builders or new owners, and always, always laughing.

He and I also spend time in the bush beyond the houses, trying to see who can climb the highest tree or cliff, or starting rock fights with the other kids. Once, Anthony jumps from a tree to a rock ledge and almost makes it but – to my horror – loses his balance and falls backwards. I see the fear in his face as he realises what's happening.

He doesn't scream, but hits the ground with a dull thump. Edging closer to the cliff edge to see if he's alive, I hear a roar of laughter.

One afternoon when I'm about 12, Anthony comes over to our house, and is crying. He's fought with his adoptive mum and tells me he hit her with a frying pan. He's got some things together and will run away. He wants to know, will I go with him?

I'm tempted, because he's a mate, but also old enough to realise something serious has happened. Our lives will head in different directions now, I sense. He runs. I stay.

He gets caught and put in a boys' home in Berry on the New South Wales South Coast.

From then on, we write letters to each other.

A Whale in the Bay

1988: three years in

I learn a different set of lessons in the cops when Jim takes a year off from the police from the middle of 1988, meaning I'm given another detective to work with as my partner.

Geoff (not his real name) is an older bloke, with maybe 15 years on me, a slumped, broken-down appearance and a lined, fleshy face. I see little of him. We often start our shifts together then Geoff will head off, saying, 'If you need anything, I'll be down at the RSL.'

Geoff used to work at Kings Cross, Sydney's inner-city, red-light district where the narrow roads are full of drunks and blank-eyed junkies, with the buildings on either side occupied by pinched-face hustlers and grinning nightclub bosses. I figure he has picked up some bad habits.

Some nights, Geoff will wander back into the Hornsby detectives' office to ask if anything is happening. I might have a suspect handcuffed to my desk and will look at him, incredulous. I'm not about to report him to our bosses – one lesson I learned in uniform is you make sure you've got your partner's back, whether it's on the street, in court, or if his wife calls the office at night to ask if you have seen him. 'He's out on a job,' you answer.

I think it's partly because each of you know what the other's witnessed. The drunks, the fights, the fatal traffic crashes. The time you were called to a house because a neighbour hears a child screaming and an adult's laughter. No one else can understand this world, certainly no one outside the emergency services. That's why so many cops get together with nurses. So, you look out for your partner without question.

When I really need Geoff, I call the Hornsby RSL and ask if the barman's seen him. As the months pass, I dial that number so often I can recite it from memory.

Sometimes, if work is quiet or before an afternoon shift gets started, I'll go for coffee with Katherine (not her real name), a young woman I know from growing up who now works in a brothel a few hundred metres from Hornsby Police Station. Prostitution's legal and, as far as most cops are concerned, accepted, as long as a brothel isn't selling drugs or operating near a school. If anybody sees us, no one questions why she and I are sitting down together. All I have to do is tell my sergeant or make a note in my duty book that I'm meeting a gig, meaning an informant.

Still, I'm disappointed for the way her life's played out. I know she had a hard childhood, her parents got divorced and her mum was a troubled soul. Katherine's a year or two younger than I am and when she complains about having to work a double shift, I tell her, 'I don't even want to know what that means.'

'I'm making money. Don't judge me,' she says. And I don't. So much of life is luck, I reckon. I've also seen enough sexual assault and domestic violence cases during my time in the cops to wonder if what she does somehow ends up helping others. I'll never excuse a man who harms a woman, but without this kind of release for some of those who need it, this might be a more dangerous world.

As cops, despite their legal status, we do keep an eye on the local clubs and brothels, just in case any of them get caught up in the drug trade, or employ underage girls. Katherine tells me that the local cops are on the take, demanding money in return for protection. I laugh and say I don't believe it. She looks at me and smiles.

In late 1988, I mention to Geoff that I know someone working at the brothel and he asks me to organise a meeting. He says it's just to gather intelligence and I don't think much about it, so I line up a drink and on one Saturday at the Pennant Hills Inn, the three of us sit down to talk.

Katherine and I use it as a catch-up, talking about family and friends from childhood, while Geoff sits there uncomfortably and, when he talks, says that he wants to know more about the brothel operation, like the number of girls and clients, or anything about the madam who runs it. Later, during a couple of night shifts when he actually turns up to work, he wants us to sit outside the building in our unmarked car and watch it, as if he's counting all the people going in and out. He never tells me what he's doing and, being the younger man, I do not ask any questions.

In 1989, after his year out, Jim tells me he's coming back. I tell Geoff that I want to work with my old partner.

Soon afterwards, the telephone rings in the detectives' office. A male voice says: 'Tell Geoff there is a whale in the bay.'

I don't understand the message but pass it on and see that Geoff looks worried. He asks me a few questions about the call, most of which I can't answer, then walks out of the office. A few days later I ask Jim what it all means and he says the call was a coded warning. It means Geoff's under investigation by police.

Eventually he is arrested and charged with soliciting bribes from the brothel. I could belt him, I'm so angry. Angry at the shame he's brought upon us detectives. Angry because we're supposed to protect people from bullies, not bully others. Angry because I could have stopped it.

Katherine was right. I should have listened.

Geoff ends up spending a few years in jail.

***

My work, the shift patterns and the things I see, begin to affect my life at home with Debbie. It feels like we are tipping out of balance. I realise I'm starting to dominate the relationship just like my father did, which makes me uncomfortable. But we're still looking to the future.

Being in plain clothes doesn't pay that well and Debbie doesn't make a fortune working as a PA, so we don't have much money, but we talk about having children.

For now, we get a cattle dog with two black patches on his eyes and call him Bandit. I take him running every morning. In the evenings, I have my soccer and kickboxing while Debbie plays netball and does her aerobics, so we don't see that much of each other. At the weekends, or when my shifts allow it, we work together on the house in Dural, but run short of cash. We want to lay paving but can't afford a compactor, so I spend two days jumping up and down on the underlay, damaging my knees so much they hurt for weeks.

In contrast, work is simple. It's a place where everything is certain and I don't have to think about whatever's going on outside it. Most days, the work itself drives any thoughts of home out of my head, like on the Saturday when I'm hiding in the dust and dirt of the crawl space beneath a chicken coop, watching the back door of a house where we believe a hardened crook is staying.

How good is this? I'm thinking as I lie there, enjoying the feeling of excitement flowing through my system and stretching out my different muscles so nothing seizes up before I need to make a move. This is what I joined the cops for. Then our target walks outside. He's a big bloke, he's on the run and he knows that if we get him, he is going straight to prison.

I use my radio to quietly tell the other cops waiting in a car out the front, 'I've seen the offender. I reckon I can take him.

'I'm going to go in ten seconds. Ten seconds and you guys come in the front door,' I say, then count to ten, crawl out from underneath the chicken shed and sprint across the yard. I'm on a high. I've found him. It's like hunting.

He sees me and turns to go inside, I smash through the back door, grab him and we crash to the floor together. I come up with him in a headlock, thinking the others will be in here any moment, only no one arrives. Instead, my suspect's mates are also in the house and now staring at me, stunned. There is an awkward silence. Then my suspect starts shouting, 'Fucking belt him! Fucking belt him!'

'Fuck off! Don't come near me! He's under arrest,' I shout back, trying to keep the bloke in the headlock between them and myself. I can't pull my gun because I need both arms to keep my suspect under control but all the adrenaline means I don't feel fear and, while everyone is staring at each other, trying to work out what to do, I start to drag my struggling suspect across the room, his feet trailing behind him. At the door, I risk using one hand to tear it open and force the two of us through it, pulling him headfirst down the steps and out across the lawn.

The other cops are still sitting in their car. They see me and pile out to surround us. His mates won't attack me now.

'Where were you?'

'Waiting for you to call. You said you'd call in ten seconds before going in.' We laugh about it later.

When our suspect's been booked and is in a jail cell, we go to the pub for lunch. I'm still on the high, enjoying myself, then start to feel sick. Telling the other blokes I'm going to the toilet, I shut myself inside a cubicle and retch. I'm sweating but cannot throw up.

I get some control of myself. I leave the cubicle, throw some water on my pale face and go back to the bar, where I don't tell anyone what happened. These guys had my back – eventually – and need to know that, next time, if it's them in trouble, I've got theirs. They don't need to know that I felt so scared afterwards I came close to vomiting.

Every shift could finish the same way if you want to, having drinks with the other cops, most often at the Hornsby Railway Hotel across the road from the train station. We talk about work and what we did on that day's chase. We make sure we have each other's backs here also.

One of the Hornsby cops lives in Newcastle, a two-hour train journey north from Sydney, so we time our drinks around his train's departure. If he misses it, we'll order a beer and wait for the next one, then the next one. One night, he misses every train and when Debbie wakes up in the morning she finds a strange detective sleeping on our lounge.

Throughout 1989 and 1990, I study again, something I thought I'd never do when I left high school. I feel a sense of shame that I didn't take my education seriously back then. I now find I am a keen student, doing an Associate Diploma in Policing, where we learn to analyse different investigations, about communication, the law and ethics. I do well enough, much better than in my HSC, but it takes time, and means another load on my shoulders while I sit up late at night in work or home with my head in a book. I write one assignment by torchlight while sitting in a cupboard at night, waiting for some suspects to break into a unit.

Outside of work in 1990, kickboxing leads me to try a kung fu class, the same instructors are teaching at the Dural squash courts. Immediately, I like it. If kickboxing is about straightforward fighting, the kind of skills I need on the streets as a policeman, then kung fu offers something deeper. It's more in the mind. I like the calmness that it gives me because, right now, it feels like life keeps spinning faster. Exercise, and particularly my martial arts, becomes a quiet place at the centre of a hurricane of working, drinking, studying and trying to be a husband. When I am training, nothing matters. The harder I push myself, the more I find that sense of quiet.

Only I keep getting sick. It is as if each time I walk past someone with a sniffle I come down with a raging cold and, each time, it knocks me out of balance.

One of the sifus – masters – in my kung fu class takes me aside and tells me I am too focused on only the hard side of training. 'Stop trying to put all your power into every kick,' he tells me. 'Stop being tense. Stop exhausting yourself.' He tells me not to force the movement, but go with it. At first, I can't work it out, but then I start to watch some of the other students doing qigong, a traditional Chinese system of slow-flowing movement, breathing and meditation.

Maybe that's what he means, I think. I start going to the qigong classes, which start at six in the morning.

I come out of them glassy-eyed. A different person. I stop getting sick.

I keep it separate from the cops, though. Qigong's the opposite of the police force's tough-guy, don't-talk-about-your-feelings attitude. If I were to tell them what I'm doing in those early-morning classes, the other cops will think I'm weird. They might wonder if they can trust me.

Instead, when work's been hard, I go home, light a candle, put on some meditation music and practise qigong. It means another thing I have to fit into the day, but it does give me a way of regaining some balance. The cost, in terms of the commitment, is worth it. I can do without some sleep, or sitting in front of the TV after dinner. When the martial arts school I train at moves from Dural closer to the city centre, a half-hour's drive from where I live, I also find time for the extra travel and keep going.

***

In March and April 1990, I undertake the six-week course to qualify as a designated detective, learning how to run investigations, prepare records of interview and what the law says is admissible and inadmissible as evidence. I know now that I never want to go back into uniform, where what you do and see at work is out of your control, like the succession of mangled, bloodied, burning bodies I've seen in traffic accidents.

I quickly learn detective work can also offer up fresh horrors. The course finishes on a Friday afternoon, 4 May 1990 and on the Sunday evening, two trains collide about five kilometres south of Brooklyn, north of Hornsby. The driver and five passengers are killed; three women, two men and a 14-year-old boy in total.

Ninety-nine other passengers are injured. I am called to the scene. Picking our way through the wreckage to investigate what happened, I look at the other cops, as well as the huddled bodies of the survivors, wrapped in blankets, and the paramedics carrying wounded people towards the waiting ambulances and realise you can't escape these sights in the police. It's how you deal with them that matters.

Some people never want to see these things. Others can't stop looking. I don't know what effect it will have on me, but I am prepared to face it. I do know that 30 years from now, I will not be able to forget what I am seeing.

Little more than six weeks later, on 19 June 1991, our son, Jake, is born. He arrives a fortnight early and I have to borrow my father's car to drive Debbie to the hospital, as ours keeps breaking down.

We are wide-eyed new parents, and I discover it is all-consuming. Debbie's given up her job as a PA to be a mum, while I do extra work on building sites outside my police hours to bring in some money. Coming home to them makes it all worth it. Debbie has a real nurturing side, she would have been a great nurse or doctor, and Jake is simply perfect. Given what I have seen in the police, I know by now that my own dad was right to teach me toughness, but I will do things differently with Jake. I will make him tough, but I will also hug him. I'll celebrate his achievements. I will tell my son I love him.

Molotov Cocktails

Mid-1970s

Growing up, I start to buck against the restrictions imposed on me at home. The little things I can rebel against, like when Dad tells me not to smoke, so I go into the shops with mates and buy Escort cigarettes. But the big things I can't control. I don't get a bike until I'm 12, when other kids had bikes at six or seven. And unlike my friends, whose parents seem to give them more freedom, I'm not allowed out after dark alone.

There is a gang of other kids, Mark, Andrew, Frank, Warren and Sue, all of them a few years older than me. We get up to trouble – though others might call it criminal behaviour. We like to roam the streets at night; I lie to Dad and tell him I'm staying at Frank's, or I go to bed with one end of a piece of string attached to my hair with sticky tape and the other tied to a rock hanging out the window. My friends creep up in the darkness and pull the string to wake me up, then I climb out and join them.

We get into shoplifting. We take our dogs into a store, and while the shopkeeper's distracted getting the animals out, we grab what we can – lollies, or even pocket knives. I discover the thrill that comes with breaking rules and risking being discovered.

Then I get caught trying to hide an ice-cream under my shirt and the shopkeeper calls Mum. When Dad comes home, he yells and screams, though by now I'm quite used to being thrown around. I have to write a letter of apology and afterwards I enjoy stealing less so we get into air rifles, trespassing and drinking instead. We shoot at birds, windows and streetlights, and on occasion at each other.

Dad and some of our neighbours bottle their own wine and store it under their houses. We steal some bottles and go down to a place we call the Pond, where there are carp swimming beneath the water. Andrew gets drunk and starts shooting at the rest of us with his air rifle. Frank and I make a run for it, and I feel a pellet penetrate my clothes and dig into my back. It's dumb, but it's exciting.

Another game is Molotov cocktails. We steal petrol from lawnmowers left in people's gardens, bottle it then soak a rag in it and stuff one end of the rag in the bottle and light the other. We throw the bottles at a rock and watch the eruption.

When the nearby Terrys Creek's in flood following a downpour, we jump in with foam surfboards. The current washes us all the way down past Browns Waterhole, a couple of kilometres away. One time I get pulled under, and my mates panic, running up to our house shouting, 'Gary's gone, he's disappeared!' Everyone rushes down to find me, then I walk up carrying my surfboard.

But the dumbest thing we do is throw metal rods onto overhead electricity wires, to make them crack and roar in fury. It's fun, until one explosion brings down some of the heavy cables. We take off back to my house, laughing. Later, we worry someone might get electrocuted, so we make an anonymous phone call reporting the damage.

***

Eventually I have a run-in with the cops. I'm not in our neighbourhood this time, but in the inner city, sitting on the grass bank at Redfern Oval with friends watching the South Sydney Rabbitohs play rugby league.

An old bloke sitting near us with an Esky asks, 'Hi boys, do you want a drink?'

When we say yes, he hands each of us a beer. We have another, maybe another two, but it might as well be 100, as we are quickly plastered.

I'm still a kid, around 13, and this is the first time I've got really drunk. I'm unable to stand up, and suddenly I'm falling down the slope, rolling towards the pitch, with sun, sky, grass and footy game all flashing past me in an orbit, and the old man with his Esky is laughing, and I have no idea what's happening or how I can control it.

Then there are blue shirts and strong hands that grab us and drag us off to their paddy wagon. They slam the door and drive us to the railway station. Once there, they open up the van and tell us to fuck off, so we stagger onto the platform and start to sober up.

On the train home, I think those cops were looking after us. Maybe, thinking about the man with the Esky, they saved us.

***

My grandfather Charles still keeps his eye on me. He's the general manager of a glass recycling plant, and when I'm 13, he finds me work delivering flyers for the business around the city centre. I always work alone because when I ask if my mates will come with me it turns out their parents don't want them to go into those places.

It feels strange, being the one with freedom, but I can't blame them after what happened when we went to watch the Rabbitohs.

On my rounds I see the drunkenness, the shouting, violence and the sadness of the inner city. I never see that in the suburbs, and I learn from the experience. How to carry myself. How to deal with trouble.

A year passes, I'm 14 now, and the older kids who were my friends – Mark, Andrew, Frank, Warren and Sue – are into their later teens. It's harder for me to keep up with what they're doing. At that age, kids discover sex and start playing around with drugs, and maybe I'm not ready. But when I turn to the kids who are my own age, I find that I've outgrown them. They're only just getting into the things my older mates have now grown out of.

I spend more time wandering in the bush near home and missing Anthony. I start to feel lonely.

On weekends and in school holidays, working for my grandfather, I graduate from delivering flyers to working in the tips and on the trucks, touring the city in the dawn light collecting glass bottles that have been left out for recycling. I work with men, and get paid adult wages, $40 a day. And I've found the perfect way to use all that money.

You Don't Give Up

May 1992: seven years in

A boy playing in bushland behind the oval at Normanhurst Park, near Hornsby, discovers a shallow grave. A dog has dug down into the loose soil and pulled free something white, like leather. Moving closer, despite the damage done by the dog's teeth, the boy sees it is the wrinkled, freckled flesh of a forearm.

The cops are called and the corpse is identified as that of 67-year-old James Kelly. A crime scene is set up with the blue and white tape running between the trees, behind which the forensic guys move in to photograph the body while uniformed police are sent to walk the surrounding streets, to knock on doors and ask people what, if anything, they've seen.

I get the call at home and meet Jim Williams at the oval. It is a Friday and, around us, people are out enjoying the beginning of their weekend. As we approach, the grave itself looks like a rushed, amateurish effort, though I imagine it would have been hard work digging through this tough earth, among the rocks and tree roots. The smell is bad enough to make me gulp with revulsion, but Jim says it could be worse. The body hasn't been here long, he says.

I know this place, I think. I've played soccer here. This oval is a part of my life. In a way, it feels good, like Jim and I are local sheriffs in some old Western movie. *This is what I've trained for.* But I don't have time to feel much emotion. I've been a detective for two years now, working mostly on robberies, street-level drug dealing and a lot of break-and-enters, but this will be the first murder case I've worked on.

Looking up, we see a fire trail running through the bush close to the grave site, and wonder if the killer drove along it to get here with James's body. As the forensics officers uncover what's left of him, we can't see an obvious cause of death, although his face and head are bloody and it's clear some badness has taken place.

'OK,' Jim says. 'We've seen enough.' He wants to go to James's home, a small house down a cul-de-sac not far from where his body was discovered. I don't question his decision. He's the senior detective running the case, with assistance from the specialist North Region Homicide Squad. I'm the young detective constable and happy to still be his apprentice on this one.

When we arrive, James's house has been broken into. It's dark inside and cluttered, with stacks of yellowing newspapers piled up on different surfaces and dating back six months or more.

I watch Jim and the Homicide detectives work their way through the crowded property, entering each room and pausing to look about them, then moving slowly into it with a meticulous care, something I haven't previously encountered on a case. *That's right*, I think. *This is different from anything I've worked on*. The consequences are much higher than any break-and-enter. A life has been taken. Right now, to me, there can't be anything more important than what we are doing.

From this moment, I want to be a Homicide detective. I'm hooked. It feels like a job in which I can lose myself completely.

Jim says that our first task is to understand the victim. We learn James drank in the Blue Gum Hotel in Waitara, so we go there and find the regulars who knew him. James fell out with his neighbour, the drinkers tell us. We speak to the neighbour at his house, who seems friendly enough, but has a strange over-confidence, as if he's got an answer for everything.

Jim and I leave thinking he is hiding something from us. *This feels personal*, I tell myself. Like it is us and him. The Blue Gum, where James drank, is also our local, where the Hornsby police drink after finishing our shifts. I'm determined to do everything I can to find who killed him.

The autopsy report comes back and says that James was physically beaten – most likely, by whoever broke into his house. It also says his heart was weak, and what killed him was a myocardial infarction – a heart attack. That finding causes problems.

In short, James died of natural causes, even if the heart attack was brought on by the beating. Jim and I argue it back and forth between us but we both know that result will make it hard for us to say that this is still a murder. If it's not murder, then our bosses won't see it as a priority. The Homicide Squad are also going to lose interest. That means we will be given less time to solve it before Jim and I are thrown back into the whirlpool of other, minor crimes that make up a local detective's work, which now seems so much less important.

The saddest part is when Jim and I attend the funeral. Even with us present, there are only half a dozen mourners. The two of us make up a third of James's funeral procession.

Months pass and we're still no closer to solving the case. It really pisses me off. It feels like Jim and I are the only two who care about James Kelly.

***

Years later, as a Homicide Squad detective, I will come back to this killing.

Jim has left the force by then and another detective, Roger, gets in contact from one of the district anti-theft units. He knows I worked the case and says one of his informants claims a local man, Paul Suters, is trying to sell a microwave, which came from James's home. It's strange but we follow it up. Suters was 19 when the killing happened, and at the time he did casual work for the neighbour Jim and I had our eyes on.

Roger and I interview Suters, who is now 23 and working as an electrical goods salesman. He admits to being involved. He says he was the lookout, waiting outside the front of James's house while a mate, just a young kid, went round the back and knocked on the door. We also match his fingerprints to those on a piece of cardboard found inside James's station wagon back in 1992.

The neighbour encouraged them to do it, Suters tells us. He told them James had money lying round the house. James was not supposed to be there – only he was. Suters says he doesn't know what happened, who came at who or whether the younger bloke panicked, but he ended up hitting James with a Maglite torch that he was carrying and the older man collapsed.

The two of them used his station wagon to drive the body to the stretch of nearby bushland, by the oval, where they buried him before making off with $120, the microwave oven and a clock from inside the house.

I tell Suters that if he wants to help himself, he needs to help us go after the younger man who did the job with him and is now also in his early twenties. Suters agrees, and we get him to set up a meeting between them at a motel in nearby Mount Kuring-Gai, which we record using listening devices.

The conversation gives us a part of what happened. The younger man admits to being there and that they buried the body. We don't get an admission that he played a direct part in James's killing, but it's enough to take them both to court.

Roger and I go back to the neighbour, expecting to bounce him. After all, Suters has told us that the whole thing was his idea. But when I ask about the killing he looks at me blankly, saying, 'I don't remember.' Looking around his house, I see notes stuck to the cupboard doors and walls, saying 'Shut fridge' and 'Turn off lights'.

He has dementia. There's no point dragging him to court.

The prosecutor, Margaret Cunneen, smiles at me when I take

the case to her, looking at the time that's passed since I first worked it with Jim. 'Jesus, you don't give up do you?' she says, laughing.

By the time both of the young men involved are tried and sentenced, it will be eight years since James was killed. Suters is charged with murder but pleads guilty to manslaughter, and the judge reduces his sentence because of what he called Suters' 'contrition and remorse evidenced in the most material manner' in helping with our investigation.

Suters gets two years of weekend detention served in a State facility beside the Hunter River, not too far from his home.

The younger man is charged with being an accessory after the killing, with Margaret telling me that there is simply not enough evidence to convict him of more. Sentencing him, the judge says that he 'presented as a young man who is now completely rehabilitated'. He isn't jailed. He still lives in the Hornsby area, working as an electrician. Afterwards, I sometimes see him driving his van to work.

I feel offended by the way the trials have played out. The two men broke into James's house. James was beaten with a torch. James died. They buried him.

Maybe they were only kids back then. Maybe they'd been manipulated by the neighbour. Maybe the judge has found it in his heart to forgive them, but to me it feels like two years of weekend detention is like saying James's life counted for nothing. Like no one in the courtroom cared for him. Like no one championed his cause.

***

Not long after James Kelly's body is discovered, a custody sergeant from Hornsby calls me at home.

'We've got someone in the cells who's demanding to see you. We can't settle him down. He's bloody assaulted everyone. Can you come in?'

'Who is it?'

'Aboriginal bloke. Anthony.'

I can't help smiling. My best mate from childhood. Of course, part of me is sad Anthony's in the cells but the fact he's asking to see me means I meant something to him. It means my memory of our friendship is real, not imagined.

'What happened?' I ask the sergeant.

'He was on a train and beat up a guard. When the cops came, he had a go at them as well.' They've charged him with assault.

I drive straight over, unsure what to expect. After writing to each other for a couple of years when he ran away from home, the two of us have lost contact. He must have somehow kept a track on me and known I joined the cops.

The moment I open the cell door and can see him, Anthony and I start laughing like we did when we were kids. We hug and sit down on the floor and talk. It freaks us out a little how, despite the time apart, we still feel the same connection.

We talk about how our lives have gone since our last letters up until this moment. He says enough for me to guess at the tough time he's had, then looks at me and shakes his head and laughs again about how crazy it is that I joined the police.

'How *did* you end up a copper?' he asks. I tell him.

We talk about how we used to steal our parents' grog and cigarettes, break into building sites and smash the windows. He looks at me, his face serious for a moment, and I realise each of us has played a part in the making of the other. He was a wild spirit and I was the voice of caution, asking, 'Should we really do this?'

'Yeah, yeah, let's do it. It will be great,' he'd tell me, and sometimes I would go along and other times he'd see that I was right. That's what made us such great mates. We balanced out each other.

Growing up with Anthony has also made me a better detective. Looking back, I can see how all the different parts connected: wanting to do bad stuff with Anthony, having a father who would kill me if he caught me, and learning to cover up our tracks in order to escape. This experience taught me how to chase crooks as an adult, because I understand their temptations and can ask myself what I would do in their place.

I walk him to the courthouse and watch as he's released on bail. He looks like the same person I knew as a young kid, only now in the dock, staring up at the magistrate. Afterwards, I help him sign his bail forms and want to ask if he will come and stay at my place, but I cannot. Before I walked into his cell, I checked his criminal record. There are a lot of violent crimes on there. He isn't the same person. Even understanding how he got here, being adopted, running away, spending time in a boys' home, and having shared a part of his history, I can't expose my family to him. At home, Debbie and I have a baby now, and we're planning for another.

I take Anthony to lunch and we promise to meet up at some point in the future, though I doubt it will happen.

This job already involves a constant battle to stop the trauma I see at work from bleeding into my home life.

And, each year, that gets harder.

Perfect Formula for Happiness

Mid-1970s

It's raining on the day it happens. I'm in my first year of high school and sport is washed out, so the teachers put us all in the big assembly hall and put on a movie.

It's a surf film called *Morning of the Earth*. I know nothing about surfing, but in those first few psychedelic minutes, as the camera shows surfers cutting white lines through blue water, while the people standing on the beaches watch them in fascination, and everything, including the film itself, seems to have been bleached by sunlight, I want to be a part of that world.

Despite living 30 kilometres from the ocean, I use my wages from working at my grandfather's recycling plant to buy a board. Like any kid, I'm looking for an identity, a purpose.

It's not like I put much of myself into my education, so long as I am having fun and doing enough not to get in trouble with my father. But I work hard at surfing. The walls in my bedroom become a mural of surfing pictures, of blue water and sunlight. On weekends, I convince my parents to drive me to the coast.

Then my sister Karen starts going out with a guy called Mark, who is three years older than me and has long hair bleached by hours in the sun and saltwater, just like in the movie. He surfs. I convince him to take me with him.

Paddling out and sitting on my surfboard beyond the breakers, where the water is still enough that you barely feel it moving beneath you, I feel at peace. Just staring at the ocean. It's a kind of meditation, I guess, though I don't go in for all that sitting-in-a-lotus-position, hippy bullshit. Even after Mark splits up with my sister, we keep on going surfing. Driving out to the beaches at Manly, Newport and Avalon, with my feet on the dashboard while Mark drives, I tell myself there might be no perfect formula for happiness, but this seems pretty close.

I keep working to buy surfboards, and in my mid-teens get a second job with one of my uncles. He's an electrician, and a good one, but we don't do much electrical work.

I think what he really wants is a companion or a lookout. My uncle has a drug habit. He takes all sorts. He'll pick me up after school and we'll go to Kings Cross, where there's a doctor he meets with. Or we'll drive around and park somewhere, then I'll sit in the car alone and wait until my uncle comes back, smiling.

What work we do sometimes takes us into the Cross's strip clubs. One time, my uncle turns up at our house with three or four strippers wanting to use our pool. He's wearing flares, with his hair long and a thick beard. To my amazement, Mum and Dad let them swim. Strict as they are, I learn that my parents are also open minded. There's no judgment. I like that, although Mum says we're not allowed to watch the women swimming.

My uncle gets on the grog a fair bit too. I'll often stay over at his place if we've got an early start the next morning, and he'll pour me Bourbon and Cokes. Not shots, either, but big glasses. I learn to pour half of each glass into a pot plant, so I don't have to match him, drink for drink. That would floor me.

I learn other lessons too, about self-reliance.

One afternoon when we are actually working, I'm up in the ceiling cavity running some cables into place when I hear banging and crashing from the room below. I hear an argument break out. When I get down out of the ceiling, my uncle is off his face and, not being able to find the wire he wanted, has smashed up the Gyprock wall to locate it.

'What the fuck have you done?' the owner demands, only my uncle is too far gone to answer.

I calm things down. Another time, I'm pulling wires through under a house and calling out to my uncle but getting no answer. When I give up and go to find him, he's passed out and collapsed, with his legs and body hanging on either side of the balcony. I call his wife, who comes to pick him up.

One Saturday morning, my uncle wants to go to a pub, an early opener, and we get there around 8am. I'm due to play soccer that afternoon and don't want to drink, so he says, 'Let's play pool', but stumbles at the table and knocks the balls flying. The blokes whose game he's interrupted tip their cues upside down and move towards him.

I step in, saying, 'Sorry guys, he's drunk. We're out of here,' and we back out onto the street again, with me between them and my uncle.

On days like this, I learn that life's not perfect and neither are people, so it's better not to judge them. In fact, over the years, I learn more from my uncle, about myself, and about people with all their different strengths and vulnerabilities, than I could find in any book.

My uncle has his faults but he is a good person who loves his family and does his best to support them.

And between working with him and at the recycling plant, I'm earning decent wages. By the time I leave Epping Boys' High, I have saved up $2000 to buy a car, a brown Datsun. It's nothing much to look at but it means I can drive myself to the beach.

I sleep in the car to extend my surfing trips over the weekends and wake with sunlight burning through the car windows, then paddle out and sit on my board looking at where the ocean meets the horizon. I surf hard, grow my hair long, taste the salt on my skin each evening and fall asleep each night exhausted. Later, I replace the Datsun with the Mitsubishi L300 Express van and fit it out with cupboards and a mattress in the back, so I can stretch out.

Leaving school at 17, I go straight into a job as an electrician's apprentice. I make $67 a week, less than I was making working for my uncle or my grandfather, but enough to support myself while living my real life at the beach on the weekend. My education's done with, and I'm not looking to replace it with anything too demanding.

You Don't Leave the Fucking Stick-Ups

September 1992: seven years in

A phone call from work on my day off rarely means something good but this time there's a tone in Jim's voice that says it's not just another drunken assault or robbery that means cancelling my plans with Debbie and going into the office.

'You've been invited to join the Stick-Ups,' Jim says. He means the Armed Hold-Up Squad. I'm stunned. To my eyes, the Stick-Ups are the big boys. If Hornsby detectives are the local leagues, then they are the first graders.

Across the state, the police force is divided into four regions, North, Northwest, South and Southwest, with the corners of each meeting in the centre of Sydney, where most of our work is, and their areas of responsibility stretching out over the vast expanses of coastline, bush and desert to the State's borders. Each region has a Major Crime Squad, which handles the toughest cases and is run by an inspector. Under the inspector sit senior detective sergeants in charge of different, specialised squads who tackle specific offences, such as Homicide, the Armed Hold-Ups, Organised Crime and so on.

'They must have seen something they like in you,' Jim says. He doesn't admit it, but I guess someone from the squad asked him for his opinion and he told them I was ready. It is to be a six-month trial.

I hang up the phone feeling 10 feet tall. The Armed Hold-Up Squad do heavy work. The number of violent robberies across the State has increased in recent years. By the spring of 1992, it feels like every week another bank or armoured van is hit, and people are regularly getting shot at.

The Stick-Ups go after the very worst of those offenders and have built their reputation on the back of serious detectives such as the squad sergeant, Dennis 'Doodles' O'Toole, who to my young eyes is a living legend.

Being asked to join them must mean that I'm a real policeman.

***

My first Monday morning with the Stick-Ups, 14 September 1992, is like being back in uniform and walking into the Hornsby detectives' office. This is the next level up and I stand there as Doodles introduces me, saying nothing and just waiting for one of the proper cops to turn around and ask me what I'm doing here and whether I belong.

The squad is based in Chatswood, closer to the city centre, and Dad dropped me off on his way into work this morning. The Major Crime office is probably six times bigger than in Hornsby and littered with paperwork from the different briefs of evidence being assembled or picked over by the detectives, who also seem bigger, smarter and more confident than anything I'm used to. But they make me welcome as Doodles shows me round.

'This is your desk, this is the meal room, let us know if you're going out,' he tells me. Leaning back against the meal room wall, he looks out into the office, nods and says, 'Round here, we work hard and play hard.'

As a detective constable, my job is mainly to help collect evidence; taking statements, going out and showing photographs to witnesses, asking if they can identify these people, chasing up CCTV footage, which is becoming increasingly available as more banks and building societies get cameras fitted, then working through the footage, looking for particular designs on T-shirts, hats, or anything you could use to link the person on the tape to a suspect. As the new guy, I watch how the older cops connect all these little pieces to build up a case.

Three days into my first week, a crook called Christopher Binse holds up a bank at a shopping centre less than two blocks from our headquarters. Binse has a reputation; less than a week ago, on 8 September 1992, he broke out of a locked ward at St Vincent's Hospital in Melbourne armed with a pistol. Today, he went in wearing a balaclava, jumped over the bank counter, terrifying the tellers and fired off a gun. He's also wanted over a string of other robberies and likes to pull stunts, like taunting the Victorian police in his home State, sending them postcards timed to arrive with each new heist, signing his nickname 'Badne$$'.

A few days later, I'm told we've got a tip-off that Binse is holed up in another crook's house. Doodles says we're going to arrest him but warns Binse is the most dangerous man in Australia and sure to want to shoot it out if he gets cornered. We set up a surveillance unit in an electrician's van outside the house and surround the property with cops, all heavily armed. I'm sitting in a car parked around the corner, carrying a shotgun. When Binse drives out, we follow him. He goes through a set of traffic lights, then slows. Two police cars slam into the sides of the saloon that he's driving. Badne$$ is pulled out of the wrecked car at gunpoint.

I quickly learn the routine at the Stick-Ups: get our shotguns ready in the squad office, head out and lock somebody up, head to the Willoughby Hotel and drink, then come in the next day and listen carefully as Doodles tells us, 'OK, this is the target.' Then the cycle continues.

There are no niceties in the way we go after criminals. Our listening devices record them talking about operations I am part of: 'That fucking Armed Hold-Up crew, they hit us. Came in with fucking sledgehammers and shotguns. They're hard cunts.' I love it. We are hard cunts. We work hard and play hard.

But work and play start to merge into each other. You might be drinking to celebrate an arrest or to meet an informant. On any given afternoon, some toughened, veteran detective will look up from his computer, which are starting to replace typewriters in the Major Crime Squad, and call out: 'It's two o'clock, why aren't we at the pub?' In answer, other office chairs will be pushed back, desk drawers will open and close as pistols are taken out and put in shoulder holsters, someone will stand and stretch and I'll look up from whatever running sheet or arrest report I'm working on, and grin, then follow them.

Sometimes, on our way out, I might look back at that unfinished paperwork and worry I am picking up bad habits.

Working with Jim, being a detective was all about sitting down and talking to a suspect. The Stick-Ups seem to prefer coming into the interview room shouting or slamming their hands down on the table. While elsewhere in Australia, the police have been using audio tapes and even video to record interviews for years, in New South Wales this technology was only introduced a year ago, in 1991, and there are no laws saying we have to use it. Instead, the Stick-Ups make the most of recording confessions in their notebooks. One might read: 'I asked him, "Did you commit this crime?" and he replied, "Yes I did. You've caught me."'

Sometimes, I might hear other cops saying, 'We should fucking flog him,' when talking about interviewing a suspect. I try to argue, 'If he's me and you flog me, then I'm not going to talk to you for the rest of my life.' Or take a crook like Badne$$, I say, who during the interviews that follow his arrest seems crazy-smart, impulsive and already as traumatised by his own life as he is used to traumatising others. Unless you're prepared to kill someone like that, I don't think a beating's going to work.

Better to sit down and talk.

Sometimes, after the squad's gone in firing, I'll look around after the gunsmoke clears and think, *Jesus, that took some balls.* At other times, when that same crook is sitting mute inside the interview room and I know he's not going to sign any confession we put in front of him, I wonder, *How will this stand up in court?*

I get used to appearing in the witness box and having defence lawyers rip into me:

'You're in the Stick-Ups aren't you?'

'Yes.'

'And you threatened the defendant?'

'No.'

'But that's what you do in the Stick-Ups isn't it? Your squad has a reputation.'

I stare at him in silence.

'Roger Rogerson was in the Stick-Ups wasn't he?' the barrister continues. 'He's seen as a hero?'

It's true. Roger 'The Dodger' was in the Stick-Ups and, for years, was seen as someone to look up to. Even before I joined the cops, he'd become a poster boy for policing, with comfortable, you-can-trust-me features like an old black and white movie star, sharp suits and an instinct for knowing where a newspaper photographer's camera was pointing. His reputation was as someone who was unafraid to pull the trigger to deliver justice. The morning papers filled their pages with his exploits in the Stick-Ups, describing them as High Noon shootouts in lonely city lanes.

I'd fallen for that storyline, like others. Rogerson had won awards, including in 1980, the year I got together with Debbie, for arresting an armed robber, Gary Purdey. Then he got caught. The Dodger was dismissed from the police in 1986, the year we got married. Soon after, he was sent to court on a drug charge and convicted, though he overturned that verdict on appeal. At this moment in 1992, he's serving time in prison for a different offence – perverting the course of justice over an attempt to hide $110,000 in a bank account under a false name.

All of this has dragged the Stick-Ups' reputation downwards, which I hate, because these are men I've learned to trust when people start firing their guns at us. In court, when the lawyers ask if Roger is my hero, I give them nothing: 'Look, I know who Roger Rogerson is. I haven't worked with him. As for a hero, I don't think so in light of what's gone on.'

What I don't say is, 'Look, who is doing wrong here? Me, who's trying to put crooks in prison. Or lawyers like you, who are trying to let criminals walk free?'

There is no easy answer to this question. One time, at the Stick-Ups, we arrest an armed robber who regularly shoots people. He will walk into a bank and shoot someone just to get attention. I'm not convinced we have the evidence to charge him, but when I speak up, the response is, 'What do you want us to do? Wait until he goes into another bank and shoots somebody else?'

He pleads guilty. To my mind, the Stick-Ups made a judgment call and it paid off. Back at the Willoughby Hotel, after his conviction, I drink my beer and ask myself who's the better public servant – the Stick-Ups who played hard and stretched the rules this time around but took a bad crook off the streets, or me, Mr Cautious, who might have left him free to kill an innocent person?

Maybe there are no answers, only other questions. It's easier to do your job than think about it sometimes. It's easier to order another beer.

***

Debbie's pregnant again and, as 1992 comes to an end, I'm more determined than ever to find the balance between home and work I'm seeking. The prospect of a bigger family on a police wage makes it harder to justify why I've spent $150 on a Monday night drinking with the Stick-Ups. Debbie doesn't like it and, when she confronts me, I admit that I don't like it either.

One job, chasing a pair of brothers who've done some bad armed robberies, takes me away from home for four weeks to Coffs Harbour, six hours' drive north of Sydney. I say goodbye to Debbie while loading my surfboard into the car next to another detective's golf clubs. We can't work all the time we're up there and I've got so used to the work-hard, play-hard attitude that I don't question it. I'm looking forward to the release of getting back into the ocean to go surfing but I can see in Debbie's face as she and toddler Jake wave me goodbye that this situation isn't working for her.

In Coffs, we work, we drink, we work, repeat. And it is hardcore drinking. We're downing shots in nightclubs. After we arrest the brothers, I walk in to interview the older one one morning with another detective who's been out on the piss until 4am.

My exercise means I don't bottom out that badly. I drink less because I want to wake up early to go running or do floor exercises, trying to lose myself and my concerns by pushing myself harder. I do handstand press-ups on the motel carpet while the other Stick-Ups watch me through their hangovers. They groan or laugh but it's good humoured. The deal is you can do what you like as long as you show up at work.

Still, during those weeks in Coffs, it feels as if the threads are coming loose within the squad, and it would be easy to get tangled up completely.

I come home to Debbie and Jake, and feel like a stranger in the house at first. The two worlds, police and family life, seem to move at different speeds. I keep training, soccer, running and kung fu. More and more, I rely on my qigong to slow myself down and bring the two worlds back into alignment, but it gets to the point where I can feel myself tensing up in the evenings at home if I do not get the chance to practise these calming movements daily. It feels self-defeating.

Once again, I get sick and am diagnosed with shingles, an infection where your skin erupts in red, angry blisters, caused when your immune system is too weak to defend you.

I realise joining the Stick-Ups had felt like a dream, but now I want to get out of it. It's meant giving up too much. My family's suffered and I've lost the simple, honest faith in being a good cop I found when working with Jim Williams. I've had to ask myself too many questions about police work and, when I tried to answer them, have only come up with more questions.

I know it won't be easy.

By now, my six-month trial with the squad has dragged on for a couple of months longer but eventually I go to Doodles O'Toole and say, 'Just to let you know, I'm going back to Hornsby.'

'What are you fucking saying?' He looks at me, as if he can't work out whether I'm joking or if he should be offended. 'You're part of the squad now. You don't leave the fucking Stick-Ups.'

I struggle to explain my reasons, if I even fully understand them. I can't be part of this and still be everything I want to be outside it. I've not been able to find the balance between being a detective and a dad, a husband and a hardarse cop, between drinking till 4am and getting up at 5am each morning to go running.

I also worry that there's some other undercurrent flowing beneath the surface at the Stick-Ups. Something that can pull you out into the deep water. After only several months with the squad, I am not yet committed. The current hasn't caught me.

Other cops tell me I'm mad. They say that if I leave, there'll be no going back to Major Crime. I will have burned my bridges.

I've made my choice.

'I'm going,' I tell Doodles. He shakes his head.

I transfer back to Hornsby.

Do What Your Mother Tells You

August 1993: eight years in

On Saturday 28 August 1993, my soccer team are playing a grand final, but I cannot enjoy the game, or the celebrations after, knowing Debbie is so close to giving birth. She goes into labour hours later and our daughter, Gemma, is born on 29 August.

We now have a son and a daughter, our family feels complete and the next day I make plans to go out and celebrate with Dad and some mates, just like after Jake's birth. Mum chastises me, telling me I need to be at home, that Jake is still so little and will need me while his mum is in the hospital.

It's a moment of realisation. If I now have two children, then I need to put twice as much effort into being a good father.

With Gemma, Jake and Debbie, we are a perfect, self-contained family. I have more time to be with them since transferring back to Hornsby and it feels like we are settled, with a clearer barrier between work and home. Until one job breaks through it.

***

Soon after Gemma's birth, I'm asked to take a look at Nora and Reg Irish (not their real names), a mother and son who've been trouble around my suburb of Dural. We've had complaints about them moving into rental places, trashing them, refusing to pay any money and that Reg then stands over anyone who tries to challenge them, making violent threats.

Talking to the landlords who have been affected, I can see that they're shattered: not only have they lost their money, they're also terrified of talking to me. They worry Reg will find some way to punish them. He's got a gun, they warn me.

This is suburbia, I think. *It's where my children live. This should not be happening.*

We've got the evidence to charge them and I find that Reg and Nora are now living in an isolated cove overlooking the water at Woy Woy on the Central Coast. I drive up from Sydney, knock on the door and walk into a small, dark apartment, where Reg is lying spread across the lounge, his pale belly spilling out from underneath his T-shirt.

'Get up,' I tell him.

'Make me.'

'Look, you're under arrest, so I can if I have to, but it would be easier if you cooperate.'

'Make me,' he repeats.

Nora tells her son to do what I'm asking.

'Why don't you do what your mother tells you?' I ask, taking a step closer. I want to offend him. He's a bully and I want him to know what it feels like being stood over.

He scowls and climbs to his feet. I charge him over the unpaid rental payments and the damage to the properties. At court, he is convicted but let off without a prison term.

Afterwards, I don't think much about it, until I get a call from the North Region Major Crime Squad. Reg has been handing out my home address and phone number in pubs around Dural. He knows where my parents live. He calls them, saying he wants to speak to me. He turns up at the home of Debbie's parents, who have also moved to Dural and live next to our house. According to what he's saying in the pubs, he's found out where Jake goes to preschool.

He wants me to know he can get at my family. I'm furious.

My boss, John, tells me to let it go, and says Major Crime will handle it but a marked police car will be parked outside my home from now on as a precaution.

That means I have to tell Debbie, who must be afraid but says she trusts me to do the best for the family. It eats at me, I know I can protect them at home, but during the day, when I'm at work, she is in the house, alone with the children. We talk about moving the kids back into our room at night. I start getting off the bus a few stops early and walking, to check if anyone is coming after me.

Then Reg turns up at Hornsby Police Station.

'You are *not* to go out there,' John tells me firmly. 'I'll go and speak to him. You stay where you are.'

He heads outside, but there's no way I'm staying in the detectives' office. I burst out of the front door onto the road outside.

'Hey, fat fuck, you come near my family and you'll regret it.'

'Are you threatening me?' Reg asks, sneering.

'No, I'm promising you. You come near my family and it will be the last thing you do.'

Maybe he thinks that I will be unable to touch him because I am a police officer, but I don't feel any inhibition. I feel that old anger deep inside me and am prepared to let it loose.

Reg hesitates, and I can see that he is frightened. John puts himself between us and starts to walk him away. I stare after them, not moving.

When Reg is gone, I tell John I'm sorry.

'Mate, I would have done the same thing,' he says. 'I just don't want him making a complaint against you, that's all.'

'Let him. I'm more than happy to justify why I said that to him.'

I mean it: I will not play by the rules if my family is threatened. Reg gives us no more trouble.

When word gets back to the Stick-Ups what has happened, they tell me not to worry and that they will fix him. I interpret that as saying Reg is fucked; that they will find something to charge him with. And, frankly, I don't care.

***

Somehow, this crisis helps bring Debbie and me closer. It makes me see that, while I've been off playing cowboys in the police, she has become vulnerable. I learn a new respect for how she handled the pressure. It also means Debbie has seen something of the world I walk into when I leave the family home and go to work. Hopefully, she also saw that I'll do whatever is required to protect her and the children.

We feel like a good team, though work can still take me away at all hours, with little warning, meaning the full weight of bringing up our children always falls on her.

The kids know none of this, however. They're growing up and every moment we are together as a family we are happy. It's a happiness forged in hardship, maybe, and tested by having a fat, standover man turning up outside her parents' house but all this has hammered out the bond between us, making it stronger. It feels like, whatever test comes next, I can be both a good cop and a husband.

Don't Hurt Him

Late 1993: eight years in

A call is put through to me in the Hornsby detectives' office. A woman's voice, nervous and uncertain.

'I'm calling because I know your family.'

'How can I help you?' I ask.

She says her name is Sharon (not her real name). 'I've got this information. I wasn't sure whether to pass it on, but I feel I have to.' A relative has told her I'm a cop. That I am someone she can trust.

'What information?' I ask.

'I need you to promise me that you'll handle it delicately.'

'I need to know more about it before making any promises.'

'It's about my brother.'

'OK –'

'I think he's done an armed robbery.'

That gets my attention. Eight years into the job, over the past few months I've been getting flogged: break-and-enters, frauds, assaults, as if every job that came into the Hornsby detectives' office I seemed to end up doing. Most of these are straightforward, volume crimes, the constant whip of work that keeps me running without feeling I am moving forward. But I want to get off the treadmill.

'You're doing the right thing, passing this information on,' I tell her. 'Let me know the details.'

She says her brother's name is Isaac (not his real name). She's seen his photo in a wanted ad or something in the papers. He's a good man, she says, but he's been through some bad times and got into drugs.

Both she and I are now committed.

There is enough in what she's told me to make me want to meet her. Heading out of the office, I ask a young, plain clothes constable if he'd like to come along.

He nods, saying 'Great.' He's smart and keen, fresh out of uniform. Just like I was a few years ago.

We meet Sharon at her home and sit together in her living room, where she and I make small talk about our families at first before I ask her to talk about her brother.

She gives me details of the robbery, in a building society on Sydney's northern beaches. Isaac walked in during the day, when the place was full of people. He hid his face – most armed robbers used a bandanna or a stocking – and got away with the money. Fortunately, no one was hurt. Sharon doesn't know if Isaac has a gun. He might have.

'You won't harm him?' she asks.

It isn't a dumb question. The New South Wales Police Force are not famous for being caring, sharing types.

'Please treat him with respect,' she asks. 'He's my brother, I love him.'

I ask her where he's living.

She tells me and repeats her request, 'Don't hurt him.'

I look her in the eyes, and tell her, 'Don't worry, you can trust me. We won't hurt him.'

Before we leave, I try to reassure her, 'You've done the right thing.'

***

We ask a magistrate to sign the warrant authorising us to do a search of Isaac's unit, and to use force to get inside it if we have to.

'Make sure no one gets killed,' he says, handing over the thin sheaf of papers.

I laugh. I've been in the cops long enough to know how to execute a search warrant.

'What could possibly go wrong?' I joke, but he's already turned away to deal with something else.

***

We form up beside a nearby cricket oval to go over my plan for the operation. I've seen what can happen when you don't plan for a job properly; a year ago, during a covert search for a marijuana plantation in remote bushland to the north of Sydney, I'd heard someone call my name, then gunshots. Sprinting over, I saw another cop, white-faced, with blood smeared across his shirt.

A guard dog had attacked him and he'd pulled his gun but shot his own fingers off while wrestling with the animal. He collapsed and I kneeled there, with my shirt wrapped around his hand, trying to stop the bleeding.

It felt like hours before anybody came to help us.

Standing beside the oval, I recognise the familiar mix of fear, adrenaline and excitement I always feel before a big job. The other cops are waiting for instructions, among them Jon, the plain clothes constable who came with me to meet Sharon, and a couple of detectives from the Armed Hold-Up Squad, which is known in the force as the Stick-Ups.

One of these guys I know, a tough unit who played reserve grade footy but still has a boyish face, earning him the nickname Strongboy.

The others I haven't worked with, although I know the sergeant leading the surveillance team; he served in Vietnam before joining the cops and has the nickname Agent Orange.

Despite the twisting in my stomach, I'm not going to show weakness. The plan is simple, I say, 'We'll go straight from here. It's a minute-, two-minute drive. It's a housing commission place, so we won't hang around because we'll stand out like dogs' balls. I'll go in with Jon and you blokes from the Stick-Ups. We'll knock on the door while the surveillance team covers the back in case he throws something out or tries to bolt.'

They nod. They understand their roles. We roll out and drive to the brown-brick, 1970s apartment building, three or four storeys tall where Isaac has his apartment. Pulling up, we quickly move across the ground and into the shade inside the building. Climbing to the first floor, I put my ear to the door of his unit and, hearing somebody moving about inside, signal to Strongboy for us to take up our positions on either side of the doorway with our backs to the brickwork, in case whoever is in there starts shooting.

Jon and the second cop from the Stick-Ups shelter in the stairwell, ready to follow us when Isaac opens the door.

***

'Get fucked!' he shouts again from inside the unit.

'Drop the knife!' Another voice.

What's going on?

The quick sound of a gunshot.

Silence.

A woman screams.

We start kicking the door – only it doesn't buckle.

With Strongboy, I shoulder-charge the door, one at a time at first, then both of us together, until it breaks off its hinges and falls down flat, sending the two of us crashing into the apartment.

Inside, the woman is still screaming. We're in the living room. The woman's on my left, bent over, hands clawing at her face. A knife is lying on the carpet, beside an outstretched hand.

Facing me, is Agent Orange, with his gun still pointing at the body.

Fuck, I think.

It can't have been more than a minute or two since I knocked on the apartment door. No more than 10 since I was standing on the footpath beside the oval.

A stream of unlikely thoughts flows through my mind: *How do we make this go away? Remove the body. There's a rug, wrap it up in the rug. Cover it up. This hasn't happened.*

I come back to my senses, and Strongboy and I drop to our knees on the carpet, examining the man lying on the floor. There is no pulse. The bullet has gone into Isaac's chest – *right through his nipple*, I think. *That looks strange* – but when we roll him over there's no exit wound, so there isn't much blood.

How can he be dead when there is so little blood?

I hear the other cops we'd left outside in the stairwell come crowding through the doorway. 'Jon, get out of here and use the radio,' I shout. 'Let them know someone's been shot during a police operation.'

Looking up at Agent Orange, I ask him, 'What happened?'

He says that while we were at the door, he heard the shouting, climbed up to the balcony and got inside the unit. He says Isaac came at him with a knife.

The knife is lying on the floor, reflecting the sunlight coming through the window. A long blade. A kitchen knife, perhaps. I can see specks of dust sparkle in the air above it. My mind's in chaos.

I didn't plan this.

The woman, Isaac's girlfriend, is led into another room, still screaming. An ambulance arrives, as do the uniformed police, who string blue and white tape across the stairwell, trapping us inside the crime scene. Soon, my sergeant, John, arrives as does Doodles, the sergeant at the Stick-Ups. They speak in low, serious voices, 'What's gone on?' 'Are we good on this?'

A police shooting means the commissioner is notified. There'll be an investigation. The press will be all over it.

I was talking to Isaac when we shot him, I think.

***

We're driven to the headquarters of the Major Crime Squad in Parramatta, as the shooting took place in that part of Sydney covered by the police force's Northwest Region, not my own North Region, which means everything there is alien to me.

When we walk into their offices, it isn't what people say but what they don't say that I notice.

'What happened?' someone asks.

'We shot a bad guy,' I tell him.

'No worries. How you going?'

'Good.' It is a stupid, macho, self-protective answer.

He looks at me and nods.

Each of us who was on the raid is kept separate from the others, in different corners of the office. Everyone else is busy; on the phone to the coroner, the magistrate, the morgue, or following some hurried order from the ranks above us. I sit at an empty desk and no one speaks to me, until a female detective notices I am alone and comes over to ask how I am coping.

'Good,' I say, but this time grateful for the question.

I call my wife, Debbie, at home and can hardly get the words out, 'This job I've done, you've probably seen it on the news. Just wanted to let you know that I'm OK. The crook I was going after, he's been shot. He's dead.'

'Are you sure you're OK?' asks Debbie.

'Yeah. Fine.' I want to keep the conversation short from fear that, if I speak to her for longer, I might break down, so I hang up, saying, 'I don't know what time I'll be home.'

It's hard to know how quickly the time passes. I am numb. As I'm being questioned by the blank faces of the detectives leading the internal investigation, someone interrupts us: 'The psychologist is here. You need to go into the briefing room.'

Inside, there is a ring of chairs. Each of us who was on the raid takes a seat facing the shrink, who looks at us in silence before speaking.

'This is probably traumatic, what's happened,' he says. 'You've been processing a lot. Has anyone got any problems?'

Like I am going to put my hand up in front of the group and tell him what I'm feeling. *Yeah, I've got a problem, because the target's sister told me not to hurt him, and I was talking to him when we shot him, and right now I don't feel good about it.*

Instead, I say, 'No problems.'

'Your instinct is going to be to get on the drink,' the shrink continues. 'But right now that's the worst thing you could do. The best thing you could do is something physical. Go to the gym.'

We nod. No one makes eye contact.

Then we go out drinking.

Once drunk, I am a tough guy again. I'm a detective, a hardarse, 10 feet tall, I work hard and play hard and laugh off tragedies that would swallow a civilian.

As the hours pass, we start back-slapping, watched by the barman, barmaids and the tradies crowding the front bar, many of whom are regulars and recognise our faces. Many of them must know about what happened from watching the TV news.

A police car drops me home around midnight and Debbie meets me at the front door, sleepy-eyed.

'Are you OK?' she asks again.

'Yeah, it's all good. It happened.'

It isn't true. I'm sick. The alcohol was medicine. I want to sleep, but not with Debbie and the baby. Not now. I feel dirty. When I get sick, I'm like a dog. I want to crawl under the house.

'I'll sleep on the lounge,' I tell her. She goes back to the bedroom, where our daughter, who is just a few months old, is sleeping.

When I lie down, I cannot sleep. My thoughts chase each other through the early hours of the morning: *I was talking to him when we shot him.*

I picture Isaac lying on the ground, with just a little blood flowing from where the bullet entered. *I promised not to hurt him.*

I tell myself that I will leave the cops.

***

The next day I go to work and write up what happened. I'm counting on seeing Jon. He and I went through this job together. We both met Sharon. We were both there when she asked us not to harm her brother.

Jon calls in sick.

Days later, when he does make it in to work, I take him into one of the interview rooms and lose control of my anger.

'You didn't fucking turn up!' I tell him. 'I really needed you. If you come out on a job like that, you've got to see it through.'

'I phoned up, I was sick,' he says.

'I don't give a fuck! You could have called me if you were sick, if you were genuinely sick. You could have found me, but you just didn't turn up.'

'It mucked me up.'

'It mucked me up too.' The sound of my voice is harsh inside the bare walls of the tiny room. 'I needed to speak to you. I needed help with this and you just left me on my own.'

I can see that he's upset, and that I am not helping, but I can't stop myself. I like Jon and respect him but I can't stop the anger coming out.

'If you want to do this type of work, you've got to be prepared to front up and to fucking turn up,' I lecture him.

But who am I to talk? I'm going to leave the cops, I promised myself that.

***

I call Sharon. To say I am sorry. To ask her for her forgiveness.

I barely get my first words out before she interrupts.

'I don't want to speak to you. I told you not to hurt him and you killed him.'

'But –'

'You killed him. I don't want to hear anything you've got to say.'

'I'm sorry.'

'You killed him.'

'I'm so sorry.'

Saying sorry just feels lame, it turns out. It doesn't explain what happened, nor make it right, nor even describe how I'm really feeling.

I don't know what I'm feeling. I don't know who I am. I'm a detective, but am I a good person? Am I helping people, or just playing cops and robbers? I can't make sense of anything right now.

Later, walking back from the courthouse where I was filling out more paperwork about the operation, I meet Agent Orange, who asks me: 'How you going?'

'Not real good, actually. I feel pretty bad about what happened.' Speaking to Sharon stripped away my bravado, I don't feel like pretending I'm a hero. For the first time, I can be honest with another cop.

'You get used to it after the first few,' he says.

I nod.

For a moment, I resent him. Shooting Isaac wasn't following the plan. But I know he made a split-second decision under pressure. It was my operation, which makes me responsible for what happened.

The narrow pathway from the courthouse leads to the red-brick, single-storey Hornsby Police Station.

At the front door, I realise I don't have to go back through it. I look at the run-down building, picturing the over-crowded, poky little rooms inside it, the concrete walls, the way that it is always hard to get away from other people in the corridors and offices. I could keep on walking. *This could be the moment that I leave the force.*

I could go home to Debbie.

Debbie doesn't know what I am feeling.

I push open the door and a bell rings. The station sergeant at the front counter looks up. I walk past, into the offices behind him. *This is all part of being a cop,* I tell myself. *Other cops, like Agent Orange, know this. It's tough, but I can do it.*

This is the price to pay. I've paid it.

I walk back into the detectives' office, with its ringing phones and desks piled high with paperwork and occupied by other cops who kick down doors and carry guns, who lock up crooks, get on the drink and never talk about their feelings. But who at least know what it takes to be a policeman.

I'm one of you, I think.

For the first time, sitting down at my desk, I am a cop, completely.

You Don't Go Straight to Homicide

1994: nine years in

The regional boss of the Major Crime Squad, Ron Smith, walks into the Hornsby detectives' office on a Friday afternoon, as I'm finishing my shift. Soon to mark my ninth year in the force, which means I will attain the rank of detective senior constable, I'm still a junior cop and so I keep my head down. It's not unusual to see Ron here as our office is on his way home from his headquarters in Chatswood. He might be here for work or for a catch-up with one of the senior detectives, like calling into the pub with mates before the weekend starts.

'Have a drink,' he says to me.

'I wouldn't mind,' I tell him. There's a fridge in the office full of beer. Although the rules around drinking have tightened up since I was first in uniform, when station cops might have a schooner standing behind the front counter, the detectives are still seen as responsible enough to manage our drinking. We won't get on the drink at 10am but if it's 4pm and we've just done a lock-up, we might shut the office door and open the fridge.

I fetch two beers and hand one over, wondering what he's here for. Major Crime includes the Armed Hold-Up Squad as well as other elite squads, including Homicide. That's where I want to get to, but I don't know how, particularly after walking away from the Stick-Ups.

Other detectives join us. The fridge empties but someone goes out to buy another carton.

'When are you coming back?' Ron asks me.

'I wouldn't mind,' I say again. I'm feeling cautious. Ron and the others keep drinking. I do the same. We get through four or five beers each. I'm not legless but on the way, and well aware that Debbie must now be sitting outside, waiting, thinking that I am up here finishing off my work.

'I think we can find you a spot,' Ron says, and my heart leaps. 'Come and see me next week in the office.'

When I make it outside to see Debbie, I know I've been a cockhead, leaving her sitting with the kids while I was furthering my career. I throw my hands up to apologise and she is shitty with me for a while on the drive home, but she can see I am excited.

'Look, Ron Smith was there and he's offered me a place in Major Crime again and I just had to speak to him and have a drink,' I tell her.

'Well, if that's what you really want to do, I understand,' she says.

I think she's happy for me. She's known me long enough to know it's what I want, that one day I hope to be a Homicide detective. We both know going back to the long hours and high-stress jobs will impact her, but I tell her that it won't be like the Stick-Ups. I'll make it clear to Ron that I don't want to go back into that squad. She nods and looks at the road in front of us. I guess she thinks if I'm happy at work then the family will benefit or, if she is uncertain, she won't stop me from moving forward.

A week later, in his office, Ron asks me, 'Where do you want to go?'

'Homicide,' I tell him.

Ron smiles. 'You don't go straight to Homicide.'

Instead, he offers me a place on the Organised Crime Squad, responsible for extortions, large-scale thefts and fraud cases. Their jobs are mostly property offences, not the offences of violence, like armed robberies, sexual assaults or murders, I get satisfaction out of. It's hard for me to cry tears for a company that's been defrauded, but if I'm going after a crook who's assaulted somebody inside their home, then however much of myself I put into catching that offender, it's going to be worth it.

It needn't be forever, I tell myself. If I want a place in Homicide, then maybe I can earn it.

***

This time, I work harder to find the balance. Instead of beers on Friday afternoons, I'll be at home, mowing the lawns, fixing up the yard, washing the car, getting all my chores done so I can spend the weekend focusing on Debbie and the children.

But, as the weeks pass, I get bored as shit working Organised Crime. We do work some good jobs. One gang target the blocks of newly built units being built across the city. When the building is ready for people to move into, with new stoves, ovens, fridges and water heaters fixed in place, these guys come in the middle of the night to strip out all the whitegoods and take them away to sell them.

It's interesting. At least they are good crooks and we have some fun chasing them. They know we're watching, so when we try to keep them under surveillance, they find ways to avoid it, or we might spend the night sitting in one block of units only to find out the next morning they have robbed the one next door.

But it's not enough. Having committed myself to the cops following Isaac's shooting, I want more. I want harder, more demanding jobs. The kind of cases that make my commitment worth it.

Looking for something that can give me more of the adrenaline I'd grown used to while working on violent crimes, I qualify for the State Protection Support Unit, who get called out wearing ballistic vests and carrying shotguns or semi-automatic rifles to armed sieges or high-risk arrests. Those jobs feel like real life. I guess at heart, I'm still the four-year-old who watched *Combat!* on television and used to sit out in the garden at night, wearing an army surplus uniform, telling my parents I was guarding the family.

But those jobs are always over quickly, then it's back to Organised Crime and the pursuit of stolen fridges. At home Jake is getting bigger, while Gemma will soon be walking. Each weekend, I take them over to my parents, where Dad lets them climb all over him and play stupid games together, while Mum will spend hours with them cuddled up. My dad has mellowed as a grandfather, I think, and I understand him better now I am a parent. While Mum fusses over the kids – to them, my parents' house is always 'Grandma's' – he and I spend the days sitting on the back deck together, talking.

Debbie and I still don't have much money, but my parents have bought a weekender up the coast in Port Macquarie, which means not paying for accommodation. We often head up there and spend our days on the beaches. Jake and Gemma show me just how much there is to live for as I hold their hands and we run in and out of the surf.

I meditate each morning. Through my qigong, I have started to see the benefit of these breathing exercises and the discipline of emptying my mind. It helps me find the same peace that I remember from sitting on my surfboard looking out at the horizon. Funny, I used to laugh at hippies meditating in the lotus position. Now it's become something I rely on, before the next wave of work, or life with the kids crashes down on me again.

***

I don't see it coming. Sure, there have been whispers for as long as I can remember, but I haven't been listening.

Sometimes those hushed voices, hinting that certain cops were involved in something dirty, did get louder. Right through the

1970s and 1980s, when I was at school, out surfing, or starting out in uniform, there were State Government inquiries investigating police links to organised crime and allegations of corruption. But back then I was too caught up in what I was doing to pay them much attention.

Even during the early 1990s, when I was working with Geoff in the Hornsby detectives' office, I managed to ignore the whispers. None of the cops who I respected, the people like Jim Williams, were ever mentioned and, unless somebody had the guts to stand up in public and speak plainly, I was not going to let it trouble me.

On 11 May 1994, an independent New South Wales MP, John Hatton, takes to his feet in the State Parliament and accuses the police force of corruption. He calls for a royal commission to investigate, saying we are 'out of control'.

I read about it in the morning papers. The police top brass packed the public gallery in their blue uniforms to watch as the police minister, Terry Griffiths, called Hatton 'paranoia personified', 'a poor man's Sherlock Holmes', and 'a disgrace to parliament'.

'There is no need to investigate the New South Wales police,' said Griffiths. 'I've said they are the best in the world. They are.'

Hatton called on Griffiths to resign.

After nine hours of debate, the motion to hold a royal commission into corruption in the police force passes. By a single vote.

Griffiths, along with several former premiers of the State and the police top brass, calls it a waste of time and money. Our commissioner, Tony Lauer, calls a press conference to say the force has reformed already. 'We're clean,' he tells the reporters. We've dealt with any organised corruption.

Reading the next day's paper at my desk, I am not so sure.

A Supreme Court judge, James Wood, is put in charge. He is a thin, precise man. A predator. His royal commission will not work like a trial, where the prosecution and defence make their arguments and the judge is strictly neutral; instead this will be an inquisition. Justice Wood gathers together an army of lawyers and cops hand-picked from the other states outside of New South Wales. They are serious detectives. This time, we're the suspects.

But, it seems like nothing happens. There are no public hearings. No arrests. We sit, and read the newspapers, and wait.

Like every other detective, I keep on working. And while we do so, the royal commission begins its covert operations. They go to Kings Cross, where I used to work with my uncle. There, they find a bent detective sergeant, Trevor Haken, who is already under investigation over his dealings with a drug trafficker.

A detective with almost three decades in the force behind him, Haken had been part of the same work-hard, play-hard culture I'd seen at the Stick-Ups, but had given up the grog to help save his fractured marriage. At the Cross, he was introduced to what they called the *Laugh*, where the senior cops received regular payments from those running drugs and prostitutes through the nightclubs and strip joints in return for police protection.

Haken became the bag man, picking up money and sharing it out among the other detective sergeants. Most of the payments were for leaving those who had paid up alone. But the police could also gut briefs – removing evidence – to make sure someone got a not guilty verdict, provide tip-offs of impending raids, put on raids that were really done for show and made no real effort to search a property, or divert other cops to those crooks who hadn't paid them.

Some criminals were given the green light to do what they wanted on the basis that at least the local cops knew who they were and could keep a leash on things. If the Kings Cross detectives stood up and sent these guys to prison, according to this thinking, whoever came in to replace them might be uncontrollable.

I guess, maybe, it didn't seem so wrong, at first.

With my uncle, I'd seen what the world of the Cross was like inside the strip clubs, with their free-flowing booze and gaudy lights that hid what was sitting in the shadows. I'd learned the sense to stay away.

But when Haken started out in the police, as a traffic cop, he learned that tow truck operators and undertakers would pay kickbacks in return for getting a referral from the scene of a local accident or a grieving family. Later, doing plain clothes work at 21 Division, he watched as one businessman who was linked to over two dozen gambling clubs would visit each week with a bag of cakes for the detectives and a bag of money for their bosses.

I guess that when you do take that first step and find you don't get caught, while the world seems to keep on turning, it must become easier to keep on walking downwards.

Then the further down that slope you walk, the more acceptable each little sin becomes, until you've fallen headlong down a pit where anything's allowed.

The royal commission waits until Haken is at his lowest, when he is being questioned by another law-enforcement body, the New South Wales Crime Commission, over his dealings with a man called Robert, a former club doorman who's now selling cocaine out of a budget motel above a strip club known as the Pink Panther.

As their interrogators go hard at Haken, asking, 'What do you know about Robert?' 'Have you ever taken money from Robert?' 'What do you know about Robert's operation in the Cross?', the royal commission's lawyers are sitting in a separate room, watching a live feed of his denials play out on a TV screen.

On the afternoon of Friday 2 September 1994, the royal commission speak to Haken in person. They say, 'You are in a very serious position.' They talk about a possible indemnity from prosecution if Haken agrees to cooperate with them in their investigation of corruption.

Haken says he will.

His car is fitted with a microphone and camera that record his meetings with criminals who hand over thousands of dollars, which he then shares out among the other bent detectives, who call themselves the A-Graders. The camera mounted in Haken's dashboard records their faces and the banknotes changing hands. It also records Haken and the other Kings Cross detectives as they drive themselves to work each morning to do a few hours in the office, then drive to the pub at lunchtime to drink into the evening. Each day the pattern is repeated. Bribes are taken. Criminal investigations thwarted. Crooks are given the green-light to keep on selling drugs, running extortion rackets or carrying out shootings.

In late 1994, Haken starts to approach more senior police officers, including the superintendent in charge of a drug task force, and records the conversations. After listening to the tapes, the royal commission begin to gather evidence against cops up to the level of chief superintendent and assistant commissioner.

As detectives, we know nothing. In the pub after work, we shrug our shoulders. Then, at the end of 1994, the royal commission holds its first public hearing. The TV cameras show that it is set up like a courtroom. James Wood sits, angular and attentive, facing the ranks of lawyers opposite. Only, in court, criminals have a right to silence. Not so the cops brought before the royal commission.

Instead, police brought into the witness box can be compelled to answer questions. If they decline, they can be arrested. If they lie, they can be jailed for perjury. The media pile in and, once again, police corruption is back on the front pages.

During those early hearings, I recognise some names, although none of them are cops I've worked with. I feel that sense of shame I remember from when my old partner, Geoff, was arrested at Hornsby. At the Blue Gum, no one wants to talk about the royal commission.

In April 1995, almost a year since it was established, the royal commission begins a public hearing on the Kings Cross detectives. We follow it on the nightly TV bulletins and in the morning's papers, as detective after detective is called to give evidence and denies any knowledge of corruption.

On 5 June, the head of the detectives, Graham 'Chook' Fowler takes the witness stand and is asked if it is his position that he never received corrupt money.

'That's correct.'

'Corruption and you are strangers?' one of the royal commission's lawyers, Gary Crooke QC, asks him.

'That's correct,' says Chook.

Crooke says he wants to play a video, making clear that this is just one excerpt from some of the royal commission's holdings – meaning they have a lot more evidence. The black and white film shows Chook sitting in the front seat of a car, facing towards the hidden camera. It shows Chook's face and the bare legs below his shorts. It shows the banknotes as Chook takes them. Afterwards, in the hearing room, there is a moment of silence. People are stunned.

Chook says they must have got an actor to play him.

'Why can't you be man enough to admit your involvement?' Crooke asks.

This is Not Right

1995: 10 years in

Am I man enough to admit my involvement?

Like those Kings Cross cops, I've been drunk on duty. On my first day as a probationary constable, a busload of us were driven up to Brooklyn, in the north of Sydney, where the wide Hawkesbury River flows down towards the ocean. The officer running our induction asked us, 'Who's going to buy the beer?' so I went into the pub and bought a carton. We spent the day on the police boat, drinking. But I was never on the take.

Throughout 1995, the royal commission starts to expose another kind, where cops weren't simply allowing crooks to break the law but were themselves committing crimes to make sure crooks get caught.

The newspapers call it 'noble cause' corruption. Looking back, I realise we were first warned about it at the police academy, when I was training to become a police constable and they asked us, 'If a child has been murdered and you find the offender standing over the dead body can you bash him?' The instructor winked.

It was accepted – even laughed at. If somebody was bad, we made sure he got punished. In plain clothes, I heard stories about suspects being loaded with false evidence. When I was studying for the detectives' course, there was an old joke going round about a magistrate telling a cop in court that he'd seen the same gun used as an exhibit once too often and didn't want to see it again.

Later, when I rode out with the Stick-Ups, I sometimes had doubts about the strength of the evidence we collected, but it still seemed to get convictions. When I went back to Hornsby, working as a detective, I'd learned from these experiences. I sat with the older cops in the back bar of the Blue Gum Hotel, and started to hear more in the silences between people than in what they were actually saying.

To be honest, I don't think there's a cop who signed up when I did who hasn't heard something, whether it's detectives holding a scrum down to agree what version of events to give in court, or carrying a spare pistol on certain jobs, so they can plant it on a suspect.

But there's a difference between hearing things and acting.

At Hornsby, I arrested a real hard head over a break-and-enter. When I asked, 'Are you prepared to make a statement?' he said he wouldn't mind a last beer before prison. He knew he was going down. We also had a stack of reports of other local break-and-enters we suspected he might have been involved in. That night, the station supervisor came into the interview room to check on us and nodded; the crook was sitting having a beer, I had another open bottle beside me on the table and he was signing up to all the offences he'd committed. He got four or five years.

I am happy to sit in an interview room for eight hours, telling a suspect I'm not going anywhere until I get a confession. One afternoon shift, the uniformed cops arrested a man who took a machete to hold up a shop. Two days before, another store got robbed in the same way and whoever used the blade had taken chunks out of the shopkeeper. After one unsuccessful attempt to get our suspect to confess to the earlier attack, I told my partner 'This is not right. We're going back.' I was let into his cell and lay down on the floor to talk to him. I wasn't going away, I told him. He confessed.

I arrested a firebug over a series of arsons at a nursing home, a hospital and at a block of units, where a blaze was set at the bottom of both stairwells, preventing people from coming down the stairs. I didn't have the evidence to charge him so I led him on, leaning close to him in the interview room and pretending that I really liked him, that I was getting just as excited about the fires as he was, until he said, 'I can really trust you, can't I? I feel a strong connection to you. We're the same.' This was going one step further than what Jim Williams taught me about shaking a crook's hand if he offers it, but I led my suspect on. I let him believe I was just like he was.

He admitted the attacks.

If I get called before the royal commission could they say I was wrong to offer a crook a beer, or that I had pressured a suspect? At the time, I saw all this as good police work. I've never seen a cop use a phone book on a suspect. I've not seen a suspect loaded up, but I can see how it happens. I understand the motive. I can also see how you might take that one, first step, like Trevor Haken, and then think, *Well, that wasn't so bad*, so you do something worse.

But if those detectives who verbal suspects, or load them with false evidence, are corrupt, then so are their bosses. I once heard of a task force formed from every known lunatic from different regional squads and sent out to hit a crew of violent crooks. The officers above them, all the way up, must have known that if you put those cops together they were going to get the job done, but not according to the rule book. And they let them.

I've also gone into court for cases where a suspect has confessed but, because police interviews were not routinely recorded, their lawyer is now saying they deny it. More often than not, the prosecution lawyer ran with the case anyway and the magistrate accepted my evidence over that of the accused man.

It's this hypocrisy I cannot stomach. Those prosecutors and those magistrates, just like the reporters sitting in those courtrooms, all want the bad guys to be punished. Those guys were in on the giggle as much as the cops were. Yet, after the royal commission, they shake their heads, or write their articles condemning 'fat, beer-swilling cops' and 'the code of silence'. And they pretend they didn't know what was going on back then and silently allow it?

That's bullshit.

***

It's March 1995, and 81-year-old Eileen Cantlay has been strangled. Her hands and legs are bound and her body left lying on the floor of her home in Asquith, north of Hornsby.

Jim Williams will lead the investigation. I am sent from the Organised Crime Squad to help him out. And we think we've got a suspect dead to rights for the murder.

The force is now using DNA technology, and the forensic technicians explain to us that, as Eileen's attacker masturbated on her either before or after he killed her, we now have DNA from the crime scene to compare with our suspect's. They tell us everyone has a unique DNA code and show us what it looks like – a vertical strip of horizontal black lines, a little like a bar chart printed out on a slip of paper.

But when we get our suspect's DNA, we're told it doesn't match.

'Hold it,' we say to the technicians. 'Everything else is telling us it's him, but because this chart is telling us it's not, we just have to accept that?'

They tell us, yes. You have to.

We shake our heads. After more work we come up with another suspect: Salvatore Previtera, a 35-year-old still living with his mother, who was Eileen's neighbour. We get his DNA, and this time the forensics guys say: 'That's the person. That's his semen.' We wonder at this new technology.

'You can charge him with that,' they tell us.

Technology is also making more changes to how we go about our business. The law has changed this year and interviews about serious crimes must now be recorded by an ERISP machine, which is short for Electronically Recorded Interview with a Suspected

Person. It's a combined film and audio recorder that puts an end to the practice of recording unsigned confessions in police notebooks. Watching the tape, the camera makes the interview room look like the inside of a goldfish bowl, with two detectives sitting facing each other on either side of the TV screen and the suspect sitting between them at the far end of the table, facing the ERISP.

As the tape rolls, I know the camera will record how Previtera looks physically unimpressive. He's a loser, the kind of person who, if you saw him in the street, you wouldn't take a second glance at. But Jim wants us to be friendly and to build up a rapport. The DNA proves only that he masturbated on Eileen, not that he killed her, Jim says. We need Previtera to open up.

And so we empathise with him. We say that we know how he's feeling. We want to make him think that we are weak like him, that we're the same, we all have our temptations. Yes, we have his DNA to help us but, as detectives, there is pride at stake here. We want to show how we can take that evidence and go one better. We want to get him to confess.

Previtera starts to get excited. He trusts us and he wants to talk about it. He desribes how he saw Eileen come home and watched her through the window inside her kitchen. He walked over to her door, intending to rob her, and Eileen let him in because he was her neighbour's son. Inside, Previtera says he wanted to grab her only something didn't feel right. He left, then returned later the same night, this time forcing Eileen down onto the floor and tying her hands and legs together.

He asked her if she had money and took $50 or $60 from her handbag. Then he started stroking her skin. It felt soft to touch, he tells us.

Listening to this makes me feel sick. It is offensive, having to sit there with a straight face while images of what he's done invade my mind. The worst part is the sense that he's enjoying telling us about this, and that we cannot stop him, because we need him to tell us everything that happened so we can use it as evidence. It's like we've become complicit.

He tells us how he strangled Eileen with a table lamp cable. That's it. That's all we need. The interview can stop. We turn the ERISP machine off.

Normally after an arrest we'd celebrate, but this time we don't. We feel dirty. Neither Jim nor I wants to talk much. The experience of getting that confession has taken something from us that we can't recover.

***

At Previtera's sentencing, a Victim Impact Statement from Eileen's son John is tendered, describing the effect of her murder on the family. It's something else I haven't seen before, as the legislation allowing it to be presented only came into effect a month ago.

I believe in the idea of Victim Impact Statements, that those who've suffered from a crime should have a chance to say what it has cost them, and am disgusted when the judge, David Hunt, makes a point of refusing to take this one into account.

He says he sympathises with the family, but the new law is 'poorly drafted'.

'The task of the criminal court in imposing a sentence is to punish; it is not to compensate,' he says.

'It would therefore be wholly inappropriate to impose a harsher sentence upon an offender because the value of the life lost is perceived to be greater in the one case than it is in the other.'

Outside the court, John Cantlay tells the gathered reporters he provided the impact statement 'so I could let the court know how my family has felt over the last two years and the pain and grief that we have gone through'. Doing so has helped him manage his grief, he says. It's not about trying to influence the judge, or claiming that his mother's life was worth a tougher sentence than that of any other victim.

'Personally speaking, I am a Christian and I think vengeance is in the hands of the Lord … whatever the courts do, it isn't going to bring my mother back.'

Previtera gets 20 years, but I wonder if it might not have been longer. This was an awful murder. Did the judge let Previtera off relatively lightly to demonstrate that he won't be affected by these new Victim Impact Statements? I don't know the answer. We don't get to ask questions of the judges, but it is as if someone has inserted a knife and opened up another chink in my respect for the court process.

I have worked on two killings now – those of James Kelly and Eileen Cantlay – where it's felt like nobody in court has stood up for the victims. Instead, the judges and the lawyers, wearing their wigs and robes, speaking a language few of us sitting watching them can understand, have done all the talking for them.

Well then, I am a detective, I think. I can catch the killers, but I can also listen to the victims. If no one else will take a stand, then I will.

Scar Tissue

Late 1995: 10 years in

The royal commission reveals that cops from the Armed Hold-Up Squads in other regions, were crooked. Once again, suspects were loaded up. Detectives lied in court to get convictions.

It feels like the rot is getting closer. At least, if I get called to the witness box then I could say, on oath, I saw nothing. But the truth is I knew enough to suspect it. I never got deep enough, unlike the Stick-Ups' old poster boy, Roger Rogerson, who's this year made more newspaper front pages, linked to allegations of drug dealing and murder.

Maybe I was fortunate Dad was so strict with me growing up. Although I defied him at the time, maybe it was enough to stop me wading out further into the darker waters. At work, I'm still in Organised Crime, but after working another murder with Jim, I'm even more convinced I want to be a Homicide detective.

Towards the end of 1995, I'm approached by Detective Sergeant Paul Jacob from the North Region Homicide Squad, a big, garrulous man who everyone calls Jaco. He'd been a year ahead of me at Epping High School and knew some of my friends. As a cop, he'd advised us on the Eileen Cantlay murder case and I'd made no secret of wanting some day to work in the same squad as he did.

Over the months since, whenever I pestered him about it, Jaco always smiled and told me, 'We'll find a place for you, little buddy.' I realise now he meant it. He gives me a heads up that there might be a place on his squad coming up. He's asked around about me and put in a good word with his boss. As far as I can tell, the transfer seems to happen solely on Jaco's recommendation.

It's everything I've wanted.

The squad's led by a gruff hard man, Detective Senior Sergeant Paul Mayger. He calls me 'son'. Some people find him difficult to get on with, but I respect him: he always backs his troops when we're in the firing line from our bosses or the newspapers.

And our cases are always in the papers. If we're called to a crime scene inside an inner-city housing commission block at night, it's no surprise to walk out into the glare of the photographers' flashbulbs and be on the next day's front pages. Politicians read the papers, which means our bosses, right up to the commissioner, always want to know what's happening, because each of them is only a phone call away from some MP or minister demanding to know why it's not been solved yet.

As the boss, Paul has to deal with all of that exposure, and I quickly learn to trust him to make the right decisions. It only gets harder when we do make an arrest because, unlike in other squads, our work will always be examined in public. Each Homicide case means giving evidence either during an inquest or at a trial in the Supreme Court. And that means more newspaper attention.

It's high stakes, and addictive. Each homicide means someone's life. You can't afford any mistakes. Within the squad, we work in teams, with one detective sergeant to two detective constables. I'm grateful Jaco is my sergeant. It means he's there to lead me through it.

Jaco becomes my mentor, in the same way as Jim Williams at Hornsby. An understated man, though always well-dressed in a dark suit and a white shirt with cufflinks, he seems to radiate calmness. Even his smile is reassuring. Following him through the corridors of our headquarters in Chatswood, I watch how he brings people together, greeting everyone from the region commander to a junior analyst with a handshake or a hug, and even stopping to talk to the bloke guarding the boom gate outside, 'Hey champion, how you going?'

Like Jim, Jaco's also meticulous, ruling off each task as it gets done in his red job book. And, like Jim, he is driven. We work long days and right through weekends. If we're preparing a case for court, we might work until midnight, when we're dead on our feet under the office lights, then come back the next day at 5am. Somehow, Jaco is always there before us. His goatee hides a double chin and he chain-smokes, while I'm younger and training every day but I look at him and wonder, *How does he outlast me?*

It's mental toughness, I realise. Jaco can stand things that would break me. Six years ago, as a detective constable like I am, he worked a serial murder case, where six elderly women were bashed to death across Sydney's north shore. The newspapers called it the work of the Granny Killer and Jaco was part of the team sent to catch him. The longer that they took to do it, the more people would be murdered.

Jaco was there, outside the house, when their main suspect, John Wayne Glover, killed his last victim, Joan Sinclair. Jaco went in with the other cops to find her killer lying in the bathtub and arrested him. It was a good result in one sense, but they had to live with the fact Joan might still be alive if they had moved a little faster.

Like Jim, Jaco knows how to work an interview. A gentle soul himself, he's not afraid to be ruthless or put somebody under pressure. If it suits him, he'll bring me in as the attack dog and the two of us will work the interview together. Some people weep. Some people sit in silence, terrified. One time, I watch a suspect's nose start bleeding when we tell him we suspect him of a murder.

And if it takes a toll on us, and on our suspects, it does the same at home as well. Working a case, we might be gone for days or weeks. Debbie gets left alone at home with two young kids. She says she's losing me to the Homicide Squad and though I tell her that she isn't, I know there's some truth in what she's saying. I am making more money now than when we got together, which makes things easier in some ways, but we both know that if I have to choose between a weekend at home and working a murder, or between sitting up all night at our kitchen table preparing for a court case and going to bed with Debbie, then that choice is easy.

If I lose myself in work, I figure, it is justified because I'm trying to catch killers.

And I love it. I just can't get enough. In Homicide, we take a lot of pride in our work and wear dark suits, partly because Jaco does and partly to intimidate the crooks, so they know they are dealing with professionals. We look the part, and pretty soon, I feel it. We're the elite. We solve the worst crimes you can think of.

When we arrive in some quiet country town to investigate a killing, you can see people thinking, *The A-Team are here.*

I don't realise how the job is changing me in other ways. Ways that nobody expected.

***

We only get the bare details at first: Martin Davidson, 60 years old, medium build, grey hair, blue eyes. Last seen in Waitara on 18 September 1995. The Homicide Squad is given the case and Jaco is asked to lead it.

We base ourselves in the nearby Hornsby Police Station, where I started out in the police, near where Martin ran a slot-car track that kids would visit in the evenings and at weekends to race electric cars around a giant, twisting indoor ring. The kids' parents tell us Martin always told them not to worry when they dropped their kids off, that he would look after their children and they were not to hurry back. We go to the track and find a cardboard box on which someone has scrawled: 'You paedophile.'

One boy tells us Martin was having sex with him. That makes the boy a potential suspect. I've seen enough in the police by now that an allegation of child sexual assault no longer shocks me. I also know that, even if it turns out Martin was a paedophile, we can't let sympathy for his victims stop us finding out what happened.

Then we look at Martin's business partner, Bruce Matthews, who first reported the 60-year-old as missing. Matthews also reported his own wife missing, about eight years before.

Her name was Bernadette. The missing persons file says she was 33, a medium build, with brown hair and brown eyes. Last seen in Belmore, southwest Sydney, on New Year's Day, 1987. Last seen by her husband.

I speak to the cops who followed up her disappearance. They say they suspected Matthews was good for her murder but never managed to lock him up for it. When I ask, it turns out they never even did an interview with him.

I don't understand it. It scares me that any cops could leave a case like this without working it harder. Maybe it was because Bernadette was only listed as missing, not murdered. Surely, they would have done more if her body was recovered. I can't help wondering how many other cases like this there are out there.

Like Jim, Jaco encourages me to trust my instincts. While, publicly at least, the police treat Matthews as the worried business partner, we call him in and this time, Jaco says I should lead the interview.

I plan an ambush, politely inviting Matthews to sit down in the interview room and go through the formalities of asking if he can confirm his name and telling him he's not obliged to say or do anything, then run through the details of his business partner's recent disappearance, before dropping it on him about his wife's disappearance.

There's no reaction. It's like a light has suddenly switched off behind his eyes.

Matthews and I sit in that room for hours, long into the night, as I try to lock him into his version of what happened. When exactly did he last see her? Had they argued? He gives me little more than the bare facts we know from the missing persons report; Bernadette just disappeared.

Afterwards, Jaco suggests we try increasing the pressure, and put listening devices in Matthews' home to start recording his reaction.

We turn up without warning to question him about both his wife's disappearance and Martin's. Jaco makes no secret of the fact we think he was involved in both. Every time, Matthews just stares back at us in answer, perfectly calm, saying sorry but he can't help us. Like there is nothing going on inside his head. No panic. No emotion.

We are convinced it is an act, only we cannot prove it.

We search his home and find a hydroponic cannabis setup, so charge him with drug offences. It's another way of building pressure. We intercept his phone calls and listen as he telephones a store to organise a purchase and gives his name as 'Paul Jacob.' It's strange, but what does that tell us?

One night, Matthews builds himself a bonfire in his backyard and just stands there, watching the flames.

Then he also goes missing. He's on bail over the drug charges, so we circulate his details nationally and the cops pick him up in Innisfail, a small town in Far North Queensland. Jaco and I fly there, along with Glenn, the third member of our team. Knowing Matthews must be feeling the pressure now, and hoping he is close to buckling, when we walk into the local police station, I say: 'Surprise! We're here! You can't run from us, Bruce.'

He sits there with his vacant look as we lay out the facts: he's facing trial, he's now skipped bail and we also know he previously used a false medical certificate to get out of attending court over the drug charges.

And then there's his links to the disappearance of both his wife and his business partner. 'We're not going away,' I tell him.

Once again he sits and stares at us. It's frustrating. If he killed them, we need to understand the motive. Was it financial? Did they argue? We need to get inside his head.

We put Matthews back in the cells and watch to see what he does next. Maybe he'll arc up, we think. Maybe he'll pace up and down. Maybe he'll ask to speak to someone. Any one of these things might give us something to work with, an insight into his mind, or another opportunity to keep pushing down on him. But Matthews just looks around blankly, lies down and closes his eyes. He starts to snore.

I turn to Jaco, saying I understand that everyone is different. But sometimes when *I'm* under pressure, whether it's guilt about something I've done or something different, it's just easier to sleep.

The next day, Matthews sits in court as we get the extradition warrant to take him out of Queensland. He sits between us on the plane as we fly with him back to Sydney. During the flight, we try to talk to him, to keep the pressure up, but he only gives us flat, unemotional responses to our questions. At home, it's my son Jake's fifth birthday, 19 June 1996, and I'm missing his party for this?

At least getting Matthews back and into a prison in Sydney will be another shock to him, we figure. A few nights inside may change the dynamic. He'll be vulnerable and frightened. More willing, perhaps, to cooperate in the hope of not being sent there again.

After leaving him to stew for a few days, I telephone Corrective Services, asking them to let Matthews know Glenn and I will be coming out for another interview this afternoon. I want him to get the message: *We're coming. It's a matter of time before we get you.*

As we're about to leave the office, another detective, Andy Waterman, calls out, 'Where are you off to?'

'To see Bruce Matthews.'

'Oh. Well, I don't think he'll be talking to you.'

Andy's a detective sergeant and I'm just a detective constable, but I'm certain I know how to play this.

'That's up to him,' I say. 'He's definitely going to see me.'

Andy's grinning, like I've said something funny. 'But I don't think he'll be talking,' he says. 'He's necked himself.' He says it like the punchline to a joke.

Corrective Services just called, he tells me. Matthews has taken his own life. He won't be talking to anyone.

When we leave work, Jaco takes us to the Blue Gum Hotel, and I suppose it's a celebration. The case is over. Only, with one suicide, two people still missing and no bodies discovered, I am still unsettled. I shift in my seat and Jaco looks at me as if he knows what I am thinking.

While I have little sympathy for Martin, who may have been a grubby paedophile if you believe the boy at the slot-car track, I do care about Bernadette, and about her family. Over the months, I've become close to her parents and sister, who've gone through so much pain and have so many questions without answers. For years they have suspected Matthews played a role.

During our investigation, we spoke to an old neighbour who remembered seeing Matthews digging in the backyard of a house where he and Bernadette lived at the time. We went in with a forensics team to dig it up, I was wearing my suit, but asked them for a shovel and started tearing at the earth.

Without warning, someone called a halt. They'd found some teeth. A chill ran down my back to think this might be her body. As it turned out, they were just old dentures, nothing to do with Bernadette.

For the investigation to end this way feels worse, somehow, than if she'd been the victim of a clear-cut murder. Maybe Bernadette's family have been spared the full horror of what happened, but they are left with only questions, still unable to grieve.

Night falls outside the hotel and, once again, we do start to enjoy ourselves. As cops, we go through these investigations together and each one ties you more closely to the people who you work with. I'm proud to have worked this one with Jaco. We talk about the note that Matthews left, a note saying he's innocent, only we don't believe it.

I'm sure his suicide is an admission of guilt.

As we keep drinking, I've no desire to go home. Not this evening. I don't ask myself if we pushed Matthews too hard but, still, I know that I'm a different person from the man who woke up this morning. Looking up, I recognise an older bloke who walks into the Blue Gum. Years ago, he sexually assaulted someone I grew up with, someone I am close to, although she never went to the police.

When I found out, I made a promise to myself that I would throttle him if I ever saw him. But tonight I don't do it.

I've already killed one person today, I think. *I can't bring more grief into the world.*

The Path That You Have Chosen

1996: 11 years in

While we're out working murders, the royal commission keeps on investigating the detectives. It's like a door was opened when it revealed the corruption at Kings Cross and people are now racing to go through it. Trevor Haken has named names. Dozens of them. Other witnesses come forward, some of them offering to give evidence against others in return for not facing punishment themselves.

The royal commission's investigators keep spreading their attention outwards, looking into police units across the State. Any cop in New South Wales could be under surveillance and I can see the effect it has; we can't stand it.

Every morning, I pick up the newspaper and ask myself, *God, what have we done this time?* Cops stealing money, cops running protection rackets, cops selling heroin out of the back of police stations. The worst humiliation is suffered by the Gosford drug squad boss, Wayne Eade, who's shown on tape discussing drug deals and the purchase of a child abuse video with a prostitute, who turns out to be an informer for the royal commission.

The tape is released to the press and shown on prime time news.

The royal commission is also investigating claims paedophile rings are operating among the highest levels of politics, media, the judiciary and the police. I know nothing about any of this but, still, the feeling is of distrust and vulnerability. Each whispered conversation in the corridor or silent exchange of glances between other detectives takes on a new meaning, and helps feed the sense of paranoia. I find myself asking who might crack and what they might be saying.

As an investigative strategy, I can see that it is working.

'Give me the commission's powers and I'll lock up every crook in Sydney,' I joke in the Homicide Squad office, but I mean it. The royal commission is aggressive, they can coerce evidence from suspects, they're unafraid to use both undercover tactics and the media to provoke witnesses into talking, and they record those conversations on listening devices. Watching them go about their investigations, I'm not prepared to celebrate what they're doing to the cops, but I do think we can learn from them.

Outside of work, I'm keeping up with my studies, doing a Bachelor of Policing, not because I want to get ahead of other people at work, but out of fear of being left behind by my colleagues. A lot of my assignments are about the royal commission, arguing the police should be given the same coercive powers.

The feeling of being exposed only gets worse as the royal commission investigators work their way higher through the police hierarchy. In February 1996, the police commissioner, Tony Lauer, resigns.

The same month, the royal commission is extended and given another year to complete its investigations. It feels inescapable. I find myself unsure if I can trust my own defences and suspicious of others in the force.

***

Looking for someone to rely on, I turn to Ben (not his real name), the sifu who trains me in kickboxing, kung fu and qigong. I've known Ben since the early 1990s, when I started training with him and the two of us have grown close over the years since.

Ben's new gym has a boxing ring and I recognise the feeling from those police jobs where we go in with guns; it's the same rush of adrenaline, excitement and, only after, sickness in my stomach.

With Ben, I'm training harder than I ever have before, but when I watch him fight I still see he can do things that I cannot. I ask him, 'What's the secret?' and he talks about using the body's natural energy rather than its muscle, only I don't really follow what he's saying. Then, during one class, with the lights off and our eyes closed, we go through a series of gentle movements, opening our arms wide, then bringing them together, repeating this over and over before standing in silence with our hands about 15 centimetres apart. I can feel a resistance between my hands. It's like a ball of energy, about the size of a beachball. I start playing with it, moving it, pushing it and feeling it push back, almost disbelieving.

That is my natural energy, my chi, Ben says. I learn to feel it flowing through my body. Ben teaches me to channel it. If there's a blockage, I can feel it grinding.

He and I also meditate together, emptying our minds of everything except our breathing. Afterwards, I feel refreshed. My doubts and my uncertainties are quieter.

Ben talks about yin and yang, the two opposing principles of nature in Chinese philosophy. It's the same thing the hippies used to talk about around the campfire when I was a surf bum, only Ben tells me that while it sounds like hippy shit, it isn't. He says that when you're fighting and you throw a punch, that blow starts out weak – that's yin – then it grows strong at mid-range – yang – before its force fades at the point of full extension – yin again. I can use this against my opponent: when he throws a punch and misses, he moves from yang to yin and is at his weakest. Then, Ben says, I should feint to throw my opponent off balance, and attack. Drive over him before he can recover.

That isn't hippy shit. Each time I walk into his gym, I bow to Ben and he returns the salute. He is a few years older than me, and when he speaks, I listen. He talks about how a warrior must have honour, and how honour is founded on justice and on your obligation to others. Quoting Confucius, he tells me, 'To see what is right and not to do it is want of courage.'

After training, the two of us sit cross-legged on the floor and talk, sometimes for hours. Often, we're still sitting, reflected in the gym's mirrored walls, long after everybody else goes home. We talk about fighting, police work, how the royal commission has shown me things that make me ashamed to be a policeman and how it's changed the way I think about my colleagues.

He tells me to hold up my feelings of shame and anger at what I've seen, look at them and ask myself if they're the right reaction.

'Maybe I should say something if I suspect that stuff's been happening,' I say to Ben.

'That's not the path that you have chosen,' Ben says. 'Your path is to endure this. The only thing you can control is what you do yourself.'

Once again, I consider leaving the police and he offers me employment. I think about it. I feel comfortable sitting with him on the bare mats in a way I don't always feel going to work as a detective amid this long-running scandal. I am certain what Ben's teaching me is important.

One night, the telephone keeps ringing from his office but we don't answer. After three or four calls, I say to Ben, 'I think that's probably Debbie looking for me.' She understands the importance I place on my training and the influence Ben has on me, but she is still a young mum, at home, alone. Eventually, I answer. It is Debbie.

***

In September 1996, Detective Sergeant Wayne Johnson shoots his estranged wife and then himself after being named at the royal commission. Another detective jumps to his death from the seventh floor of a building. Other cops are found hanged or gassed in their cars. The stories start to multiply of grown men breaking down after the royal commission's investigators arrived at Christmas time, on wedding anniversaries or at children's birthday parties.

Just like it did with Trevor Haken, and I did with Bruce Matthews, the royal commission wants to take advantage of its suspects when they're vulnerable and more likely to cooperate. The price is paid in careers, hopes and shattered marriages.

In May 1997, the royal commissioner, James Wood, hands down the first volume of his final report, which is bound in red and as thick as the phone books we are supposed to use to beat our suspects. Over the past three years, hundreds of cops have had allegations made against them and dozens will now be referred to the Director of Public Prosecutions for potential criminal action.

The worst of the allegations, of a network of high-ranking paedophiles who protect one another, are found to be unproven, but the royal commission does accuse the police of failing to protect children across the State from being sexually exploited. And there is no avoiding the other evils it's uncovered. In his report, Justice Wood finds 'the only conclusion open on the evidence ... is that a state of systemic and entrenched corruption' exists within the force. 'The consequences of corruption are devastating for a police service as a whole, and for its individual members. They are similarly devastating for the community which police are expected to serve.'

It's hard to learn that some of those you looked up to were crooked. Harder still to live with the way the newspapers, defence lawyers and politicians seem to treat every detective as if we are just as corrupt. This job is hard enough, and it only gets harder when the people we rely on, like our victims' families and witnesses, become afraid to trust us. Justice Wood says there's no such thing as individual bad apples, but no one seems prepared to go out in front of the media cameras and explain that the whole barrel isn't completely rotten.

In fact, it is the opposite, it feels like our top brass desert us. One deputy commissioner goes so far as to say publicly that we are all a disgrace and should be sent back to uniform.

It makes me realise I can't trust our bosses.

Our new police commissioner, Peter Ryan, talks about wanting to 'draw a line in the sand' and leave history behind it. But over the past three years I've learned that you can't simply draw a line and say, 'That's it.'

Take the example they taught us about at the police academy: 'If a child has been murdered and you find the offender standing over the dead body can you bash him?' The answer you're supposed to give is 'No'.

But what if the child is still alive? What if only the offender knows how to save that child, but he won't talk. Would you be prepared to bash him then? If it saved that child's life, then who would not forgive you?

Every one of us goes back and forth across the line, sometimes. In the court cases that follow the royal commission, a few of their own investigators are accused of supplying and encouraging a heroin dealer in order to further its investigations, and of falsifying evidence that led to some cops' dismissal.

If true, that is surely noble-cause corruption too.

In the end, only seven cops are jailed as a result of the royal commission's work, including the former chief of the Kings Cross detectives, Chook Fowler. Instead, I watch as hundreds of cops are targeted for dismissal or internal investigation. Others retire, disillusioned.

A generation of detectives, good and bad, is lost and a link to our past goes with them. These were veterans, toughened investigators who'd seen the worst the world can offer and learned their lessons from the generation before them. Some of the younger cops who come in to replace them are good enough, but they're different. More polished. More professional. I fear the force risks becoming too safe, too risk averse. Within the Homicide Squad, I notice how our ranks become depleted as those detectives who are left get promoted or moved to fill the gaps left elsewhere, or simply walk away saying they've had their fill of the police force.

The murders never stop though. The few of us detectives who are left have a responsibility, I think, to reach back to the past and try to mend that broken chain together.

In the end, I never got called to give evidence before the royal commission. After it finishes, a new, permanent watchdog is set up in its place, called the Police Integrity Commission (PIC). One afternoon, I'm driving home, listening to the car radio when I hear news of another investigation. They play another undercover recording and, this time, I recognise the voices. They are from North Region. My region. There's talk of suspects being loaded and of guns being dumped in the Hawkesbury River. Several detectives I've worked with, including Strongboy, who went with me through the door of Isaac's apartment, are among those said to be involved in it.

Strongboy ends up rolling over and becoming an informer. Later, a good friend of mine gets caught up with the PIC and I drive him to the hearing at their offices in central Sydney. 'Mate, I don't know what to say,' I tell him. 'I know that you're honest.'

***

Looking for something to hold on to, I find it in my cases. At home, I might struggle to explain this to Debbie, but if I could, I'd tell her that, at least in Homicide, it's black and white; good guys and bad guys, a killer and a victim. Everything is certain.

***

By chance, I bump into Geoff, my old partner who was jailed for soliciting bribes from a local brothel. I've bought a beer and am turning back towards my mates when I see Geoff standing there alone, a broken man and a sad one. He's drinking at the Hornsby RSL, of all places, the same bar he would disappear to when we were supposed to be working a shift together.

To my surprise, I no longer feel any anger towards him.

'Hey, Geoff,' I say. 'Long time no see.' Knowing he's spent time in prison, I make a joke of it: 'What have you been up to over the last few years?'

He laughs a little. I laugh. We shake hands and have a short, awkward conversation. Maybe I've become more forgiving. After all, while Geoff has been inside, I've seen so many different people in so many different situations. I've helped put some of them in jail and seen them come out having served their sentence. Some of them I've even had a beer with afterwards. I've learned that luck, like who your parents are, what your childhood was like, who you end up working with, plays a huge part in everyone's life story.

Everyone has failings, I think. Maybe some of the idealism that once made me so angry with Geoff has since been tarnished. Maybe I'm just a rougher, beaten and battered version of myself, still shell-shocked by the impact of the royal commission.

Geoff's served his time, I think. *The justice system's had its piece of him.*

The differences between us, cop and criminal, seem small and unimportant as we stand there in the RSL together.

At the same time, they are everything. I am a cop; he is a crook.

I am a cop, and I still have other cops, like my sergeant, Paul Jacob, to look up to. Like me, Jaco survived the royal commission with his integrity unquestioned. If working Homicide is simple, it is also demanding. It's like a contact sport and Jaco goes in hard, but fairly. I'm on his team. He is my coach, my captain. During a case that comes to dominate the next two decades of my life, I will rely on his example.

I have to believe the justice system works.

Bowraville

December 1996: 11 years in

Right in the middle of the royal commission, Jaco is given an unusual job. He spends a week working alone on a cold case: the disappearance of three children in a small town called Bowraville, which sits on one of the slow rivers that run down from the Great Dividing Range through the rich, green cattle-farming country on the Mid North Coast of New South Wales. His task is to establish whether there are grounds to reinvestigate the case, following a formal request from a local cop who once worked it, without success.

We talk about it in the office. Jaco says the first victim was Colleen Walker-Craig, a pretty, popular 16-year-old who disappeared just over six years ago, on 13 September 1990. Colleen was at that point in life when she was becoming independent; she'd left school and moved between her mother's home and the houses of relatives. That September, she arranged to meet her mum at a local footy tournament, which was when her family realised that she was missing. After seven months, in April 1991, her clothes were dragged out of the local river.

Three weeks after Colleen was last seen, on 4 October 1990, four-year-old Evelyn Clarice Greenup also disappeared. She was a quiet girl, not the sort to run off, her family said. Photographs show her wide-eyed, with chubby cheeks and a bow in her hair, or wearing a pink cardigan. Her remains were found later that same April, dumped in the forest near a dirt road running through the hills above Bowraville.

Evelyn's skull, found lying on dried leaf litter in the bed of a gully, showed what looked like a stab wound to the right temple.

Sixteen-year-old Clinton Speedy-Duroux was the third victim. His family described him as being a Pied Piper, someone who all the other kids would follow. Clinton loved dancing, turned somersaults off the bank of the Nambucca River and, when he played footy, scored two tries to help his team win the local grand final. He disappeared on 1 February 1991, four months after Evelyn. His body, or what was left of it given the heat and the animals around that summer, was found just over two weeks later, lying near the same dirt road where Evelyn's body was found.

The autopsy found Clinton's left jaw had been broken, as if by a blow, and there was a narrow hole in his cheek, just below the right eye socket. The pathologist believed the same implement could have been used to kill both Evelyn and Clinton.

Each of the three went missing following a party in Bowraville. All three kids were Indigenous.

When Colleen disappeared, the local cops did nothing, Jaco told me. Her family said the police told them, 'Maybe she's gone walkabout'. No crime scene was established. No search was carried out.

Evelyn's family said they were told the same thing although, at least, given her age, this time the police did go out looking for her. But they were looking for a missing person, a little girl who had got lost. They weren't looking at human intervention, or trying to recover forensic evidence. No one linked her disappearance to Colleen's.

Clinton's family told a similar story. This time, the local detective was called. He interviewed a white man from Bowraville, James Hide (not his real name), in whose caravan Clinton was sleeping before his disappearance. But still there was no crime scene, no forensics. Clinton's family, too, say the cops told them maybe he'd gone walkabout.

It was only when Evelyn's and Clinton's bodies, and Colleen's clothes, were recovered, that the police could no longer ignore them. Three local detectives were told to take a look. They had little support, few resources and no access to computers, which by then were starting to be used across the force, particularly on complex cases, like multiple murders. Instead, they took their witness statements on a typewriter one of them carried round with him in the boot of his car. They were also told to keep on working their other cases.

On 8 April 1991, James was arrested and charged with killing Clinton. On 16 October he was charged with the murder of Evelyn. The 25-year-old worked in Bowraville's tanning factory, dragging bloodied skins around. It's heavy work, and he was big and powerful.

A judge ruled that the two cases – Evelyn's and Clinton's – would be heard in separate trials, meaning each jury would be told only one child had disappeared from Bowraville, not three.

In February 1994, on the third anniversary of the day Clinton's remains were discovered, a jury found James not guilty of the murder. Soon after, the State Director of Public Prosecutions (DPP) decided to drop the charge against him over Evelyn's murder.

Colleen's body was never found and no one charged over her disappearance, Jaco told me.

He filed his report in May 1996 for review by the Major Crime Squad, North, commander and the commander of the North Region. It described James as the 'suspect' despite the verdict of the court, saying, 'In my opinion there is certainly no question that all efforts should be made to investigate these very serious criminal matters to a successful conclusion.

'If it is accepted Hide is responsible for each of these deaths he is a "serial killer" who may escape prosecution for these crimes if no further effort is made'.

The report made it way up through the police hierarchy to our new commissioner, Peter Ryan. In December, I'm allocated to a dedicated task force, called Ancud, set up to reinvestigate the killings.

This time round, we have eight detectives and two full-time analysts to go through the folders full of evidence and documents produced during the first investigation. Being in a task force is new to me and when I ask what the name means, someone laughs and says it's a small town in southern Chile but don't worry about it, the names are randomly selected. I should pay more attention instead to the choice of commander – not Jaco this time but Rod Lynch, a veteran of the police force's most high-profile recent investigation, into the serial backpacker killer Ivan Milat, who was convicted of seven murders only a few months earlier.

Rod is a serious cop and knows how to work a serial murder, so I don't feel too bad about not having Jaco here to guide me. I've served my apprenticeship under him in Homicide, I reckon. I owe him. I'll only be a junior investigator on this task force, following Rod's instructions, but if I do it well, I like to think that will reflect well on Jaco. He'll always be my sergeant. My sifu.

***

At home, nothing is so simple. As 1996 draws to a close, I am increasingly unsettled. Finding the balance between work and home is hard and likely to be harder still working on this task force. I'm missing out on seeing the kids grow up. Already, work regularly means getting home too late each Friday to do my chores and dedicate the weekend to the family, as I promised myself. Often, we're working through the weekend.

Debbie is always patient, but it feels like we're in different worlds. She's at home with the children while I'm standing in bloody crime scenes. I'm struggling to unite the two sides, the light and dark. I carry too much darkness home with me. I'm still doing qigong and meditation, still running and playing soccer, pushing myself harder, trying to balance this darkness, but it's not always successful.

I have a growing sense that something needs to change. The year ends and, once again, I decide to leave Major Crime and go back to plain clothes work in Hornsby.

I type up the green transfer request. Only, I don't hear back. And soon the Bowraville investigation leads me to forget it.

***

Bowraville is a long drive, on lonely roads through thick green bushland, from our offices in Chatswood. I head up there for the first time with my new partner on the task force, Tony. When we arrive, we drive down the high street running between two hills through the centre of the town, watching the heat shimmer in the air above the baking bitumen.

Most of Bowraville's roughly 1100 inhabitants live close to the high street, in a cluster of pretty, pastel-coloured brick and timber houses. Most of these families are white. Bowraville's black population live either on the fringes, or in a strip of single-storey houses lower down, strung out along the unmarked, pitted ribbon of road leading to the town's cemetery. This area is called the Mission and it's where the three children were staying when each of them went missing. Maybe it's because I'm a city cop, or just because I'm naïve, but I wasn't expecting the town to be so segregated.

A few months later, in May 1997, a report presented to the Federal Parliament helps me understand what I am seeing in Bowraville. Called *Bringing Them Home*, it causes a sensation, explaining to people who, like me, were never taught this stuff in school, how Indigenous people were forced to live in missions set up by the churches, supposedly for their own protection, and how their children could be taken from them by police and State officials, and sent to live instead in white homes and institutions.

These people are from what is called the Stolen Generations, and were still being taken in places across Australia when I was growing up in North Epping, only, again, nobody told me.

Driving around the Mission with Tony, the black children playing footy in the park stop their game to watch us. We get out and have a look at the house where both Colleen and Clinton were staying when they disappeared. Other little faces peer round the door. A collection of old car parts is propped up along the fence and plastic garden furniture is scattered in the front yard.

Three doors up, at Number 6, is the house from where Evelyn went missing. The front window opens on to a room in which she had been sleeping.

It hits me in the stomach: the houses are so close together. Three kids, all staying on the same street, disappear over five months, during the course of one long summer. Two of their bodies were found dumped beside a dirt road in the bushland I can see behind the Mission houses. The third child's clothes – Colleen's – were dragged out of the water, near to where that dirt road crosses a bridge above the river.

I look again at Number 6. A bedsheet is pulled across the window as a curtain. At home, my own kids are five and three, making them one year older and younger respectively than Evelyn was at the time she went missing. It isn't hard for me to think how little she was then, to picture her walking or talking, or reaching up to her mother for a cuddle. To see how easy it would be to harm her.

The sound of laughter tells us the kids in the park behind us have restarted their footy game. In other houses, other children are watching us through the windows. Turning, I see two boys, maybe 12 or 13, walking down the road, loose-limbed and grinning, their arms around each other's shoulders. *That's Anthony*, I think. My childhood friend. We were just as close as those two boys are. I remember what it felt like then, to have your whole lives ahead of you.

If only it could stay that way. If only.

People on the Mission rioted after James was found not guilty of killing Clinton. They marched on the Bowraville Police Station, breaking windows in the white people's houses as they passed. One group, led by the women and including several schoolchildren, gathered outside James's mother's place, just around the corner from the Mission, throwing rocks.

Knocking on doors in Bowraville, we find we are met with hostility and suspicion. It is as if the town and its police force have turned against each other and, six years after the murders took place, their memory is still hanging heavy in the air. Most of the time, we breathe it in without noticing but on others, particularly the hottest, humid days when the air feels thick with misery and trauma, or when some redneck on the high street wants to know why we're bothering trying to find the killer – 'What are you trying to find this bastard for, to thank him?' – or someone on the Mission shouts at us to fuck off because they won't talk to a white policeman, I feel trapped in an endless jungle summer, wet with sweat, exposed to a world we thought we knew, but didn't.

What I see in that small town makes me ashamed to be an Australian.

The only way out of this is to solve the murders. But finding the people we need to talk to isn't easy. On the Mission, things don't work the same way as they do in Sydney. You can't work to city time. For starters, no one on the Mission makes appointments. Instead, we turn up at an address and ask whoever we find there if they've seen the person who we want to speak to.

'He's been up that way,' somebody will offer, waving a hand towards the town or, in the other direction, the cemetery. We head off, following where they're pointing, only to find someone else who tells us he's been seen at Top Pub, and so we drive up there, and so it goes on.

It's not always a bad thing. It slows me down and helps me take a more thoughtful approach.

Outside the Mission kindergarten, behind the house where Colleen and Clinton were staying, I approach one of the community's female elders. She watches me walk up, and before I say anything, she snaps, 'Why should I trust you? You're a cop.'

I stop and look at her, then say, 'I understand.' Only I don't. *We're the good guys, surely?*

'White cops like you came here and took our children,' she says.

I say that I just want to find out what happened to Colleen, Evelyn and Clinton.

She looks at me. I can see the sorrow in her face, beneath the anger.

Later, I'll learn this woman is Aunty Elaine Walker, Colleen's aunt, and one of those who led the march on Bowraville's police station. I'll go back and talk to her again and she will tell me more about being an Indigenous person in Australia than we learned at school in Sydney: like how her people have been bullied, beaten, shot at or raped, forced from their homes and, even during my lifetime, barred from the local shops and pubs in Bowraville.

She tells me no one listened to the families when they said their children had been murdered. The families know the reason, she says. 'It's because they're Aboriginal.

'Things only happen when we get the media's attention or we protest,' she says.

As the months pass, Aunty Elaine helps me get to know the murdered children's families, including her sister Muriel, Colleen's mother, who is like a rollercoaster, driven to extremes of high and low emotion by the loss of her daughter. She introduces me to Evelyn's family, and I quickly form a friendship with the four-year-old's aunt, Michelle Jarrett, a big, bossy woman whose wide smile disarms you. I like her immediately.

Clinton's father, Thomas Duroux, also lives in Bowraville, though he's separated from his son's mother. He's quieter than Michelle and Muriel, seemingly a man of few words, though always polite and respectful.

Sitting with him in the shade of the big, old white mahogany tree opposite his house, I'm almost afraid to ask Thomas about Clinton, as if he finds what happened too painful to talk about and having to answer will release all the emotion he is carrying, tearing him apart again.

The Mission is unlike anywhere I've known. There are different tribes, the Gumbaynggirr and the Dhanggati, different traditions, different laws and different ways of asking questions. Aunty Elaine tells me that, under Aboriginal law, anyone responsible for another's death accepts there must be payback. So far, the Australian justice system has given them nothing, she tells me. Their children have been murdered and nobody jailed as a result.

As a white policeman, how do I navigate this difference between the two worlds we inhabit? Aunty Elaine teaches me to change the way I ask my questions. Don't force somebody to make eye-contact, she says. On the Mission that's seen as impolite and confronting. Take the time to sit and talk with people, and offer something of yourself up first, so they can judge if they want to trust you.

Under her guidance, my communication skills increase and so do my responsibilities. Choosing which witnesses to believe and which I think are mistaken or lying, could decide the route of the investigation. Getting that judgment right might mean the families get justice. I make mistakes. Sometimes, I don't understand what people tell me, because I'm used to asking direct questions, not the roundabout way that they talk on the Mission. Too often, early on, I don't listen properly to what they're saying because that isn't how people talk in the city, or I misinterpret their answers due to my own unconscious biases.

I spend hours sitting under that white mahogany, which Aunty Elaine says is called the Tree of Knowledge, just talking to the people on the Mission. They start to open up.

Aunty Elaine walks past and sees me sitting on the grass in my suit. She laughs and says, 'You've got so much to learn, whitefella.'

I tell her that I want to learn. There's something different about this case. It overwhelms me. I like the fact that, the more work I put in, the more Aunty Elaine seems prepared to trust me.

I want to repay that trust. Growing up, I made a choice. I could have been a surf bum but I became a cop, which meant giving up that freedom. There'll always be a part of me that loves to surf and drink with my old mates, or dreams about travelling the world searching out the perfect break, but I want something more from life. I want to be the person people turn to when they really need somebody.

I don't think I ever spent a minute once I'd joined the cops asking myself why I did this work, or whether it was worth it. Sitting under the Tree of Knowledge had its emotional cost, but it also had its rewards. At home, with Debbie and the kids, my family rely on me. Now, on the Mission, these other children's families were relying on me, too. It was my job to find their loved ones' killer.

That is what makes working Homicide so important, I realise. It is the ultimate responsibility. It is a heavy burden.

I tell Aunty Elaine I'll do everything I can to get justice for the children.

She looks at me as if to say, *Don't fuck with me, policeman.*

***

Rod Lynch tells us not to focus on James Hide, who's already been found not guilty of killing Clinton. So, instead, we look at a local white man who's recently got out of jail and is rumoured to have been involved in the children's disappearance. The yellowing, old files from the first investigation are also full of other details, possible leads and rumours about what might have happened. One theory says a carful of blackfellas who'd driven up from Sydney were responsible. Another, which seems to have been provoked by local gossip, backed up by confidential reports from the State Department of Family and Community Services, says Evelyn's mum was a drinker who could not look after her daughter properly and so other members of her family had hidden the four-year-old, to prevent her being taken into care.

The cops who worked the case at the beginning followed that lead up, setting up surveillance on a house in another country town where they thought Evelyn might be living. Only, as it turned out, she wasn't. They also pursued reports of a stranger seen making an approach to three young Aboriginal girls during the school holidays, and of a white man seen driving with a dark-skinned girl sitting in the front passenger seat, who had something tied around her mouth.

Rod warns us that the Milat investigation was led astray in the early days by rumours and false sightings. One by one, we rule each of them out.

Reading through the boxes of old witness statements is equally confusing. Different people claimed to have seen each of the children alive *after* the dates on which their parents reported their disappearance.

One witness said she'd seen Colleen the day after the party from which she supposedly went missing. Another witness saw her at 7am on Saturday 15 September, two days after the party. A third said Colleen was sitting in a white Commodore parked outside the party, a fourth that Colleen left in the early hours to catch a train to Sydney. According to this version of what happened, she was then going to travel with some other people from the Mission to the small inland town of Goodooga, up near the Queensland border.

It was the same with Evelyn and Clinton. Three people said they'd seen someone matching Clinton's appearance hitch-hiking out of Bowraville on the morning after his father said he went missing. Around a dozen witnesses claimed to have seen four-year-old Evelyn at different places on the day after her mother said she disappeared.

These sightings created problems for the original detectives. No one saw James carry out the murders, although he had been at each of the parties from which the children apparently went missing. If the children had, in fact, been seen alive after these parties happened, then there was nothing to link James to their disappearance. If these witnesses were right, then we could rule him out.

But not every witness sighting can be trusted – that's something else they learned on the Milat investigation.

I remember Andy Waterman, the detective sergeant who told me Bruce Matthews necked himself in prison, telling me he learned that lesson when he, too, spent time on the Milat task force. Andy was a dedicated detective and said they spent ages chasing up false sightings. Memory plays tricks on people. And sometimes the way police ask the questions can cause a witness to think they've seen something they haven't.

In Bowraville, it turns out, the cops had gone around with photographs of the missing children, asking if anyone had seen them. Do that, and you risk prompting someone's memory. They're likely to believe the person in the photograph is the person they saw, even if it is now weeks or months after the event. What they should have done was ask these witnesses to pick the person they remembered out of a collection of different photos.

I shake my head at this. It's basic police work. And now, so many people claim to have seen the murdered children after the time their parents insisted they'd gone missing that it feels like we are chasing ghosts.

Rod Lynch also wants us to test these sightings of the children, to see if we can trust them. We go back to these witnesses, sometimes driving across the State to find them, and they start casting further doubt on their own recollections. According to their written statements, different people saw Evelyn at James Park, Lanes Waterhole and in the Reibels supermarket on Bowraville High Street, places further apart than you could expect a four-year-old to walk to. But we find some of these witnesses were children, interviewed without adults present. Some admit they didn't know Evelyn themselves but only thought they'd seen her later, after they heard the four-year-old was missing. Others are uncertain of times and dates, or say the first police to interview them themselves suggested the day on which the sighting had occurred.

The sense of shame I feel as we start to unpick the first investigation is not so different from the feeling of watching what the royal commission uncovered. In both, the police failed to do the job they were supposed to. In some ways this is worse than those videotapes of cops taking backhanders. Here, the police force had a responsibility to the families of the victims and we ducked it. We moved too slowly when the children first went missing and then too few resources were dedicated to the investigation. It should have been led by Homicide detectives, but it wasn't.

Even Colleen's mother, who first reported her daughter missing, had to wait six months before the police took her formal statement. No wonder the families believe they have not been properly listened to.

***

By late 1997, my request for a transfer out of Homicide and back to Hornsby seems to have been lost in the never-never and, instead of spending more time with my family, I'm now working full-time on a serial killing that took place about six hours north of Sydney. Debbie seems to be happy at home and I'm caught up working on the murders, but it means long periods of separation. Our team works 10 days on and four days off, and each time I drive away from Debbie and the kids, it feels like I'm leaving behind a part of me. When I come back, it feels as if I'm a stranger. After my four days at home, I start to feel like we are sort of back together, and then it's time to leave and drive back to Bowraville again.

I'm probably away for about half of the first year I work on the murders. With Christmas ahead of us, I fear that Debbie and I are becoming different people. How can we not be, when her life is caring for the children while mine is finding a child killer? *I am the one to blame*, I tell myself during the long drives back towards the Mid North Coast from Sydney. *I'm the one who's changed, not Debbie.*

***

Our bosses are starting to complain that we've made little progress and the Ancud Task Force starts to be cut back. Our commander Rod Lynch is promoted; others leave or are rotated out. They're not replaced.

Eventually, by the autumn of 1998, it's just me and a young detective, Jason Evers, who got put on the task force as a reward for bringing in a big drug bust, which seized four kilograms of hashish from a hotel in Gladesville. The first time I go to Jason's house to pick him up, an irate woman answers the door in her dressing gown.

'Is Jason here?' I ask politely.

'No, he's not!' She slams the door.

It turns out Jason's marriage has just ended. For the next six weeks I pick him up in a park in North Ryde because he's staying in different places until he finds a house, and the easiest place for him to park his car is behind the toilet block at the oval.

I like him, though. Jason is raw, a plain clothes constable and not yet a designated detective, but he's smart. He smiles and swaggers like a natural comedian, which balances out my seriousness, and he cares about the victims – a few years ago, Jason was a victim himself, when a man forced him to lie on the ground during a robbery and put a loaded shotgun to his head, not realising Jason was a cop at the time. A week later, the same crook did another hold-up, during which he shot somebody. To Jason, working on a murder case means standing up on behalf of those who didn't get the same chance he did.

We spend days together driving across the State, trying to track down witnesses who've left Bowraville since the murders happened. There is now enough evidence, I am certain, to discount the witnesses who claimed at the time to have seen Evelyn after the night of the party on which her mum said she went missing.

That puts James back into the frame.

In May 1998, we ask the DPP to reverse the decision to drop the charge against James for the murder of Evelyn. I spend months working alone on the submission, while Jason is caught up completing his detective training. The room set aside for Task Force Ancud is the largest I have ever worked in and, with no one else working on the investigation, I get so lonely during the days that I start phoning up to take part in the competitions broadcast on the radio, just to get some human contact.

After a year of waiting, in May 1999, the DPP comes back to us. They're not convinced. The lawyers refuse our request to put James on trial.

We have to break the news to Evelyn's mother. I feel that we have failed the family. Aunty Elaine had asked me, 'Why should we trust you?' and I hadn't come up with an answer. Worse, after the DPP's decision, my bosses decide to shut the investigation down.

I lie awake at night and think about the case; not putting somebody in prison means a serial killer is still out there.

It could have been different, I think. The decision to separate Evelyn's and Clinton's trials when James was first arrested means no court has ever heard about the deaths of all three of the children together and about the similarities between them. *Look at the Ivan Milat case. If they had also broken all the murders of his seven victims up into separate court hearings, he might have been found not guilty.* Instead, he was tried on all seven at once and convicted. Staring at the darkened ceiling, it seems so unfair.

During the days, I try to lose myself in work and training, pushing myself harder, seeking complete exhaustion. And if work is hard, then life at home is harder. I'm not the person Debbie married any longer. Instead, I want to be this person I've become, the Homicide detective. I want more of this life, more of the intensity, more of this sense of purpose, more of the bright lights – not that there are too many of those in Bowraville.

But I don't think Debbie has changed with me. I start to resent the way that her life seems so perfect. She does aerobics every morning, then hangs out with friends while the kids are at school.

Hoping to recapture the carefree, surfing lifestyle we shared when we first got together, in the winter of 1999 Debbie and I move to the Central Coast, to be near the beach. It ends up putting more distance between us. Copacabana, where we find a house, is a long, 80-kilometre commute to the Homicide Squad's offices in Chatswood, and the constant driving kills me. There just isn't time for anything except work, sleep and commuting. I leave home before the kids are up, and after two hours of wrestling with myself through the traffic each morning and evening, am too tired to enjoy the family when I get home.

I feel unfit. Without the time to practise, my martial arts and meditation suffer. A nerve in my back flares up from all the constant sitting in the car. Everything is slipping out of balance. During the long hours of commuting, I start to question if I really want to be married, then hate myself for asking the question.

At the worst times, awake in bed, listening to Debbie's gentle breathing, I start to think that she's holding me back from being the person I want to be. For our anniversary, 21 November, we go to watch a movie then to a Chinese restaurant. My nose is bent out of shape from where I broke it sparring the day before. We sit there together eating and I realise that we've become one of those couples who have nothing to say to each other.

I start to look for reasons to stay longer at the office. In the Homicide Squad, each of the detectives rotates through on-call duty, meaning we spend a week where we will handle any fresh report of murder across New South Wales. When a new job comes in at 5pm, I think, *Happy days, I don't have to go home.*

I feel like all these thoughts mean I am not a good person any longer. I can't breathe. I'm suffocating.

Debbie and I talk about splitting up. During one of these unhappy conversations, she gets into her car and drives off. I get the kids together and we go after her, eventually finding her in tears at Avoca Beach. I think she wants me to say we can make the marriage work, only I cannot say it.

Early in 2000, I tell Debbie I need a break.

'What are you doing?' she asks me.

'I don't know,' I say, and tell her I will stay at my sister Karen's.

The day I move out will always be the darkest in my memory. The kids are hanging on to me while I pack my bags into the car in our driveway. As I'm about to drive away, Jake, who's eight, is standing at the door saying 'Daddy, where are you going?' Debbie stands behind him, crying.

I stay in contact with the kids. Speaking to six-year-old Gemma on the phone, she asks me, 'Daddy, why can't you come home?' and I sit there thinking: *What sort of a human being am I?* My kids have always looked at me as someone to rely on, and I've failed them. I know I'm the one who wrecked this family.

Only later will I ask myself: if I had my time over, would I make the same decision? Those years we had together as a young family are the happiest I remember.

But I can't know the answer. Right now, this seems like the path I have to follow.

Round Two

No Good to Anyone

1 June 2001: 16 years in

This is hell on wheels, staring at the chain of brake lights stretching out in front of me on the road, mind numb, shut in by grey buildings on either side, skipping through radio stations searching for a distraction.

Wishing I didn't have to take this three-hour drive to and from work every morning and evening. Reminding myself that this was my own choice.

Behind me is the Central Coast, which I left before 5am. At the house in Copacabana, Debbie and the kids might be just waking up; only their home hasn't been my home for over a year now, not since I walked out on our family.

I stayed with my parents in Dural for a couple of months afterwards, but that became uncomfortable. Not that they made me feel bad – when I told Dad about the separation he asked, 'Are you sure this is what you want?', but did not try to stop me – the problem was that I started to get comfortable having my dinners cooked for me and Mum doing my ironing. In my mid 30s, I was becoming a child again.

My parents' place was also too far from Jake and Gemma, who have to be my priority. So in the spring of 2000 I found the cheapest place available in Copacabana: a granny flat that I rented for $105 a week. I scrounged up a bed and a tiny black and white TV that I sat on a cardboard box taken from the office. I had one suit and two shirts, which meant I was constantly washing shirts then hanging them out to dry for the morning.

It wasn't nice being in the dog-box but that felt right, because it felt like punishment.

After separating from Debbie, I was full of self-loathing. I didn't really understand my own decision to break up our marriage and didn't seem to recognise the person I saw in the mirror every morning. Searching for some inner peace amid this turmoil, I bought a stone statue of Buddha sitting cross-legged, which came cheap as the head had broken off and been fixed back together. It looked like I felt, beaten up and shattered, and I would sit and meditate in front of it for hours.

Other times, I would stare out at the calm water in Copacabana bay, beyond the white lines of advancing waves, and find some peace in that, too. At least my dog-box overlooks the ocean.

The old friends Debbie and I shared stopped calling, as if they also thought I needed to be punished. We used to go on holidays together but now I wasn't asked to join them, although Debbie and the kids were. That hurt. Some of them were schoolmates.

I told myself that they were right to rally around Debbie and knew I was strong enough to look after myself. I could live with that explanation, though it was painful when I found out two particularly good mates had been up to the Central Coast to see her but not told me they were in the area. I was best man at both of their weddings.

I've thrown myself completely into my work, instead. Last year, I took two weeks off and shut myself inside the unit, studying to pass the test to become a detective sergeant. I got myself so focused that I didn't watch TV or pick up a newspaper, so I had no distractions, and walked into the interview like I was heading into combat. I won the promotion. It means I now lead Homicide investigations, just like my old mentors Jim Williams and Paul Jacob.

Jason Evers, who I worked with in Bowraville and is now himself a designated detective, has come over to the Homicide Squad and works on my team. He's still got the same swagger to him and on our jobs he is the yang to my yin, the light to my darkness. We worked closely together on the first case I led from start to finish, investigating the killing of Barbara Saunders, a blameless 53-year-old, a devoted wife and mother of twins, who was shot on her way home from Normanhurst Railway Station on a Friday afternoon two weeks before Christmas 2000.

Jason and I were standing at the crime scene when Barbara's husband, Keith, turned up, looking for her, that evening. We treated him as a potential suspect, sitting him down for an interview at the police station and going in with aggression, looking to unsettle him so if there was a lie in what he was saying, he would be more likely to stumble over it.

Keith seemed to shrink before us, already traumatised by his wife's death and now with two detectives coming after him. In that moment, I was the avenging angel. I wasn't looking to his feelings, or at his past, at the memories he and Barbara made together, I was looking to the future, to an arrest, to an appearance before a Supreme Court jury, to a possible prison sentence.

Later, when Jason and I were satisfied of Keith's innocence, I apologised to him for how hard we went at him. He shook his head, saying, 'At that moment I knew the right people were working on this investigation. I knew how far and how hard you would go if you thought someone had murdered Barbara.' I took heart from that.

The killer turned out to be a 19-year-old, Nicholas Grayson, who had a long history of petty criminal offences, which got more serious as the years passed, until he was doing break-and-enters, stole a gun, then used it to shoot Barbara in an attempt to steal her handbag.

He denied shooting her at first, but we could show he'd used Barbara's stolen credit card after her death. When he claimed to have been somewhere else that Friday afternoon, we interviewed the people he claimed to have been with, and they did not defend him.

In court, Grayson pleaded guilty and was jailed for a minimum of 12 years. It didn't seem like much in return for taking someone's life and we apologised to Keith again after the verdict.

He said it didn't matter how long the killer got, nothing was going to bring his wife back. I carried those words around with me afterwards, feeling their heavy weight. It made me question if you can ever trust the courts to deal with a murder fairly. You can't balance out the result of Barbara's killing; her killer gets 12 years inside, her family get a life sentence.

Inside the car, I stare at the road ahead, where the red tail-lights of the close-packed cars are edging their way forward. *Fucking hell,* I think, *I've got work to do today.* On these long drives, when you've heard the same news on the hourly bulletins at six and seven, the radio can only keep you distracted for so long before your thoughts take over and then you're stuck in the car with them.

Today, Jason and I are working on the killing of a toddler, one-year-old Jayden March. Ten days ago, on Tuesday 22 May, his foster mother, Linda Wilson, took Jayden into his local GP's practice saying she couldn't wake him up and he wasn't breathing properly, but the doctor couldn't save him. Jayden died. His body was covered with bruises.

Working the case means being based in Sutherland, close to where Jayden was living, but which is on the south side of Sydney and a three-hour drive in traffic from Copacabana. The tail-lights on the road ahead come to a halt.

Until recently, Jason and I were working at Kincumber Police Station, just 10 minutes' drive from home, trying to catch a serial rapist. There'd been five, brutal attacks across the Central Coast that we knew of, as not every rape victim chooses to come forward, and we threw everything we had at trying to find him. Brave undercover policewomen were sent in to sunbake on the beaches where he targeted his victims. We spent days walking the nearby bush tracks, stopping any man who was out alone to ask for his details. We used the media to make sure the rapist knew we were looking for him.

The attacks seemed to stop, although we hadn't caught him. Not getting a result means always living with the knowledge he might hurt someone else and I was sorry to see that job end. Being based so close to home had also meant I could wake up and go for a surf with Jake as the sun rose, then afterwards we'd have breakfast together before I'd drop him off at Debbie's on my way into work.

Work and family life rarely seem to balance out the scales like that. At its worst, when it was my turn to have the kids and I was stuck at work, the kids ran loose, occupying themselves photocopying their heads on the police station photocopier, but at least I was close to them.

I think I am a better parent for moving out of the family home. I've learned how to plait Gemma's hair, iron their clothes, pack their school lunches and help them do their homework. All things I would have relied on Debbie for if we had stayed together.

The traffic isn't moving and my eyes are starting to close, so I crack open another can of the sickly sweet energy drink I've started to rely on to keep me awake during these drives. *This morning,* I tell myself, *I need it.* Jason and I are on call this week, meaning we respond to any murders happening across the State, whenever they come in. I managed about two hours' sleep last night. I'll spend three times that sitting in traffic before this day is over.

It will feel good to get home tonight. A year after splitting up with Debbie, home is still the dog-box unit with two work shirts drying outside on the verandah. But at least Pam will be staying over with me tonight, which means she'll be driving the same road back from Sydney this evening and the two of us can sit together and look out at the ocean together when we get there.

***

For a few years now, since around 1998, I've been lecturing on Homicide investigation as part of the detectives' course run at the Goulburn police academy. At first, I'd been nervous at the prospect of standing up in front of a room full of people and uncertain what I really had to offer.

The experience reassured me. It made me realise how much I'd already learned in the police and more comfortable about my ability to stand up and talk in public. The other benefit of lecturing on the course was Pam. She also lectured on the course and was one of very, very few women to prove themselves in the alpha-male world of the Homicide Squad, although we hadn't worked together as Pam was part of the force's Northwest region, while I was in North. There was something about her; she had poise and a don't-fuck-with-me look, as if sending a warning to any man who tried to hit on her that she could bite his head off, but when you got past that, she had a deep compassion.

It was Pam who came over to me years before, to ask how I was coping after Isaac was shot while I was talking to him outside the front door of his unit. After that, I'd seen her around at work every so often, but usually across a crowded office and was pretty sure she hadn't noticed me.

Like me, Pam wore dark suits, but hers were more elegant. She had fine cheek bones like a china sculpture, a graceful way of moving and deceptively soft blue eyes which had seen as many bodies as I had at work. In the past, she'd worked Arson, then the Breakers Squad, going after safe-breakers and professional thieves, and now she was one of only two or three women among the dozens of male cops who worked murders for a living. That took courage.

Pam was tough and I respected the way she went after what she wanted in life. I recognised something of myself in her, and started thinking she might feel the same way.

Work threw us together. Around the same time I started lecturing at the academy, the police force restructured into 80 Local Area Commands, with the four different regional Major Crime Squads brought together in one building in central Sydney under the new title of Crime Agencies. It meant the Homicide Squad was now a bigger, single unit, divided into six different teams, each led by an inspector, under which we still typically worked in threes of one detective sergeant and two detective constables. Pam and I were in different teams within the squad, but the change meant I still saw her in the office every day.

Lecturing also meant we were both away from home for at least a night every few months. After spending our days teaching, we didn't want to hang out with the students, so we would go out for a drink or dinner. I hated myself for my weakness, but, looking across the table, I could see she was different from Debbie. Pam understood what it took to be a cop and what the job took out of you, while Debbie was my childhood sweetheart. She was part of the world I came from before joining the police.

Pam represented all the excitement of police work. If working homicides had been the current that carried me away from family life, then listening to Pam lecture or talking about her cases at the bar afterwards, was a voice calling to me to go deeper.

Eventually, I betrayed Debbie in my mind. One night, after dinner in Goulburn, Pam came back for drinks in my motel room. We shared a six-pack and when it was finished, I told her, 'You don't have to go.'

She laughed, stood up and said, 'I will be going.' The next day I apologised, saying I hoped she'd not taken offence. She hadn't but said she didn't think staying would be a good thing for either of us at that moment. 'You do your own thing, but don't factor me into it,' she told me, which I took to mean that it was up to me to choose which path I followed. Pam didn't want to be the one who broke up a marriage.

I left Debbie. Afterwards, Pam and I started to go for drinks together, both at the big, raucous police functions, like when another detective retired, and during quiet evenings in bars where it was just the two of us and we would not be seen.

I know I'm falling for her. We've both got broken marriages behind us. We both understand the pressures on each other. We both know one of us might be called out at any moment on a job, but we're together because we want to be and we think it is pretty cool that way.

We each have our own places. At first, Pam had an apartment in Epping and now has a flat in Chinatown, in Sydney's centre, which means when I stay over we can walk to work in the Crime Agencies office in Strawberry Hills, rather than drive hours every day to get there.

Days like today, Pam stays at my place on the Central Coast. She gets on well with Jake and Gemma, which she needs to, not just because she knows how much I care about them but because there have been days when the four of us have all been spending time together, crowded into my tiny bedsit. Eventually, the owners could see it was awkward and let me convert their garage into a second bedroom. Now Pam's saying we should move in together, further up the coast. There's a bigger place at Avoca I like the look of, which also overlooks the surf.

At home, Pam helps me balance out my days at work, leading investigations, making constant decisions, aware that every choice, if it is wrong, could mean a criminal walks free, or worse. She asked me once what my favourite food was and I said, 'Toast,' meaning, I like it because it is convenient. Eating toast means I can fix a breakfast within minutes when I get up at 3.50am ahead of the long drive to Sydney.

So she drags me to restaurants. To galleries and theatres. She tells me I'm entitled to enjoy my life. She says I'm too austere, that I don't expect enough from life, or allow myself to have it.

If I get up at five o'clock on a weekend morning to go training, she'll say, 'Just stay in bed, read the papers. We don't have to do anything today.'

I try just sitting there, but I don't find it easy. I ask myself: *Is this what life is actually about? We can just do what we want?*

It freaks me out. It comes with guilt. Easier to keep moving, which means working hard and training, and I am now getting private lessons in kung fu and qigong from Ben, the sifu who I met in Dural. Once, when I was sick in bed, Pam tried to put an arm around me but I pushed her away. I didn't want her to see me when I was ill. She told me my weakness is that I will not accept weakness, in others or myself.

With Ben, I still talk about yin and yang, but I recognise that life is out of balance at the moment. I have my work. Pam shares my job. Between the two, I don't have the time to surf, or meditate like I used to, because I spend my hours instead sitting in a line of cars, struggling to get where I am going but halting, stalling and jerking forward, just one link in a chain of tail-lights.

But soon I will arrive in Sutherland where I can start work, which means thinking about someone else; in this case, little Jayden March. It's easier to keep moving forward.

Like I tell Ben, there might be too much yin, the darkness, in my life right now, but it makes me a formidable detective.

***

It's Friday 1 June 2001, and the plan is to interview Wilson on Monday. We've already got her phones off, meaning under surveillance, but now I want to put listening devices in her home as well, so we can listen before she does the interview and after, to see how she reacts.

Jason and I are dealing with the police lawyers, formally declaring that our application for a listening device warrant is true and accurate before it goes to a judge, when I get a phone call from Pam.

'Do you want to go to Paris?' she asks.

I struggle to make sense of the question. I've had so little sleep and have so much to organise, how can I go to Paris? I ask Pam, 'When?'

'This afternoon.' She's been asked to escort a prisoner who is being deported, and it means a free trip to France and back.

'I can't, Pam, I'm swearing out a warrant for Linda Wilson.'

'Jubelin, you know I love Paris. We can go to *Paris* for the weekend.' She's trying to make me understand this is what couples do, they go on romantic holidays to Paris, but I'm still not thinking clearly.

'Pam, I can't. I've got the kids this weekend. I've got Linda Wilson. We've got to get her house off and I've got to prepare for the interview on Monday.'

Pam starts to reply, but I cut her off. I tell her, 'I just can't,' and hang up.

Jason has overheard my half of the conversation. When I explain what Pam was offering, he looks at me like he wants to slap me.

'You're fucking mad.'

'I'm not mad, Jason. I've got the kids tonight, I've got to take Jake to swimming practice. My passport's up on the Central Coast. We're doing Linda Wilson on Monday. How the hell can I go to Paris?'

'You're an idiot,' he tells me. I stare at him, still trying to process everything that's happening. I wonder if he's right.

Pam will understand, I think. She is so similar to me, so ruthless in the way she goes about her work as a detective. I've seen her nearly destroy herself working cases, including serious, gangland murders. She'll understand why I have to be ruthless now.

What is there to understand, you idiot? Our relationship isn't some sort of mutually assured destruction pact. She's right to want some time off. She loves Paris. And I know how long it might take to get this warrant issued and then organise getting the technical and surveillance units ready to fit the listening devices. We could fly to France and be back before it happens. Then I'm not sacrificing anything.

You can't just drown yourself in work because you walked out on your family. I've got Pam now. She can keep me afloat.

I tell Jason: 'You're right.'

He offers to work through the weekend on the listening devices and I tell him to call me when everything is ready. I call Pam back and tell her, 'I'm in. I don't want to pass this up. I'm coming.' She doesn't react. She just says to be at the airport for eight.

I drive back to the Central Coast, through the same damn traffic heading out of Sydney. At home, I rush inside and grab my passport and some clothes, then pick up Jake and Gemma from Debbie's, take

Jake to swimming practice, phone my parents and ask them to take the kids for the weekend, and arrange for Dad to pick them up from me during a hurried meeting at Hornsby Police Station on my way back to Sydney.

This is nothing new to Jake and Gemma. With me on call one week in every six, they're used to being bundled into the back seat of the car at short notice, sometimes still half asleep from being pulled out of their beds at night, while I drive towards a new crime scene, calling my sister Karen or my parents to ask if they can take the children.

Sometimes during these journeys, if we are on the freeway with no other cars around, I'll put the siren on to distract them. Once, before Debbie and I split, I was looking after Jake and had to go into the police station one night to deal with a crook. Jake sat alone at a desk in the darkened office while I was in the interview room, until I needed to leave it to use a computer. Light spilled out from the open door, giving Jake a view of the crook sitting inside, at the table. I had to walk about 20 metres away to get what I needed, so I told Jake, 'If that person moves, you yell as loud as you can.'

He sat there in silence and only told me later he was terrified.

***

I meet Pam at the airport and we take custody of an angry Frenchman. He fights me the whole way to France.

At Charles de Gaulle Airport, after a 30-hour sleepless flight spent trying to restrain him, the other passengers get off the plane and he and I wrestle in the aisles, ripping his shirt, before we hand him over to the gendarmes. I'm so tired that when we get to our motel, I drink glasses and glasses of water from a tap without noticing the sign saying '*Eau non potable*'. 'Water not for drinking'.

Pam takes me out to enjoy the city. When I wake up on Sunday morning, not only am I feeling the effects of a night out drinking, but I'm also sick from the bad water. That evening, I call Jason from a payphone in the street outside to ask how everything is going. It's Monday morning in Australia and he tells me the listening devices warrant has been authorised and the technical and surveillance cops are on standby.

Christ. I have to go back. The job's ready to start. I can't leave the other cops waiting.

It's like having an addiction, doing this work. I simply need to be there.

I tell Pam: 'I'm going back a day early.'

'Jubelin, we've got two more nights' accommodation here in Paris paid for and you're telling me we've got to go home?'

'I've got to. I've got to do Linda Wilson.'

She's furious, but we fly home together a day early, on Monday. Pam says she doesn't want to stay on in Paris alone. I spend the flight to Sydney preparing for the interview, while Pam ignores me. I tell myself that if this was her case, she would do the same.

We get to Sydney on Wednesday morning and there's fog, so we're diverted to Melbourne and sit there on the tarmac before flying back to Sydney. From the airport, Pam and I go into work.

I've barely slept. I'm fucked. Jason takes one look at me and says, 'Go home and sleep. You're no good to anyone.'

I drive back to the Central Coast and sleep, then fight my way back through the early-morning traffic on the Thursday to do the interview with Wilson.

Innocent Little Boy

7 June 2001: 16 years in

'How would you describe Jayden to me as a child?'

Linda Wilson looks at me with calculating, piggy eyes. 'Very happy,' she says. 'Content, lovable. Great eater.'

That's good, I think. *You're talking*. Right now, I just want her to feel comfortable. I want her to underestimate what she's got herself into by sitting down to talk.

We're inside one of the small, windowless interview rooms in Sutherland Police Station, just before 8pm on a Thursday night, because Wilson agreed to be here. As it stands, I don't have enough evidence to arrest her, which means she can walk out of here whenever she wants. I don't want to let that happen, and the best way for me to prevent it is to make her feel confident. To make her think that I cannot hurt her.

We're like two boxers, circling each other. In this fight, I want to let her get confident, make her commit. Let her think that I'm just a bumbling detective and the best thing she can do is give me her version of what happened.

Then I can contradict it.

I smile and ask another fluffy question, 'In saying that, a great eater, what was his favourite food?'

Wilson reels off a list: 'Spaghetti bolognese, um, chicken, ah, loved vegies, fruit, yoghurt.' Her mouth is set in something like a smirk. 'He was always looking for more food.' I nod encouragement.

'Yes.' *Keep talking.*

'Give him dessert, like yoghurt or custard or something, and he would wander off to the fridge and maybe point as if he wanted more food.'

Wilson had been uncertain when I called her this evening, asking if she could come and answer a few questions. 'I don't know,' she told me. 'Maybe later.' She and her husband, Tony, had just ordered a pizza.

'Finish it,' I told her. 'Take your time.' It was important I did nothing to alert her.

I don't want her to suspect that I have any real interest in the case, let alone that I had been there during the one-year-old's autopsy, or spent the days following it hassling a paediatric surgeon to shift his focus from the lives that he might save just long enough to concentrate on this life already lost, to help me understand the bare, clinical descriptions of Jayden March's injuries given in the autopsy report.

I asked him what force would it take to cause those bruises? How long would they have been visible before Jayden died?

I want to know if what Wilson says now will contradict his explanation. Because then I'll know she's lying to me. And a lie can be exposed in court.

That's the tightrope she and I are treading, as I try to tempt her out over the void.

'Would it be fair to describe him as always hungry?' I continue.

'I don't know, maybe,' she says. 'Each child's different.'

The wheels of the ERISP machine's three audio cassettes turn slowly, recording our conversation. The only other person in the room is Jason Evers, who's silently making notes, looking down at the paperwork in front of him, but who I know will be feeling just as strained and taut as I am. As partners, we've spent so much time together over the past few years that I know him almost as well as I do Pam, if not better. I rate Jason for his big heart and his determination to stand up for victims. That heart will be beating just as fast as mine right now.

Wilson looks at me, at Jason, at the ERISP machine camera opposite where she is sitting, then away, at the four cream-coloured walls on either side, each of them so close that any of us could easily stand up and touch them.

'A happy child?' I ask her.

'Very.'

'How was he in terms of communication? I understand he was one month short of turning two?'

'Well, he couldn't talk. He was calling us Mum, Mum, Dad, Dad.'

You weren't his mum and dad, I think. *You were his foster parents. I've spoken to his real mum.*

The State Government's Department of Community Services (DoCS) had taken Jayden from his mother. They thought she wasn't a suitable parent. Being Aboriginal, he should have gone to an Indigenous foster home, but for some reason that hadn't happened. Working this case, it has been hard to escape the thoughts of those other three Aboriginal children who disappeared from Bowraville. Whose bodies, or the two of them that were found, had suffered awful injuries – just like Jayden. Whose killer is still out there.

But I don't let my face reveal my thoughts – or Wilson doesn't notice.

Her own face is a mask of innocence, the turned-down mouth and double chin framed by long, bleached hair, its natural colour showing at the roots. 'That's basically all he could say,' she tells me. 'I didn't know if he wanted something really or he didn't. Because he couldn't talk, he couldn't express how he was feeling. Or I just had to use my imagination as a mother.'

You weren't his mother. You didn't protect him. Wilson talks about her experience of caring for her own young children, who are no longer living with her. I listen, reliving the experience of watching Jayden's autopsy. The smell of antiseptic. The little body lying on the huge steel tray made to carry an adult corpse. The helpless feeling of wanting to protect him.

The pathologist found bruises on both sides of Jayden's head, bleeding inside his skull and in both eyes, a swollen brain, a ruptured stomach and bruises to his penis. Those were just the recent injuries. There was evidence of others, which could have been weeks old.

Jason and I had stood there, watching on in silence. Both of us had seen other bodies, and other autopsies, so we'd had some preparation. The days when I could simply gloss over the mention of a 'post-mortem' in a newspaper report of some killing or accident are gone. Now the word triggers an explosion of senses; the black and white tiles leading to the mortuary, the whine of the trolley wheels, the scalpel making its incision, the drill, the crack as a section of skull is lifted clear, the revulsion in my stomach.

Every one of those experiences hardened me. Becoming hard has helped me to stand there, unmoving, during the next autopsy, because as Homicide detectives, they are a part of every job we do.

Inside the morgue, I won't let anyone, not Jason, the pathologists nor the forensic technicians, see my disgust, my weakness. My job is to be the hardcase, the Homicide detective. There's no way I will let anybody see how Homicide could break me.

And so I'd stood there, wearing the blue surgical gowns they give you to wear, watching and listening to the pathologist describe what he was doing. At one point, Jason pointed to a bruise and asked, 'What's that?'

'That's a pinch mark,' the pathologist replied. It seemed sadistic.

We needed to be hard to stand that sight.

Wilson tells me Jayden and his three-year-old sister needed close supervision. 'Just rough playing with each other,' she says.

'Right.' I nod encouragement.

'She started turning on the hot plates at home and just running from one side of the lounge room to the other side and banging into Jayden. I felt as if you know, if something was going to happen, it would be an accident.'

What game is she playing? I think. *Is she trying to make Jayden's sister a suspect?* I know that the autopsy showed Jayden was hit with a force equivalent to those felt in a high-speed car crash. There's no way, surely, those injuries could have been caused by his sister playing.

Wilson says Jayden was often sick when he and his sister got back from access visits to their birth mother. 'For a few days, he wouldn't want to eat.'

I ask, 'Was this a regular thing?'

'Yeah, it happened. I'm not trying to put the blame on anybody.'

'No, no,' I say.

'I'm not blaming anybody,' she continues, the pink skin of her cheeks wobbles under the ceiling light as she is talking. 'But he was fine up until he started having access visits.'

You are trying to blame somebody. Or at least trying to make me think there are other people worth blaming. But all I say is 'Right.'

We have looked at other potential suspects. We looked at Jayden's birth mother, but it did not make sense. She last saw Jayden during an access visit five days before his death, while his injuries are more recent.

Wilson says how, three times in the three months Jayden was living with her, she took him to hospital saying he had vomiting, diarrhoea and abdominal migraines. 'I suppose I'm an overprotective mother.'

'Yeah.'

'You know, especially not being your own child.'

After their third visit, Wilson says that she complained to the hospital in writing. 'They were very rude.'

'Yes.'

'I felt insulted with some of the questions they'd been asking. The doctor there, he said to me, "Oh, you're back again."'

'Right.'

'I felt highly insulted.'

'Right.'

'He turned around and said, "How long have you been fostering?" and "Do you enjoy fostering?" and "Would you rather look after older children?"'

'What do you think he was alluding to with those comments?' I ask her. I know the doctor reported his concerns to DoCS.

'I don't know,' she says. 'That's why I wrote the letter.'

'Obviously you were insulted.'

'Because he was questioning my parenting.'

'Right.' I think about the listening devices we put in her home and how they recorded the visits of other men, while Tony was at work. About how the kids were tucked away in the flat while Wilson entertained them.

Jayden died on a Tuesday, I say. Can we go back over her movements during the previous days?

On the weekend, she and Tony took the kids out, but she can't remember where.

'If you did take them out, you'd have constant care of them?' I ask.

'Just the four of us went out.'

'OK. So you don't leave them in baby crèches, movies or wherever?'

'No,' she says. They were always with her.

If they were always with you, no one else could have harmed them.

On the Monday, Jayden's last full day alive, Wilson gave him a bath. I ask, 'Did you notice any injuries on him?'

'No.'

'Would that stand out, was it normal for him to be bruised?'

'I've never seen a bruise on Jayden.'

'OK.'

'Never seen a bruise on Jayden.'

'Right.'

Wilson is less certain what happened on the Monday. The kids had been watching TV and playing together. If she went out, it would have been after 10 o'clock, when their cartoons had finished.

'I'm always home by lunchtime because I watch the soapies,' she says. *Days of Our Lives* and *The Young and the Restless.*

'Can you recall that particular day, on Monday?' I ask her.

'That's probably what happened.'

'Yes, but let's take that word "probably" out.' I've seen too many good court cases lost because the defence lawyer argued his client had only said that something 'probably' happened. We're nearing the end of the tightrope. I don't want either of us to slip now.

'Well that was my routine,' she tells me.

'You did not differ from that routine on that Monday?'

'No.'

'So, at no time was Jayden in the custody of any other person?'

'No.'

Got you. Wilson has limited the pool of potential killers to herself and her husband.

As if she realises her mistake, she starts talking quickly, telling me that when Tony got home from work on Monday evening, Jayden was sick, flopping around, and she couldn't get him to stand up.

But she'd previously said Jayden was playing around the flat on Monday.

'How were the kids playing if Jayden couldn't get up?' I ask her.

'Just playing around like, on the lounge or on the floor, in the bedroom, whatever, like that.'

'Just so we're not misunderstanding ourselves here, you told me that Jayden couldn't get up?'

'Yeah.'

'Then you're saying they're running around the house?'

'Yeah.'

She's shaken. She says Jayden was sick for four days running, since the Friday.

I ask her why, if Jayden was so sick, did she not call an ambulance, as she had with the previous hospital visits?

Is that a flash of anger? How good is she at hiding her feelings? 'Maybe he was just being stubborn, it could have been anything,' she says.

We move on to the Tuesday. The day Jayden died. That morning, he woke up as usual, she says.

'What was he doing?' I ask.

'He was running around fine, he was OK.'

Running around? The doctor said that with his injuries, he would not have been running anywhere.

Wilson bathed Jayden again, she says, and dressed him, then left him on the floor.

'I was only gone for a couple of minutes or so.' When she came back he was making funny noises. So she ran with him to the doctor's surgery.

'Why did you run?'

'I wanted to get there quickly because he was sick.'

'I'm just trying to paint a picture here … it's important to me, how you got there. So you describe it, how you got there.'

'I wasn't just walking, I was running and walking very fast.'

The ERISP machine interrupts us with a beeping to tell us the cassettes need replacing. I breathe out and suspend the interview as Jason changes them.

Five minutes later, we resume. I'm focused.

'You are particular about your supervision of Jayden?'

'Yeah, yeah.'

'You have no knowledge of any injuries?'

'No.'

I picture Jayden lying on the steel tray.

'OK. All right. We'll just move on to a different section now. Just so you understand … myself and Jason, we are from Homicide,' I tell her.

'Mmmm.' She's noncommittal, unsure what to make of the change in my voice.

'We became notified of this matter when the autopsy was being performed.'

'Oh. OK.'

'The autopsy found out how Jayden died,' I tell her. 'There is no way the one-year-old was running around on that morning.' I tell her how the doctors say some of his injuries look older than the others. These would have been visible before his death, including when she gave him a bath on both the Tuesday and the Monday.

The atmosphere inside the room now is electric. Having brought her out above the void on her tightrope, I want to shake her off it.

'I'm just in shock,' she says. 'I can't believe it. It's heartbreaking.'

I don't believe you. I ask her directly, 'How did he suffer those injuries?'

'I couldn't tell you. He didn't have a mark on him while he was in my care.'

'Is your husband capable of inflicting these injuries?'

'No. None whatsoever, not at all.'

'What do you base that on?'

'My husband and I have never hit a child, especially foster children. We took on fostering out of the goodness of our hearts, and to hear this, I'm just, it's just, it's very hard for me to believe.'

Maybe you didn't hit him, I think. *Did you shake him?*

'Now in terms of taking Jayden up to the doctor the day Jayden died, you and I went through it in detail about how you got up there. You said you travelled briskly?'

'That's right, yeah.' She doesn't know where this is going.

'A run–walk, a fast walk?'

'Yeah.'

I lay out six photographs on the table, each showing grainy, black and white CCTV footage of Wilson carrying Jayden to the doctor's. She doesn't look like she is trying to move quickly. I ask her what is in the photos.

'That's me,' she says, pointing at one. She looks at the next. 'Maybe the railway station. It's probably me and Jayden. Yeah, that's Jayden and me.'

'Is there anything that looks like, if that image is you, that you're running?'

'Oh.' The look on her face changes, like she's been struck. 'No, not really, no.' She knows now that I suspect she has been lying.

Part of me would rather not have these suspicions. Whether it's instinct or some old-fashioned value I learned growing up in the suburbs, where women were expected to be only wives, mothers and home-makers, but I still find it difficult to think I'm going to charge a woman with killing a child she was looking after. It's like some of my own innocence has been lost during this interview.

I want to give Wilson a chance. An out. A way to explain this. I ask her, 'Is there anything you want to say in relation to this matter?'

Her face settles back into the same, blameless expression she wore on her way into the interview room. 'I'm just in shock. It's just hard to believe. He's just an innocent little boy.'

He was.

'OK. This interview is now concluded. The time is now 10.13 by my watch. OK?'

'Ah, hmm,' Wilson mutters.

I lean forward, stretching out towards the ERISP machine. 'Right. I'll just turn that off now.' *You have one last chance to explain this.*

'OK,' says Wilson. The interview is over.

Paris. London.

July 2001: 16 years in

I'm on a high after the interview with Linda Wilson, and I stay there. Once a case reaches the threshold where I think I'm going to get a result, I feel like I am flying.

These are the moments that make up for the lows the job brings with it. Like Pam's silence. She doesn't talk to me for days after I chose working little Jayden's case over a third night together in Paris.

She'll calm down, I tell myself. She knows the rush of working a case, when the chase is on and you are getting close and nothing else exists outside police work. When your senses are fired up, so even the light shining through the office window as you type up the paperwork for an arrest seems brighter than it's ever been and you can think more clearly than you ever have before, or work for days while barely sleeping.

Pam knows how a case consumes you.

At work, we collect the final pieces of evidence we'll need before a final decision on whether to charge Wilson over Jayden's death: the listening device recordings from her home, which need to be monitored in real-time and then transcribed, and a formal, written report from the paediatric surgeon who helped me understand his injuries.

I chase the doctor for days, calling him, visiting the hospital and following him around. He keeps saying he has other work to do. Other, living patients. I don't give up and eventually, he says he's going to take out a restraining order if I keep on harassing him, but I get the paperwork.

The listening devices are less productive and give us little evidence against Wilson. Instead, while we are working back one night in Sutherland Police Station, the detective who's monitoring this surveillance comes up and tells me he's worried about her.

'What's she saying?' I ask.

He says she sounds like she's drunk or has taken something. He can hear her talking to herself, alone in her apartment, and fears she might hurt herself.

Everybody in the office looks at me. It is a judgment call. As police officers, our first responsibility is to preserve life, not to avenge it, and so we have to act. But move too soon and we will blow our surveillance operation.

I ask for the local uniformed police to be sent to her unit, ready to go in if we need them. We keep listening to Wilson's voice, unaware that she's being recorded, while I sit and ask myself if I can keep this running or if now is the moment I need to send the cops in or even call an ambulance.

The minutes pass.

We hear a key turn in the lock. Her husband, Tony, is home. Whatever's happening in their apartment, he can face it. I exhale. I can feel my heartbeat thudding in my chest. The surveillance continues.

At home, Pam and I reconcile. I keep making the long drives between Sutherland, her apartment in Chinatown and my place on the Central Coast. Jake has just turned 10 and Gemma will soon be eight. I flog myself to make it back from work for their school sports days and concerts.

I want to show how I am committed to them. On Wednesdays, I drive to Sydney for work, drive back, pick up the kids and drive them down to Sydney for their kung fu class, then we stay at my parents' place in Dural, then on Thursday morning I drive them up to school in Copacabana, then drive back to work in Sydney.

One evening a week, I pick Gemma up from ballet and drop her home. Mostly she just sits in the back of the car talking to friends, not giving me a second thought. Twice a week I spend the night standing on a cold soccer field coaching Jake's soccer team, then drop him home, then often drive to Sydney and stay at Pam's place.

It's manic but work sustains me. I'm still high when the doctor's report finally arrives and we go to Wilson's apartment near the railway station in Sutherland to arrest her. I knock on the door and can hear her moving around inside. She doesn't answer, so we wait, knocking again and calling out, 'We know you're in there Linda, come on out.' The last thing I want to do is turn this into another siege, like what happened with Isaac.

Eventually she does open the door, wearing tracky dacks, a T-shirt and a look of innocent surprise.

'You're under arrest for the murder of Jayden March. You're not obliged to say anything unless you wish to do so, but whatever you say may be used in evidence,' I tell her. He response is shock, horror. She says she can't believe it.

We walk her to our unmarked car, drive to the police station and I charge her. I still feel good but the next morning, at Wilson's first court hearing, I start to come down. The court seats are hard and uncomfortable. These cases leave you low sometimes, sickened by what you've seen in the morgue or the interview room, or by what one person will do to another.

You carry that tragedy around, the trauma, anguish and anger. You learn to use it as a motivating force that will carry you through the many court hearings and meetings with lawyers ahead, which can last months or years, before the person you've arrested faces trial. But it still weighs you down. You miss the simple, clean excitement of the pursuit, of the arrest.

So you are always looking for another case, to start the chase again. You start to crave another Homicide investigation.

At home, Pam and I take our phones to bed, and both reach out beside us in the darkness when one rings. We're used to these constant interruptions, which often send one of us stumbling to the shower, then to throw on some clothes before hurrying out of the door, heading for another crime scene.

Cold, exhausted or reluctant to leave your bed and a warm embrace behind you, there is always that excitement you've been craving. If this job is an addiction, then you are getting another hit.

Sometimes, the chase does not begin with a phone call. In July 2001, it begins with an email waiting for me in the morning, when I arrive at work. It's from Interpol, the International Criminal Police Organization. We'd asked them to help track someone down and they say it looks like he's in London.

The email has a phone number for a contact in the local cops, so I go into Kincumber Police Station near my apartment on the Central Coast late that night to call them. They say they're confident he's there; they've checked his post and even done physical surveillance. We have to move, I say to Jaco. He agrees. Jason and I will fly to London.

Pam's not impressed when I tell her I'm taking a second trip to Europe within weeks, but she understands it. She simply nods when I tell her we've found where Gordon Wood is living. Of course we have to go, she knows that. Working Homicide, when the call comes, you answer.

Pam also knows the case; the death of a young woman, a bright, popular 24-year-old who was the third child in a family of four and moved to Sydney hoping to make it as a model

Her body was found at the base of The Gap, a towering, dark cliff standing at the entrance to Sydney Harbour, in the early hours of Thursday 8 June 1995.

I'd only got to know Caroline Byrne in death, during the years since, from her family and friends and from looking at photographs. Tall and blonde, with wide brown eyes, it's easy to understand how she did find modelling work, while also teaching deportment for Sydney's famous queen of etiquette, June Dally-Watkins.

This is our job. As detectives, we meet people for the first time in death. We often get the call to go to work at night and when it comes, we head for the door and drive towards the crime scene.

We go where no one else will. Not knowing where the chase will end when we begin it.

Over the years, I'd also noticed how, in almost every photograph I've seen of Caroline, she's smiling.

***

I said 'I'm in' the moment I heard Paul Jacob was leading the reinvestigation. That was mid-1998 and we were to be a team of six, including myself and Jason. By then, the case was already making headlines.

At first, in 1995, the local police had found Caroline was depressed and likely taken her own life. They interviewed her fiancé, Gordon, who told them he'd been at home the evening before and fell asleep in front of the television. Waking after midnight, he realised Caroline wasn't there and went out searching for her. Driving around the places they'd often been to in the city's wealthy eastern suburbs, he ended up at The Gap. Caroline's car was parked in a back alley, close to the cliff edge.

Gordon telephoned her father and brother, waking them up to tell them she was missing, then drove across the city to collect them before returning to the cliffs. He told them he'd last seen his fiancée the day before, showed them her car, with Caroline's brown leather wallet inside it, and led them up the rough, stone steps towards the cliff edge.

Borrowing a fisherman's torch, Gordon searched the darkness. Caroline's father, Tony, thought that it was hopeless and turned back. Gordon led her brother Peter to the edge and they peered down, using the handheld torch to look into the void below. Gordon thought he could see something. Peter couldn't.

The cops were called, bringing more powerful lighting equipment to pierce the darkness, without success, while Gordon stood with his head and hands on the rail that ran along the clifftop overlooking the black ocean. 'I can't believe she's done it,' he told one cop, and another, 'I'm pretty sure my girlfriend has jumped off The Gap.'

It seemed that he was right. Caroline's body was recovered beneath the place where Gordon had pointed over the cliff edge using his borrowed torchlight.

In January 1996, Caroline's father wrote to the cops, saying they had given up too quickly and suggesting Caroline was murdered. That June, the cops spoke to Gordon again. He repeated that he thought she'd killed herself. Her mother had done the same thing a few years before, he said.

An inquest into Caroline's death was held in November 1997, and the media loved it. A young, blonde model made for good pictures in newspaper pages and on television bulletins. They also loved the names of those from the big end of town who were mentioned in evidence.

When he was called into the witness box, Gordon said how, at the time, he'd been working as a personal assistant and chauffeur to Rene Rivkin, an eccentric businessman who made his name share-brokering for genuinely big names like Kerry Packer and Sir Peter Abeles.

Rivkin himself was also colourful, and caught up in a scandal. He'd made a fortune when his Offset Alpine Printing business burned down in 1993, after being insured for several times what he had paid for it. Asked where he was on the day before Caroline was found, Gordon said he'd been to a restaurant where his boss was having lunch, then drove one of Rivkin's friends into the city. This friend was Graham Richardson, a former federal minister in the Hawke and Keating governments and a Labor Party numbers man. His name alone made headlines.

Gordon denied any involvement in Caroline's death. When the inquest ended, with little or no evidence of her last hours to go on, the coroner could not decide whether it was a murder, suicide or accident.

But the headlines continued. In March 1998, Gordon gave a television interview, in which he again denied involvement. Asked 'Do you accept that you are under suspicion in this affair?' Gordon replied 'I'm not under suspicion by the police.'

By April, hounded by the media, he'd sold his car, cut off his phone, broke the lease on his flat in Bondi and left Australia.

Now the coroner wanted the case investigated again and Jaco had been asked to lead it.

Jaco encouraged us to spend time with Caroline's family,

learning to like them as people and to grieve for the trauma that her death had caused them. We re-interviewed old witnesses and spoke to others who the police had never dealt with. Our job was to talk to everybody who might know anything about her. After that email from Interpol arrived in 2001, we decided it was time to talk to Gordon.

At first, the senior bosses who allocate our resources are reluctant to let us do it. Two return flights to the UK would cost a lot, and they doubt it is worth it.

'Why would Gordon talk?' they ask. He'd spoken to police before. He'd already fronted the inquest and the media.

'Get us there and I guarantee he will do an interview,' I argue. It is a risk. If I am wrong, and Gordon won't talk, the case could stall. After three years without any obvious result, there's pressure coming on us now to drop it. In Homicide, each week means new cases to solve and there are only so many detectives. Pursuing even one old death like Caroline's means leaving questions hanging over a more recent case, for lack of anyone to answer them.

But, like Jaco, I care too much to let this investigation go. The Byrne family are good, gentle and decent people. Caroline was their sister and their daughter. We'd sat in her father's home and seen the photos that he kept of her. Whether she died in an accident, a suicide or something else, her family deserve to know what happened.

That was our job, to follow where the case led us, even if it meant flying halfway around the world to do it.

***

In person, Gordon Wood looks just like Chesty Bond, the cartoon character who used to advertise white singlets when I was growing up.

Like Chesty, Gordon is groomed. He has that same wave of blond hair, bulging muscles and square jaw. Watching him carrying a gym bag back to his apartment in Chelsea, southwest London, I think of Chesty's smiling, easy confidence. He seems at home here, walking between the rows of tall, grand properties with big bay windows, which go for a small fortune. I put the thought aside. This morning, Monday 23 July 2001, Jason and I are sitting here inside a borrowed, unmarked police car, watching Gordon walk towards us, for one reason only.

He stops as we get out and stand on the footpath. I introduce us, saying 'Look, Gordon, we're from Australia. We're here about Caroline Byrne. We'd like to interview you.'

'No, I don't think so,' he replies.

'But she was your fiancée. We're investigating her death.'

He shakes his head and turns towards the apartment building, but doesn't hurry away. He still has that same, assured self-confidence about his movements.

'Why are you worried about speaking to a couple of cops from Australia?' I ask him.

Gordon pauses. We try to make something from his hesitation, giving him a phone number for the nearby Kensington Police Station, where we've based ourselves with help from the local cops.

He looks at it and I smile at him before we leave, trying also to look confident.

The truth is, I still fear we have come all this way for nothing. We can't make Gordon talk to us. He'll only do so if he wants to.

Soon after, Gordon calls. He says he's considered our offer, spoken to his advisors and decided to accept it. We arrange to speak to him in the afternoon and, when he arrives, I see he's changed his clothes, he's looking dapper and carrying a bag of muffins and take-away coffees, which he offers to us.

I take them and throw them in the bin.

'Now, we're here to talk to you about the death of Caroline,' I tell Gordon.

I Don't Think It's Going to be Easy

23 July 2001: 16 years in

The paint is peeling from the four walls of the interview room. Jason and I open the door and walk in behind Gordon Wood. He sits. We sit. We look at each other.

Outside, the streets are full of fierce summer sunlight. In here, Jason and I are weary, having not slept for days. We spent the whole of the flight over from Sydney awake, reading the different witness statements, phone records and investigator's notes produced during the different police investigations, and kept on working through them last night in our hotel.

This morning, spinning with exhaustion, I ran through London's Hyde Park, then swam in the Serpentine, a narrow lake inside the park, where the grass and trees come down to meet the water. Pulling myself out, as the cold water dried in the early sunlight, it felt as if some of the stresses I carry on every investigation – Will we solve this? What if I do the wrong thing? What if the answer escapes me? – were carried away also.

I found a place on the grass to practise my qigong, away from other people.

Caroline's family, I thought, had spoken of Gordon's big personality. He was likely to bring that energy to our conversation when we met him. With no authority to make him sit and answer questions, I could not expect to dominate him or match his energy with mine in a confrontation.

I had to find a way to balance our energies instead, to make him want to engage in this. Just like the yin-yang symbol, where both yin and yang reach around and complement each other.

First, I had to find my own balance. Starting my qigong, I stood shoulder-width apart, hands cupped near the centre of my body, raising them, palms upwards, almost to eye-level, before turning the palms over and lowering them until the fingertips were almost touching near my belly again.

My breathing was in time with the movement. Breathe in when my hands come up. Breathe out when my hands return to my centre. With each breath out, I let the tensions built up during those sleepless nights pass out of my body. My heart rate slowed.

I felt ready.

Inside the interview room, Jason checks through the stack of witness statements and other documents we've brought with us from Sydney. If I forget to ask a question, he'll point it out.

'All right,' I say, looking at Gordon. 'Let's start the interview.' Jason starts the ERISP machine recording, a transcript of which would later be tendered in court, at Gordon's trial.

***

'Do you agree that on 12 June 1995, you provided police with a statement in relation to your knowledge of issues surrounding the death of Caroline Byrne?' I ask Gordon.

'I have no recollection of when it was.'

'I agree it's a long time ago. Perhaps I'll be able to assist by showing you a copy of a statement in your name, Gordon Eric Wood.'

I give him a copy of the five-page statement, as well as the three-page transcript of an interview he did with police a month later. I also hand Gordon a longer transcript from another interview done the following year, a copy of his evidence to the inquest in 1998 and a transcript of his TV interview.

Tired as I am from the sleepless nights, I feel alert. I watch Gordon as he lines up the sheets of paper around him on the table.

'Mr Wood, can you describe to me your relationship with Caroline Byrne?' I ask him.

'She was my fiancée.'

'Could you expand on that?'

He continues: 'She was the love of my life. I believe that I was the same for her. It was a very magical and special relationship with a special woman, and I was a very lucky man for three years.'

'Right,' I say. 'Can you tell me what impact Caroline's death has had on your life?'

'No, I can't actually. Not in words.'

'Mr Wood, it's been documented' – I point at the piles of paper between us – 'that you believe Caroline committed …'

I pause. He's starting to break down in tears.

'Sorry,' he apologises.

'No, it's quite all right. Take your time. Do you need a tissue?' I ask, and there is some water, if he needs it.

'Thanks.' He takes a breath and says again, 'I'm sorry.'

I wasn't expecting this. *Try to keep your balance*, I think. In qigong, you learn how the slightest difference in the positioning of a foot, or even of your weight within your foot, can leave you unstable and quickly exhausted.

'You understand that we are going to be asking a lot of questions today?' I ask.

'I know.'

'We'd like to cover all the issues.'

'Go for it, mate.' He looks at me across the table. 'Go for it,' he says again.

I ask why he believes Caroline took her own life. He tells me she'd once attempted to kill herself before. He says her mother's suicide meant Caroline might have had a 'congenital predisposition'. Two days before her death, she'd seen a doctor who diagnosed depression and referred her to a psychiatrist.

'Through the course of our inquiries, and they've been fairly substantial …'

'Mmmm?' he says, looking at me calmly.

'… you appear to be the only person that believes Caroline's taken her own life.'

'I would say that most people in their heart of hearts, who are close to Caroline, would believe she committed suicide,' he says. 'I would say her family probably, you know, at the Pearly Gates, talking to God, would say, "OK, yeah, I buy it. She committed suicide."'

'I'll stop you there,' I say. I need a moment to gather my thoughts.

'It's not just her family,' I say. We've interviewed her friends. Her workmates.

'Yeah.'

'It's been a long, protracted inquiry.' We've spoken to her doctor, Cindy Pan, who said Caroline seemed calm, almost serene. Yes, Gordon was right – Cindy did refer her to a psychiatrist. But, 'No one there has indicated to us that they believe Caroline was suicidal.'

'Yeah.'

'When you provided police with a statement on 12 June, five days after her death, you were so confident that she took her own life that you didn't even want an inquest. How were you so confident?' I ask him.

'I can't imagine,' he says. He also seems calm. 'I can't think of a single person or good reason as to why it would be anything else.' He frowns, as if turning his thoughts inwards to make sure he is certain before continuing: 'There's certainly nobody I know who'd ever want to harm her.'

He leans forward: 'Who would kill her and why?'

I don't respond.

It feels like an age has passed since I was in the park this morning, practising qigong. Back then, continuing the form, I moved on to a smaller, equally controlled movement, raising my hands, palms upwards and bending my arms at the elbows until they were flat in front of me, then turning my hands over and moving them down, repeating the movement. I felt controlled. I could feel my chi energy move through me.

The slow cycle of the ERISP machine's cassette tapes brings me back into the present. Continuing the interview, I ask about Caroline's scheduled meeting with the psychiatrist. 'I believe you said she had an appointment on the day of her death?'

'If my memory serves me, it was on, was it four o'clock on Wednesday, her appointment?' asks Gordon.

Inside, I cringe because I don't have the answer. I tell Gordon, 'I, I'm not sure.' Jason flips through the papers in front of him.

'OK. I think it was something like that,' says Gordon.

I try again, saying Caroline's family told us she was uncertain about marrying him. That they thought he was the one pushing the idea.

'Her family were very accepting of me,' he says. Caroline's father was going to lend them money for an apartment. 'At the time, I remember him as saying, you know, I'm paraphrasing but it was like, *Well, she's yours now.*'

'Yes.' I'm on the back foot, out of balance.

'Not that Caroline was a chattel.'

'Yeah.'

'But, you know what I mean, it's like "She's in your care" and so on. Acceptance of her being under my stewardship.'

'Right.' I don't know where this is going.

Gordon says he never told his friends that they planned to get married. 'We were very homey, couple-y sort of people. I don't know, Gary, if I did tell some of my very, very good friends. I may have.'

Breathe out, I think, let the tension flow out with each exhalation.

I ask about his previous descriptions of the week leading up to the discovery of Caroline's body, starting with the Monday, two days before she disappeared.

'The thing I remember is that she told me she had been to the doctor. She was explaining why she was depressed,' says Gordon.

'Yes.'

'She said, "I don't think I've come to terms with my mother's death."'

I ask about the Wednesday, the day before Caroline's body was discovered, when Gordon's boss, Rene Rivkin, had been having lunch with Graham Richardson at a restaurant in Darlinghurst, in Sydney's inner east.

Gordon told the inquest Rivkin asked him to pick up Richo after the meal and drive him back to work in the city centre.

Only, I tell him, we've spoken to Richardson, whose diary shows he was having lunch that afternoon with someone else.

'You're a smart man,' I tell Gordon. 'I'll be clear with you, what we're trying to establish here is your movements on the day Caroline died.'

'I understand that.'

We've also spoken to another witness, who claims he saw someone who looked like Gordon at The Gap that afternoon, arguing with someone who looked like Caroline. 'So it's very important that we lock in what your movements were for that particular day.'

Gordon repeats his previous account. 'I appreciate that it's fucking awkward for me.'

He says that just because Richo's diary says he had an appointment elsewhere, doesn't mean he wasn't actually with Rivkin.

I tell Gordon we also have a Diners Club statement from that day in the name of rugby league executive Peter 'Bullfrog' Moore, the person Richo's diary says that he was having lunch with.

'Yeah.' He pauses. 'So Peter Moore could have eaten with anybody, right?'

He's right. I'm just asking for his explanation.

Gordon continues, 'The question is, who did Peter Moore have lunch with? Richo can't tell you he was definitely with Peter Moore, 'cause he could've done something different to his diary.'

'You say that with a degree of certainty,' I tell him.

'No, I don't say that with a degree of certainty, I say that with a degree of defensiveness, because at the moment, you know, you're questioning what I did.'

'Yes,' I say. It's not a personal attack. I'm just presenting the facts. The only movement in the room is the ERISP cassettes recording our conversation.

'You understand why I take it personally?' he asks. 'I lost my fiancée and six years later I'm still embroiled in this, which is not pleasant for me.'

'You're still maintaining that your recollection of the day is that you picked up Graham Richardson,' I say. 'Is that correct?'

'Yeah. I mean it is correct.' Gordon continues: 'I don't want you to take this the wrong way, but you know, maybe I got my days wrong.'

I tell him, 'I'll explain it simply.' A witness says he saw two people matching the descriptions of Gordon and Caroline arguing at The Gap on the day before her body was recovered. 'And now we can't establish any form of alibi for your whereabouts that afternoon.'

He understands: 'People are wondering how I found myself at The Gap.'

Right now, nothing exists outside these four bare, peeling walls.

'Why did I know to go to The Gap?' Gordon says he simply ended up there, after driving round his and Caroline's favourite places. 'But it's also a good place to go to if somebody is in a depressed way, to look for them, isn't it?'

'Well –' I start to answer, but he interrupts me. 'Excuse me, Mr Wood –' I try but we are talking over each other.

'I didn't drive to The Gap. That's the point I'm trying to emphasise, Gary. Everybody's assuming I just poodled off to The Gap. I know I didn't do that. I didn't poodle off to The Gap.' His voice is rising.

I let him talk.

'So, yeah, I'm getting agitated,' Gordon says. 'I'm getting agitated because six years later, my life is sort of in a mess and I'm meant to sit here. I'm just trying to help you guys, I'm trying to help myself.'

Moments later, Jason hands me an aerial photograph of The Gap and I ask Gordon to show me where he found Caroline's car, and to mark the spot with a blue pen.

'No, I won't mark it,' although he points. 'That's in the vicinity.'

'And you won't be any more specific than that?'

'No, sorry mate, but I feel a bit under attack here.'

'I –'

He interrupts: 'You know, I'm getting scared now.'

'I want you to be accurate, Mr Wood.'

'I'm scared to talk to you, 'cause you're having a go at me.'

'No, I think what –'

He interrupts again: 'Can you just hit pause?' He means on the ERISP machine. 'Because I want to talk to you about how I'm feeling.'

'I would rather continue talking on tape,' I say. I do not stop the recording. He looks at me. I'm feeling more balanced now. Gordon says it has been so long since Caroline's death.

'Can you understand why … it's difficult for me, emotionally? It's difficult for me to trust you. I met you out the front of my apartment and my instinct and my belief in truth and honour and justice and all those noble values,' he continues. 'I am trying to help you because I'm hoping that you're going to help me.'

'I understand.'

He tells me that, not only is he innocent of any involvement in Caroline's death, but he's actually a victim as well. 'It's doubly worse.' And yet, he says, he still came here to talk to us.

We go over the facts again: Gordon's fiancée disappeared; he found her car; he thought he could see something from the clifftop using only a handheld torch while Caroline's brother, who was with him at the time, saw nothing. Gordon was right. That was where Caroline's body was recovered.

'Are you saying that I'm present when she goes over the cliff?' he asks me.

'I'm saying that they are the facts, the way that they present themselves,' I answer him.

He denies any involvement.

'You're certain on that?' I ask him. 'Don't take offence.'

'It's massively offensive.'

***

After almost five hours, the conversation returns to whether Gordon was driving Richo back from lunch with Rivkin on the day before Caroline went missing.

'I have often wondered, or sometimes wondered since then whether I got confused,' he says. 'I'm dropping off, picking up people all the time.'

I do not commit myself, saying only 'Mmmm,' and 'Right,' while he keeps talking.

'I'm trying to be honest,' says Gordon. Maybe he got his days wrong, and it wasn't Richo in the car with him. Maybe it was Rivkin. Or maybe someone else. 'I'm not helping myself here,' he says. 'I'm sorry it isn't very clear, but I am human.'

In fairness, nothing he has said is evidence that Gordon was involved in Caroline's death. He says that there are lots of other things that he might want to clear up with us, only he hasn't had much time between first seeing us outside his home and now. I tell him that he has our number. If there is anything else while we're in town, to contact us and we will try to clarify them.

'That will be it,' I say. 'The time now is 7.05pm. I'll suspend the interview.' I switch off the ERISP machine.

The three of us sit back and I breathe out, exhausted.

This morning, after finishing my qigong, I sat, cross-legged, on the grass to meditate, facing the sun. I felt centred, more able to notice the details of what was going on around me than before; the light playing on the water, the sound of children's laughter, my own breathing. Even though it was a hot day for London, the sunlight seemed weaker than at home, I noticed. The colours around me were less bright than I was used to. The edges of the shadows less certain.

***

You don't normally get to pick and choose your jobs in Homicide. Mostly it's luck. If you're on call, which you are one week in six, you work whatever murder happens.

But, in November 2001, when I first hear about the disappearance of Terry Falconer, a prisoner working on day release, I'm interested. Then Jaco is sent up to the Mid North Coast, where a body's been discovered, and I want to know more. Jaco is already handling a lot of cases at the moment. We speak by phone and he tells me he's overloaded. Someone else will have to take on this one.

If it is what I think it is, then straightaway I want to lead it.

Despite a decade working murders, and even doing time in the Organised Crime Squad, I've never had the chance to take on a real gangland killing. This has all the hallmarks; sawn-up pieces of the victim's body found inside blue plastic bags floating in the Hastings River near Port Macquarie, a few hours north of Sydney. Whoever could do that to another human being is no ordinary criminal.

I'll need to talk to the squad commander, but first, I ask Jason and our other team member, Nigel Warren, if they're up for working on the case. The three of us have worked together since the first murder case I led, the shooting of Barbara Saunders, and I trust them. If I'm being honest, it goes deeper than that; I need them.

We joke about it between ourselves. When we get called to the scene of a new murder, I'll introduce us to the local police commander, saying we balance each other out: 'I'm the serious one, Jason's the joker. I charge ahead, while Nigel is more cautious. He's analytical while I am physical. And you can tell by his name that he's the nerd, he'll take charge of the computers.'

Jason will usually chip in with a smartarse comment: 'Don't listen to Gary, he's got no personality, and he looks like Monty Burns when he's naked.' But the truth is, we do each balance the others out. Each of us has strengths where the others have weaknesses.

All three of us also have lives outside of work, and this looks like the murder could take us away from home for weeks. Christmas is coming up, though personally, I'd welcome the chance to avoid it. Last year's was my first since leaving Debbie and I chose to go into the office and work rather than stay at home and face up to how our family is splintered.

But not everybody has my problems.

Nigel and Jason may not share my motivations but they still say yes.

I knock on the door of the Homicide Squad commander, Nick Kaldas. He's only recently taken over the squad but I already rate him, he's worked the streets, spent time on undercover operations and has a politician's charisma. I can see how the commander's job will be a step he climbs on the ladder to higher things.

Nick looks up. 'Come in, Jubes.'

'You know that job up at Port Macquarie, the body in the bags?' I ask.

Nick nods. 'Yeah, he's been identified as that prisoner, Terry Falconer. Jaco's up there working the on-call response.'

'I know, I've spoken to Jaco and he can't keep the job because he has some other matters he's working on. I'd like the job.'

Nick frowns. 'Are you sure you want it?'

'Yeah.' I tell him Nigel and Jason are also available, that the Caroline Byrne investigation is moving slowly and that Grayson, the suspect in the Barbara Saunders murder from a year ago, just pleaded guilty, meaning we don't have to prepare for a trial, so have the time to spare.

'That's great,' says Nick. The case is ours. 'Thanks for putting your hand up. I don't think it's going to be easy.'

Nick turns back to the paperwork waiting on his desk. I walk back into the squad office to pass on the news to Jason and Nigel, wondering what I've just got us into.

***

A week later, early on Sunday 2 December, Paul Jacob picks me up for the drive to Port Macquarie. We're both working overtime and Jaco's on his way back to the crime scene after picking up a change of clothes from home. When we get there, he'll conduct a one-day handover to my team before returning to Sydney and, while he's looking tired from all the work and travel, he still has that same old, reassuring smile.

This should just be two mates on a long drive together, a chance to spend some time with the guy I consider a mentor – but I'm wound too tight to enjoy it. Right now, the Australian boxer Anthony 'The Man' Mundine is fighting for the super middleweight world title against the German hard man Sven Ottke. I promised myself I'd watch it; for me, boxing means memories of childhood, practising punches with my grandfather or sitting on the lounge with Dad to watch Mundine's own father box on *Friday Night Fights* while I was growing up.

As an adult, I love the way the boxing ring is a test of character. You get in there and face your fears. Mundine has passed that test repeatedly. I've followed his career ever since he switched over from rugby league.

The drive means I can't watch the fight, so I'm hanging on every update I can get from the news bulletins on the car radio. In the early rounds, Mundine's looked good. He's tough and fast, giving the champion problems.

'Listen, buddy,' Jaco says, bringing my attention back to the murder. He tells me how the body was discovered, when, on the night of 25 November, a fisherman found a plastic bag floating in the river and cut it open, seeing something that looked like skin, tattooed with a pair of lips, some sharks and a woman lying with her hands behind her head and a towel round her midriff.

The fisherman called the police, who went out in a boat in the early hours of the next morning and found five more bags, each bound up with silver duct tape like the first, wrapped in chicken wire and weighed down with a round river stone.

Jaco says the gases produced by decomposition caused the bags to float and, without that, we might never have found them. Inside, the body had been cut up with a handsaw. It was the tattoos, still visible on the victim's skin, that allowed police to find a match to descriptions kept in custody records, allowing Terry Falconer to be identified.

The people you are looking for are brutal, Jaco says, but I'm distracted. I ask him to pull into a club just off the highway and head inside.

'Are you showing the Mundine fight?' I ask the barman. He shakes his head.

Back in the car, the radio is saying things are heating up in the fifth round. 'He's gaining confidence,' I say to Jaco, who looks at me and smiles, then shakes his head and turns back to the highway.

I've got this, I think. *I'm no longer just Jaco's apprentice. I've led the Barbara Saunders murder case. I've led the investigation into the death of Jayden March.*

We talk through what Jaco's team have done in Port Macquarie. Normally, with any new murder case, you start with the crime scene. You get photographs, forensics, expand the area cordoned off with police tape rather than contract it, make sure you gather every single piece of evidence.

Only, we don't have a crime scene. We don't know where Terry was butchered. And the stretch of river where the bags were found isn't going to tell us much.

After learning everything you can from the crime scene, you move on to the victim. Who was Terry? What did he do? Who did he know?

These questions we can answer, thanks to his criminal record, which shows how Terry's life has been played out before the courts.

As a young man, he worked as a miner and panel beater. After that, he was in tow trucks at a time when the industry was both corrupt and violent.

Terry suffered a brain injury after being shot by rivals, but it didn't stop him. He wound up making methamphetamine, the highly addictive drug known as ice, and was linked to two bikie gangs, the Gypsy Jokers and the Rebels. Terry used to drive ute-loads of meth down to Sydney from his property at Brewarrina, in the far north of New South Wales, and made a lot of money from these runs.

He married and later split from his wife. He got busted for drug production. Aged 53, he'd been due to be released from Silverwater Prison within weeks.

As part of that process, Terry was on day release, working at a smash-repair workshop run by one of his mates in Ingleburn, southwest Sydney. Ten days before his chopped-up body was discovered, three men dressed like cops arrived and showed Terry a police badge before one put on surgical gloves to search him. Witnesses said they put Terry in handcuffs and took him away in a blue Ford or possibly a Holden. Either way, the witnesses said it looked like a police car.

It wasn't. Or at least, not a car belonging to the New South Wales police. Jaco checked more widely but none of the other, different law-enforcement bodies knew anything about what had taken place.

So had Terry faked his own arrest and gone on the run? Some in the cops believed it at first, but it didn't make sense. Why run, says Jaco, when you're about to be released?

That's all we have. If it wasn't the authorities who took Terry and he didn't run, then he must have been abducted. It's not much to go on, but it does tell us something: if Terry's killers wanted him dead, they could have just walked up and shot him. It looks like they also wanted him alive first.

The fact there are at least three men involved in Terry's disappearance also gives us a way in, if we can exploit it. Find one of those three and maybe he'll roll over on the others. The third thing in our favour is the simple fact Terry's body was discovered. 'That's a huge fuck-up by the offenders, buddy,' says Jaco. Without that, the cops might have kept on thinking Terry staged his disappearance. Without a body, Homicide would not have been called.

I ask Jaco to pull up at an RSL, hoping to catch what is left of the fight, but when we arrive the place isn't open. The radio says Ottke was landing body blows on Mundine in the seventh, but then the Australian came out with more aggression, advancing on the champion and getting in two right hands that put Ottke on the floor.

Jaco and I look at our potential suspects.

'Buddy, there's so much going on, we haven't even got it all on e@gle.i yet,' says Jaco, referring to the new computer management system being introduced for major cases that I'd used for the first time a year before. It's a more efficient way of managing the vast amounts of information, such as phone records, telephone intercept transcripts, photographs and witness statements that a big case collects and a big improvement on the systems that went before it. The difference from the old days, like in the beginning of the Bowraville investigation, when cops relied on card indexes, is vast.

Too often, back then, a suspect could fall between the gaps in these filing systems, such as when the list of names provided by a witness was not cross-referenced against a printout of vehicle registrations for example. The idea is that e@gle.i will stop that happening, but even so Jaco says, 'We're just being overwhelmed with information.'

The list of potential suspects he's drawn up so far looks like a Who's Who of the worst people in New South Wales: bikies, murderers and organised-crime figures. Being a crook himself meant Terry mixed with plenty of other crooks, which is dangerous enough, and Jaco says he was also an informant for seven different law-enforcement agencies.

Seven! If any one of those connections had got out, it would have made Terry a target.

Our job will be to work through this long list of suspects, looking at which of them had the motive, opportunity and capability to carry out the killing. For starters, Jaco says, the Rebels bikie gang are said to have somehow got hold of a police document suggesting Terry was an informer.

Near Kendall, just south of Port Macquarie, I ask Jaco to pull off the road outside the Kew Hotel and run inside. At least they're open, but not showing the boxing.

Jaco can't stop smiling as I walk back to the car, shoulders slumped and finally resigned to missing the match's conclusion. As we head back onto the Pacific Highway, he says Terry's name also came up on e@gle.i as a person of interest in another unsolved murder: the killing of a seemingly blameless old couple, Anthony and Frances Perish, shot dead in their backyard in Leppington, southwest Sydney, almost a decade earlier, in 1993.

It's a strange case, he says. Both victims were shot outside the house then carried into their bedroom and left lying on their separate beds. It is a strange way to finish off a killing. Almost touching. No one knows who did it.

Jaco's already spoken to one of the detectives who worked on the case, who told him one of the couple's grandsons, Andrew Perish, believed that Terry was the killer, though if he was, any motive is uncertain. Perish is also a former president of the Campbelltown chapter of the Rebels.

The cops interviewed Terry about the killings when he was in prison earlier this year, after an anonymous caller to a local police station also claimed he was responsible. He denied any involvement, claiming his ex-wife was spreading rumours following their breakup. Terry said she was trying to get him knocked.

There was no evidence to back this up, says Jaco, but it widens the pool of potential suspects even further.

From Kendall, the road runs through thick, deserted forest before turning east towards the white beaches and blue ocean that run along New South Wales' Mid North Coast. It's a beautiful stretch of country and one I know well from the years spent driving up here to work on the Bowraville murders, which took place just over an hour away from where we are. I also have happy memories of holidays in Port Macquarie with Debbie and the kids. Days spent running in and out of the surf together, or just hanging out as a family in the garden. I know the place, it's comfortable. It feels good to be returning.

That feeling ends when we arrive. By the time I find a pub to watch the fight, it's over. Instead, on the car radio, I hear how Mundine looked to be one punch away from defeating the champion. In the tenth round, he was trading blows with Ottke when he caught a short right to the temple. The Man fell onto the canvas and could not get back up.

Disappointed, we drive to the town's police station, which overlooks the harbour wall that marks the mouth of the Hastings River.

Here, in a long room on the first floor, Jaco's been setting up a room for the strike force, which is what task forces are called now, after some decision by the police bureaucracy. I don't mind the change, it makes us sound aggressive, which I welcome, but doesn't make any difference to the work involved.

'Welcome to Strike Force Tuno,' Jaco says. 'Sorry about the mess.' There's paper everywhere. The room is missing the computers, printers, in-trays and white boards that we'll need to make sense of the investigation. Looking around, it's obvious that Jaco has, rightly, been prioritising getting information in and our first job will be to make sense of it. The older I get, the more I understand how being a cop isn't all about chasing crooks, kicking down doors, and sitting face to face with criminals – the way I imagined it when I joined up. The job *is* all those things, but only rarely. Most of the time, solving a murder is about making sure you control the tide of information flooding in, so that nothing gets lost.

There's going to be weeks of dull office work just making sense of everything and I wonder what to use for motivation. Like Jaco, I usually think about the victim. It helps to get close to their family, so you can feel their emotion. This time, Terry was a crook, so maybe he's not a big loss to society, but he still had people who loved him. And whoever killed him is still out there, laughing.

'Mate, we should take this personally,' I say to Jaco, breaking the silence between us. The worst thing is that whoever took Terry dressed themselves up as cops. They used our badge. They made it look like *we* killed him. 'You dress up as cops, kidnap someone and cut them up?' It's only a few years since the royal commission made crooks out of the cops. These people now are mocking us.

I feel a flame of anger rise inside me. I'm ready now. Whatever it takes. I'll show everyone it wasn't cops but crooks who were the killers.

***

Over the next week, I watch the strike force room fill up. All up, there will be about 30 of us working on it, including detectives from several different squads and local area commands, as well as the police analysts who do the vital work of going through witness statements, phone records, property documents and other sources of information, trying to find connections.

Privately, I compare the crowded rows of desks and growing piles of equipment with the resources put into the Bowraville investigation after the children went missing. Back then, the case was run by only three detectives, who drew up their own timelines in black Texta on butcher's paper stuck on the wall of a spare room in the tiny local police station. Unlike me, the officer-in-charge had no experience in leading Homicide inquiries.

I think about how, only two years ago, senior police shut down the reinvestigation of those murders, after the Director of Public Prosecutions declined our request to put our main suspect on trial again over the killing of four-year-old Evelyn Greenup.

I argued for it to be re-established, saying we still had to take the children's deaths to an inquest, and they agreed, but didn't give us any resources to do it. It was still just Jason and me. Now, those same bosses have decided that the killing of one white man, a criminal, deserves a bigger strike force than I know what to do with. *It's offensive*, I think, then put that thought behind me and get on with the job.

My first priority is setting up e@gle.i to ensure that everything coming in about the roughly 70 potential suspects in Jaco's Who's Who of the New South Wales underworld is properly understood.

Jason, Nigel and I spend our first weeks inside the strike force room, collating evidence, ensuring everything is recorded and allocating tasks for the others. Watching the hours the pair of them put in, and the intensity of their concentration, I hope that everybody on the strike force – many of whom have never worked a murder – looks up to them as examples.

They're smart, which you need to be in Homicide, both book-smart and street-smart. You've got to be able to talk to people at different levels, because you never know what type of killing you'll be working. It could be a professor who gets murdered, or a street-corner junkie.

They're confident, which is vital. You need an ego, even something close to arrogance, because it's a massive thing to charge someone with murder, and it's also a life-changing decision *not* to go after someone because you think that there are better suspects. You have to back yourself to make those calls, and deal with it if they are wrong.

Jason and Nigel can also handle the emotion. You need compassion to do this job properly, but having it means you will never forget what it feels like to sit down with a murder victim's family. They won't forget you either.

And, like the two of them, you've got to be prepared to put the hours in, even if that means day after day of information management. At first, our approach comes in for ridicule from some of those on the strike force, and other local cops who aren't involved. A fortnight in, I start to hear people are bagging us, saying, 'You're not going to catch anyone sitting behind a computer', or suggesting we don't have the guts to go out and rattle the crooks involved.

I can't stand that kind of lazy thinking, so I front some of those who are the source of this poison. I don't care if it gets me a reputation as a hard man to work with. But unless you've worked Homicide yourself, you don't get to criticise me, my team or the way we do our work.

The way I see it, you have to earn the right to walk around calling yourself a Homicide detective and the only way to do that is through the work itself. I know I ask a lot, in terms of hours, effort and constant attention, but if you're prepared to do that, the way Nigel and Jason are, then I'm a real softie. On this case, as the first few weeks turn into months, I start to realise how much work it will involve.

U Love Me

29 August 2002: 17 years in

We're almost nine slow months into the investigation when two Strike Force Tuno detectives, Glenn and Luke, walk up to the front door of a potential witness in one of the hardscrabble suburbs that are a part of Sydney's western edge, a long, dull drive from the bright lights of the city centre.

This is only the latest of many similar, so far largely unsuccessful calls and the two detectives knock, half-expecting the bloke inside to ignore them, half-expecting him to tell them to get fucked. Rocco – which is what his mates call him – is a member of the Rebels, and that's what bikies usually say to the police.

The door opens, although a locked security screen means they still have no real view into the house. All they can make out is a large figure standing in the shadows.

'What do you want?' he asks.

They say that they're from Homicide and want to talk about Terry Falconer's murder.

'I know who's done it, and *why* they've done it,' Rocco tells them.

Glenn and Luke can hardly believe what they're hearing.

Rocco tells them to come back tonight, alone. When they do, what he tells them is a revelation. It's everything we've been hoping for, and more.

***

Since last December, our strike force of around 30 has been steadily cut back by the bosses, who also told us that the New South Wales Government was close to broke, so there was no more money for overtime or travel allowance payments.

To save on travel, a few months ago, the strike force was moved down from Port Macquarie to the Crime Agencies' headquarters in central Sydney. It was probably a good thing; although the extra payments helped as I'm still short of cash following my separation from Debbie and the kids, I was sick of the travelling. Except, I found we didn't have a room to work in.

Soon after the move, I walked into the office of Wayne, the acting Homicide Squad commander, and told him, 'I need a room.'

'We haven't got one,' Wayne told me. Wayne is a decent, honest bloke and I knew it was the truth, but I wasn't going to accept it.

'Well, I'm just going to follow you around all day until I get one.'

Wayne thought I was joking – until I started following him in and out of his office, up and down the corridors, repeating, 'I need a strike force room, I can't do this without a strike force room, you've got a fucking strike force here but no room for us to work in.'

Eventually, Wayne laughed. He got it. The way I deal with challenges like this might not always work, but he found us a room. We kept working. The next challenge was our lack of any real progress.

The pressure wasn't only coming from our bosses. Sometimes, when I was on call, I'd stay over at my parents' house in Dural to avoid the long drive to and from the Central Coast. My dad would watch me being interviewed about the murder on the TV news and ask me, 'So, do they know who's done it?'

'Dad, who do you think "they" are?' I'd reply.

'The blokes working on this investigation.'

'Dad, you've seen me, I'm on the TV, talking about it. Do you understand that I am "they"?'

He was the same when I did a short stint in close personal protection for dignitaries back in 2000, around the time of the Sydney Olympics. Working for the Prime Minister, John Howard, meant joining his early-morning walks, so I'd stay at my parents. Dad would ask me: 'Who actually looks after him?'

'Dad, *I'm* looking after him.'

'Yeah, but who else is there?'

'No, Dad, *I'm* looking after him. *I'm* his close personal protection.'

I'd laugh about it afterwards, but it made me feel like I was five years old again.

With Strike Force Tuno now short on resources, I told the team to make the most of what we had. So if they went to a country town to interview a witness, they were to drive around the streets and make sure people saw them. During media interviews, I tried to give the sense we were a big, remorseless investigation. I wanted to put pressure on anyone who knew about the killing, to make them think it would be better to come forward than wait for us to find them.

It hadn't worked. For nine months we'd got little, and that upset me.

But that all changed once Rocco decided to talk.

***

Glenn and Luke go back to meet Rocco in a granny flat out the back of another property, a small place so crowded with junk they have to clear a space among it to sit down. They get on well enough to arrange another meeting, at which Glenn introduces me to Rocco, sitting inside an unmarked car parked near a servo in southwest Sydney. He's big and physically imposing, somewhere in his thirties and with a menace about him – as well as a manslaughter conviction, over his part in a fatal brawl.

That's good, I think. *He's the real deal.* He's only going to know about what happened if he is a genuine crook, not someone who's pretending.

Rocco says little at first and I guess that he is also working out what to make of me. It will take a long time and many meetings to gain his trust and hear everything he has to tell us. After all, as he points out, the men who kidnapped Terry were dressed as cops. What's to say they weren't the *real* police? Both of us remember Roger Rogerson and the royal commission into police corruption. What if I'm another corrupt cop, who's coming after *him*?

After every meeting, Glenn and I complete a formal investigator's note and a contact advice form, documenting what Rocco told us, and entering the details into e@gle.i. As his story emerges, what I like most about it is that it isn't perfect. It doesn't try to answer all our questions, which makes it more convincing. It won't solve the case alone.

Rocco says he was approached by a woman, someone he knew to be the girlfriend of one of the Perish brothers' associates. She gave him $1000 in cash, telling him to buy some decent cloths to wear for dinner. A few days later, Andrew Perish picked up Rocco and drove him towards the city, saying they were heading for Newtown. When they got there, Anthony was waiting.

This in itself is a shock. As far as we knew, Anthony, the elder brother, is a ghost. Known by his nickname, Rooster, he's been on the run for 14 years over a drug offence, without the police catching him. Rocco knows little about what Anthony got up to all that time, except it was unlikely to be good, and the idea of him sitting openly in an inner-west restaurant, inviting people to dinner, is disturbing.

The close relationship between the brothers is also concerning. Word has it Anthony was the first person in Australia to produce ice, and made himself a fortune. Andrew, the younger brother, runs an agricultural goods store in the city's southwest suburbs and is an apparently legitimate businessman. We have no evidence these two businesses are linked.

Rocco says the three men sat and talked. Anthony ordered wine. During the meal, he raised the subject of his grandparents, asking Rocco if it was true that Terry Falconer once told him in jail that he killed them.

Rocco said he hadn't.

Later, Anthony wanted to talk business, asking, 'So, Rocco, what can you do for the company?' – meaning, Rocco thought, the Perishes.

'What would the company have me do for them?' he asked, testing the waters.

'You've got a boat?'

Rocco did, but said it needed fixing.

'If the boat was fixed, would it make it out to the shelf and back?'

Rocco guessed he meant the continental shelf, way out in the Pacific Ocean. He said it would.

'I want you to put the boat in,' Anthony continued. 'Come up the Karuah River to Bulahdelah.' Bulahdelah is a town on the Mid North Coast, an hour and a half's drive south of Port Macquarie. 'There's a wharf up there. Come up to the wharf and I'll be waiting for you just like a fisherman with a couple of Eskies because the cunt might be in a few pieces.'

'Who is the cunt?' asked Rocco.

'Don't worry, it's not you,' but Rocco was still uncertain. The more we learn about him, the more we realise how deep his suspicions run. He insists on meeting us at 10pm in isolated parks around western Sydney suburbs like Mount Druitt and Blacktown, where Glenn and I will go and talk with him, while Jason Evers and Luke sit in a nearby car, worrying about our safety.

Or Rocco will call late at night, saying he's seen a car go by and wanting us to check it out. We also learn that he is right to be paranoid. He'd fallen out with different members of the Rebels over time and, underneath his leather jacket, carried the scars of seven stab wounds he got while serving time in prison.

The Perish brothers offered Rocco $30,000, as well as the cost of fixing his boat. They gave him a prepaid mobile phone so they could contact him without the call being traced and, after their meal, both of them visited him in person to check on the repair work.

Rocco, who still worried he was being set up – or worse, he might be the real intended victim – tells us he filmed these visits. Hearing that, my first thought is exultation; it would mean concrete evidence to back up what he's saying. Then Rocco's paranoia starts to infect me. Is he trying to set us up? Could he have faked the tapes?

We can check the dates of the recordings. It's now over a year since the meetings he describes took place. How likely is it he would plan a conspiracy over that length of time, just to ensnare some cops he doesn't know, who turned up at his door one morning uninvited?

Rocco shows us a tape of Anthony's last visit, which took place a few days before Terry's abduction on Friday 16 November 2001. In it the two men are walking together to the gate of what looks like a rural property, where they stop to talk. There's no sound, but Rocco tells us Anthony was saying: 'You'll come up, you'll pick up a couple of Eskies, you'll go out and take them out to the continental shelf, you will empty out the contents over a big hole using a depth sounder. On the way back, wash those Eskies out halfway back and throw them over the side. When you get back, wash the boat out with ammonia.'

'Huh?' Rocco replied. This wasn't the plan that they'd discussed.

'If you wash it out with ammonia, they can tell there's been blood in the boat but they can't tell whose it is. It fucks the DNA.'

'What, you're not coming with me?'

'Nah, that's what I'm paying you for.'

Playing for time, and with his mind now twisting with worry that he was being set up, Rocco said his boat was fixed but still needed to be run in before it could make the journey.

'Get on with it,' said Anthony. 'Hurry up because this cunt goes Friday regardless.'

Rocco says he had to get out. He wasn't going to go through with it.

After Anthony's visit, he switched off the prepaid phone. He says the Perish brothers didn't visit him again, although rumours started going round that the Rebels were demanding his colours back, meaning the patches worn on a bikie's leather vest identifying them as a gang member. Handing your colours back could also mean the gang forcibly burned or cut off your identifying tattoos. Rocco was too ballsy to go into hiding, but his paranoia grew.

Among the strike force, we also asked ourselves how much we could trust him. Running an informant is common practice in the cops, but it is rarely easy. To start with, they're criminals and their world is an extreme one. I try to look past that background. The real question is why they're helping you. Often, an informant only offers information to get themselves out of trouble. That makes it difficult to respect them, because informing's un-Australian. It means dobbing on your mates. Informers get called dogs, and are treated worse if the people they inform on are able to catch them.

But Rocco isn't asking us for anything. We know he's not an innocent – he tells us stories about armed robberies, drive-by shootings and drug dealing – but when I ask him why he wants to go down this path, he says he needs a change of direction. He'd only recently got out of jail when the Perish brothers approached him and hadn't planned on going back to his old life, but being a crook is like smoking: *I'm gonna give it up, but I'll just have one now and then I'll give up later.*

Rocco needed something to make him quit for good. Informing on the Perishes will do it.

He knows what that decision means. At the least, he'll have to abandon his old life and cut the connections to everyone he knows. But fail to take that step and his old life will likely lead him somewhere fatal, he says, either dead in a fight or back in jail where he was stabbed before, and neither prospect looks attractive.

We decide to trust him. I ask Rocco to wear a wire and approach the Perishes again, recording the conversations. The risks are huge, but so are the rewards if we can pull it off, and keep him alive. At the least, it will help to check the truth of what he's told us. At best, we might gather more evidence.

At first, Rocco refuses. Wearing a wire goes beyond simply telling us what he knows about the killing. I tell him that it's only one more step along the path he's chosen. Eventually, he says that he will do it.

Rocco sets up a meeting with Andrew Perish for 30 September 2002. The two men will meet in Andrew's store on a dusty stretch of highway outside Sydney. Rocco's cover story will be the inquest that is soon to hear evidence about the deaths of the Perish brothers' grandparents. This inquest will later prove to be inconclusive, but at this moment, we think, the Perishes must be uncertain about what it will find, particularly if Terry Falconer's murder is related.

We tell Rocco to say he's received a summons to appear as a witness.

I like the plan, but we run into a problem. It relies on Rocco going alone into Andrew's South Western Produce store, where he'll be out of sight. A listening device normally has both a recorder and transmitter, so we can listen to the conversation as it happens, but Rocco says Anthony is wise to this and always carries something in his pocket that vibrates if there's a transmitter near him. We don't know if Anthony will be at the meeting

'If I walk in there and that goes off, I'll be a fucking dead man,' says Rocco.

I tell him we have his back.

'You know as well as I know if they wanted to do me, they'll do me and you'll only get in there after I'm already done,' he says. He's right.

The risks are getting bigger. We send him in alone, with just the recorder, and wait nearby – just close enough to be able to hear a gunshot.

***

'Bullshit, isn't it?' we hear Andrew saying when we play back the recording later. This is the first time the two have met since Rocco switched off his mobile phone, but so far Andrew doesn't seem suspicious. Rocco is playing his part well. When he mentions the summons to give evidence at the inquest, Andrew says, 'Did you get it today?'

'Yeah, about 11 o'clock at my girl's –'

'Fucking can't, mate,' Andrew interrupted. 'You go there and fucking …'

'Yeah, they're going to ask me that shit and what do I say, man? What do you want me to say?'

'Fuck, just something like –'

'Want me to say that fuckin' Terry told, told me that he'd done it or what?'

'No, no. Don't fuckin' –' Andrew replies.

'Well, I dunno, that's why I'm asking. That's why I'm here to fuckin' see ya, Andrew.'

Listening, we have to give Rocco credit. He has balls.

It seems like Andrew's trying to calm him down: 'I know they're not going to want you to say nothing about knocking the other thing. They're not going to learn nothing.'

'Knocking' means killing, I think. That's good, but it is not nearly enough to use as evidence. Hoping to hear more, I'm disappointed when the conversation veers off into more general discussion of bikie life, filled with rivalries, conspiracies and violence.

After a quarter of an hour or so, Andrew says, 'I gotta let you go, mate, all right?'

'All right.'

'Have a good afternoon.'

Throughout September and October, we send Rocco back half a dozen times to talk to Andrew. To get it on tape that the Perishes did give him money in connection with his boat, we get Rocco to say that he wants to repay it, and give him $1000, which he gives to

Andrew to pass on to Anthony, saying, 'Give that to him. I promise to round off what I owe him.'

Andrew says he'll talk to his brother. Rocco says he'll pay it back in stages.

'Yeah, no worries,' Andrew says. Meeting by meeting, recording by recording, we are getting closer. But whether Andrew trusts Rocco or not, he never actually admits to any illegal activity.

By mid-October, the strain's getting to Rocco. He is smoking cones to help him sleep as well as giving the amphetamines a decent going-over. One day he finds four Jatz crackers floating in his swimming pool and says they're evidence that someone has broken into his property. When a car with the rego plate HSV-DNA goes past, he believes it's part of a plan to break into his house and harvest his DNA.

Another time, Luke and I are at his place when he tells us, 'Here you are, you can have this', and hands me a metal pipe about 30 centimetres long, just too wide to get your hand around, and heavy.

'What is it, mate?' I ask.

'A pipebomb. Rigged it up in case some fucker breaks in,' he says. Then, seeing my expression, he adds, 'It's all right, I've disconnected it.'

Luke and I look at each other in silence, then leave, carrying the bomb back to our car. If we call the Bomb Squad, they're going to block off the road and it will be on the evening news, but we don't want anyone to know we're talking to Rocco. So we put the bomb in the car boot and drive away, hands sweating on the steering wheel, to a deserted oval. When I call the Bomb Squad and explain what we've done, they royally abuse me.

On 16 October, as Rocco prepares to head into the South Western Produce store one more time, I can see the stress he's under. It's not just his paranoia, and his legitimate fear of being found out by Andrew Perish, it's like he's also wrestling with his conscience.

I have to respect that. Rocco's been living by his outlaw code since he was a teenager, meaning it's what's guided him all his adult life. It's like how, in the cops, you always have your partner's back. For Rocco, even *talking* to police means going against the code. Wearing a wire is a complete betrayal.

***

Glenn and I wait in our unmarked car while Rocco is inside the store, coiled tight with the tension of not knowing what's going on, half-expecting to hear the shot that means Rocco's been found out and has paid the price, something for which we'll ultimately be responsible.

Each of us is lost in silent thought. *Is it right to ask someone to risk their life to help you solve a murder? What if you end up with two bodies here, not one? What price are you prepared to pay?*

Any price. Murder cannot go unpunished.

This is my job. This is my role as a detective to sit here, hands sweating, inside a dusty car making these calls. Rocco's job is to go into that store, one crook talking to another, and risk his life. If we are lucky, and we get it right, we'll one day go to court where a jury will listen to this evidence and decide on their verdict. A judge in a white wig and black silk gown will pass sentence. Everyone has a part to play, but neither judge nor jury has to make these real, life and death decisions.

This never gets easier, no matter how many times I do it.

A text message arrives. It's Rocco.

'U love me don't you? ... Don't you!! ... I do belive that I have admis.'

I breathe out, sinking my head back into the car headrest. I'm just happy he's alive. *Fuck. Yes, Rocco, I love you.*

We see him turn into the car park and get out of his car, face hidden in the shadow of a baseball cap, head turning from side to side to see if anyone is watching. He approaches us and tells us what happened.

He says that he and Andrew had another quiet conversation about the inquest, which starts next week.

Andrew said, 'Yeah, you don't know nothing, right.'

Rocco said he was worried about a police running sheet Andrew had once shown him, which the Rebels had got hold of and which suggested Terry was working as an informant for the cops. If this document exists, it would confirm the rumours about it which Jaco heard at the start of the investigation. Rocco was worried the paper would still have his fingerprints on it and this would come out at the inquest, linking him to Terry's murder.

He tells us, Andrew whispered, 'Rocco, nobody knows we done it.'

A smile cracks the toughened bikie's face as he waits for our reaction.

We look at him and then we're high-fiving, ecstatic.

'Great mate, well done! You've got it,' I say, thinking, *Thank fuck, I can relax now. It's over.*

But it isn't.

We take the tape back to the Homicide Squad office and listen to the recording. To my horror, the listening device Rocco was wearing has failed.

A backup device, less well positioned, picked up part of the conversation, but at the moment Rocco says Andrew admitted his involvement, a whirring air compressor starts up in one of the nearby store fridges, drowning out what he says.

What the fuck? I think. *A man risks his life and this happens?*

The lesson is that listening devices can fail you.

For one, final, attempt, Rocco goes back into the store at the end of October, telling Andrew he'd heard Anthony might be in Sydney.

This time the wire works. It records Andrew making a phone call, saying, 'Hey mate, how you going? ... Uh yeah, I got someone here, OK ... Have a little talk you know. Are you there? Yeah, he's here now, yeah.'

Listening to the recording later, we can hear Rocco take the phone, 'Hey buddy, how ya going? What's happening. Ah, fuckin', fuck all mate.' The other voice on the phone call is not recorded, so we only hear Rocco's half of what is said, 'So we fuckin' need to have dinner, mate ... Fuck, just give Andrew a ring and organise it with him and he can let me know yeah, pick us up or whatever.'

That dinner never happens, though, for weeks, Jason, Luke, Glenn and I take our guns and Kevlar vests home with us every night, in case we get a call from Rocco saying it's on, meaning we'll need to rush across the city to seize Anthony. As the months pass, I have to accept the Perishes must have decided to cut contact.

Rocco gets worse. He insists on meeting other crooks, saying he'll be able to judge by their reaction if his cover is blown. One time, he calls me up saying he's been asked to get involved in a beating. Someone owes one of his mates some money.

I tell him, 'Mate, you can't do that. I can't have you getting involved in illegal behaviour.'

'But if I don't go, they'll know I'm off.'

In the end, the debt gets paid, meaning the beating doesn't happen. But keeping Rocco in check is exhausting. In December 2002, he calls Glenn, saying a helicopter has been circling his house and demanding to know why. He thinks it's the police checking out his place before launching a raid on it. He crashes his motorbike and the uniform cops who respond find $20,000 inside his panniers, along with videotapes of his meetings with Glenn and me at his house, filmed using a camera hidden inside his television.

He says he was worried that we might betray him after everything he's done, and the tapes are his insurance policy.

***

No matter that I'm trying to manage a paranoid bikie and investigate a murder, life at home doesn't let up.

One morning in early 2003, I walk outside the flat in Copacabana where I'm living and look down at the ocean, close enough to just make out the surfers cutting through the water. I like it here. For eight months, Pam and I were living in the rented place we found together near another surf beach, Avoca, but the commute got too much for her and she moved back to Sydney, while I got this flat to be near the kids. She and I still spend most of our nights together, staying over at one another's units.

It feels like I've got some balance in my life again. Pam and I are going well and I'm also secure in my relationship with Jake and Gemma. Last year, the townhouse behind where they live with their mum, my ex-wife, Debbie, came up for sale and I bought it. It's rented out, I don't know if I'll ever live in it, but what it does is show the kids that I'm not going anywhere.

Pam could have doubted that decision, but she didn't. She's never been jealous of Debbie and is always graceful in the way she lets me prioritise the kids. *She's a classy lady*, I think, walking to get the post. Life's working out. Looking out at the ocean, I watch a surfer ride one of the lefts that form near the north edge of the bay.

Looking down, I see divorce papers waiting in the mailbox.

My first reaction is overwhelming sadness. Yes, it was me who walked out but the uncaring lawyer's letter enclosing the formal paperwork is a stark statement that our marriage is now over. I failed. This isn't the life I had imagined growing up.

'I'll sign the papers, but you could have told me they were coming,' I say when I next see Debbie, to pick up the kids. She nods.

Getting divorced so soon after buying the townhouse also means I'm still struggling for money, and relying on overtime payments from work. Fortunately, we get a lot of overtime in Homicide.

***

Throughout October 2003, Jason and I are kept busy with the trial of Linda Wilson over the death of one-year-old Jayden March, making sure witnesses turn up at court and answering the prosecution lawyers' questions about this or that piece of the evidence.

In November, we finally convince Rocco to sign a formal witness statement in relation to Terry Falconer's death and Glenn, Luke, Jason and I spend a week of 10- to 12-hour days holed up with him in a rented house north of Sydney, getting his account down on paper. It runs to 87 pages and he is at his worst throughout this time, his paranoia crawling up the walls.

It's taken us so long to get this done because Rocco understands that this is the moment he loses control of the whole process. Before now, when he agreed to work as an informant and even during the meetings when he was wearing a wire, there was always the slim chance that, if discovered, he could try to talk his way out of it. Signing a witness statement means there is no such explanation. He can never go back.

If we take this to court and the Perishes are not convicted, he's a dead man.

'If you fuck this up, I'll kill you,' he tells me.

'Mate, I always knew that was the case. I'm not gonna fuck it up,' I try to reassure him.

Rocco refuses to take part in WitSec, the witness security program, because he doesn't trust it, so instead the police force pays for a one-way flight out of Sydney. The cops on the strike force also chip in what we can out of our own pockets, so Rocco has about $2000 when he gets on board the plane. It makes me deeply uncomfortable, after everything he's been through, that this is all he gets in return. Should this case get to court, the barristers involved will make more than that much daily.

Yet Rocco doesn't think that. The day before his flight, he comes to our offices in Strawberry Hills, and when we hand over the plane ticket, he looks at it like he can't believe it.

'Mate, I didn't think you were going to do this,' he says. 'I didn't know if I could trust you but you've given me a shot at it.'

He reaches beneath his shirt and produces a loaded automatic pistol with a laser sight. 'I suppose you can have this now,' he says, laying it on the table.

***

Linda Wilson is sentenced two days before Christmas 2003. In the end, she's found guilty of manslaughter, not murder, and the judge is more understanding of her than I was.

He finds that the injuries to Jayden's head were caused by 'impact and shaking'. He says the jury's decision not to find Wilson guilty of murder means they 'must have rejected the hypothesis in the prosecution case that it was the offender, and the offender alone, who inflicted all the injuries'.

It is a 'reasonable possibility' that Wilson's husband, Tony, actually inflicted some of these injuries, says the judge. She's 'had a troubled life'. There's evidence of a personality disorder: 'she was unsuited to the task of foster carer and ... sooner or later, she would have been demonstrably unable to cope with her responsibilities'.

It's worse than that, I think. Jayden's death could have been prevented. There were warning signs flashing, if only anyone had noticed. Like the fact Wilson and her husband, Tony, applied to be foster parents in Queensland but were knocked back, so they moved south and tried again in New South Wales, where they were accepted.

Like how Jayden had been taken to hospital more than once before he died, where the doctors had told the Department of Community Services (DoCS) that they were worried about him. Two DoCS workers visited Wilson's house and spent hours with her and Jayden just days before his death. Yet they saw nothing.

As a Homicide detective, I cannot protect the victims in my cases. I get involved only after they have died. Hoping to prevent another similar tragedy, after Jayden's death, I filed a report saying, 'There are a number of issues involving DoCS that have been identified. These issues might require further investigation.' I met with the coroner to tell him about how DoCS had handled the case and he wrote to the minister.

In response, the department told me to ease up. 'You've got to think bigger here, Gary,' they told me. 'Do you know how many other kids we have in care? It's thousands. We don't want all those parents to worry. We don't want to generate more fear.'

To my shame, I believed them. It was the first time I'd been caught up in politics. Sitting in court, I think I was mistaken.

The judge gives Wilson nine years in prison, with a non-parole period of six years and 11 months. An appeal court will later reduce this to six years with a non-parole period of four years and six months.

Four and a half years. A boy is dead.

I watch Wilson as the judge stands and leaves the courtroom. She doesn't blink. I think of all the other children, like the thousands in DoCS' care, or the three children in Bowraville for whom it is already too late.

In this case, I played by the rules. I shut my mouth.

You don't fucking do this on my watch, I think. *This doesn't fucking happen.*

I won't make the same mistakes again.

Walking Evil

1 January 2004: 18 years in

The phone rings before dawn on New Year's Day. Pam and I wake, but I'm on call, so I know it's for me. Despite not drinking last night, we still sat up until midnight to see 2004 in, and I can feel how little sleep I've managed. It's not yet five o'clock.

Pam smiles and rolls over. It will be her turn to answer soon enough. Her turn to spend a week responding to every fatal brawl or suspicious-looking suicide in New South Wales, every drug-related robbery gone wrong or bloodied body discovered stabbed to death in the back seat of a Holden, every call-out to a fly-blown house whose neighbours have finally decided that they can't stand the stench during this run of 30- and 40-degree summer days. For most of these on-call cases, we oversee the initial investigation and maybe advise the local detectives on how to take it forward, then hand the work over to them. The tougher ones, where the crime is particularly awful or looks like it will need specialists to track down the killer, we keep.

Maybe this isn't one of those, I think, reaching for my notebook in the darkness. Maybe this is a straightforward case. An open goal. I ask for the details.

They're brief – a man, deceased, maybe a shotgun to the head – but enough to tell me my night's sleep is over.

I call Nigel Warren and Luke, who's come over to Homicide since working on Strike Force Tuno, and tell them to get moving, then grab the clothes I lay out ready every night when I'm on call, fall into the shower, then the car, making more phone calls as I drive down the empty highway to Sydney.

More information is coming in: the victim was a 54-year-old, Michael Davies. He ran a cleaning firm. About 4.30am, his wife got home from work to find Michael's body in their bedroom. She called 000 and the operator dispatched an ambulance, as well as the local police.

When they arrived, the room looked like a nightmare. As the forensics team started to look at the blood spatter, they realised Michael wasn't killed by a shotgun. It was more likely something blunt and heavy. But only a frenzied attack could do that kind of damage to another person.

I'm facing something evil and the new year is only a few hours old.

In Campsie, west Sydney, I drive down roads of unsuspecting, sleeping houses, until I see the blue lights. I duck under the crime scene tape and am shown into the bedroom. Michael's body is still lying where his killer left it. A camera flashes as the forensic technicians record the scene as evidence. Down the hall are children's bedrooms.

I'm told that when Michael's wife came home, she found their two-year-old daughter and four-year-old son, who seemed unharmed. But her 10-year-old daughter, from a previous relationship, also lives in the house and, right now, she is missing. The property has a garage out the back. Inside, some cushions and discarded children's nightwear are lying on the floor.

By mid-morning, I'm facing a row of grim faces at the first of the day's briefings at the nearby Campsie Police Station.

'This is as real as it gets,' I tell the uniformed cops gathered from five different local area commands, as well as detectives from some of the other specialised squads and tactical police from the State Protection Group.

I explain how the four-year-old boy said he saw a man inside their house last night and recognised him as one of his father's mates. The dead man's wife has told us her husband invited the man to stay with them over Christmas, but he stormed out after a few days. He was a strange man, she says, with a black beard and tangled hair. He worked as a cleaner with her husband sometimes. His name is Jeffrey Hillsley.

Nobody speaks. The room is small and cramped, with people standing shoulder to shoulder against the walls.

Hillsley is reason for us to worry, I say. He's 52, with a string of child sex convictions. In 1984 he was jailed for the abduction and sexual assault of a child. Released on parole in 1986, he was later found with a young girl, locked in a toilet at his workplace. Jailed again in 1990 for assaulting two girls, he briefly escaped before being recaptured and sent back to prison. Over the years he's sent a series of letters to the parole board, including one that read: 'A message for the community – I will be back. Thank God for the little girls.'

He signed it 'Walking Evil'.

Eyes harden all around the room, but it gets worse. A report from a former prison officer says Hillsley told him something. He claimed to have been mistreated while in prison, saying, 'The screws have bashed me and the more that happens to me the more the kids will suffer. They won't find me next time; it will be another Samantha Knight.'

Samantha was a nine-year-old girl who disappeared in 1986 and has never been found, though another serial paedophile was recently convicted of her manslaughter.

Hillsley's now been released from prison, I tell the team. Earlier today we got his address and I was there when the tactical police broke down his door. We didn't find him or the girl, but we did find handwritten notes containing references to the missing 10-year-old, which made me even more worried. The fear is that he's planned this. We have to find her.

'A child's life's at risk,' I urge them. 'I want everyone to switch on.'

I speak to one of the bosses at police headquarters, which recently moved out of the city centre to a new, glass-fronted office block in Parramatta, western Sydney. What used to be called Crime Agencies is now State Crime Command and the Homicide Squad has a big, dedicated office on the eighth floor. Inside the glass doors, the wall of the office is covered with yellowed newspaper clippings of famous old cases, with headlines like 'Murder hunt' and 'The killer who came knocking'. At any time, the squad might be working on over 100 open cases and have another 600 which are still unsolved and being regularly reviewed. Even in this context, what's happening this New Year's Day is different.

'It's fucking big,' I say on the telephone. A young girl is missing. And, from what I've seen so far today, people don't come much worse than Hillsley.

The commissioner will be briefed on this, as will the police minister. The press will also want a piece of it, which always makes the bosses nervous. I say we have to use that as an opportunity. We need the missing girl's description on TV and the radio. It might mean somebody comes forward. At the same time, we have to protect Michael's family from reporters, who will soon have their phone number, will have parked their TV trucks outside the crime scene and will be knocking on their neighbours' doors.

'We have to get the media solid.'

***

The day passes in a blur of decisions and it is dark again outside.

The 10-year-old is safe. She managed to escape from Hillsley somewhere in the streets around her home, running alone down the empty roads as everybody else enjoyed the New Year holiday, until she got back to her family. It's a godsend. Having seen the damage Hillsley had done, I couldn't bear to think of that happening to a child.

A medical examination showed she'd been sexually assaulted. Hillsley himself is brought in around 9.40pm, smelling of sweat and dirt, and dressed in filthy jeans and a grey T-shirt. He says that he's been walking the streets since the murder happened, and was arrested while hiding in a stormwater drain behind the Sunbeam factory in South Campsie, near where the 10-year-old ran away from him.

When Luke and I walk into the interview room, Hillsley is waiting for us inside it. His long, unkempt Ned Kelly beard curls down towards his skinny stomach. I notice there's a graze on his head and that his teeth are bloodied. Outside the room, he has already told me he went to Michael's place to bash him because he had the shits with him. But I need it on tape. An admission isn't worth much without a record.

Luke and I sit facing each other, the ERISP machine facing Hillsley. Luke looks as serious as I feel right now as he prepares to make notes of the interview. He's a good fit for me on this job, a deep thinker, the kind to ponder case law rather than charge in headfirst. We need that calm in here because, outside the room, there are a lot of tough guys walking around saying that Hillsley should be bashed, or even gelded. If they just had five minutes in a room with him ...

Maybe, I think, *there might have been a time for that, but it's not now.* I don't know how I would have acted if we hadn't found the 10-year-old. If Hillsley had been sitting here, refusing to say where she was, would I have crossed the line? I think I would. I would have bashed him to make him talk.

Afterwards, I would have put my hand up and said, *This is why I did it. We were trying to save a girl's life.* But now she's safe, I never have to know what I'd have done. My job instead is to put him in prison.

I switch on the ERISP machine and start to talk, 'This is an electronically recorded interview between Detective Sergeant Jubelin and Jeffrey Hillsley.'

Hillsley smiles.

I try to control my emotions. If I lose it with him, like those tough guys outside say that they want to, I risk losing his confession.

I continue, 'The time this interview is commenced at is 10.05pm.'

My daily meditation helps. At home, I use it to re-centre myself, to bring myself back into balance from the wild highs and crashing lows of a cop's life. I'm finding the same discipline can help me deal with work itself. Hillsley's smiling at me – so what? I just accept it.

That ability to become detached, to relax into a zen state is becoming my confessional priest, a way to reconcile the pressure calls I am constantly making.

I ask him, 'Can you tell me the circumstances of how you came to be at Michael Davies' place in the last 24 hours?'

'The reason why?'

I don't react.

He starts to talk. 'I was over at Michael's place over the Christmas break, he asked me to come over for about three to four days. We were putting some mulch on his garden. And Michael likes to get into your personal life. I was telling him about a friend of mine who had three strokes before it actually killed him and Michael started joking about three strokes, you know, and I thought that was a bit of, um, no respect for my friend, no respect for my personal life. And that's what really pushed me over the edge.'

He looks at me. *Is he enjoying this?* It's like he wants me to react. I need to show him that isn't going to happen.

'Where did this conversation take place?' I ask him. I want him to know I'm only interested in the facts.

He says in the front garden.

I ask him for the time and date.

He wants to talk about the killing, saying, 'I'm afraid after that day in the garden, Michael was heading for it.'

'Explain that to me,' I say, trying to unpick what he is saying. 'When he was heading for it, what exactly do you mean by that?'

'I only wanted to bash him. I didn't want to kill him. I mean, Michael's got a lot of goodness in him too, you know.'

'Right.' I keep my voice level.

'He's got a lovely family and a lovely wife and, I mean, I didn't want to take him away from them. It was just, I really just wanted to bash him.'

This is perverse. It's like he's trying to push my buttons.

I stare at him, expressionless. His eyes flicker away, as if he finds my lack of response a disappointment.

He tells me how he walked from home to Michael's house on New Year's Eve, carrying a knife and a hammer in his rucksack. He's savouring the details: a dark blue bag with two pockets on either side; a claw hammer with a yellow shaft; a knife from his drawer at home with one sharp edge. He says the knife was for his own protection.

It took Hillsley three hours to walk there, he says, and then he walked around for several hours more, 'thinking about if I was going to do it or not'. His mind made up, around 10.30pm, he let himself into the garden, checked the back door and found it locked, then saw that the bathroom window was open.

He wants to relive the crime, I think. *As if he's feeding off the moment. He knows he's never going to do anything like this again. He'll be in a prison soon and, once inside, he'll have only the memories to sustain him.*

Hillsley says he piled an outdoor chair on top of the outdoor table and climbed up, then reached in to pick up the toothbrushes and bathroom things left lying on the windowsill.

He's friendly now, almost boastful. 'If you go there, you'll find them under the back bush up in the left,' he tells me. 'In the right corner, that's where I threw them.'

It seems unreal that he is offering this evidence. No normal crook would offer up the evidence I need to jail him. But it's like Hillsley's trying to co-opt me. Like he wants me to witness what he did.

He describes climbing through the window and pulling out his hammer.

'I still didn't know if I could go through with it,' he says, and pauses, inviting me to move the interview forward.

'Was anyone awake at the time?' I ask.

'No, no one was awake.'

For half an hour, Hillsley says he wandered around the sleeping house. He made himself a drink of Ribena. When Michael's four-year-old woke up and saw Hillsley, with his wild hair and hammer, standing in the darkness, he told the child to go back to bed.

I don't allow myself to think about my children. About how they might one night wake up and discover an intruder. Empathy is important as a cop, but too much of it will not help you. A good detective won't let themselves feel emotions at a moment like this. Jaco wouldn't do so, if he were here. The interview is too important.

I'll process those thoughts later.

Hillsley says he walked into Michael's bedroom, where his victim was sleeping. He woke him up before starting to hit him.

'Can you demonstrate how you were holding the hammer and how you struck the blows, just with your hand?' I ask. It sounds banal, but I want to see if he'll admit he knew what he was doing. When his case goes to trial, I don't want Hillsley to hide behind a claim of ignorance to get a lesser sentence. I want to see if he knew a hammer could kill.

'I grabbed it right down at the base,' he says. 'Because I know that's where the power is.'

OK, I think, *you've no excuse.* 'The power is down in the base,' I repeat.

'Yeah, of course, that's how I've always learned to use a hammer.'

'Right.'

'So I just, when he woke up, I just went, bang, bang, bang like that.'

This is horrendous. He's having too much fun with this. I pull him back.

'You've learned to use a hammer?' I ask. 'Have you a trade or a background?'

'No, my father had a scaffolding business and we used to put the bindings on the end of the new planks when they came in.'

'So you understand the power of the hammer?'

'Well, I think most people do once they've used one.'

Hillsley tries to take the interview back to where he wants it. He says he only wanted to pay Michael out. He thought Michael would go to hospital and be fixed up. Then Hillsley could tell him, *That's what you get for being an arsehole.*

I'll leave it for the jury to decide. On Hillsley's account, the death was an accident, but there's no doubt he meant to attack Michael, and to harm him badly. In New South Wales, the law says murder is killing done with intent to kill or inflict grievous bodily harm, or with a reckless indifference to human life. Whatever Hillsley thinks, I believe he'll go down for murder, not manslaughter.

But now I have to ask about the 10-year-old.

I caution him again. He's not obliged to say anything but whatever he does say may be used in evidence. 'You understand that?' I ask.

'Yes, I do.' He smiles again. This is something he wants to talk about. 'That was further payback to Michael really, apart from my sexual attraction to her.'

I let him talk. He describes how she was screaming, how he pulled the knife out. He walked her out to the garage. I wonder if the other children heard.

Hillsley tells me how he assaulted her.

I listen, feeling horrified, knowing I'm complicit in what's happening between us. *Each of us is getting what we want from this*, I think. *I'm getting his confession. He's enjoying telling me about this.* Again, I'll deal with all these thoughts later.

Hillsley says he asked the girl to leave the property with him. 'I just told her that I loved her and I was sexually attracted to her and sorry what's been happening to her but, um, she willingly wanted to come with me, so …'

Fuck this, I think. *I can let a lot slide, but you're not going to tell me that this girl, after you've just murdered her stepfather, is enjoying having your grubby hands all over her?*

I almost spit the words out, 'When you say willingly, do we agree that that was a result of the threat that you made towards her life with the knife?'

'Yes.'

'So in terms of willingly, she was compliant because of the fear that you had instilled in her. Would that be fair to say?'

'Very fair.'

Good. Now, when you get to court, your lawyer can't stand up and say, 'My client believed these acts to be consensual.' It happens. I've seen lawyers saying worse than that. I've seen lawyers saying the victim led her rapist on.

Hillsley continues, explaining how the two of them started walking towards the city centre. They asked for water at a house because they were dehydrated. They were going to catch a train but didn't because he thought a woman who sat down near them on the platform was acting suspiciously. They got lost. Hillsley assaulted the girl again.

'In terms of sex with a 10-year-old girl, you realise that's wrong?' I ask him.

He says, 'With paedophiles, they know it's wrong but they've really got no control over it to be quite honest with you.' He is almost convincing.

'Talk me through what you mean by that, from your perspective?'

He pauses. 'Well, you know it's wrong. You know it's going to hurt the child but it all comes down to that self-gratification and that is stronger than what harm you are actually doing to the child.'

I think about it for a moment. *He has urges he can't control.* I put it aside. Someone smarter than I am can decide, or if it matters.

Hillsley says he was always going to give himself up. Then the girl ran away from him. 'I told her not to go because if you do it this way, they're gunna get me and kill me.' A whining sound has entered his voice. It grates.

I ask him who was going to kill him.

'The police.' He says he always gives himself up. If I look at his record, I'll see that for myself.

'But the way it turned out was not the way you wanted it to?' I ask him, disbelieving.

'Yeah, well, that's right, because, you see me face and teeth and everything' – he points to his injuries – 'so, I mean, you know, I know what it's like in jail, when you come into a police station, how they knock you around severely.'

'Just so I cover this, that graze to the side of your head, that appears to be a graze under your hairline.'

'Yes.'

'Was that incurred during your arrest?'

'Yes.'

'And how did that happen?'

'By an officer.'

I tense. I need to deal with this. The days of phone books might be over, but if Hillsley says that he was beaten, then when this gets to court, a smart lawyer might claim he gave his confession under duress. If I do anything tonight, I will make sure that doesn't happen.

I ask if anything took place during his arrest that forced him to take part in this interview.

He shakes his head. 'Oh no,' he says. 'The interview's not a problem.'

I stop the tape and walk out of the room, to clear my head. I'm pissed off that any cop might have beaten Hillsley. I understand that they'd want to but it doesn't help. It's like with forensic evidence, it just contaminates the interview.

Outside, Luke and I talk to Nigel, checking if anything new's come in while we've been inside the room with Hillsley. No new crime scene discovered. No new physical evidence. Nothing that we need to put to him. It is a brief break but I need it. It feels like several days have passed since that phone call this morning.

We walk back in and Hillsley watches us in silence.

I tell him we'd like a sample of his DNA. Will he agree to that?

'As long as the person doesn't start bashing me before he gets it all done.' *He's back on this. He's trying to provoke me. He wants to get inside my head.*

'There will be no one bashing you.'

He says that he could hear us talking outside the room. Talking about the 10-year-old. He says I was trying to incite some other cop to go down to the cells later and give him a caning.

Is this a fantasy? Is he imagining this? Or is this just how he wants to play it, casting himself as the victim?

'I heard her name,' he says again, nodding at the door through which we've just entered.

'Most definitely you've heard her name,' I say, because we were talking about what happened to her and what happened to Michael. I want him to drop this.

I raise the DNA test again. 'I was asking are you prepared to participate, or for us to –'

He interrupts, 'Well, see, I've done those sort of examinations before and what are they doing there? They're hitting me in the guts and everything. I mean, Jesus.'

I stare at him. I get the creeping sense that he *wants* us to bash him. It's like another way of him savouring his crime. If he provokes me into violence, it proves how bad he is. He'd relish it. *This is a man who signs his name as 'Walking Evil'.* Bashing him would show that he is special.

'You've busted my teeth tonight, so you're going well,' he says.

'How did we bust your teeth?' I ask, swallowing my anger.

'Well, the officer there, they rammed me head into the brick wall there, so they've busted all me teeth up the top here.'

'Well, there's no excuse for assault any time,' I tell him, flatly. 'What I want to clarify here, because you've raised it, is that the answers you have given in this interview haven't been clouded by any concerns or fears that you've got?'

'No.'

'Your fears haven't impacted on you participating in this interview?'

'Oh, no, the interview's not a problem.'

'OK. Now, can we get back to the original question ... are you prepared to participate in the forensic examination?'

'Yes, I'm here to cooperate as best I can. There's no lies and I've got no problem doing the test.'

'Thank you.'

That's it. That's everything I need. Exhaustion overwhelms me.

He has confessed, but there is nothing in his gaunt face that looks like remorse. If anything, he seems almost disappointed.

I look at the time: 12.28am. New Year's Day is over. *No other year will ever start as badly as this one has.* I did my job. I didn't react. I didn't let my disgust or anger overwhelm me.

Jeffrey Hillsley, you only made me tougher. It is as if the job keeps asking me, *Do you give up?* Not yet, I don't. What's next?

Later tonight, I will tell every other cop in the station not to talk to Hillsley. I'll stand in front of him while he is in his cell, just so he can hear me ask another detective about the cricket. Not because I'm really interested in how Australia have battered India, but to show Hillsley that I'm not interested in *him*. That he has not provoked me. Talking about the cricket tells him that he is not important to me. That I do this every day, and he is just another number.

At 12.31am on 2 January 2004, I switch off the tape. 'Interview between Detective Sergeant Jubelin and Mr Hillsley concluded.'

Luke and I stand and walk out of the interview room, leaving Hillsley behind with just his thoughts for company.

Just Pure Anger

9 February 2004: 18 years in

On Monday 9 February 2004, the inquest into Evelyn's and Colleen's deaths begins in Bellingen, a little country town not far from Bowraville, with an old-fashioned courthouse at its centre. A few months before, I drove north from Sydney on the Pacific Highway, heading for the hardscrabble cluster of houses where James Hide is now living, taking with me a court order to appear at the inquest. I wanted to deliver it in person.

Staring at the empty highway, I thought back over the past decade, since James Hide was found not guilty of murdering Clinton. It was almost eight years since I became involved in the reinvestigation. It's five years since the Director of Public Prosecutions (DPP) refused our application to restart the prosecution of James over the charge of murdering four-year-old Evelyn, which was dropped after he was acquitted of Clinton's murder.

After swallowing our disappointment at that decision, Jason Evers and I had tried to use it to our advantage.

The following year, in 2000, we approached the State Coroner, arguing that there was now no prospect of a criminal trial, which meant the children's deaths in Bowraville remained formally unexplained. While inquests had been held into Evelyn's and Colleen's deaths in 1991; the former was halted when James was first charged with the four-year-old's murder and the latter ended in an open verdict, meaning the coroner had not been able to find whether she was killed, had killed herself or died by misadventure.

The inquest into Colleen's death was reopened in 1994 but ended with the same result. There'd never been an inquest into Clinton's death. In the strange bureaucracy that governs inquests and criminal proceedings, the fact someone was put on trial for Clinton's murder meant no inquest was necessary, even though the trial led to an acquittal. Officially, despite the suspected murderer being found not guilty, the state still accepted the victim had been murdered.

But, Jason and I argued, there was still no formal explanation of what happened to Evelyn and Colleen. We told the coroner we also had new evidence from our investigation. Would he hold a new inquest, into these two deaths, to hear it?

Justice is delivered slowly – a coroner has to be available, an unbooked courtroom found; plans were made to hold an inquest into the children's deaths but these fell through due to the pressures of another hearing – but, in 2003, the State Coroner, John Abernethy, agreed that he would do it. That meant we had to provide a formal brief of evidence and, by that time, Strike Force Ancud existed only on paper. Jason and I weren't given any new resources, so most of this work was done at night, on weekends or during office time that we were able to steal from other investigations.

Finally, the inquest into Evelyn's and Colleen's deaths was scheduled to begin in February 2004. This would be the first time evidence about all three of the children would be heard together in one courtroom as differences in the law between criminal trials and inquests also meant the coroner could hear the details of Clinton's disappearance. I hoped it would provide the children's families with some answers. I also hoped it might put some pressure on the DPP's office to overturn its own decision and send the murders to trial.

Throughout the years it had taken a long time to get to this point – longer than Evelyn's lifetime – and the decency of the people I met in Bowraville had left me humble. Despite enduring a trial and two inconclusive inquests, so far, they'd always done the right thing, never taken justice into their own hands, and were now prepared to put their faith once again in the police and the courts.

The children's parents, brothers, sisters, aunties, cousins often called me in the evenings. I listened to their stories of the children. I also spoke to the children's friends who, by now, were adults. When Jason and I visited Bowraville, we could look at Colleen's younger sister Paula and think, *That's Colleen.* Clinton's nephews, who were growing up fast, were Clinton. We saw Evelyn in the young kids running around the Mission.

When they called, we'd sometimes talk on the phone for hours and my own children soon realised what I was discussing. They'd grown up with this investigation, just like the missing children's families. If ten-year-old Gemma was sitting in the next room when one of these calls came in, she'd sometimes turn down the volume on the television just so that she could listen.

It wasn't like the missing children haunted us, it was more like we now knew them. Driving north from Sydney to James's house, this gave me a sense of purpose. Taking the sharp right off the main road, I looked over at the back of where he was now living, wondering if he'd be there when I arrived at his new home. Another turn, then another, and I was pulling up on the narrow, comfortless road outside it.

Walking through the wooden gate, I passed a bulky air-con unit bolted to the brick wall and headed up the steps to his front door. We'd met only once before this, years ago, when I visited him to see if he would talk to the police about Colleen and Evelyn, because he had only ever been formally interviewed about the death of Clinton. Back then, he told me, 'No, I'm not saying anything.'

This time, James answered the door and I could see that he was older. He was in his early 40s, and the muscles in his arms and shoulders, which had once been strong from working at the Bowraville tanning factory, had grown soft.

He invited me into his house. Inside, it was small and dark. We sat facing one another.

I told James about the inquest. 'I'm basically accusing you of being a serial killer. Where do we go from here?' I told him.

'You think I've done something I haven't done.' He said that he'd already been found not guilty. 'I just need to be left alone,' he said.

We stared at each other.

I told him this wasn't over. He didn't blink.

During the long drive back to Sydney, every time I caught a glimpse of my own eyes in the rear-view mirror, I could see him looking at me.

***

Inside the Bellingen courthouse, the children's families are crowded between walls lined with rich, dark timber. On one hangs the New South Wales coat of arms, showing a rising sun above a shield decorated with sheep fleeces and sheaves of wheat, held upright by a kangaroo and a lion. Underneath this is the latin motto 'Orta recens quam pura nites', which translates as 'Newly risen, how brightly you shine'. It is a world away from the Bowraville Mission.

After two brief weeks of evidence about the children's disappearances, the inquest is adjourned on Friday 13 February. It won't resume until August. I feel embarrassed. I don't know how the families of murder victims can withstand all the delays and the waiting involved in the court system. I guess you do it day by day. You have no choice. This is how justice is delivered.

Jason and I go back to work. Nine days later, on Sunday 22 February the body of a 13-year-old, Michelle Pogmore, is found, dumped in a council refuse bin. I'm driving back from lecturing at the detectives' course in Goulburn with Pam, and we have Jake and Gemma with us, when I get the call. I drive them home, then turn the car around, heading for the crime scene at the Town Centre Reserve in Mount Druitt, western Sydney

It is a hot summer's day when I get there. Michelle's been missing since leaving a nearby street party two days earlier. It is another sight that I know will never leave me.

The next day, after Michelle's identity has been confirmed, I pull up outside her family's home to break the news, knowing the 13-year-old's mother must be watching as I walk up to the door. I try to keep my face expressionless, not giving anything away, so she doesn't guess at what has happened until I am there to tell her in person. As detectives, we meet people at the most real, vital moments, when life and death collide, and it is sometimes our job to make the collision happen: *Your daughter has been murdered*.

As a young cop in uniform, I failed in the task of delivering news of a child's death to a parent. Back then, I was overwhelmed. I didn't understand my role and stood there mute and uncomprehending while the mother broke down in front of me.

This time, I get it right. I'm older now and have seen so much more emotion. After saying that we've found Michelle, I stay with her mum, providing what little support I can offer. There's nothing wrong or weak, I've learned over the years, about a detective offering somebody a shoulder to cry on when they have lost a loved one. I wish that I could swallow all her pain, but my duty is to offer only the prospect of some understanding: *this* person did it for *this* reason. I tell her I'll do everything I can to find the killer.

Making this promise means leaving a piece of yourself behind with every victim's family. It goes back to what I learned in Bowraville; you have a responsibility to those people whose trust they place in you to find their loved one's killer. It is a heavy weight. Picking up another person's cross means that sometimes it will crush you.

Years before, during one of our visits to Bowraville, Aunty Elaine Walker had approached Jason and me and said, 'One of the old boys wants to see you.' When we asked why, she said, 'It's men's business.' She couldn't talk about it.

We were to go down to the break wall at Nambucca, where the green river that flows past Bowraville empties itself out into the ocean. The old boy met us there then took us down to the water's edge and told us to look out at the horizon. We stood together in silence.

Jason may have been sceptical but I recognised something. This was like some of the meditation classes I'd done with Ben. We stood and listened as the old boy spoke about his people and their country. He spoke about justice, and what this investigation meant to them, and us. Some of what he said I understood, some I did not, but I realised he was giving us a gift.

He wanted us to understand this place as he did. Afterwards, driving back, I thought about different trips I'd taken in recent years to Hong Kong and Vietnam to practise meditation, like I was chasing some secret knowledge round the world. Here it was at home.

And that made sense. After all, as Indigenous Australians, the Bowraville mob were part of the oldest living culture on the planet. Being invited to take part in this ceremony gave me confidence. It made me feel accepted. It made me feel that we were on the right path.

As white cops speaking to blackfellas, we still had a wall of colonial history to break down between us but, the more we understood each other, the more information was handed from one side to the other. Sometimes, Jason and I would spend hours on the Mission, not because we had specific questions we wanted the people there to answer, but just yarning with the elders.

It worked. One day we spoke to a woman on the Mission who told us how she'd woken up at night to find James Hide standing in her bedroom, watching her and her sleeping children. Another told us how James had chased her friend across the golf course, only he couldn't catch her.

One man, Hilton, said that he'd been drinking with James after the children's disappearances, when James whispered something like: 'I've got bodies. I've killed people and their bodies are out on the Congarinni Road near my crops.' Both Clinton's and Evelyn's bodies were found dumped beside the Congarinni Road, with Clinton's body near a crop of marijuana plants.

We asked Hilton why he'd kept this information to himself for years. He said he didn't think the cops would believe him. When we asked why, he said it was because he was Aboriginal and James was white.

Among the old paper records from the first police investigation, we also found witness statements from people on the Mission who said that, in the months before the children disappeared, they got into an argument with James. He brought a golf club to their house, they said, and started smashing the front, shouting: 'I'll get youse, you two fuck heads, I'll take youse out to Congarinni Road and use youse for fertiliser, under the ground.' These witnesses were never mentioned during the trial over Clinton's murder.

They will be heard at the inquest, though. When it resumes, in August 2004, it feels like we are making progress.

We never do find out who killed Michelle Pogmore.

***

The inquest will also hear from another, unidentified witness; a criminal informer. Like Rocco, in the investigation into Terry Falconer's murder, he is risking his life by coming forward, so the coroner agrees to identify him only as Mr X. Jason and I know him by another name. We call him Axeman.

We first learned his name from a neat, handwritten letter that was already old when we found it in 1997, buried among the stacks of paperwork collected by the detectives who led the first, unsuccessful, prosecution of James Hide over Clinton's murder.

The letter was a warning, sent by a prisoner who James had got to know after being arrested and briefly held. While James had been released on bail, awaiting trial, the letter said there was a rumour going around the prison that the cops were planning a covert operation to gather evidence against him. It named a former prisoner who was planning to approach James to talk about the killings.

That prisoner was a dog, the letter warned. He'll be wearing a wire. It was signed, 'Your mate forever, Axeman.'

As a prisoner himself, a copy of Axeman's letter was made by the prison authorities and passed to the cops working the first Bowraville investigation. Going through the files again during our reinvestigation, we learned that the covert operation it described hadn't gathered any useful evidence against James but the letter itself was interesting. On it, Axeman had written his inmate number, which allowed us to find out his name. He'd been released since the letter was written but we'd flagged him, meaning if he ever got arrested again, I'd get a call.

The telephone rang on Easter Sunday 1998, which meant I was in trouble with my family. They'd gathered at my parents' place in Dural for a barbecue to mark the holiday but I told them this was too important. Making my excuses, I drove a couple of hours north to Belmont, where I met Jason and walked with him into the local police station. They took us to the cells.

Behind the cell door, Axeman was six foot three and skinny, with scars on his hands, and arms covered in rough tattoos that looked like they'd been done in prison. He looked like a typical crook, and reading through his criminal history confirmed he was a bad one; he'd been charged with murder once, a brutal killing which gave him his nickname, although he was later found not guilty. There were also convictions for break, enter and steal, supplying heroin, malicious damage, some serious assaults – what he described as 'ultra-violence' – and perjury. Since first being caught, for passing dud cheques as a 17-year-old, he'd spent most of his adult life in prison.

Look at it one way, I thought, *and all that means he's a long way from being the perfect witness. Look at it another and, just like Rocco, it means that he's the real deal.* To my mind, his criminal past was what qualified him as a potential informer. As a real crook, he would have genuine knowledge of other criminals.

It also meant that Axeman had some seniority within the justice system – which is why, he told us, James approached him in Maitland Gaol asking for advice after he was arrested.

'He was just a mellow, fat little pig that was running around the jail,' said Axeman in a thin, rasping voice. But James could snap. 'Someone was having a piss in the shower and pissed on his leg. Well, he just attacked the bloke in the shower and smashed his head in, then jumped on his head while he was on the ground and, oh mate, went off, right off, just frenzy. Violent. Yes, full attack mode.'

I asked him if James ever talked about the murder he'd been charged with: the death of 16-year-old Clinton Speedy-Duroux.

Axeman nodded.

I said we'd like to talk about it with him.

He shrugged, as if to say, 'I've got no objection'.

I asked why he was prepared to talk.

'The fact that a child was killed', Axeman said. 'Look, I'm a crook. I'm scum, I'm this or that – but I just had a kid.' Becoming a father had changed him. His way of looking at the world had shifted. It sickened him to think of children being hurt.

We asked if he would wear a wire, like Rocco. If he would, I figured we could play on the letter Axeman sent to James, the one we used to find him. He could use that letter as an excuse to seek James out, telling him the cops had been in touch about it. Axeman could claim they wanted to charge him with hindering a police investigation, because he sent James a warning letter.

He said he would do it. We wired him up and arranged for a female undercover cop to play his girlfriend, thinking that made him look more credible than if he was alone. I drove them out to Bowraville, where Axeman walked into the local stores and asked people, 'I'm looking for James Hide.'

They told him James left town, but to try his mum's place, where he'd been living at the time the children were murdered. Axeman knocked on her door and told her he was a mate of James's and needed to speak to him about some shit that's going down.

We already had her phones off, so when James's mum called her son, we listened. She was cautious. She warned him, remember how the cops tried to fit you up before.

'Look, it's really OK. I trust him, he helped me out a lot,' James told her.

Listening in, I was thinking, *Happy days.*

***

The first time James and Axeman met, they sat and talked for hours. Listening in to what they were saying, I didn't think James had any suspicion he was being recorded.

Axeman offered to fix him up with marijuana, which he could then sell on. James said he'd done a little dealing: 'In the last 12 months I've only had about three ounces, and that I got rid of pretty quickly.' Just enough to make a little money and keep some back to smoke himself.

But when Axeman tried to steer the talk towards the murders, James denied his involvement. He also denied admitting anything in prison, saying, 'When I was there at Maitland, I didn't ask anyone about anyone else's business and I didn't tell anyone else about mine.'

The meeting ended with us gathering no new evidence against James. Two weeks later, we tried to raise the pressure by sending Axeman back to try again. This time, we told him to claim the cops had told him they'd got evidence from someone else saying James admitted to the murders while in prison. I gave Axeman a copy of a fake record of interview, which we had done with him, making it look as if we pulled him in for questioning. I wanted James to think we were closing in.

Once again, James denied making any admissions. Listening to the surveillance recording, I could tell something had changed over the past fortnight, because he was now clearly suspicious. James talked about how the police might be using high-tech equipment to listen to his conversation with Axeman. 'I'd be even more worried if I was fuckin' guilty of something and had to be careful what I said in my own house,' he said.

After that, my bosses shut down the operation. I tried to say it was the wrong decision. If we could do this properly, I argued, have

Age 4, playing at being a soldier defending the family home.

Who is this Santa character? With my sister Karen, 1964.

Finding freedom on a surf trip, age 17.

Endless Australian summer, holidaying on the coast.

Some academy mates (I'm on the right). We had no idea what we had gotten ourselves into.

With my parents on the day I passed out of the police academy in 1985.

With Debbie at the academy on the same day, also my 23rd birthday.

Training to deal with the worst of the worst, 1998.

With Jason Evers outside Buckingham Palace, during a trip to London in 2001 to investigate the death of Caroline Byrne.

Tony Byrne in 2012, holding a photograph of his daughter Caroline.
Stephen Cooper / Newspix

With my kids, Jake and Gemma. Teaching them to find the same sense of freedom I have in the water.

At my wedding to Tracy in 2011, which coincided with a flash flood.

Speaking to the media after the Perish brothers were sentenced over the murder of Terry Falconer, 2012. *Simon Alekna / Sydney Morning Herald*

The families of the murdered Bowraville children march on Parliament House, Sydney, 2013. *Dan Himbrechts / AAP Image*

NSW Police Commissioner Andrew Scipione apologises to the Bowraville families, 2016. *John Feder / Newspix*

Flowers left outside the Lindt Chocolate Café, Sydney, following the fatal siege in 2014.
Dean Lewins / AAP Image

The boxing ring exposes any weakness.
Gary Jubelin v Mark Bouris, 2018.
Robert Gibbs / Beaches Images

With Matt Nable (from *Underbelly*) and some of the Bowraville mob, after fighting in a police boxing event, 2017.

During a 2015 search operation in the bush near Kendall, where William Tyrrell went missing. *Nathan Edwards / Newspix*

Speaking at one of the events to mark the first anniversary of William's disappearance. *Nathan Edwards / Newspix*

Finding Matt Leveson's body, with his parents, Mark and Faye, 2017. *Dean Lewins / AAP Image*

I've learned to find the same sense of peace while surfing and through meditation.

Surfing mates on a trip to Lombok.

Practising qigong in the Blue Mountains, outside Sydney.

With Gemma and Jake, as adults. I am most proud of my relationship with my children.

Leaving the Downing Centre Local Court in April 2020, having been found guilty.
Joel Carrett / AAP Image

Starting a new career after the police – working in media.

Axeman move in somewhere near James, find him some work, let them hang out and become mates, then maybe we'd get something.

I failed to win the argument. I should have argued harder.

***

But we still have Axeman's account of what James said to him in prison. It's not as good as a recorded confession but it is still evidence and will be heard when the inquest into the children's deaths resumes in August.

Between Axeman and Rocco, I'm now using serious crooks to pursue two separate investigations. One of them has beaten one murder charge while the other's been convicted of manslaughter.

The fact they were both prepared to wear a wire does give me some comfort, because it means they were prepared to let us test the truth of what they're saying. And, on a personal level, I trust them. Neither is gaining anything from their cooperation. In fact, both their lives have been made harder by the decision to come forward. Both now live in fear some other crook will find out they turned dog and decide to come for them.

Both of them are outlaws – an alleged killer and a convicted killer respectively. Their values might be different from my own – ask Axeman and he'll tell you all the violence he's done was righteous – but I can still identify with them, thinking back to my own wild youth, breaking into building sites and bringing down power lines. They live in a different, mixed-up, shadow world from the one I inhabit. It is a tougher world, where the first commandment is Thou Shalt Not Talk to Cops. But both of them have broken that, not for reward, but because they think it's right to. In that sense, they are both moral people.

All this is a long way from when I joined up. Back then, everything seemed simple; we were the cops, we caught the crooks. Even during my first years in Homicide, I saw things in black and white: good guys, bad guys, killers, victims. Now I'm older and I see the world in shades of grey, as if a fog of different, conflicting instructions is clouding my vision. Without a clear choice between black and white, I have to use my own moral compass to find the way forward.

By the time the next inquest hearings loom up ahead of us, calling Axeman feels like a simple decision. If, for him, informing is the moral choice then, for me, it is the moral choice to use him. My job is to catch killers. In Bowraville, I'm looking for a child killer. If that means using one crook to catch another, then so be it.

The inquest resumes.

***

On 3 August, when Evelyn's mother, Rebecca Stadhams, takes the stand, the counsel assisting the coroner, police sergeant Matt Fordham, calls her 'ma'am'. That's respectful, which I like, but no one calls Rebecca 'ma'am' at home and hearing it here, the word has a formality about it, just like the coat of arms, which says, *This world is different from your world.*

Rebecca looks so small and alone in the witness box, and when she starts to talk about her daughter, the coroner asks if she wants to stop because there are so many tears.

'No, I'll be right to go,' Rebecca says.

Others among the black faces watching in the courtroom are also crying. I hate seeing them suffer. I notice Rebecca is looking down, not at the sergeant asking her the questions. Before going to Bowraville, I know my instinct would have been this meant she was hiding something.

She also takes long pauses before answering the sergeant's questions, during which I can hear the other family members breathing. Before going to Bowraville, I would also have suspected this meant she was choosing her answer carefully, and maybe even lying.

Today, I know that both these things are just seen as good manners on the Mission. Sitting on the hard wooden bench of the courthouse, I can imagine how this subtle form of racism might have impacted on the early police response to the murders and also how witnesses like Rebecca, who are so clearly uncomfortable within this environment, might still be easily misunderstood.

Rebecca explains how she was drinking on the night before Evelyn went missing. They were at a party at her mum's house and she can't clearly remember going to bed. She'd been drunk before, she says, but this night was different. She had all three of her children sleeping in the same room as her and normally would wake up to give the youngest a bottle. This night, she didn't.

'Just as soon as I hit that bed I never moved.'

'Was that strange?' the sergeant asks.

'Very strange,' answers Rebecca.

'Why was it strange?'

'You wake up the next day and find out that your pants, trousers, your jeans is halfway down your legs and your underwear's been interfered with. I reckon that would be strange.'

Chastened, the sergeant tries to clarify his question, asking if there was anything strange about the way she slept?

'I felt really sick and that the next day,' Rebecca tells him.

Later, he asks her about James Hide. Has she seen him with tablets? Rebecca says she has, at parties.

'Have there ever been occasions where you think that Hide might have put a drug in your drink?'

'Yeah, I reckon I was drugged or spiked or something.'

'What is it that makes you think you'd been drugged that night?'

'Because I didn't wake up and I never heard nothing in that room. And I usually get up and make my baby a bottle and that and go to the toilet and that. It was just when I got on that bed, my mind was just completely blank. I didn't hear anything.'

The sergeant finishes his questions. Before she steps down from the witness box, he looks up and tells her, 'Thanks, Rebecca.'

***

The inquest continues through the cold, first days of August. Rebecca's mum, Patricia Stadhams, gives evidence about how James was at the party that night and brought some spirits with him. He was drinking, she says, they all were. Patricia saws she saw James in the bedroom with Rebecca, arguing with another man. She says she went in there and moved them out, so Rebecca and the kids could sleep. She says the door had a lock, but you could open it from the outside with a knife if you knew how to.

Soon after, the party wound down Patricia says. 'Everyone was gone then, by three, and only him was around, James Hide.'

Another relative of Evelyn's, Fiona Duckett, is called to give evidence and describes how in the night, after the party finished, she woke up to fix her infant son a bottle and saw James walk out of Rebecca's room, alone. He walked down the hallway. He didn't see Fiona and by the time she'd followed him to the front door and looked outside, James had disappeared.

On 10 August, Axeman is called to the witness box. The police sergeant runs through his criminal history, saying, 'Sir, is it the case that the offences which you have been dealt with by the courts include "Break, Enter and Steal", "Fradulent Misappropriation", "Supplying Heroin", "Possessing Heroin", "Stealing", "Malicious Damage", "False Pretences", "Forgery", "Offensive Behaviour" and some quite serious assaults?'

'Certainly is,' Axeman answers. *At least he isn't hiding anything*, I think.

The sergeant asks what James told him in prison.

'He just commented that he'd been charged over the death of a young fellow. I didn't know the name of the bloke.' The sergeant nods, inviting Axeman to continue. 'He said that they were trying to pin him on it and they had him on the grounds that, it was something about a blanket.'

Sitting in court, watching, I'm thinking how, with an informer, you're always looking to see if they can provide details they couldn't have got from media reports. I've heard a lot of Axeman's story before, but the reference to a blanket is potentially interesting: a stained, blue-and-pink striped blanket was found near Clinton's body. A pillowcase matching those in James's caravan was stuffed down Clinton's shorts.

'They'd had a knife fight and what-not and he'd buried him out in the marijuana patch,' says Axeman, recounting what James told him. That's also interesting. Clinton's body was found near a small plantation of marijuana plants growing in the forest. We'd checked if it was mentioned in the trial over the teenager's murder, or if that fact had made its way into the newspaper and TV reports. It looked like it hadn't.

'Did Mr Hide describe to you where the fight with the male took place?' the police sergeant asks Axeman.

'It was in a caravan.' Clinton was last seen in James's caravan.

Axeman says James told him Clinton had pulled a knife during an argument over a drug deal, but James had taken the weapon from him. 'And, yes, he dealt with it.'

This version of events just doesn't fit with what we know about Clinton. According to his family, the 16-year-old was a decent young bloke, not even much of a drinker, although he was drinking at a party on the Mission before going back to sleep with his girlfriend in James's caravan.

Clinton was only in Bowraville for a short time, visiting his father, Thomas Duroux. It seems unlikely he'd got into drug dealing.

Another possible explanation might be that, if James did it, he would be reluctant to tell anyone in prison, *I murdered a kid*. Child killers become targets behind bars and, big as James was, he wouldn't have wanted to attract that kind of attention. Maybe he lied about what happened, saying, *There was a knife fight and Clinton came at me. I stabbed him in self-defence.*

'Did Mr Hide describe where on Mr Speedy-Duroux's body he was stabbed?' the sergeant asks.

'No, he didn't no. Just said he give it to him about the head,' Axeman replies. Clinton was stabbed in the head.

I know none of this is direct evidence James was the killer, and that Axeman's account is not enough on its own to convince a jury but, like everybody else in the courtroom – the police sergeant, the coroner, the children's families sitting silently behind me in the public gallery – hearing him give these details on oath, I can't help but want to know what else he says that James told him.

He says he did not want to hear more. Knowledge is dangerous in prison – 'Hear enough and you become involved.' Though James did say he was confident he'd never get convicted. He claimed the Aboriginal witnesses were drunks, says Axeman, looking out at the children's families.

'What did he say about them?' the sergeant asks.

'Just they were going to be hopeless in court and said it wouldn't make the grade and wouldn't get up there.'

The sergeant asks if James talked about any other murders.

Axeman looks like he's weighing up whether to hold back or continue. After a pause, he says there was another time, when James came back from court after being charged with the murder of a young girl.

Evelyn, I think. The case that was dropped after James was found not guilty of killing Clinton.

Axeman says James approached him after arriving back at the prison.

'What did he say?'

'Not to get the wrong idea about the young girl's death … he went into a bit of detail and I had to cut him off but she'd had her head smashed against a wall.'

I sit up and lean closer. Axeman cannot know this, but when I sat down to interview Evelyn's grandmother Patricia Stadhams in 1997, she told me how, on the night her granddaughter went missing, she woke up and heard Evelyn crying. Patricia went to the locked door inside which Evelyn and her mother were sleeping. She heard her crying, 'Mummy, Mummy.' It sounded like the child was scared and Patricia started shaking the door and yelling out to Evelyn to open it.

She said she heard a thud, then silence. *Like the sound you'd make striking a crying child against a wall?*

'I can just hear her screaming and screaming every time I think about it,' Patricia had told me. 'I could tell by the sound of her voice that she was scared.'

I'd asked her why she hadn't come forward with this before.

'I told my people that I just heard her crying but didn't tell them all that I knew and they put me through hell,' she answered. 'They accused me of having something to do with it. If I told them all that I knew, if I told them how she was screaming for her mummy, they would have blamed me.'

A child screaming. A thud. Then silence. In the inquest, the sergeant asks Axeman if James told him what was happening when he attacked the girl.

'No, no. I cut him off, mate. Yes, I didn't want to know about it,' he says.

'Did he talk to you about the reasons why he had to –?'

'He was trying to justify himself but it was over anger. It was just pure anger, mate.'

'Did he say what he was angry about?'

'No, no. He didn't.'

'Did Hide talk about any other children?' the sergeant asks him.

'There was something about a 15- or 16-year-old white girl.'

Colleen? I wonder. She was 16, with pale skin. Her mother said the family had some white in it, but you wouldn't describe her as white.

Axeman scratches his chin with his long, scarred fingers. 'Yes, it was a white, young girl, Woolgoolga, Maclean, something or other,' he continues. Woolgoolga? Among the different, conflicting accounts of Colleen's movements on the night she disappeared was that she was planning to travel to Goodooga. It is a stretch, but could Axeman have misheard, or misremembered? The information about Colleen's travel plans has never been made public. Or was James talking about something else?

***

The day after Axeman gives evidence, James himself is due to take the stand, so Jason and I drive to the nearby motel where he is staying to pick him up and drive him to the courthouse. He is alone, without a lawyer to represent him. During the journey back, I try to start a conversation, but he offers only one-word answers.

Once in the witness box, the coroner asks James, 'Have you had legal advice in this matter?'

'By phone, yes.' His voice is flat and hollow, echoing off the timber walls.

'We'd like to hear from you but is the legal advice to the effect that you've been advised not to answer any questions if the answers you give may tend to incriminate you?'

'That's right, your honour.'

'And do you want to exercise that right?'

'I do, your honour.'

With that, the sergeant assisting the coroner says he has no further questions. James steps down from the witness box and walks out across the courtroom.

***

James does not come back a month later, on Friday 10 September, when the coroner announces his decision. Despite Colleen's body never having been recovered, Abernethy finds that she was murdered, but that there is not enough evidence to say who it was that killed her. He formally suspends the inquest into Evelyn's death, saying he is 'satisfied firstly that there is evidence capable of satisfying a reasonable jury properly instructed of her murder and secondly, that there is a reasonable prospect that that jury will convict a known person of her murder'. It will now be for the criminal courts to decide what happened to Evelyn.

'A known person has been given every opportunity to make submissions before me and has chosen not to do it,' says Abernethy. Afterwards, he writes to the State DPP asking him to reconsider whether there are grounds to charge James with killing Evelyn.

I keep working the Bowraville case, both on and off duty, preparing a submission to support this. At first, the DPP remains unconvinced. Then, in May 2005, I'm walking through Hyde Park in the centre of Sydney when I get a call from one of the DPP's lawyers, asking me to clarify something in the submission.

'I'll come over,' I say.

'There's no need –'

'I'm just outside. I'll be straight there,' I interrupt. Inside their offices, I spend three hours arguing that they should take the prosecution forward. I try to make them understand the humanity of the decision they are making, like how Evelyn's grandmother Patricia is the most credible witness you could hope for – if you meet her. I talk about how Hilton, who said James whispered to him that he killed people and buried their bodies, had not come forward before because he was a black man who feared a white policeman would not believe him. I tell them that we'll never have this chance again.

The DPP agrees. I start preparing for court.

You'll Have to Wear a Uniform

March 2005: 19 years in

The black suit jacket feels comfortable. Well worn. Beneath it, a white shirt and knotted black tie. Black trousers. Non-regulation leather boots. My Glock 22 in its holster tucked into the small of my back.

I should be putting on a uniform, but I don't want to. I haven't worn one for 20 years, not since I became a detective.

The only reason I'm even thinking about a uniform now is that a new anti-corruption policy introduced after the royal commission means every detective in State Crime Command now faces being rotated to a new squad every few years. It's meant to stop cops from building corrupt relationships with the crooks they meet through work, but I think it's a mistake. In Homicide, we work a case, then move on to the next one, not like the old Kings Cross detectives, who spent their days surrounded by the same club bosses. Nor are we like those cops fighting the War on Drugs, who might regularly walk into crime scenes where there's a pile of money sitting on the table. When the Homicide Squad get to a crime scene, there's most often just a body.

Rather than be rotated out, during 2004 I jumped instead, winning promotion to detective inspector and a position working as Crime Manager for the Chatswood local area command, on Sydney's lower north shore. The pay's good, which helps with my money worries, but it's a desk job with a huge range of responsibilities. I oversee the local intelligence, crime prevention and transit cops, the beat police officers who patrol the local streets and shopping centres, as well as the local detectives. It means 7am briefings and evening Neighbourhood Watch meetings, sitting on the human resources committee and overseeing the station rosters. Shopping trolleys are one of the big issues I deal with. People don't like it when they're taken from shops and left lying round the streets.

I try to stop the admin work from taking over, so I can spend more time with the detectives, or working on the Bowraville case, even if that means doing it in my own time. It's a way of staying faithful to who I am at heart, a Homicide detective, but it isn't always easy. On my first day, Doreen, the local area commander, told me: 'You'll have to wear a uniform.'

I said I didn't have one. She asked someone to sort it out. As each item came in – hat, jacket, pants – I'd throw it under my desk.

After a few months, Doreen asked me again to wear a uniform. I wore it for a month or two, more out of respect for her than anything, because Doreen was a good boss, then took it off and went back to wearing my suit.

My happy place at Chatswood is the station gym, where I can train or meditate. The other cops have got used to coming in and seeing me with my eyes closed in lotus position. Like with the uniform, it is another way of keeping balanced; OK, I'd been forced to take a different job, but that didn't mean I was a different person. That sense of sanctuary I found in the gym might help explain my actions when someone violated it.

One day I smelled something foul in the changing rooms. Taking a look, I found someone had shat in the shower. The cleaner said it wasn't the first time it had happened, and that made me mad. We're cops. We have real responsibilities to others – we can take away other people's freedom. For a cop to do this was mocking those. It was perverse.

At the next morning briefing, in front of the whole station, I walked in and told the assembled officers, 'No wonder people call us pigs, because we *are* pigs. We're dirty, rotten pigs. Someone shat in the shower, and I'm going to use every ounce of my investigative skills to find that person.'

I wanted to shock them. To drive the message home, I kicked a chair and stormed out of the room.

Later, I had blue and white crime scene tape put up around the gym shower block, then emailed every cop at the station saying I was disgusted. The email said I'd called in forensics and that, yes, stupid, you could get DNA from human faeces.

Word came from one of the older guys that a young cop went white when he read this. I had him brought up to my office via the stairs, so he was out of breath when he arrived, then shut the door and stared at him.

'Why did you do it?'

'Do what?'

'Don't fucking muck around, someone shat in the shower and you're the person that's done it.'

It only took a couple of minutes to break him. He confessed, but there was something weird about the way he did it. It felt like he was getting off on telling me the story.

'Give us your gun and get out of the police station,' I said. He went. I didn't have a clear idea if I was sacking or suspending him, and probably I broke some rules, but he didn't come back, so that wasn't an issue.

Looking back, I can accept it seemed extreme, but I was happy to be seen as a hard man to work for if that meant stopping other cops from taking the job less seriously than I did. Getting older, and being stuck behind a desk not out there chasing crooks, I have less patience for those who don't see that police work is life and death. At its extreme, in certain situations where it is justified, being a cop means you can kill someone and the law will defend you.

Yes, afterwards, in the pub, I laughed about the Mystery of the Phantom Shower Defacator, but in the moment I was deadly fucking serious. For me, it was partly about dealing with someone who I thought had no right to call himself a policeman. And partly it was proving I have more to offer than shift rosters and pushing back the tide of abandoned shopping trolleys.

***

Sometimes, you have to take this seriously.

On one job in 2005 I oversaw a kidnapping: a father disappeared with his child and was calling the mother demanding a ransom to reunite them. She walked through the front doors of Chatswood Police Station to ask for help and, given what was at stake, I referred the case to State Crime Command. They said it was a civil matter not a criminal one, and so they couldn't touch it.

Fuck that, I thought. *We'll do it.*

The father kept phoning, making more demands, so we traced the calls. The New South Wales Crime Commission, a powerful and largely secretive law-enforcement body, stepped up to help. They had better equipment than we did in the cops, so we eventually tracked the calls to Thailand. Working with Interpol and the Thai police, we got the child back and were in the process of extraditing the father when a federal politician called me and tried to vouch for him, saying surely there was no real need to do this?

The politician called back later, drunk, apologising in case I misunderstood what he was asking. The Thai police put the kid's father on a plane and we arrested him when it landed.

***

Later that year, another father abducted his children after stabbing their mother, although she survived. We worked all night, putting out an Amber Alert broadcast across the news networks to say the kids were missing, and dealing with the phone companies, trying to triangulate his mobile phone signal to work out where he'd taken them.

We kept trying to call him but the phone was switched off.

Just give it one more go, I thought, dialling the number again. The father answered. He sounded reasonable but wouldn't tell me where they were and, as we spoke, he started getting agitated.

I tried to talk him down. 'Look, it might seem bad now but it's not bad. The main thing is your kids.'

'No, I'm going to go,' he said, hanging up. I stared at the phone, consumed with panic, and dialled the number again. No answer. I dialled again. He answered.

'Are the kids OK?'

'Yes.' I felt relief wash over me.

We got those children back as well. This time, I kept the father on the phone. We traced the signal, and I also managed to get enough details about exactly where he was for a tactical team to storm their motel room while I was talking to him.

***

Around midday on Thursday 24 March 2005, a woman called Natasha Ljubic comes to the front desk of Chatswood Police Station, saying her husband, Bob, has disappeared. She says the 44-year-old deals in luxury cars, and runs two dealerships, Mosman Automobiles and Sydney's American Imports. He got a call at 9pm last night from someone asking him to go and look at a damaged red Ferrari F355 Spider. He didn't come home.

I recognise the name: Bob Ljubic was someone we looked at in the last on-call murder I dealt with at Homicide. A former employee of his, Franco Mayer, was shot dead days before being due to appear in the New South Wales Industrial Relations Commission to pursue a $650,000 claim against Bob over alleged loans and unpaid wages. The case was unresolved, but I remember that we'd looked at him as a potential suspect.

It's interesting but I've got a holiday booked with Pam, the first trip we'll have had overseas without having to escort a prisoner. Just like our Paris trip, we've used these deportation flights to visit Fiji and Hong Kong together, but only for a few days. This time, we're going to Vietnam for a fortnight.

The plan is to escape the intensity of work and home life where, being both cops, work tends to follow us. This time we can relax and enjoy each other. We'll visit Saigon, Hanoi and go trekking in the mountains. I love the different Asian cultures and, given Pam loves France, I've sold her on the history of French colonisation, saying we'll still be able to find her a baguette.

Two plain clothes constables have been dealing with Natasha and I tell them the disappearance should be reported to State Crime Command. Given Bob's possible link to the Mayer killing, Homicide should deal with it, I tell them.

Two weeks later, when Pam and I return, I get an update from the constables, Ben Walsh and Andrew Brennan. They're both good, keen young cops but say that Homicide worked on the case for only four days before handing the case back, effectively leaving them in charge. Despite this, between them they've made real progress.

The call Bob received at 9pm on 23 March was traced to a prepaid SIM card, registered to a false name and address. The car he was driving that night was found at The Gap – by chance, the same suicide spot where the body of Caroline Byrne was discovered a decade ago. The car had unknown fingerprints inside it.

Bob's body was discovered on 28 March floating a kilometre out to sea, wearing only his shoes and socks. A large shark was spotted circling nearby. We were lucky. Much longer and we might never have found him.

Ben and Andrew say that Homicide reckon it was a suicide.

'That's not a suicide,' I say. 'I'll make some calls.'

I call Paul, the new Homicide commander, who has replaced Nick Kaldas, and tell him they've got it wrong. Paul's response is flat and unmoving. 'We've assessed it and our assessment is it's a suicide,' he says. I tell him, 'All right, Paul, then just so you know I'm not going behind your back, I'm going to go above you.'

My next call is to his boss at State Crime Command who says, 'Gary, it's not a murder, and even if it is, you're not gonna be able to solve it.'

'Fuck it, OK, thank you,' I say.

I know it's going to enrage them, but I'm not comfortable with writing this one off as a suicide.

I pull in Ben and Andrew, as well as some other detectives and plain clothes constables from different local area commands, telling them: 'Guys, we're going to treat this as a murder because it *is* a murder, and we're *going* to solve this because State Crime has told me we're not going to be able to.'

I get the plain clothes guys to wear dark suits when they turn up at people's doors, to say they're working a homicide and never smile. It'll help reassure any potential witnesses, but it's also a threat. It's saying we're serious about this case and will hopefully get back to those who are responsible. We need a break, and I want those crooks to make mistakes. I want them to panic, thinking, *Fuck, these guys are coming after me.*

We open up Bob's life: his medical history and business dealings, including his assets, property interests, loans, debts and transactions. We plan physical surveillance as well as listening devices and telephone intercepts. We discover that Bob knew some interesting people: a SIM card found in his abandoned car is registered to a suspected drug importer, and a street directory on the front seat contains the name and contact details of a member of the Comancheros bikie gang who has a murder conviction. We speak to one informer who tells us Bob was involved with people who ran a cocaine importation racket. Other bikies turn up at Bob's funeral, including the National Sergeant at Arms of the Rebels.

So, maybe Bob was not an innocent. But, like Terry Falconer, he was still someone's son. He was still someone's husband. He's still somebody's father.

I like the energy of this strike force. The young guys, particularly Ben and Andrew, drive the investigation forward and we do get our break. Road toll records show us that on the night Bob went missing, his car crossed the Harbour Bridge just ahead of another car driven by a man called Jason McCall. We follow this up and discover McCall is a bear of a man, who once worked in security, and receives $500 a fortnight in unemployment benefits yet shells out $2100 a month in mortgage repayments. He reported his car as having been broken into on the same evening as Bob's disappearance.

Once again, I ask the New South Wales Crime Commission for help and they start tracing the spider's web of phone contacts between McCall and others. We learn some of these people don't seem to get along – the house of one is destroyed in an arson attack and we suspect another might have been the one to do it.

Ben and Andrew argue the arsonist might have stopped for fuel on the long drive to Goulburn, where the attack took place, asking if they can visit every service station in the almost 200 kilometres between the city and Sydney for CCTV footage. I like their ambition so say to go for it, though when they return with a pile of tapes, I reckon we're long odds of finding anything.

'Mate, this is a needle in a haystack,' I tell Ben.

'Oh no, boss, I'll do it.' He's keen.

I'm wrong to doubt them. On the first tape, they find a man who went into the servo to buy a jerrycan of fuel and a lighter. The CCTV camera catches his rego plate, so we get a name, Tom McCartney (not his real name) and pull him into the Crime Commission for questioning. They lay out the evidence against him and, unlike with us, it is a crime not to answer their questions. The flip-side of these powers is that the answers can't be used in any criminal trial, but that doesn't stop us using them as intelligence.

I hope the examination will shake Tom and, after, I take him to a separate room and offer him a deal; I say we know what he was up to, but will offer him immunity from prosecution if he chooses to cooperate.

It's exactly the same tactic the royal commission used to hook their main informer, Trevor Haken. Tom lays it out. He didn't only do the arson. He was there when McCall and another man kidnapped Bob. They beat him up, blindfolded him and drove him to The Gap, where they marched him up the steps towards the cliff edge. The plan, Tom says, was just to scare him – they wanted money off him, while he and Bob had had some kind of argument in the past – but McCall lost it when they got there, and threw their victim over the fence.

For me, it isn't a decision. Tom is a crook, no doubt. He was involved and his own account puts him at the scene of Bob's murder. But, as it stands, we don't have enough without his evidence to charge anyone. That means that we won't solve this case without Tom's help and the price of his cooperation is that he doesn't face criminal charges.

More than that, we will have to protect him, give him a new name, move him away from Sydney and help find him work. For McCall to go down, Tom must get a new life. I make the call. We'll sink McCall and give Tom a life raft. That's what I mean when I say police work is life and death. That's why I take this job so seriously.

McCall's no mastermind. Searching his home, we find records linking him to the burner phone used to call Bob and lure him from his home that evening. Tracing the movements of this phone and others he used, we find that they match Bob's own movements.

Whether he realises we are getting closer, in July 2005, four months after Bob went missing, McCall gets his car professionally cleaned twice in a week. The first time, we have an undercover cop do the work and search it. The second we seize it. There's nothing there, except some rope, but we're still satisfied we have enough on the car's owner now and can afford to change our focus.

I'm interested in the third man Tom said was involved. Tom said his job was to drive Bob's car out to The Gap after the others kidnapped him. I ask Tom to wear a wire and he arranges a meeting in a club not far from Chatswood Police Station.

It's high-risk stuff. Unlike with Rocco or Axeman, where we had a cover story that allowed them to go back more than once to try to get more details, I reckon Tom's got one chance at this before he risks raising suspicion. Our technical guys don't share my sense of urgency, however. When the day comes they seem more interested in reading the papers and mucking around than checking their equipment.

When Tom gets back, he tells me he got everything we wanted. The two of them discussed the kidnapping. The third man talked about how he drove the Porsche Cayenne four-wheel drive that Bob was driving and dumped it at The Gap. I'm satisfied. If we can get two convictions over this, then allowing Tom to walk away without arrest was worth it.

Driving home, one of the technical guys calls me, saying the recording equipment failed.

I tense up, gripping the steering wheel. 'What are you saying?'

He plays it down. 'Look, whenever you want to send him in again, we'll be there. And we'll make sure it's right.'

I snap. 'Are you fucking for real? You're telling me to send him in again? Send someone in to talk about a murder again and *just repeat the whole thing*? You're telling me that this whole fucking thing has been a waste of time?'

The anger's natural enough but misdirected. I'm really angry at myself. It is my job. I should have got them to check their equipment.

We never do arrest the third man. I'm sick at the fact that, after all the work, and the big calls, part of this case will fall down over something so stupid. Particularly after the equipment problems with Rocco, it's also sickening to think that someone might get away with murder just because we don't have good enough technology.

Still, we do have one good informer and I'm determined to make the most of him. I remember how vulnerable we felt in the police during the royal commission, when their investigation seemed to be unstoppable. It felt like they were talking to everyone, which made you look at even your old friends with suspicion. Over the next few weeks, we plan to do the same thing when we arrest McCall, by using a show of force to simultaneously interview every close relative, business associate or crook we know he deals with.

For each of them, we prepare separate interview plans. We get warrants to search their properties. The whole thing will take between 30 and 40 cops, working together, as each of these different interviews is to take place at the same time. Not every person that we speak to is a suspect, but each of them, we will tell about the others. I want them to feel that same suspicion of their friends and what they might be saying. I want them to think, *Do I need to tell the cops something first, just to protect myself?'*

On Monday 8 August 2005, we launch these coordinated raids. We call it Operation Day.

McCall denies everything in court. It takes another two years to advance through the rounds of preparatory court hearings and other legal processes but eventually, the jury go against him. In November 2007, McCall gets 29 years and four months for Bob Ljubic's murder, with a non-parole period of 22 years. It is a victory for Bob's family, but I'm left with the knowledge that it isn't perfect. I never did find out who murdered Franco Mayer. Out of the three men who were involved in Bob's kidnapping, only one – McCall – went down. Tom got immunity from prosecution over his role in the plot, as well as the arson. The third man, who the wire failed to record and who drove Bob's car to The Gap, was never caught.

We got one man. A life for a life. In that sense, we avenged Bob's death.

'I'll fucking get you, you cunt!' McCall shouts at me as he's led away.

***

Sometimes, cases make you ask yourself too many questions. At other times, they're simple. On 4 July 2005, a month before McCall's arrest, Jeffrey Hillsley was sentenced to 30 years' jail, with a non-parole period of 25 years, for the murder of Michael Davies and sexual assault of his 10-year-old stepdaughter. We challenge the sentence in the appeal court, and on 28 September 2006, the judges agree, saying instead that Hillsley should never be released.

Their judgment reads: 'There are some crimes which are so wicked that a sentence less than a life sentence cannot adequately reflect the community interest in retribution and punishment.'

I have to agree. I saw the trauma that man caused. It's like the Bible says, 'thou shalt give life for life'.

That's why I do this job. That's why I care so much about it. Murderers can't walk free to kill again. They must be caught.

That's what I do. I catch killers.

Double Jeopardy

February 2006: 21 years in

I spend the hot summer months at the end of 2005 and beginning of 2006 preparing for the trial of James Hide over the murder of Evelyn in Bowraville. In the first week of February, days before the trial begins, the families of the three children gather at the medical centre on the tiny patch of park in front of the Mission for me to explain what to expect. Even for those who there at the inquest, or the trial over Clinton's murder, the court is such a different world from theirs, it's worth repeating its procedures: how a jury is sworn in, the barristers will walk around in robes and wigs, how you have to stand and bow when the judge enters. How, often, they might not understand what's being said but that Jason Evers and I will be there to answer any questions.

There is a face I do not recognise among the crowd. A psychologist called Tracy, who's been employed by the State Government to work with the families. A lean, athletic figure – I later learn she is a sprinter – she stands out. She's beautiful. During the trial, we go out for a drink and she tells me about her childhood growing up in a remote community on the far edge of Western Australia. We sit up talking late into the night. She's smart and funny, and she really seems to care about the people she's working with in Bowraville.

She says I'm rare, that she's never seen an Aboriginal community trust a white policeman. It gives me some encouragement at a time when I need it.

***

The trial, which starts on 7 February 2006 and is held at Port Macquarie Supreme Court, is exhausting. For Jason and me, a big part of our work as detectives is making sure the witnesses turn up at court. It means driving back and forth from Bowraville, tracking down people who have different ideas of time and appointments from those the court is working to and for whom, the prospect of giving evidence itself can be confronting.

Axeman, our star prison informant, has been drinking again and refusing to give evidence. I follow him, a bottle in each of his hands, along the beach shouting: 'Mate, come on!'

'No, you'll get me killed!' he shouts back. That's possible, I think, but then again, over the few years I've known Axeman, I've started to think of him as a cat; he's got nine lives. What's certain is that Axeman is always trouble.

A few years ago, shortly before the 2004 inquest into Evelyn and Clinton's death, I got a call from witness security, asking if Jason and I could look after Axeman for a night. Some bikies were going after him, they said, though with Axeman you never knew the whole story. We should get him out of Sydney. They said they'd come and get him from us the next day.

Four weeks later we were still washing his clothes, or he was wearing *our* clothes, and we were travelling round the State with him on jobs, like he was our enormous, tattooed son. On the long drives he'd stick his head out of the car window and I had to tell him: 'Sit down, stupid!'

In the evenings, we'd put him up in a motel room and hang out in there with him so he didn't head out to the pub, where he'd only get into trouble. At seven o'clock the next morning, he'd be in the motel pool, sculling a bottle of bourbon.

'Can we leave you? We've got to go and do some work,' we'd ask him on our way out. He'd still be floating round the pool when we got back in the afternoon, staring up at us as he downed another drink.

Another time, Jason and I arranged to meet him in a country town but when we got to his property, it was empty. We stayed a week, going back each day until he turned up. This time, when we parked, he started walking to the car, revving a chainsaw he was carrying and looking at us with a strange, violent expression.

Suddenly, he laughed. We lived. We still needed to stay close to him, because he was a witness. Like any couple, he and I fell out at times. He called me once to say that he was muscling up, 'And then I'm fucking coming after you, cunt.'

'Really? You're muscling up? You're coming after me? Well, fucking bring it on.' I hung up.

A week later I got another call. 'Oh, sorry, mate. I probably overstepped the mark a little there.'

Nothing has changed. I walk behind him on the beach at Port Macquarie, shouting, 'Mate, come on!' He waves a bottle of bourbon. 'Mate, I love you like a brother. I'm not going to let anybody hurt you,' I tell him.

Eventually, he takes the stand.

But Axeman is only one part of the nightmare.

***

The trial lasts a month and I can feel it slipping away from us before the first week is over. I'm used to prosecution lawyers having questions for the detectives about different pieces of evidence, or how a certain witness is likely to manage in court, but we're asked nothing.

One morning the prosecutor says he wants Evelyn's father, Billy Greenup, to give evidence. I try to say Billy's been hit hard by the trauma of his daughter's death. He drinks, and he and I have barely spoken. The prosecutor won't hear it, so I drive to Bowraville, where it's baking hot and find Billy, but he won't do it. He's nervous and horrified at the prospect of going into a court full of strangers and talking about his daughter. I try saying he should do it for Evelyn and do get him back to Port Macquarie but, while Billy and I are sitting outside the court on the footpath, talking through what him going inside the building will involve, he throws up all over my feet.

Inside, the prosecutor says that we don't need him now. I tell Billy, feeling rotten at what I just put him through and am shocked when he grabs me and wraps me in his arms. He says he's sorry for not talking to me, and for the vomit.

'I know what you blokes have done for us,' he says and we hug it out.

Another evening, I head into the local police station to do some work when a local cop in uniform comes up, smiling, and says, 'Are you the ones bussing in all the Abos?'

'What?'

'Bringing all the Abos in for the trial.' He laughs.

'You're a fucking disgrace,' I tell him. 'Get out of my sight.' His laughter dies.

Back in court the next morning, I look at the jury, who are all white, and wonder if they feel the same way.

How much does racism, or at best, unconscious bias, come into their decision-making process? I'll never know because, as a cop, I'm not allowed to speak to them. They're the ones who get to judge the evidence Jason and I have collected. They have to choose whether to believe the black witnesses, who often look so out of place and nervous on the stand, and say Evelyn had disappeared on the night of 4 October 1990, after a party on the Mission, or the white woman who ran the Reibels store on Bowraville's main street and swore she saw the little girl inside her store several days later.

This matters because if Evelyn did not disappear on the night of the party then there is no connection to James Hide, who was also in the house that night. In his closing speech, James's barrister tells the jury the white woman's evidence was 'absolutely like a beacon'. It could guide you.

'Ladies and gentlemen,' he says, 'the death of Evelyn Greenup, there is no doubt it was a tragedy.

'It is a fact that the Crown case comprises in large part the evidence of a large number of people who were extremely drunk at the time. It includes the evidence of a prison informer who has been convicted of perjury,' – that's Axeman. 'And it includes the evidence of someone who you could only characterise as being a drunk now, and he has been for many years,' – that's Hilton, who said James had whispered to him about killing people and burying their bodies.

'You simply cannot make a silk purse out of a sow's ear and you might think that is the reality that the Crown is inviting you to embark on,' James's barrister continues. Listening, I feel all my certainty about the case drain out onto the courtroom floor. Jason's shoulders slump forward. It's taken us almost 10 years of work to get to this point and we are both exhausted.

According to court practice, the prosecutor has already given his closing speech, which means the defence lawyer's is the last voice the jury hears, other than the judge's. James's barrister knows what words to use. These are decent, ordinary people. Port Macquarie is a small town set amid farming country. It isn't the big city. 'In all, it's my submission to you that the evidence that you have received in this trial doesn't amount to a hill of beans when you look at it objectively, as you will, and in those circumstances it's my submission that you will have no problem at all returning a verdict of not guilty.'

Gary, Gary, Gary

3 March 2006: 21 years in

The jury walk out of the courtroom to decide their verdict, and I head back alone to my motel room, crashing out, fully clothed, on the bed.

I'm sleeping when a strange voice wakes me: 'Gary, Gary, Gary ...'

I look around and there's no voice, just a panicky feeling that threatens to overwhelm me. It's like I'm in the ocean, having fallen off my surfboard, and am being tumbled underwater.

Walking into the autumn sunshine, the colours of the motel walls are more vivid, and the shrieking of the lorikeets in the gum trees behind it sharper than I remember. I walk up the road towards the courthouse. I should feel comfortable in Port Macquarie, but I do not. I know this town. I brought the kids up here for weekends on the beach. The first few months of the investigation into Terry Falconer's death was based in the police station. The place feels alien today. Arriving at the courthouse, I climb the steps and go inside.

The jury are coming back.

Too soon, I think. It's rarely a good sign when they come back this quickly.

***

There are riot police in the courtroom. A decision had been made above our heads to send them here in case there's trouble at the verdict, and I think that it is shameful. For the past month, the courthouse has been full of all three of the murdered children's relatives and no one has caused problems. Now there are rows of big, intimidating cops in black uniforms taking up the chairs at the front of the court, so that some of these family members cannot even find a space to listen to the verdict and have to wait in the hall outside instead.

It sends a message that the police don't trust the victims' families. Jason and I are caught in the middle and, frankly, feeling closer to the families than we do to the cops right now.

The jury walk in and take their seats. They find James Hide not guilty.

James doesn't react.

I look at him. There is no way of knowing what's going on inside his head. He's big, a beast to look at, but he's no dope.

As one, the children's families stand, turn their backs on the judge and jury and walk out of the court. I am so proud of them; it is the powerful peaceful protest I can imagine. Outside, one of the older women collapses and the others form a circle around her. They weep. They shout, but there is no violence.

***

It feels like somebody's reached in and ripped out my guts. I can accept defeat, but the experience of letting those families down is more than I can manage. Their pain pours out and fills the courtroom.

Jason and I feel the water level rising. We told the families to trust us and we've failed them. The water is above our heads.

Leaving the court building, I'm still kicking beneath the surface. All the effort we've put into the trial – organising witnesses, answering the families' questions, trying to motivate the prosecutor, who never seemed to care about the case like we did – has left me with little strength.

I've given everything I could to bring this case to trial. It's cost me my marriage – I've drowned myself in work and now all that I can see is blackness. And for what?

I walk away from the court.

***

'Not guilty' is a result, I think. It doesn't mean 'innocent'. Like the judge told the jury, the defendant doesn't have to prove his innocence in court. Instead, the prosecution has to prove his guilt, and prove it beyond reasonable doubt. We failed. That is the justice system. It gives you a result.

***

The children's families ask us, 'What can we do now?'

I tell them, 'Nothing.'

Once somebody's been tried for an offence, that's it, you can't put them on trial over the same offence again. The lawyers call it double jeopardy. There's nothing you can do unless you want to change the law itself.

'Let's do that, then,' the families say.

I love their courage and determination. But I doubt that I can help them any further.

***

Jason and I load up our cars to drive our separate ways, him north to Ballina, where he has taken a promotion to detective sergeant and is living with his new wife, and me down south to Sydney.

'Yeah, all right. See you.'

'See you.'

We don't know how to talk about it. We don't know how to deal with the emotion.

The two of us have been partners now for almost a decade. It's been like a marriage sometimes, in the way it was 24/7 on jobs, living with each other for weeks at a time while working in Bowraville, or driving for half a day to other crime scenes, working a full day when we got there, then checking into some cheap motel, trying to keep the cost down because we're on a travel allowance, so we would get a double room and move the furniture around so the beds were further apart and the wardrobe in between us, to get an illusion of private space.

Jason knows my family. He plays football with some of my cousins. He's got so close he ended up marrying my younger brother's ex-girlfriend. He's smart, he's diligent. He cares about the victims. He's one of the few people I can talk to about my father. Despite all that, I think we both find it easier to walk away because we remind each other of this verdict.

We don't talk for six months.

***

Not one of my bosses calls me to say 'Good effort', 'You did your best', or ask how I'm doing. When I get back to work in Chatswood, people joke, 'How was your holiday in sunny Port Macquarie?' I get a message from the Homicide commander, telling me not to talk to the media about the case.

***

At home, I start to fight with Pam. It's like I'm on auto-destruct. I don't care about myself right now, so I don't care about our relationship.

One day, the two of us are walking along the beach near home when Pam tells me, 'You just have to let it go.'

She's right, and her advice is well-intentioned, but it has the reverse effect. I want to scream. *Fuck you*, I think. *You don't know anything about it.*

We have a huge fight and Pam leaves for a few days. It feels like our relationship is over. I'm stuck at home alone, thinking about the murders.

If I had the time or ability to realise what I'm going through, maybe things might be different. But I'm not making rational decisions. Instead, my attitude to every choice or obstacle in life right now is, *Fuck you, I'm happy to take myself to the bottom*. I'm dragging Pam down with me.

Soon afterwards, I tell her I've had enough. The two of us together are too intense. While I've been working on the Bowraville and Terry Falconer killings, Pam's been solving gang and bikie murders. When each of us wanted some down time, the other was working. There'd been too many nights when one or both of us was out, working on different cases, or the phone rang and she would tell me not to answer it, but both of us knew I would.

Pam tells me I'm an extremist. That I need to feel pain and can only feel compassion for murder victims, not the people around me. That I treat witnesses, bosses, suspects, even my own family, like they have no value other than to help me solve cases. That it's like an addiction.

We decide to call it quits. I tell myself our breakup will protect me, that I've let life get out of balance again, with too much work, too much darkness and not enough light. Pam tried her best with me, and we loved each other, but both of us were Homicide detectives. Being together meant there was never any respite from our jobs.

***

You can't escape your cases. One month after the not guilty verdict, on 4 April 2006, Gordon Wood is arrested in London over the alleged murder of his fiancée, Caroline Byrne. It has been five years since I interviewed him in London during 2001.

Over that time, Caroline's father, Tony, has protested at the slow pace of the investigation, even getting it raised in the State Parliament in October 2002. Like with the Bowraville murders, this case, too, has been a constant battle for resources. In February 2004, we'd sent a brief of evidence to the State Director of Public Prosecutions (DPP), asking for their advice on charging Gordon with murder. Paul Jacob, who is still leading the investigation, went back and forth with the DPP for years, revising the brief, until in March this year, the DPP gave him the go-ahead.

The case made more headlines, with one photographer even getting on the plane carrying Gordon back to Sydney.

***

I keep looking backwards. I'm frustrated that so long after Caroline's death and the deaths of the Bowraville children, their families still don't have an explanation of what happened. I dwell on the fact that, around the same time as the Bowraville murders, I was working an hour away in Coffs Harbour with the Armed Hold-Up Squad, one of a dozen cops chasing something else, who could have been better used investigating the children's killings. After a decade spent trying to put that right, I'm ashamed not to have jailed whoever killed Colleen, Evelyn and Clinton.

Within weeks of the verdict, I am approached by a woman from Bowraville, who wants to ask about Clinton, the third of the murder victims.

Have I heard about the truck drivers who saw a white man standing over the body of a black teenager lying in the road, on the morning after Clinton disappeared?

'No,' I tell her. 'I haven't.'

Norco Corner

19 September 2006: 21 years in

'We're in the delivery truck, coming along here quite early in the morning,' says Michael as we retrace the route he took 15 years ago, on the morning 16-year-old Clinton went missing.

One of the former truck drivers I've been told about, he shows me how they drove into Bowraville from the southeast, where Wilson Road takes a blind left-hand turn known locally as Norco Corner.

My bosses told me to leave this case alone after the not guilty verdict, but I can't do it. When you've been here and driven these roads, when you've looked up at the dark forest where Evelyn's and Clinton's bodies were found on the hillsides above the town, it's impossible to leave it.

Only now, with Jason's move to Ballina and the way the case has broken our relationship, Strike Force Ancud is me, working in my own time, or when I can justify getting away from work at Chatswood to come back here.

'It's 3.30, quarter to four, maybe 4.30, in that pre-dawn time,' Michael goes on. 'It's dark, with no street lighting.' He was one of two men delivering meat to the butchers in Bowraville that morning. The other, Greg, was driving the truck.

'We've got quite powerful driving lights, so we could see him. The guy was lying with his head facing down by the hill.'

I turn to look at where Michael is pointing. 'We had to go around him, pull in hard at the corner,' he says.

Greg swore and yelled at the person lying motionless on the bitumen. He didn't answer.

They saw another man, standing beside a stationary car with no lights on and its boot open. He walked towards them, out of the shadows and round to Greg's window.

'I leaned across and said, "Mate, what's going on? We could have hit that guy, he's lying in the middle of the road there."'

The man told them it was all right, that the figure lying on the road was blind drunk but not to worry about it, he'd already called the police.

At the time, they just accepted it. There were no payphones on that road back then, and this was before anyone had mobiles, but maybe he'd used a phone in someone's house.

Michael says the car looked like a Galant. It was a mustard colour, he says, somewhere between a yellow and an orange.

I think, *James Hide's mum drove a Chrysler Galant.*

Michael says he didn't know why the car had its boot up. Maybe the man standing in the road had been trying to put the sleeping man inside it, or maybe he'd just pulled him out. The man standing in the road was white, says Michael. The early-morning twilight made it hard to tell his age, but maybe somewhere between his mid-20s and early 30s, stocky, with brown hair and a little chubby in the cheeks.

Like James.

The figure lying on the bitumen was Aboriginal, and younger than the other man, says Michael. Maybe 18 to 25, slim build, long scraggy hair. He didn't have shoes on.

Clinton fits that appearance, or close to it. And he wasn't wearing any shoes when his body was discovered. Surely, this is important. I don't like being on my own, without Jason to ask what he makes of this. For so long, it has been the two of us fighting together and now I feel lost. This evidence raises more questions than it answers.

Why have I heard nothing about this before? Returning again to the files from the first police investigation, I find that Greg and Michael *did* speak to police at the time, but no formal witness statements were taken. Worse, during our reinvestigation, another detective looked at their evidence again, but it was not followed up.

Why not? I can only guess, but maybe because back then we weren't focusing on Clinton's murder, since it had already resulted in a not guilty verdict. Looking at the name of the cop on the paperwork, I also remember how, when we were away in Bowraville together, I saw more of him in the pub than out, chasing up confusing leads.

There are other questions to be answered. Michael says this happened on the morning after Clinton slept in James's caravan, the morning his family say they realised he was missing. But the old files suggest the first police investigation thought it might have been a week later, when there is a record of a similar call being made to the local police. Michael also talks about seeing a dog, when neither James nor Clinton owned one. But still, why was none of this heard during the trial over Clinton's murder?

These are the questions I'd like answered. Call them a case theory:

What if James bashed Clinton while the teenager was sleeping in his caravan? That would account for Clinton's broken jaw when the cops found his body. Maybe James knocked him unconscious. Maybe the blow killed him outright.

The distance from James's caravan to Norco Corner is a few hundred metres. James matched the description of the man seen by Greg and Michael standing over the body lying on the road that morning, which matched Clinton's description.

Did James put Clinton's body in the car and drive to Norco Corner?

Did he drag Clinton out onto the road?

Norco Corner's a blind turn. It would have been dark – Michael and Greg's truck had powerful driving lights and they only just managed to avoid the figure lying on the bitumen. Another car or truck might have hit him. If it was Clinton lying there, the collision might have disguised his injuries. What happened after Michael and Greg stopped? After they asked the white man what was going on, and he assured them that he'd called for help and they drove on?

If that white man was James, did he then load Clinton back into the car and drive up to the forest? Did James dump Clinton's body beside the Congarinni Road, near his crop of marijuana plants?

I'd love to ask James those questions. Only, he isn't talking.

***

I can't leave the case alone for another reason, also. It's still affecting my life at home.

When I met Tracy, the psychologist helping the Bowraville families, I knew we got on well but didn't think we had a future. Our homes were more than 3000 kilometres apart, on opposite coasts. After I broke up with Pam, Tracy and I began to speak more often on the phone. Sometimes we spoke for hours.

In October 2006, a month after I met Michael in Bowraville, Tracy starts to spend more time with me in Copacabana.

She's different from Pam. Tracy is different from anyone I've ever known. Born in the northwest corner of Australia, she grew up near Shark Bay, where her father was a station manager and her mother a shearers' cook. As a child, her family moved to nearby Useless Loop, a closed community town servicing the salt harvesting operation, and lived in a shack with a dirt floor, before settling in the mining town of Tom Price, 500 kilometres northwest. These experiences gave her a sense of drive, and an empathy for what other Aboriginal people have been through. Tracy had seen the effects of the Stolen Generations, the poverty, the booze.

She became the first Aboriginal person in the country to complete a combined masters and PhD in clinical psychology, and then she started her own business. She's won awards for her research into mental health in Aboriginal communities.

Tracy says she can keep running the business from the east coast, and so we set her up in my home. It's hard yakka and means she's travelling across the country every couple of weeks, but when we are together it's great. She gets on well with Jake, who's now 15, and 13-year-old Gemma, and we start to build a life together. She runs, so understands the importance to me of my training. Like the kids, Tracy gets used to waking up and finding me doing press-ups, weights or yoga. All three of them laugh about how they can tell how my day went by watching the way I rip into the punchbag hanging on our balcony. But all three of them are serious about their sport as well.

Jake and Gemma both do kung fu and I also encourage them to play one team sport and one individual sport, so Jake plays soccer and goes surfing – just like I do – while Gemma does ballet and netball.

I push them hard, but for their own good, like my dad did. Which makes me shake my head to see how soft he is with them.

One time Tracy and I go away for the weekend, leaving Dad in charge, with a list of instructions: the kids can only eat healthy food; they must do their training, and their homework when they're not doing that; they absolutely cannot go to McDonald's; and are *not* to spend the day at Aunty Karen's, who lives about an hour away from us.

Dad ignores everything I say. The kids eat Macca's, go to Aunty Karen's house, and do no homework and no training. They do everything I've told him that they cannot. Now that he's a teenager, Jake's also started to defy me, trying all the same tricks that I used to with my own parents.

He'll say he's staying at a mate's house while his mate claims he's staying at ours, then they'll go out together, knowing that if I catch them, there'll be trouble. Jake's mates call me The Unit, joking that I look like a utility and I'm capable of anything.

One night, I'm driving home from work at about 2am in an unmarked police car to find a mob of drunk kids spilling across the roads in Copacabana. The local cops had been called in to break up a house party, leaving the kids to roam the streets. They're still over-excited. One teenager puts his face up to the car window to give me a razz, freezes in horror and pulls back, shouting: 'It's Jubes's dad! It's Jubes's dad!'

The crowd scuttles. Jake jumps behind a bush to hide. Suddenly the road is deserted.

***

While I follow up the Norco Corner evidence, the murdered Bowraville children's families are campaigning for a change to the laws surrounding double jeopardy.

It seems impossible: a small group of blackfellas from the Mission, where broken-down cars are left to rust on pitted roads, seeking to pull down one of the pillars that supports the white man's justice system, a pillar that's stood in place for as long as the convict-built sandstone columns supporting the State's old Supreme Court building at Darlinghurst in Sydney.

The families shrug at this. It's not *their* law, they tell me. Black law says anyone who kills another accepts there will be payback.

At the heart of their campaign is a woman called Leonie Duroux, the no-nonsense daughter of a conservative Baptist minister who grew up in Sydney but defied her parents and left the city before getting together with Clinton's brother, Marbuck. Physically, Leonie is small, her head barely reaches my shoulder, but you wouldn't mess with her. She carries the weight of the world around on her shoulders like it's barely a burden. For years now, she's been writing letters about the children's killings – hundreds of letters, to victim support groups, to the Aboriginal Land Council, to Members of Parliament, to the New South Wales Governor, asking for their support. Recently, she's started writing letters about the double jeopardy laws.

A campaign group is formed, called Ngindayjumi, which means Truth Be Told in Gumbaynggirr, the Aboriginal language spoken in Bowraville. It gets the attention of journalists and is featured on the ABC's *Australian Story* TV program in September 2006. The families are getting themselves heard.

Leonie goes with Marbuck and Clinton's father, Thomas, to meet their local MP, who arranges for them to travel to Sydney and meet with the head of the New South Wales Premier's Department. When they get there, the politicians tell them the judges are against a change. Leonie argues that the same law was changed a year ago in the UK, after an inquiry into the death of another black teenager, Stephen Lawrence, which found the police investigation into his murder suffered from institutional racism.

The world is changing, Leonie says, to anyone who'll listen.

When anyone asks *me* about the law, I say look at DNA technology. When the Bowraville murders happened, we didn't have the ability to test a bloodstain or a strand of hair and say who was at a crime scene. Surely, the courts have to accept this technology might mean it's possible an old exhibit could throw up some fresh DNA evidence, meaning a verdict has to be reconsidered? We're all after the same thing, I say, which is justice.

In December 2006, the State Government announces it will change the law. The Mission families have knocked down the sandstone pillars.

Smiling at my own lack of faith in this community, I think it's only right if the Bowraville case is the first to take advantage of this earthquake. Reading through the new legislation, it says that somebody who's been found not guilty of a murder can now be sent back for retrial, if 'fresh and compelling' evidence is found against them.

DNA evidence would be 'fresh and compelling', but we haven't got it. Too many years have passed and what little physical evidence we have has degraded. The first investigation of the murders found a tiny red stain on the headboard of the bed in James Hide's caravan. Today, if DNA testing could match that to Clinton, it might prove he was attacked there. At the time, all the police could do was confirm it was a bloodstain, and in the process of running that test, the stain itself was destroyed.

I wonder if the Norco Corner evidence is 'fresh and compelling'. It's never been heard in court before. If so, this is our chance to solve this case; it means the appeal court could overturn the previous not guilty verdicts over Evelyn's and Clinton's deaths. We'd have the chance to run the trials again. And that means a chance to overcome the other, fundamental problem in the prosecution – the decision of the judge at the time James was arrested to separate the cases, so each jury could only be told one child disappeared from Bowraville, not three.

These laws have also changed since that decision was made. It's now much more likely the courts will accept what they call 'tendency and coincidence' evidence about the similarities between separate crimes that show they may be linked. That means a new trial might be able to hear evidence about Evelyn's and Clinton's murders, and maybe even Colleen's, which has never been presented to a jury, all together. *That might be enough*, I think.

I am excited. This might be a chance to right a historic wrong. *Three children were murdered in Bowraville*, I tell myself. On that basis alone, I can't think of a more important case in New South Wales.

And I'm supposed to work it on my own, without a strike force.

Standing on the balcony of my townhouse in Copacabana, I call Linda, the acting Homicide Squad commander.

I tell her that I want to put in a submission to the State Director of Public Prosecutions (DPP), seeking a retrial of James over the murders of Evelyn and Clinton. As I'm still the crime manager at Chatswood, I'll need assistance from Homicide.

She says there isn't anyone available.

I put in written requests, and get nothing. Years ago, Linda and I worked together as detectives at Hornsby and were friendly, which makes her refusal feel worse.

Weeks later, when work at Chatswood takes me to the police headquarters building in Parramatta, western Sydney, I go to visit Linda, catching her in the corridor just as she's leaving the Homicide Squad office.

'Linda, I need staff,' I tell her, the anger rising in my voice. 'I'm sick of fucking around trying to get staff.'

'You can't speak to me like that,' she says, but I've exhausted all my reasonableness.

'Fuck off, I'll speak to you any way I want!'

She stares at me. She says there are other cases, other murders, with a much better chance of being solved than the Bowraville killings. Those cases need resources too, she says.

Then let the cops working those come in here and fight for them. 'Let's go up to level nine,' I say. That means the senior bosses. 'Let's go up there and sort this out. You explain to them why I'm not getting any staff to help me with a triple murder investigation. Come on, let's go now.'

She walks away. I know I've gone too far. I know I always over-escalate and usually regret it. But this time, I don't feel regret. I know there are people at work who say I am a zealot. I hear the rumours going round. Well, fucking let them. I know I'm doing the right thing. And I know that the Bowraville families accept me.

The case is too important. If it means a falling-out with the acting Homicide commander, then so be it.

Hours later, I get two people assigned to work the case: Bianca Comina, an analyst I've worked with before on the Caroline Byrne investigation, and Jerry Bowden, a Homicide detective.

Right, let's fucking do this.

***

Our first job is to prepare a formal submission to the State DPP, asking him to send Evelyn's and Clinton's cases to the appeal court. Jerry is a character, with an easy smile and tireless energy that I'd been missing in Jason Evers' absence. He's the yang to my yin again, without which it had been hard to lift myself up and stop from being swamped.

Without Jason, I'd also lost his uncanny ability to remember the details of the investigation. If I couldn't remember a name among the different folders full of witness statements we'd built up over the years, Jason would always be able to remind me, and say where I could find their evidence. While we use the e@gle.i computer system, I still like to have a hard copy of everything printed out and now it looks like a mountain to dismantle, but Bianca comes in to move it. She breaks down folder after folder of documents, working with a tireless determination that also gives me strength. I don't know if I could have continued with those files if I was on my own.

Together we draw up a 61-page affidavit, outlining what we know about the case to date, including the Norco Corner evidence. It also includes a list of 20 examples of the 'tendency and coincidence' evidence linking the murders together, including that James had previously expressed a sexual interest in Colleen, Evelyn's mother, Rebecca, and Clinton's girlfriend, Kelly Jarrett, who was also asleep in the caravan on the night Clinton disappeared.

Colleen had previously complained to a friend that James had pulled her pants down and 'mauled' her while she slept in his caravan two nights before she went missing. Both Rebecca and Clinton's girlfriend also woke up following Evelyn's and Clinton's disappearances to find their pants had been pulled down.

Another example of 'tendency and coincidence' evidence is that James's mother's red Galant was seen by witnesses near where each of the children went missing. And, after James was charged with murdering Clinton, the third of the three children, no further similar murders happened in the area.

We also ask the Australian Institute of Criminology to analyse the data held in the National Homicide Monitoring Program (NHMP), which lists every such death nationwide, to see how likely it might be that the three children were killed by separate offenders.

We want to show the DPP that we are dealing with a serial killer, and that the version of events presented to each jury in the separate trials over Evelyn's and Clinton's murders was therefore misleading.

'Based on the interrogation of the NHMP database covering a period of 16 years, the murder of three children from a small town over a period of 6 months by different offenders to date has not occurred,' our affidavit argues.

I sign the affidavit on 31 January 2007.

On 4 June, the DPP writes back, saying that 'even accepting that any admissible evidence concerning the Norco Corner incident is fresh, in my view it is not compelling', and declining to let the case be reheard.

***

Throughout my separation from Pam and the disappointment of Evelyn's trial, I've grown closer to my sifu, Ben. He sometimes comes to Chatswood Police Station to give me private classes or for meditation. When it has felt as if life might tip me over into darkness, he's reached out to help me rebalance and find the sense of purpose I need to keep going.

But, in the middle of 2007, a cop who I don't know comes to the martial arts gym where Ben teaches and confronts him, saying he's not happy.

The cop is worried about his daughter, who he says has thrown her life away to follow Ben's training. She is under 18.

Ben introduces me, saying I'm a fellow officer, that I'm at the gym a lot and I can tell him what's been going on. I say I know Ben well and that I've seen his daughter at training. Everything I've seen has been legitimate, I say.

He's being asked to take my word, as one cop to another. He leaves, but I'm not certain he's convinced.

The experience makes me watchful. I start to look at Ben differently and, for the first time, I see how he's lost some of his humility. He boasts about the champion fighters who've trained with him. I ask myself if I can be so sure that he's trained under this master or that master, as he claims.

I also watch the cop's daughter and see the way she looks at Ben, and the way he acts with her in training. I see how they spend so much time together, despite the difference in their ages. I start to feel uncomfortable.

I call Ben out and he begins to protest, saying, 'Oh, but –'

'There's no fucking buts,' I tell him. 'It's like me getting into a relationship with a victim.'

'Listen, Gary –'

'You've taken advantage of her. There are no excuses.'

I tell him I don't want to see him or to speak to him. She is a child. It's a betrayal. It's a betrayal of me also, because I believed him.

I walk out of Ben's gym and don't go back. I've lost my faith. Once again, life feels as if it's slipping out of balance. I work longer hours. With Tracy away in Western Australia so often for her business, there is less reason to go home.

***

The Bowraville families refuse to accept the DPP's decision. Leonie Duroux starts calling lawyers, asking if there is anyone who can help them. She writes more letters. Soon afterwards, in July 2007, we arrange to meet in my office at Chatswood, and she walks in carrying a plastic bag bulging with paperwork.

'Have you got any folders?' I ask.

'I can't afford that.' So I go to the station storeroom and get folders, files and plastic sleeves.

Between us, we start another campaign. Leonie finds a barrister, Chris Barry QC, and a city law firm, Allens Arthur Robinson, who agree to look at the case without payment. Professor Larissa Behrendt and Craig Longman from the Jumbunna Indigenous House of Learning at the University of Technology, Sydney, also offer to help.

The lawyers need to understand the history and the evidence, Leonie tells me. I think about the 61-page affidavit the police submitted to the DPP as part of our last, unsuccessful application. It is a confidential document and, as a cop, I'm not allowed to give it to her. So, in November 2007, I suggest she make a Freedom of Information request and, when that is successful, provide my affidavit to the lawyers.

Between them, they decide to go above the DPP and write to the State's Attorney General, asking him to send the case to the appeal court. I love it. I'm now actively conspiring with lawyers outside my own police force to overturn a State Government decision. Leonie and I spend hours on the phone together, talking strategy. Her fierce determination gives me strength.

The lawyers tell her it would help if I could find a senior police officer willing to support their application. I follow an assistant commissioner into the car park to get him to sign it.

This isn't over, I think, as I walk away across the car park. *We're not finished yet.*

Stone-Cold Killer

September 2008: 23 years in

It's Friday afternoon and the road is full of people heading up the coast to start their weekends as Flatline and I are battling through the traffic, trying to catch up with a contract killer.

We've had Brad Curtis (not his real name) under surveillance over the Terry Falconer murder long enough to know he's tough and smart. Smart enough to talk in code over the phone even though he hasn't realised we're listening. We know he used to be an army commando, trained in weapons and surveillance. We've been told he now works as a hitman, so when we intercepted a call between Curtis and another man we haven't yet identified, talking about a job that's too good to refuse, we decided to pursue him.

When Curtis left his house in Merewether, south Newcastle, earlier today, an unmarked police car followed him onto the Pacific Highway, where we expected him to turn south, towards Sydney. Then I got a call in the office, saying he'd stopped at a McDonald's. In the car park he met another man, someone the cops running the surveillance didn't recognise. Curtis went to the boot of the second man's car, took something out and shoved it in his waistband.

It had to be a pistol. The two men left the second car and got into Curtis's together before pulling back onto the Pacific Highway, heading north, away from Sydney.

We had an armed hitman on the loose.

Glenn and I scrambled, leaving the office and driving into the pre-weekend traffic, while the surveillance team kept updating us on Curtis's progress as he drove past the Myall Lakes turn-off, Port Macquarie and further north, towards the border with Queensland.

Glenn drives, while I handle the phone calls, liaising with the surveillance cops and our bosses at State Crime Command. We call Glenn Flatline, because his pulse never rises; he's good when the adrenaline is running and can handle this kind of situation.

'What do we do, Glenn?' I ask him.

'I'm not sure,' he answers, looking at me with a faint smile, then back at the road.

The alternatives are clear: stop Curtis – which means letting him and every other target we've been chasing know they're under surveillance – or let him go and risk having him shoot someone.

I call Chris, the current acting Homicide commander, who refers it up, to assistant commissioner Dave Hudson.

When Chris comes back, he says, 'It's your decision. Keep us informed.'

Great, I think. *You heroes.* I organise to get a plane up in the air to keep an eye on our target, and we keep on driving.

***

By now, it's almost seven years since Terry Falconer's body was dumped in plastic bags left floating in the Hastings River. Before my move to the Crime Manager's position at Chatswood, we'd got Rocco's evidence that the Perish brothers wanted to use his boat, but that alone was not enough to charge anyone over the murder. Rocco wasn't there when Terry was killed and didn't know how it happened.

I told the bosses that a team of six would need to work on it for six months to get to the point where someone could be charged, but no other detectives were put on it. Jason Evers left for Ballina, so Glenn and Nigel Warren – who'd both been part of the strike force from the beginning – took charge of the case. Then Nigel also got promoted elsewhere and was not replaced, so Glenn was on his own.

In late 2005, an informant revealed where Anthony Perish was hiding, on a semi-rural block in southwest Sydney leased from the State Government. He'd built a secure compound, complete with three-metre walls, electric fencing and 27 CCTV cameras. The police attempted to install listening devices in this fortress without success due to all the security in place, so in September 2006 they stormed it, arresting Anthony over drug offences from years before.

Inside, they found camouflage gear he wore to roam the property and surrounding land at night, as well as photographs of our police surveillance teams.

With Anthony, who'd been a ghost after going on the run over a decade before, now under arrest, the New South Wales Crime Commission hauled him in for questioning. They'd also been working with police, and their analysts had traced the phone networks of those thought to be close to Anthony, intercepting tens of thousands of phone calls, to see who was talking to who and what they were saying to each other.

The Crime Commission now went at Anthony, his brother Andrew and some of their other associates as hard as they could, but got little as the Perishes faced down their interrogators from inside the witness box.

An attempt to jail Anthony over the drug offences failed, and in March 2007 he was released and quickly disappeared.

That October, while I was stewing over the DPP's refusal to send the Bowraville case to the appeal court, Glenn learned that it was now his turn to be rotated out of Homicide. By then, I'd finally got out of Chatswood and back to State Crime Command, having taken a position in the Gangs Squad.

Gangs meant bikies, warring outlaw motorcycle clubs who called themselves the one percenters, had names like the Nomads, Comancheros or the Gypsy Jokers and who fought with fists and knives and guns over pride, territory or control of the drug trade. Being in Gangs meant dealing with a lot of drive-by shootings, cowardly attacks where houses were shot up to send a message, with little regard for who was sleeping in them. On one shift I went to the scenes of seven different shootings in a single night.

Hearing Glenn was being rotated out, I went to see the squad commander, asking him to let Flatline join my team and bring with him the Terry Falconer investigation. This job will make your name, I told my boss. It's big. Let us run it and we'll lock up more murderers than Homicide.

Only, he didn't want it, and we argued. I stormed out of his office, kicking the bin for effect and telling him the Perishes and their associates were major crooks who would only kill more people.

It risked making more enemies among the senior ranks, but I was putting the case first and politeness second.

Eventually, Glenn came to Gangs and we started work, only to be told by one boss that the case wasn't going anywhere and we'd been chasing rabbits down holes for years. There was pressure to shut down the investigation.

Despite this, the investigation kept expanding: soon there would be tentative links to nine other suspected murders or attempted murders in total in New South Wales, including the disappearance of Ian Draper, a cellarman who worked at a club in Sydney's southwest, in August 2001. Ian had given evidence against Andrew after witnessing a brawl in which a man had died. Andrew was found not guilty. Six week after his disappearance, Ian's car was found abandoned outside the Rebels national headquarters in Leppington.

There were three more open cases in Queensland, including one, a fatal shooting on the Gold Coast in April 2002, which was linked by DNA to the attempted murder of a man in Sydney later that same year. While there wasn't always a link between the Perishes themselves and all these crimes, as the connections between the men

I tell her I don't know.

'But what am I supposed to do all weekend?' she asks me.

Please just give me some peace on this one, I think. I barely have a minute to spare as it is with everything that's going on. I'm in a car speeding away from home, chasing a killer north towards the State border, I can't stop and think about our life together now. I can't just move between the different worlds that easily.

Coffs Harbour call. The stop has gone like clockwork. The second man inside the car with Curtis was driving when they pulled them over and produced his licence. They did a breath test and let him go, but they have got his details.

I copy them down. It's late but I call Bill, my old police academy classmate, at home. He now manages e@gle.i, our internal computer system.

'Bill, I need this done,' I tell him. I give him the name and licence details.

He looks them up. He says the man's linked to the Russian mafia.

We keep driving, heading north.

***

In the small hours, Curtis's car approaches the State border, which means the other New South Wales police surveillance will have to drop off. Once Curtis crosses into Queensland, no matter what he does, Glenn and I will have no power to arrest him.

I call Queensland Police's headquarters. By chance, the on-call officer is a detective sergeant, Darren, who's worked on their own investigation of the Gold Coast shooting that Strike Force Tuno is investigating, so we know him. When I tell him what's going on, he is able to talk down his bosses, whose first reaction to the news an armed hitman is heading over the border is to want to force Curtis's car off the road for fear he'll carry out a killing.

That would ruin our investigation. Telling his bosses what's at stake, Darren arranges for a local police team to take over the covert surveillance, as Glenn and I are still too far behind on the road to do it ourselves. We're also given the OK to keep following Curtis, though now I have to keep the Queensland cops informed of what's going on, as well as my commanders in Sydney. At least, in Copacabana, Tracy's gone to sleep. I'll try to repair that damage when I manage to get home.

Finally catching up with Curtis's car on the Gold Coast, we watch as the two men inside it pull up outside a string of pubs and nightclubs, walk in and come back out soon afterwards. Every time they disappear from view I tense, fearing the worst.

Around 5am, Curtis and the second man stop at Jupiters Hotel & Casino, go inside and book a room. Still playing cat-and-mouse, we get access to it when they leave a few hours later, and find they've left behind the packaging for a new mobile phone. All the identifying details, which we could use to trace their calls, have been cut from the packaging and taken with them. I'm impressed at how professional they are.

By now, Glenn and I have been up for over 24 hours, are still wearing the suits we wore to work yesterday, haven't washed and have barely eaten. We book into a cheap motel and put our heads down for a couple of hours, while the Queensland Police surveillance team keep following Curtis. After a short and broken sleep, as more phone calls come in to tell me that the two men are now heading for Brisbane, Glenn and I get back in our car and follow them again, relying on the stream of updates from the surveillance team in order to stay close, but always out of sight in the city's back streets, ready to respond at any moment.

This game goes on through Saturday afternoon. Curtis and the second man visit a series of pubs, walk inside, come out a short time later and drive on. It goes on through the night. Glenn and I battle with exhaustion, taking it in turns to drive. At one point, our targets drive about an hour out of Brisbane to visit a few more pubs before heading back into the city.

It continues through a second night. On Sunday morning, I get a call saying the surveillance team are watching Curtis on Brisbane's South Bank. 'He's meeting someone. It looks like Anthony Perish.' We've shared our information with Queensland Police, including Anthony's photograph. 'They have exchanged a bag. Do you want us to take them now?'

I feel excitement, and, again, a kind of professional respect. Anthony had disappeared again following his arrest over the drug charges. We'd no idea he'd even left Sydney.

We've got a new sense of the scale of his operation. We've found a string of pubs and clubs to which he's linked through the visits of Curtis and the second man over the weekend. The second man, himself a connection to the Russian mafia, suggests Anthony's business also has international links.

They're organised. They're smart. They're proper crooks.

'No. Let them go,' I say. 'We'll keep gathering intelligence.'

Curtis and the second man drive south, back home. Over the coming months, our investigation will suggest this trip had been to deliver drugs and pick up money owed to Anthony by the managers of several businesses he owned.

Glenn and I know this is big. It's every detective's dream. *I'm coming for you Anthony*, I think. But first, I have to go home and apologise to Tracy.

***

On 21 November 2008, I'm in the headquarters of State Crime Command, working on the Perish gang, when I get a call to say the jury is coming back in the trial of Gordon Wood for the murder of his fiancée, Caroline Byrne. It's now 13 years since Caroline's body was discovered.

I head for the Supreme Court in Darlinghurst, and hear the news on the way in: guilty.

When I get there, Paul Jacob, who led the investigation, says they're in a nearby bar with Caroline's father, Tony. I join them and we raise a glass to his daughter.

This is Personal

19 January 2009: 23 years in

It's early morning and most people will still be in their beds when I stand up in front of a roomful of violent men. 'I want you to hit him and I want you to hit him hard,' I tell them. A few of those listening to me nod. For them, this is not unusual. They are the State Protection Group (SPG), the shock troops of the New South Wales police, who train for sieges, terrorist attacks and the worst, most difficult arrests.

'Him' is the person in the photograph I stuck up in my office more than a year ago now. The person I think about when I come into work and who I think about when I leave. The person whose business dealings I've taken great satisfaction in unpicking since that long drive up to Brisbane with Glenn, following Brad Curtis.

It feels like he and I have been following each other's footsteps sometimes. Last year, when one of our telephone intercepts revealed he was on his way to Mudgee, a bush town 265 kilometres to Sydney's northwest, to do a concreting job, I sent two detectives to the town, telling them to ask around the local motels with his photograph, trying to locate him.

The first motel they walked into, a man walked in behind them. Well-groomed, a collared shirt and jeans, sharp eyes, it was the face in their photograph. Anthony Perish. They followed him until he turned down an isolated road and they had to drop back for fear of being spotted.

Later, they asked around the local concrete firms and one driver described doing a strange job at a property on that same isolated road; a slab was being laid above a hidden cavity dug into the ground.

Glenn and I arranged for a police helicopter to fly us up to Mudgee and, from the sky, we saw a shed was being built on top of the slab. It was the perfect set-up for a meth lab, the kind used to produce the drug that Anthony was said to have introduced to Australia and used to make his fortune. We were getting closer, following behind him. And now the time has come to let him know I'm coming.

***

For weeks, we have been planning for this moment. Last month, in December 2008, we arrested two other associates of Curtis's in a drug bust at a self-storage unit at Camperdown, in inner-west Sydney. Inside, we found a wallet containing a driver's licence in the name of Paul Elliott, a name which meant nothing, until a search of police records showed his burned-out car had been found the week before, and his girlfriend had reported him as missing.

We've got enough, I think, *to move and need to do so before anyone else is killed.* I decide to pull everybody in at once, hoping the shock and awe will make them talk, just like Operation Day in the Bob Ljubic murder investigation.

Only this time, it's bigger. Around 100 cops have been involved in planning the operation, including the SPG, uniformed cops, surveillance teams and the 16 people now working on the strike force. Resources are no longer an issue; the more we have uncovered, the more our bosses realised how this case is important. The plan is to arrest Anthony and Curtis together. It has to be done this way, partly because if we arrest one, we will alert the other and partly because although we have surveillance on Curtis, Anthony is still a ghost. We don't know where he is.

Everything needed to be ready at the moment, day or night, when our surveillance teams learned the two men would be meeting. We've drawn up operational orders and prepared ring binders of background information for each of our targets. We have search teams ready to hit Curtis's house and his mother's house, as well as Andrew Perish's house and the isolated property in Mudgee. Another team will stay on standby, ready to move if we can find an address for Anthony.

This meant long hours. We worked weekends and public holidays through the new year to get everything ready. When the bosses denied our overtime request, we kept working.

For weeks, I've also been training hard, waking early to run up the hills round Copacabana, or boxing and doing circuits in the work gym, getting fit for the stretch of sleepless days ahead.

Each day, when I got home, I practised qigong or meditation, seeking that feeling of when you're just about to fall asleep. When my thoughts about the case crowded in, or my fears and stresses about what could go wrong became overwhelming, I tried to let them pass, as if they were being carried down a river.

This discipline of being able to clear my mind was vital. With so much at stake, I knew that when the call came, and I needed to step into the ring I could not afford to feel fear or let doubt distract me. This is between Anthony and myself, going toe to toe, and I intended to be ready.

The plan is:

On day one, we arrest them but say nothing publicly.

On day two, we arrest or question another roughly 20 of their friends, family and criminal associates.

On day three, we release photographs from the arrests, hold a televised press conference and announce rewards for information about the murders our strike force is investigating.

I want anyone connected to the Perish operation to feel fear, at first when they hear rumours about the arrests, then that fear should grow as the arrests widen before we finally reveal the scale of our operation. I want them to doubt what those other people we've arrested may be saying. It has to feel like a creeping artillery barrage, a demonstration of police power that will shake the ground beneath them.

Anthony is strong, I sense, as is his brother Andrew. Both men have faced questioning about their alleged crimes before, and neither was broken. But I'm hoping Curtis turns out to be the weak link. He's a cleanskin, with no criminal record, although we think he's good for several murders. He's never had to deal with the police before. I hope he panics when he's in a cell and learns his home is being searched, and his wife and mother questioned.

Just knowing Anthony is also in a cell somewhere might be enough.

Maybe Curtis will roll over.

***

Around 11pm yesterday, Sunday 18 January, we intercepted a call in which Curtis and Anthony arranged to meet this morning. We don't know where they'll meet, but Anthony seems to spend a lot of time on Sydney's north shore, so we've set ourselves up in Chatswood Police Station, in the same room we used for Operation Day in the Bob Ljubic murder case.

All night, as I checked through our preparations, I thought about what could go wrong. The lessons from 18 years ago, when Isaac was shot inside his unit while I was talking to him, are still painful to remember.

***

Around 9am, surveillance cars follow Curtis to the Lavender Blue Cafe close to Sydney Harbour, where he and Anthony take a table next to a big, open window. We don't alert the café owners. We can't risk it. Instead, an unmarked van parks out the front of the building and a few cops dressed as tradesmen enter, find seats and order coffee.

We've got one chance to get this right. From Chatswood, I tell the SPG commander, 'You guys take them whenever you want them.' He's in charge now. Get it wrong and Anthony will disappear for good.

The commander gives an order and the back doors of the van burst open. Men in black body armour carrying high-powered weapons race down the path towards the café, while the undercover officers inside draw their pistols. Coffee cups are knocked over or dropped as the other customers respond in shock. Anthony and Curtis are hauled out through the café window and pushed onto the ground, guns pointing at their heads as their hands are bound behind them. Everybody plays their part perfectly.

I tell the commander to keep them there until I arrive. It's a ten-minute drive and when I get to the café, they're lying side by side, face down, black cable ties biting into the soft, pink flesh of their wrists. This is the first time Anthony and I have met in person. I want to show him who's in charge. Who's in control. This is my chance to show him who he's up against and, if I can, unsettle him before his interview.

He turns his head and looks up at me in silence.

A TV crew who were filming a fire down the road have captured the arrests on tape. The arrests make the evening news. The journalists ask us what is going on, but we stick to the plan and do not give them anything. I want to allow rumours and suspicion to run wild among Anthony's associates.

So far, I could not have written this better.

Underbelly

20 January 2009: 24 years in

It's 6am and I'm back in Chatswood Police Station, briefing the cops involved in the next salvo of the assault. Around the room is a line of whiteboards on which I'll tack every arrest, each search, each interview, who's talking and what they're saying. Every piece of information or evidence gained in any one of these can then be passed on to any other team, particularly the detectives running each of the different interviews, so they can use it to gain an advantage.

Throughout the day, I'm in touch with every team by phone. Each door we go through is another heavy round fired at the Perishes and, in among all the explosions, the noise can be deafening, with different, sometimes contradictory and high-pressure decisions to be made all the time. Kaan, a junior detective with a cool head, works with me, assessing what we've learned from one interview and how we can use it to create a detonation in another. I've warned him in advance, 'It's not going to be pretty, but nothing's going to be personal.'

At times I'm yelling, 'Not good enough, I need him found now!' It's full-on, but this is a big job, it matters. Right now, I don't have the time to worry about how the people I'm shouting at react.

The plan works. Brad Curtis is clearly shocked and the cops in the interview room with him, John and Dave, push him hard to roll over. At his house, we find a hitman's arsenal of guns, as well as bulletproof vests and police identification patches. Curtis also tells them about some military-grade explosives he has stored at his mother's place in Lane Cove, forcing us to seal off the street and send in the Bomb Squad, who take them away safely. Inside, among Curtis's other possessions, we find a bag of cat skulls.

He says he'd be prepared to talk.

***

On 21 January, we plan to launch a media blitz, encouraging other witnesses to come forward. The message is: *Anthony's hold on you is broken.*

Geoff, the new Homicide Squad commander, calls me and says that he'll be doing all the interviews. After years spent working on this high-pressure investigation and three days of making nonstop decisions, I lose patience. Geoff can tell from my silence something is wrong

He starts saying it's to protect me, a way of making sure I don't say anything in front of the media that I later contradict when called to the witness box in court.

'Fuck off,' I tell him, feeling insulted. I'm not some rookie constable who needs to be looked after. 'If you want to do a media stand-up, then you do yours. I'm going to do mine.' Then I hang up.

He calls back straightaway and says, 'All right, I'll do Ray Hadley on 2GB and you can do the rest of it.'

'Thank you,' I say and leave it there. I know I will regret this exchange later. Geoff doesn't tend to hold a grudge, but I wonder if I've made yet another enemy among my own police force, to go with Anthony Perish.

***

On 22 January, Brad Curtis spends 20 minutes on the phone with his children in tears, then seven hours talking to detectives. Glenn leads the interview while I wait outside, watching it live on the ERISP machine screen. Curtis shows no remorse and rolls on his mates to get a reduction in his sentence. Like other times when I've seen informants cut a deal to save themselves, it's hard to respect him. At least out here, where he can't see me, I don't have to hide the look of distaste on my face.

Curtis says he met Anthony at a bar in Kings Cross in 1997, around the time of the Wood Royal Commission, when the area was red hot with crooks. I wonder if Anthony dealt with the bent cops who were exposed by the royal commission. Certainly, he was on the run back then, yet Curtis says he never seemed to get in trouble with the Kings Cross detectives.

Curtis started to get work carrying out acts of violence for Anthony, telling others they were doing 'black ops' together. He justified it by saying the police would be thankful to them for taking the scum off the streets.

When Glenn asks about the murder of Terry Falconer, Curtis says Anthony wanted him to look over some documents he had. 'It had got to do with the murder of his grandparents and who could have done it. He wanted to bring the people to justice.'

'Did Anthony seem quite concerned about getting to the bottom of who killed his grandparents?' Glenn asks. We'd looked at this as one possible motive for Terry's murder; another was the suggestion Terry might be informing on the Rebels.

Curtis says it was all about Anthony's grandparents, 'I think he was impacted far more than anyone else. I don't know why. I don't know why. He was hell-bent, hell-bent on getting not only anyone that did it but anyone that knew about it.'

He says that Anthony paid him to kidnap Terry. Curtis approached two other men, Jake Bennie and Craig Bottin, who was also known as Skitz, on account of his violent mood swings. The three men used Curtis's car and stole the rego plates from a police car, planning to replace them after the job was done. Anthony gave them a police uniform shirt and a bottle of something chemical.

'Perish gave me strict instructions that, "He'll put up a fight, so make sure you handcuff him and put this anaesthetic over his mouth." He told me it was kind of like chloroform and it will just help him sleep.'

Once they'd kidnapped Terry, they cut off the tracking device he was wearing to monitor him on day release from prison and loaded his unconscious body into a metal toolbox in the back of another vehicle, a van. Inside it, they drove him to a house in Turramurra on Sydney's upper north shore, where Anthony was waiting.

Curtis says when they opened up the box, Terry tried to get out, 'so Anthony grabs his head and slams it down'.

'And then what happens?' Glenn asks.

'He shut the fuckin' lid.'

'Who shut the lid?'

'Perish.' Anthony told Curtis to load the box onto a white ute, which Curtis and another man, a rough bloke called Matthew Lawton, were to drive north, for hours, to a remote bush property at Girvan, over 200 kilometres away. Early on in the journey they heard noises coming from the back of the ute, but then these fell silent.

When they arrived at Girvan, Curtis says they found a run-down house and a large, corrugated-iron shed with strip lighting hanging from the ceiling. Lawton, who was driving at this point, turned the engine off and said they should go in the house. 'I asked "Aren't we going to get him out?", and he goes "No, we'll wait for Mate",' – meaning Anthony Perish.

Hours later, Anthony arrived. He told them to put on white plastic suits and spread plastic sheeting across the shed floor. Curtis says they opened up the toolbox and hauled Terry out, but he was dead. He says Anthony told him, 'Just remember everyone last saw you with the body, they're gonna think you're the killer, even your own mates. You're the one that's been seen, your car, but I'll help ya, I'll help ya get rid of it.'

Between them, they lifted Terry up using a block and tackle attached to his handcuffs. Curtis claims he stood back while the other men cut off Terry's clothes and pulled out his teeth. 'Then they started to, you know, do the job of cutting him up.' He says Anthony told him to get involved. They packed up the plastic bags. 'I was feeling sick after what I'd just seen and had also done.'

Afterwards, the men cleaned the shed floor with chemicals, burned the toolbox and the handcuffs outside on the property and loaded the bags into the ute. Curtis says that he was scared. He says he's not guilty of murder, but guilty of abduction and stupidity. Stupidity, I guess, for getting involved.

'I never intended for that guy to die,' he says. Anthony had told him he wanted to question Terry about who killed his grandparents, but 'he didn't even ask him one fuckin' question'.

We've got enough to go to court.

Anthony and his brother Andrew are tougher than Brad Curtis. They refuse to answer any questions.

***

In the months following the arrests, in mid-2009, my bosses in State Crime Command say I should talk to a TV company. After keeping our investigation undercover for almost a decade, Strike Force Tuno was big news. The TV producers have also recently proved a sensation with their 2008 crime drama series *Underbelly*, based on the Melbourne gangland wars in which dozens of people were murdered. New series are being planned and I figure my bosses want to show the New South Wales police can be just as tough as our counterparts in Victoria.

The producers say they want to write a drama based on the case and for me to be one of the central figures. I'm excited. This was good police work and I'm not about to back away from it in public. Also, with all the fights I've had with my bosses over the years, it's started to feel like I have a target on my back and the public profile of being in a television show might make it harder for anyone to get rid of me. The politics inside the cops is fierce, especially as you climb up the ranks. A couple of mates have already warned me, 'Just be careful, they will go after you.'

The other guys on the strike force also seem flattered by the attention and the senior command approve the series. Everyone seems happy, but I start to see how this could be uncomfortable. Already, the writers are talking to Pam, my ex, and Tracy, my current partner. Pam's cautious at first, though I try to joke that our relationship is worthy of a TV series. She reminds me her life's moved on, she's married now, and says her new husband is only going to hate me more after watching the two of us on screen.

Tracy says she doesn't have a problem with it, though I start to suspect she's really less than happy with the prospect. She's a high-profile businesswoman, who travels the country for work or to give keynote speeches at conferences. She's used to being the centre of attention.

At work, people now seem to be spooked at the thought of how they will appear on screen. I don't know what's going on with Glenn; I barely see him in the office now. I try to talk to him a few times, but he's always caught up with something else.

I can understand it. I try to play it cool but I'm also wondering and worrying over who they find to play me on screen.

My heart jumps when the producers call and say they've found an actor. It's like I'm being judged – this person is the way other people will see me. They say he's called Matt Nable, a former professional footy player and boxer, who's currently in the US, filming a movie called *Killer Elite* with Robert De Niro. I look him up online and he seems tough, a hardarse, and when we talk on Skype, I can see he's smart as well. We talk about the work I've done in Bowraville and he seems to care about it. We meet for breakfast when he's next in Sydney and it feels natural talking to him.

Matt tells me he's been playing a bikie in an upcoming TV series about the Milperra massacre, when the Bandidos and Comancheros went to war in 1984, and doesn't have another bad guy in him at the moment. He says he's got a sense of who I am, and likes it. I'm flattered. I can already see him watching me, thinking about how he will put my mannerisms and character on screen.

I go to the first script reading, with all the actors sitting round a table, and I'm starstruck. But by the end of the evening I'm feeling comfortable. I defy anyone to have a TV series written about them and not enjoy the process. When they finish the read-through, I tell them to do it one more time with feeling. Jonathan LaPaglia, the actor playing Anthony Perish, quips, 'You don't look that tough.'

'I'd fucking chew you up and spit you out,' I tell him. He laughs. It's a new world, and I like it.

***

The *Underbelly* series also brings pressure with it. With the trial of the Perish brothers and Matthew Lawton coming up over Terry Falconer's death, I'm already feeling the weight of expectation from my bosses and the prosecution lawyers. While the series won't be shown until the trial is over, so as not to prejudice the court process, the TV producers are saying how they've invested all this money and really need convictions.

Other trials are also coming down the line towards us, dealing with some of the other crooks we've picked up through Strike Force Tuno's investigations, which bring with them more pressure. I try to ignore it. Pressure is what you accept in the cops and I want to bring the same single-minded focus in preparing for court that I learned from Paul Jacob this time around, despite the protests from the strike force at the pace of work, and the intrusions caused by the TV series.

Much worse, our analyst, Camille Alavoine, who's worked the case since 2001 and has already fought off cancer once, is told the disease is back. I worry about her; over the years, I've seen Camille work herself into the ground. She just keeps going and going and going.

'You don't have to work on this, you've done everything you can,' I say to her.

'This is what I've dedicated my life to. I want to see it through,' she tells me.

It's tragic, and as death approaches she's desperate to hand over her work on the investigation to another analyst. I ask the bosses if we could replace her in time for Camille to do the handover in person, so she doesn't feel all her work has been wasted. The request is refused.

One day, Camille comes into my office and breaks down, saying she is scared of dying. Having spent years dealing with death only after it happens as a Homicide detective, here it was sitting inside my office with me. I shut the door and told Camille she had every right to be scared, that it was only right to show fear after being so brave for so long.

Without Camille, and her selfless attitude to seeing someone jailed for Terry's murder, the case wouldn't be close to where we've got it, but she is not replaced before finally being admitted into the hospital. It's a hideous, bureaucratic decision. When I go to see Camille on the ward, she gives me an envelope with money inside it.

'When I die, I don't want a funeral, but can you put this on the bar and people can have a drink?' she asks. A week or two later,

Camille dies, so I get some people together and we go and have a beer with the money. Her loss rocks me. I've lost a friend. Someone I relied on. Yet, when that night is over, we still have to go back into work.

Everybody dies, I know that, and know that it can happen in a moment. Now I know it acutely. But the job has to continue. Camille would expect it. As unsteady as I feel without her presence on the strike force, there is no other way to live.

***

By the time we get to court, for a committal hearing in June 2010, it's been eight years since we first spoke to Rocco, our key informant. His evidence that the Perish brothers wanted to use his boat to dispose of a body is going to be critical; it could mean the difference between murder and manslaughter.

In those eight years, he's met someone and settled down. He's started a family. When we visit to ask if he's still prepared to give evidence, Rocco says, 'Fuck, I put my life on hold for you guys, but now I've got my life in order, I've got kids, you're going to drag me right back into this shit again?'

He's always been difficult at times. I remember when, in 2008, I got a call from him one night, asking to meet in a deserted car park. When I arrived, his car was parked on its own, with the lights off and Rocco sitting on the back seat. I got in the front and he asked me: 'How do I know I can trust you?'

My mind raced. This bloke had been charged with murder once, and convicted of manslaughter. I stared straight out the windscreen, and hoped my voice would hide my fear.

'You're asking me how you can trust me?' I replied. 'Fuck me, you're sitting behind me in a car at night in the middle of nowhere, you've probably got a gun pointed at me as we speak and you're asking me *how you can trust me*?'

Now, two years on, Rocco is working and paying taxes. He says he's enjoying a settled life, without having to look over his shoulder. It means that he's got more to lose – and plenty of time to worry about things now.

We talk him round. He tells me how it was his manslaughter conviction that put him on the road leading to this point. Years ago, Rocco was part of a bikie gang who set out to bash a bloke, only someone pulled a knife and their victim was killed. It didn't sit right with Rocco to be a part of that, even if he wasn't the one who did the stabbing. He needed to get out of the bikie world for good and cooperating with us is one way of making sure he can never go back there. But he's nervous. I tell him to trust me.

But even with him on board, the court process is slow, particularly as the prosecution barrister gets sick and has to be replaced, and it is another year before we get the Perish brothers to trial in July 2011. Not long before the hearing, I get a call from Rocco, asking for my address.

'Mate, I can't give you that,' I tell him. Home is my safe place. Cops don't publish their addresses, because catching crooks means that we can be targets. I've seen it happen, when Reg Irish was threatening my family years ago. It's not just our own safety we're protecting, but our loved ones'.

'I've put my life in your hands,' Rocco says. 'I could and probably will get killed because of this. You want me to trust you? You've gotta show that you trust me.'

Could I trust him? I tried again, 'I am a cop, Rocco. I can't have bad guys turning up at my place.'

'If you don't give me your address I won't be coming to court.'

'Fuck it,' I say, and give him the details.

A week later, I receive an envelope containing scribbled notes of the rego plates from cars he thought were following him during the investigation, and of the different times he saw helicopters overhead or footprints in the earth outside his place and feared people were coming for him. His paranoia isn't news to me, but it's impressive to see it written out, like a record of his fears over the years that we've been working together.

I call him and confirm what he has sent me, so he knows the address I gave him was correct.

'See you in court,' he tells me.

***

Shortly before the trial begins, Anthony Perish offers to plead guilty to manslaughter but not murder. Tactically, I think his offer is a dumb move; it shows us that he thinks we've got him, but I'm so tired and beaten up by the pressure we're all under, I am tempted to take it.

The *Underbelly* writers are still following the case, getting material for the series, and it feels like half the strike force are trying to hide their private lives from them while the other half are desperate to make it onto television. Glenn and I are managing to keep it civil while we work together, and I hope our friendship will repair itself once all of this is over. Every day brings another bust-up to be refereed: at one point I have to deal with a complaint that Rocco has been showing the female cops a photo of himself in a spa with a beer bottle in front of his penis.

Glenn and I talk to the prosecution barrister, Paul Leask, about Anthony's offer. He's a good, switched-on and intense lawyer, which means, right now, he is absolutely what we need.

'No, fuck it, let's run with it. We've got him for murder,' Paul says. The guilty plea is rejected.

The case runs on for months, through the winter of 2011 and into spring. As a witness, I have to wait outside the courtroom until I'm called to give evidence, meaning I sit there wondering what's going on inside. The division between Glenn and I has also seemed to spread through the strike force and I hear whispers other cops are calling me a media whore because of the TV series. It gets so bad, the lawyers representing the Perish brothers invite me to have lunch with them because they see me sitting out there on my own as they walk in and out of the courtroom.

Not that they go easy on me when I make it into the witness box. Instead, Andrew Perish's barrister, a terrier called Winston Terracini SC, focuses on the failure of the listening device when Rocco claimed that he'd got a confession.

'Did you get a report from the scientific and technical branch about this?' asks Terracini loudly, in a disbelieving tone that tells the jury, *Look at this performance.*

I reply, 'No, I didn't.'

'It must have been *so* frustrating and disappointing that, out of all the tapes, that it just malfunctions when the confession is tumbling out?' he wheedles.

'It's happened to me on other murder investigations, and I was as frustrated then as I was on this occasion,' I deadpan.

'Can you tell us one?' he asks me, turning to the jury, as if saying, *He's making this all up. Now watch him twist himself in knots.*

'Yes, I can. The murder of Bob Ljubic,' I say. 'The device failed in that case too and we still got a conviction.' That shuts him up. Terracini is too smart to let his reactions show in court, but he drops off the line of questioning.

When it is Rocco's turn to speak, I realise how impressed I am by him. He's risked his life by giving evidence, and turned his life around in the time I've known him. I can't excuse what's in his past, but that was then. I've trusted him with my life now. He knows my address. Redemption's a huge part of being a cop. Sometimes we're solving cases and helping punish crooks, and sometimes we're helping the criminals to turn their lives around. It is a privilege to play a part in someone's absolution.

Anthony Perish declines to give evidence. His version of events, according to his lawyer, is that he only wanted to kidnap Terry Falconer, but arrived at the property at Girvan and found the journey there inside the box had killed him.

Paul Leask, the prosecution lawyer, challenges this account. The case, he says, comes down to the evidence of Rocco.

As Paul says, when Rocco first told us his story, back in 2002, neither he nor we knew anything about the significance of Girvan, where Terry was dismembered. Girvan is over 170 kilometres south of where Terry's body parts were found in the Hastings River. Yet Rocco said the Perish brothers wanted him to bring his boat up the Karuah River. A tributary of the Karuah flows close to Girvan.

That shows the plan was always to kill Terry, Paul argues. Accept Rocco's evidence, he tells the jury, and you have to find this was a case of murder.

The jury believe him. After a week's deliberation, in September 2011, Anthony Perish and Matthew Lawton are found guilty of murder, while Andrew is found guilty of conspiracy to murder.

Anthony just stares at me as the verdict is read out, so I stare back. But, inside me, relief wells up. For one thing, this vindicates Rocco. For another, it means that he is surely safer with the Perish brothers in jail.

After another, months-long delay, the judge holds a sentencing hearing in March 2012, during which Terry Falconer's son James reads out a Victim Impact Statement saying his father died with 'no dignity, no respect and no mercy'. Raising his eyes to meet the eyes of the convicted men, he says his dad was 'like a lion being pulled down by a pack of sniffing hyenas'.

The judge accepts the Victim Impact Statement, acknowledges 'the grief and distress of the deceased's family', and offers his sympathy.

On 13 April 2012, the judge hands down his sentence. Anthony gets 24 years with a non-parole period of 18 years, Andrew gets 12, of which he must serve nine, and Matthew Lawton gets 20 years with 15 before he can be released.

All up, over their different trials, 14 criminals charged by Strike Force Tuno are sentenced for crimes including murder, attempted murder, kidnapping, shooting, conspiracy to murder, drug manufacture and distribution, armed hold-up and firearms offences.

Brad Curtis is sentenced over the kidnapping as well as two other shootings, and asks that a long string of a further 14 offences is taken into account. He's jailed for 20 years, having received a 50 per cent discount on what the judge would have awarded him if he hadn't cooperated with police and will later die in prison.

Jake Bennie, who took part in Terry's kidnapping from the smash-repair workshop, is sentenced to three years in prison, with two years non-parole. Craig Bottin, the third man that day, gets five years, with a minimum of three.

Every charge that Strike Force Tuno lays results in a conviction. *You don't get results like this,* I think, *unless you're prepared to pay the price to get them.* Working murders is the ultimate responsibility, and you have to be prepared to meet it, even if it leaves you with nothing. Look at our analyst Camille, whose work on this case was the last thing she did in the police, or look at my relationship with Glenn, who stands apart from me in the courtroom to watch the Perish brothers' sentencing. The friendship between us has finally been broken by the pressure we've been under. My relationships with some of my bosses may also never recover from all the confrontations sparked by my demands for more staff, time and resources to work on this case.

At home, the case has damaged my relationship with Tracy, with whom I could have spent all those evenings and weekends I instead spent in the office. Or I could simply have been a better, more balanced person if I'd had that time.

But that is what it costs to work murders, and I don't regret it. I would rather pay up than try explaining to Terry's family why we let his killers walk free.

This has been a once-in-a-career case, but just before the *Underbelly* series is broadcast in August, I get cold feet. I tell the producers I'm worried about the sex scenes they've filmed between the actors playing Pam and me. Too much of my private life has already been wounded or left exposed by my job, I tell them. They get it, and when I watch the program, on my own at home – Tracy is in Perth for work – the sex scenes have been cut.

At first, watching my life play out on screen, I want to curl up into a foetal position. Then I unwind. They've captured who I think I am; a complex person who is hard when he needs to be hard but is also vulnerable as well. My life changes with all the attention; I get more calls from journalists and there are posters for the show on the side of buses driving through the city. I go out drinking with Matt Nable and people come up to tell him how they love him in *Underbelly*.

When they are gone I look at him and joke, 'Fuck me, you're the pretend Gary Jubelin. *I'm* the real Gary Jubelin.'

Even working the perfect Homicide investigation, the one where every charge results in a conviction, is really a lose-lose, I realise, because your starting point's a killing, there's no way of changing that.

But maybe that suits me. Ever since I started to play soccer growing up, I've always performed better when I'm on the losing side.

***

Not every case can end in a conviction. Two months before the Perishes were sentenced, on 24 February 2012, the appeal court announced its verdict after hearing a challenge to the conviction of Gordon Wood for the murder of Caroline Byrne. Despite interviewing Gordon in London in 2001, I haven't worked on the case since leaving Homicide and so am not there in person as the three judges hand down their 186-page judgment.

It's devastating to the police case.

In cold, black type, the judgment details the lack of any police photographs or contemporaneous records of where Caroline's body was discovered at the base of The Gap in 1995. This led to controversy in 2004, the year I left the Homicide Squad for Chatswood, when the police were forced to change their estimate of where Caroline landed.

This in turn caused problems for the physics professor the prosecution relied on as an expert witness in court, Associate Professor Rod Cross from the University of Sydney. He'd argued Caroline could not have jumped the distance between the cliff edge and where she made impact, so must have been thrown over. His findings were subsequently disputed.

What made things worse was Professor Cross's publication of a book about his role in the case after Gordon's conviction. According to the court judgment, this showed 'he clearly saw his task as being to marshal the evidence which may assist the prosecution to eliminate the possibility of suicide and leave only the possibility of murder'.

Reading on, the judges also criticised the prosecution barrister, Mark Tedeschi QC. His argument that Gordon killed his fiancée because she wanted to end their relationship was 'entirely speculative', according to the judgment. Tedeschi had suggested Caroline might also have been killed to stop her revealing details of the Offset Alpine Printing scandal involving Gordon's boss, businessman Rene Rivkin. This, too, was dismissed by the appeal judges.

'There is nothing in the evidence which justifies the prosecution's speculation with respect to the applicant's motive,' said the Chief Judge, Peter McClellan. Throughout the judgment, Gordon is referred to not by name but as 'the applicant', because he applied to the appeal court to challenge the guilty verdict.

Without motive, certainty where Caroline's body was recovered or confidence in its expert witness, the judges were not prepared to let the guilty verdict stand. 'Suspicion and conjecture, even grave suspicion, is not a proper basis for the finding of guilt.'

Gordon's actions and statements, both before and after Caroline's death, 'require careful consideration', the judgment read. 'It would seem that he lied about some matters. Certainly his behaviour was at times unusual.'

But this was not enough. Perhaps they could be explained. The way the court system works, Gordon did not have to explain them. 'The Crown must prove its case. No burden falls upon the applicant.'

The prosecution had not proved its case. The judges ordered Gordon's conviction be overturned and that he instead be found not guilty.

That's how the system works. The highest court in New South Wales had spoken. I was still proud to have worked on that case. After the appeal court judges stood and walked out of the courtroom, Caroline's father, Tony, left with my old sergeant, Paul Jacob. I felt guilty not to be there with them. I could only guess how both men were feeling.

***

Like every other case, I carried this decision home, where Tracy has now learned to judge the way the verdict has played out from the expression on my face when I walk in. She knew not to worry, as the frown lines would relax once I'd had time to do my meditation. It is almost a year now since she and I were married, on 12 November 2011, in a ceremony held in Port Macquarie, a place full of memories for me, both good and bad – from holidays when the kids were little, to setting up the strike force investigating Terry Falconer's murder.

The two of us had found a balance between us. We've also bought an apartment together in Pyrmont, in Sydney's inner-west, near the harbour, but we still have our different lives. Tracy's business, working in specialist mental health services for Aboriginal people, was going well, although she was spending more time running it from Perth these days than on the east coast living with me. We'd got engaged among the waterfalls and vine forests of Litchfield National Park, in the Northern Territory, during a trip for Tracy to give a keynote speech in nearby Darwin.

That night, she'd gone out in the city with some girlfriends, while I went back to the hotel and watched a boxing match on TV, thinking life didn't get any better. With her often in Perth and me in Sydney, the distance separating the two cities meant that I could concentrate on work during the week then fly over on a Friday evening, switch the phone off and watch out the plane window as the red desert unfolded beneath me in silence.

In Perth, I wasn't a Homicide detective. I could relax. Selling the townhouse in Copacabana and leaving the kids behind during the move to Pyrmont had been a wrench, made easier by the fact they were older now, with Jake at university and Gemma finishing school. They're growing up, making their own way into the world and don't need me around so often.

I am excited about the future. Just before our marriage, I took a few months long service leave from the cops and spent it with Tracy in Perth, helping with her business. With the company going well, she told me how she wanted to make the wedding a big event, so we hired a rural property near the Hastings River and had a wedding planner fly up from Sydney to meet us. We brought in marquees, a bar, a dancefloor and a lighting crew. There was a boat cruise. Tracy's family came over from the Pilbara, and the Bowraville mob also made the journey from the Mission.

It was a different world for them, and for me also. It was an outdoor service, with chairs for the assembled friends and family arranged in rows on the pasture overlooking the river. Standing there in my new suit, I'd come so far since my first wedding, held near where Debbie and I grew up, where my mates cheered us on from the awning of the nearby bottle shop.

Together with our guests, waiting for Tracy's arrival, we watched the clouds gather: first bruise-purple, then black. Tracy walked down the aisle as the first raindrops started to spatter. We made it through the service before the storm, but then it was chaos, with floods of water deeper than our ankles. I took my shoes and socks off and rolled my trousers up to carry Tracy to a house on the property.

During the reception, somebody told me, 'You're bloody.' A leech had crawled up my arm and the whole sleeve was crimson.

Let's get away from here, I thought, as Tracy and I got into our chauffeured car to leave that night.

We were looking forward. Tracy was smart and fun. She stood for something. Her career was going well and at work, I'd just received an unexpected invitation from Peter, the new Homicide Squad commander, to return to it from Gangs and take up a senior role in the Unsolved Homicide Unit, reviewing old, unsolved cases that have often been forgotten – except by the victims' families – to see if new technology or sheer determination could make a difference.

It felt like the best fit for a cop with my skills and experience. I like the tough cases. Not working on fresh murders also meant fewer pressures, fewer sleepless nights and other sacrifices for myself and those around me.

Just before Tracy and I drove away from the wedding, her sister jumped into the car. She was looking for her teenage son, could we help her? Of course. I was feeling happy – freshly married, the crooks in my career case all inside prison cells, and, with my new marriage, leaving behind us a period when my personal life had too often been out of balance. There had been too much darkness over the past decade; I'd lost my sifu, got formally divorced from Debbie, split from Pam, and endured a painful break in my friendship with Jason Evers.

But I'd also formed new relationships, with Rocco and Axeman among others. Our relationships are based on the fact I don't judge them, which is something I learned in Bowraville, where both sides, the police and the Mission families, had to get over their distrust of the other.

After buying the apartment in Pyrmont, I'd also found a new sifu, Chan Yong Fa, who taught in Sydney's Chinatown and was not afraid to slap me in the face and call me an 'angry policeman' if I turned up scowling to our Saturday morning qigong classes.

Getting older, I was more confident about talking to other cops about my qigong and meditation. I'd proved myself as a Homicide detective during this phase of my life and, with that, some of my old insecurities had washed away. I wasn't worried about whether other cops saw me as a hardarse detective, which made me more willing to talk about this softer side of my personality and the benefits I'd got from it. And, the older I got, the more obvious those benefits became. When many of my generation of detectives were having to let their belts out as their bellies spread, I could still train as hard as people 10 or 15 years younger.

The noise of the wedding reception started to fade behind us. I was getting some perspective; while it had been a dark decade during which my private life had fallen apart, it had also been a time when I'd been at my most dangerous to criminals. Linda Wilson, Jeffrey Hillsley and the Perish brothers had all been jailed. *I can take it easier now*, I thought. *Maybe I can rest on my laurels.*

The car swerved. A body was lying on the road. We stopped, and I told Tracy and her sister to wait in the car before running back to find it was a young Aboriginal bloke – just like the one on Norco Corner.

It was Tracy's nephew. Like my own son, Jake, he'd drunk too much at the wedding. Drunk. I looked at him lying there, head lolling back, completely out of it and thought how this could easily have ended in a tragedy. That's the fine line between life and death. Whose fault would it have been if something had happened to him? His for drinking too much and ending up on the road, where he was so vulnerable? Ours, for allowing him to drink?

Either way, your past has a way of catching up with you. You are the product of your actions.

I helped to get him in the car.

Round Three

Enough to Walk Away

December 2013: 28 years in

The needle hurts, but not enough to make me flinch. Beneath its point, the Sanskrit symbol 'Om' is emerging in blue ink etched into the skin of my right bicep, which is my stronger arm when I am boxing. Om is a holy word, one we chanted at a meditation retreat where I spent time in Nepal earlier this year. I don't think I've ever been as relaxed as I was then, getting up early in the morning to do some boxing training on my own, then taking part in group sessions doing yoga, meditation or doing a painting of Buddha, which is now hanging in my kitchen.

When we arrived, they asked us why we were at the retreat. I said I'd taken a year off working at the police and spent the time instead in Perth with my new wife, but would soon be heading back to the world of Homicide investigation. I wanted to be prepared, to find a sense of peace I could carry with me into the battles ahead.

This tattoo is a reminder to myself of what I learned there, about trying to be peaceful. That's my soft side. To balance it, I've also had the words 'Better to die on your feet than live on your knees' tattooed on my left ribs, above my heart. That is how I intend to live my life from this moment forward.

The tattooist shifts in his chair. Behind him, the warm Perth sun filters through the glass of his dark shopfront. Over the past year, I've also taken other trips, riding a motorbike round Vietnam, surfing in the Maldives and a cycling trip through Thailand with Bill, my old mate from the police academy. Each trip was like a window into my old, hippy lifestyle before joining the cops, a world I had since pulled a curtain over. I found some of that sense of joy that I'd been missing while riding my motorbike, sitting on my surfboard looking at the horizon or cross-legged on the floor in Nepal. I started to accept I can have both sides in me: detective and hippy.

Most of the past year, though, has been spent in Perth with Tracy. She's building her business up and explained how her earning capacity is greater than mine in the cops, so the more I was able to free her up to focus on that, the more we could earn as a couple.

The agreement was it would be just for a year. I do the groceries, tidy up at home and pick up the slack for her at work, doing office administration and even getting involved in bigger decisions like the hiring and firing of people.

I still travelled back to Sydney often, staring out of the plane window at the dead heart of Australia. There are always court hearings for old cases including, earlier this month, an inquest into the death of a 33-year-old called Ryan Pringle, who was shot by police at a remote property near Tenterfield, in northern New South Wales, over a year and a half ago.

Police shootings are called 'critical incidents' and they're seen as being serious enough that the Homicide Squad investigates them. Ryan, who suffered from schizophrenia, had been staying on an isolated property as part of a spiritual gathering called the 'School of Happiness'. When we arrived, we learned that, late at night, he started making death threats against the other campers and two local cops were called out. The two cops were a couple, which is not unusual in country towns and they were thrown into a nightmare together, trying to find their way around in the pitch-black and help the other people flee, when Ryan came at them out of the darkness, carrying a crossbow.

He walked towards them, refusing to put the weapon down and at one point yelling, 'I'm going to kill you.' Carter, the police sergeant thought his partner, Karen, a senior constable, had been shot and, in his torchlight, saw Ryan a few metres away, pointing the crossbow at him. Carter fired four times. The closer we looked, the more we saw he had no choice but to do it.

After his death, Ryan's blood showed a concentration of more than 10 times his prescribed dose of anti-psychotic medication, as well as a cocktail of other chemical traces, including oxycontin, marijuana, speed, methamphetamine and alcohol. At the inquest, the coroner said Ryan 'was a man who lost his mind'. He cleared both the local cops of wrongdoing, recommending them instead for bravery awards.

Ryan's father also told the two cops he didn't blame them. 'I share your pain,' he said in the coroner's court. 'The discharge of your firearm was not only the last resort but was imperative in the deteriorating reasoning of my son.'

It was another tragedy, and a reminder of how close we tread alongside death when doing this job. It comes for you out of the darkness.

In Perth, one of the highlights of this year has been working on the renovations to the home Tracy and I share here. She wanted something special, so we designed a lap pool, a walk-in wardrobe and an outdoor gym. The house would be full of sunshine. I enjoyed working on the ideas and talking to the architects, creating something for the first time, rather than spending my days at crime scenes where we arrive only after life has fled, and in the morgue for autopsies, watching the dissection.

You can't escape this work, though. Not once you have started. One time, I sat in our house in Perth for two days and a night without sleeping to finish a report on the Bowraville murders.

Nor would I want to stay here, for it means missing my family. At home, on the east coast, my son, Jake, says he wants to join the army. I'm proud of him for the decision, and also glad that he has made a choice to see more of the world rather than simply grow up, live and die on the Central Coast, like so many others. But, as a parent, it is also sad, having to accept my boy's no longer a child, and it is no longer my role to parent him. The army will do that for me.

My daughter, Gemma, is also growing up. She's taken a year out, working in admin at her old school. The older she gets, the more she looks like her mother, Debbie, and, just like her mum, I'm learning not to underestimate her. Gemma is capable, confident and never flustered. There's a strength of character and a hardness to her. No one will walk over Gemma.

As much as I want to see more of them, having this confidence in both my kids was what made it possible for me to come to Perth in the first place. They have the right values. They're not going to fuck up their lives without me.

If anything, I've been feeling more disorientated by the move than they have. I hardly knew anybody here when I arrived in this city and have had to find a new sense of who I was for the first time in almost three decades, without being a policeman.

Since arriving, I've joined a kung fu class, working with a former disciple student of Master Chan, who I train with in Sydney. Every Sunday we practise qigong outside in the morning sun and I've started to explore this culture more, joining the other students to take part in lion dancing during the local Chinese community festivals.

I also train at a boxing gym run by a former State champion and Golden Gloves winner, David 'Iceman' Letizia. Dave's a hard man, and I had to prove myself when I first walked into his gym but now, when one of his boxers is in camp preparing for a fight, I train with them, running up hills together and living as disciplined a life as they do.

I'm proud that I've been able to earn their respect. Boxing

tests every aspect of your personality, exposing your strengths and weaknesses in public. Dave's gym is a place full of genuinely hard people and I am surviving within it. After watching me train, he invited me to start sparring and saw that I could take a hit. From then on, we'd go hard at each other and I got my nose broken again. A photograph taken afterwards, shows me bruised and bloody but smiling. I'd proven to myself that I could step out from behind the police badge.

When Tracy saw that I was thriving, she started to remind me how uncomfortable things got in the cops after the Strike Force Tuno investigation and the *Underbelly* series. She got an accountant to look at our finances, including my super. 'You've got enough to walk away and we'll do this together,' she told me. She wanted me to leave the cops and stay in Perth.

If Tracy and I were out with friends in Perth and someone mentioned *Underbelly*, she would shut down the conversation.

Sitting in the tattoo parlour, as the warm sun washes over the street outside, part of me is tempted to stay here, despite what I told the organisers of the meditation retreat in Nepal. Being here, I've reconnected with the hippy side of myself I thought I'd lost. There are new worlds to explore here. There is a freedom; I can train in the morning, then have a nice breakfast and sit outside reading the newspaper rather than heading into work each morning before most other people have left the house.

As the tattooist picks away at the final curling point of the Om symbol, I also know there's been another area of lightness over the past 12 months; not having to bear the weight of responsibility being a Homicide detective demands of you.

It is hard work. Few other jobs involve being called out in the middle of a winter's night and standing there, sleepless and freezing, looking at a broken, bloodied body while knowing that all you have to look forward to right now is an autopsy. Part of me wants to be excused from picking up that load again.

And yet – I chose to do this work because the work, to me, is sacred. It has a moral weight. The gravity of being a policeman is pulling me back to the east coast. There is also a drifting, weightless feeling to being – well, what am I? – in Perth. I miss the daily intensity of working murders and I miss knowing my role within that work. I am an expert in it. My toughness, my relentlessness, all the things that have led me to fall out with my colleagues and bosses in the past, are also advantages when your job is catching killers. Life is sunny here in Perth but I don't have a purpose.

I told them the truth at that meditation retreat among the Himalayan mountains; however far I have travelled this past year, I've always known in my heart that I was going back to the New South Wales Police Force.

I'm not done with the cops yet. Policing is the one thing I am really good at.

***

Another realisation. While I was thousands of kilometres away in Perth, my sister-in-law Lisa died in Port Macquarie after a long fight with cancer. She was a wild, loving and funny woman, who'd helped light up our family. A great mum and someone who was always laughing.

I flew back, having been so distant from my family for so long, and the suffering her illness and death had caused them threatened to overwhelm me.

With most deaths, I am fairly stoic. I can stand up at a funeral or in court and say what has to be said. This time, I saw my brother, Jason, and found it hard to talk to him. He and Lisa had three kids. Instead, I just looked at him in silence. I realised how much I admired him.

I've chosen one path in life and Jason chose another. Mine led me to a place where I had won promotions, faced down killers and got public recognition. My name was in the newspapers and on the TV news reports, but Jason has done more than I have done. He'd gone out to work each day and come home to his children. He'd fought alongside Lisa for years while she was sick. He'd held his family together.

Jason was more a man than I was.

***

I need to go back to work.

After a year out of the police, I've done what I said I would in Perth, helping with Tracy's business and the renovations. The house is looking beautiful, easily the nicest place I've ever lived in, but I know that, at work, leaving my senior position in the Unsolved Homicide Unit means I will not get it back and I resent that. It doesn't seem to bother Tracy.

It feels like our relationship's been different since our wedding. We still get on, we can sit and laugh together, but it feels as if she's trying to control me. We have also retreated from each other physically, we don't hug or kiss the same way that we used to. I need that part of our relationship and, not having it, have started to turn to my boxing instead for those bodily feelings of hitting and being hit, for that rush of adrenaline when you climbs into the ring, and that stomach sickness afterwards.

I want to feel alive. Too often, living our life in Perth, I'm missing that.

I should have faced this earlier. It's like when I was at school, if someone said something that cut me, I wouldn't find a way to deal with the injury, but would instead try to ignore it, so the wound would fester, until something erupted.

Over the past 12 months with Tracy, it's as if I've been trying to ignore the part of me that is a cop and found I cannot function as only half a person. It's like the way I meditate because it gives me a sense of peace in a life full of conflict. In Perth, I've realised that meditation on its own is not enough. To be complete, I need to go and pick a fight.

I tell Tracy I am going back to Sydney. She says she's staying in Perth. We agree to start living on either side of the country again. We can each fly over every second weekend.

In January 2014, I travel back to Sydney, alone.

It doesn't work. Every second weekend will soon become every three, or four. Or we might have a good weekend in Perth, then I'll fly back and by the time I've landed in Sydney, Tracy isn't answering my calls. There are long silences between our conversations. In Sydney, I discover I am lonely here, as well. After a year away, I've lost contact with my old mates.

We try a marriage counsellor. We try a few.

In February 2014, I put on my suit and walk back into the Homicide Squad offices, past the wall covered with the yellowing front pages of newspapers writing up old arrests, to take my place among the rows of desks overflowing with paperwork and coffee cups. I listen to the old office sounds, the telephones ringing, the keyboards tapping and voices calling across the room. They seem louder to me somehow, after a year away, and it's hard to make sense of anything amid the noise.

I haven't been assigned to any team, just given a desk and a stack of old, cold cases, to see if I can make anything of them. I feel isolated. I watch other cops go out for coffee with their teams, while I will often leave the building at the end of the day having barely spoken to anyone.

Outside work, friends and family say, 'Let's catch up when Tracy's over', expecting to see her next weekend, or the next. I don't want to say I don't know when she'll visit, so I stop trying to contact old mates. I have no time for my kids, and when I do occasionally see them, I'm not really present.

I'll walk through Darling Harbour at the weekend, see all the happy couples and think, *What's wrong with me? Look at all these people in happy relationships.*

All they see is a tall, broad-shouldered detective, his eyes hidden behind sunglasses, and they can't know what's going on inside my head, because I refuse to show weakness. I'm too proud to put my hand up and ask for help.

At home, I pull the blinds down over the big windows overlooking the bays of Sydney Harbour. Those windows should fill the place with sunshine reflected off the water, so I shut it out. I'm sick of the world. I leave the apartment only to go to work or train.

I live like this, without a view, for weeks.

One day I realise how close I am to losing myself completely.

I open the blinds. It is a direction to myself: *Get out there.*

At work, I pick up an old case file I recognise: the disappearance of a 20-year-old called Matt Leveson. It was something I'd looked at briefly before I went on leave and I'm disappointed to see nothing's been done in the time since. *Fuck this*, I think. *Someone has to do this properly.*

Matt was starting out in adult life. A young lad, like so many others. Blond hair, big smile, well-dressed, he worked for an insurance company.

Matt was trusting, blameless. He was reported missing by his parents in September 2007, after a night out dancing at Sydney's ARQ nightclub with his 45-year-old boyfriend, Michael Atkins.

In an interview with Homicide detectives during the days that followed, Atkins claimed he'd left the nightclub with Matt and driven home to his flat in Cronulla, southeast Sydney, where the two men lived together. Atkins said he fell asleep watching TV and woke up a little later, to find Matt was missing.

Already, when he spoke about Matt, Atkins used the past tense.

Also, although the police hadn't told him by the time the interview started, Matt's car had been found earlier that day, parked at the Waratah Oval in Sutherland, a 20-minute drive from Atkins' flat and near the entrance to the expanse of wild bushland called the Royal National Park that forms Sydney's southern border. Inside it was a receipt for the purchase of a mattock and duct tape from a local Bunnings Warehouse, dated 23 September 2007, the day Atkins said that Matt went missing.

The cops had checked the store's CCTV, which showed a man who looked like Atkins making the purchase.

'Is there anything you wish to say about that?' asked Mathieu, the detective.

Atkins looked away before replying, 'Ah, don't think it was me.'

After a moment's silence, Mathieu asked him, 'Who do you think it could be?'

'I don't know.' Atkins reached for his cup of water and drained it.

Later during the interview, Mathieu asked him, 'How do you feel about our belief that it's you that made the purchase?'

'Surprised.'

'Do you wish to say anything further about that?'

'Nuh.'

Watching the video recording of the interview, I cringe at how the detectives keep letting Atkins off, not demanding he explain what sounds like an obvious falsehood. Asked outright if he was in any way connected with the disappearance of Matt Leveson, Atkins just said, 'No,' and the detectives interviewing him seem to simply accept it.

A year later, in August 2008, Atkins was arrested and charged with Matt's murder. A year after that, he was put on trial. The case file on my desk contains the inches-thick court transcript. It shows how the cops also discovered a big stereo speaker had been ripped out of the boot of Matt's car, meaning there was more room in there to carry something. On Atkins' phone they found worried text messages he sent to Matt after his boyfriend went missing and, alongside them, messages showing he was also contacting old boyfriends and trying to line up dates. Matt's mobile was itself found in Atkins' car, meaning he'd been sending those text messages to a phone that was already in his possession.

Three days after Matt's disappearance, and less than 24 hours after it was reported to the police, Atkins had driven from Sydney to Newcastle for sex.

But there was still no physical evidence of murder; no DNA, no fingerprints. Juries love forensic evidence, probably because it plays such a big part in all the cop shows they watch on TV. During the trial, Atkins' defence lawyer also took issue with the discovery of the receipt for the mattock and duct tape. 'What has it got to do with this case?' he asked the jury. So what if Atkins bought a mattock and some tape at the same time? 'Big deal. He's in Bunnings.'

And then, the lawyer argued, Matt himself had not been found. 'We don't know if the man is dead.' Sparing few thoughts for

Matt's family, who sat watching from the public gallery inside the courtroom, the lawyer raised other possibilities: Matt and Atkins did a little drug dealing, which meant they knew some shady characters. Maybe Matt met with foul play during a drug deal? Or at the hands of another gay man? Maybe he ran away? Melbourne had a great gay community too.

However unlikely these seemed, or however hurtful to Matt's family, the defence did not have to prove any of these things had happened. Just like in the Bowraville case, it was the prosecution's job to prove its case. All the defence had to show was these other possibilities existed.

The defence also had another advantage: the jury was never shown the part of the recorded interview with police where Atkins denied buying a mattock and duct tape on the day he claimed Matt had vanished from his unit. The judge ruled the footage was inadmissible because the cops failed to formally warn Atkins he was being interviewed as a potential suspect, not simply a witness.

That failure meant the jury who found the case against Atkins was unproven never saw his shifting, uncomfortable explanation of why a man matching his description was buying a digging tool that morning, the receipt for which was later found inside Matt's car.

Atkins was found not guilty in October 2009.

In 2012, before I went to Perth, the new Homicide commander Mick Willing and I had met with Matt's parents, Mark and Faye.

Faye sat facing us with her blonde hair framing a careworn face and both arms folded tightly across her slender frame, as if trying to hold in her grief. It was clear that her son's disappearance had changed her. Once, she'd been a mother who gave out love and received it, like any mum. Now she was a fighter, demanding that somebody do something to find out what had happened to her son.

Mark Leveson was grieving too, although he disguised it better. A broad man who obviously lifted weights, he too was a fighter, even if you were more likely to notice his soft eyes and gentle way of talking, and the fact he seemed to have a smile for everyone.

Mick told them we would take another look into what had happened to Matt and both Mark and Faye were grateful. Looking through the file again more than a year later, I want to make good on that promise.

There's little doubt Atkins remains the chief suspect, but as with the Bowraville murders, the acquittal makes it hard to go after him again. Even since the overturning of the double jeopardy rules, he can't face another trial without 'fresh and compelling' new evidence.

There is another tragic parallel between the cases. In Bowraville, Colleen Walker-Craig's family still go out searching the riverbanks and ditches for her body. Matt's parents also go out looking for his body, digging at sites across Cronulla's coastline and in the Royal National Park. When I met them, it seemed like the only thing worse than finding where he was buried was the burden of not knowing what happened to their child. They were convinced Atkins had buried Matt – why else would he buy a mattock?

After the not guilty verdict, Matt's father, Mark, had a series of tattoos inked into his skin as permanent statements of his love and loss. Among these, on his right forearm are the words 'Death leaves a heartache that no one can heal', and on his left forearm, 'Love leaves a memory that no one can steal'. On his right shoulder is a portrait of his son's face, with Matt's date of birth and the date that he went missing.

Like Faye, who also had other, similar tattoos done after the not guilty verdict, Mark was determined not to let the court decision be the end of this. Yet, like the three children in Bowraville, it seemed to them that nobody cared about Matt Leveson – not the courts, not the media, nor the police, who had let the case drag while I was in Western Australia.

Elsewhere on Mark's left arm, are tattooed the words, 'It's not a justice system. It's just a system.' Putting the file down, I can see that he and Faye have every right to think that.

Matt should have got better attention. For starters, there was a tip-off to the Crime Stoppers telephone number, dating back to 2010. This claimed that another of Atkins' former boyfriends had a late-night Facebook conversation about Matt with someone who identified themselves online as 'MikeyBoi Atkins'.

The conversation suggested Matt was killed because he threatened to go to police about Atkins' drug dealing.

During the exchange MikeyBoi asked, 'U wanna know how he died?'

'Yeh?' replied his former boyfriend, Andrew.

'He called me a dog, and I hit him,' MikeyBoi had written.

Somehow, the cops had not followed this up. At its worst, in the Unsolved Homicide Unit, cases would be picked up once every six months, checked to see if there might be an easy way to solve them, like some new DNA and, if the answer was no, they'd be ignored until another six months had passed.

Even after the meeting between Mick, myself and Matt's parents, nothing was done. I start to follow it and find Crime Stoppers had in fact been contacted three times over the years about this conversation, but still nothing had happened. The next step is to contact Andrew, and see if he will wear a wire to record his conversations with Atkins.

He says that he will.

There is a part of me – the part that took me to Perth – that still doesn't want to pick up this burden. Another part of me knows that I have to do it.

A case like this, with a suspected murder, a missing victim and a not guilty verdict, is going to be difficult. A case like this will give me the motivation I need to leave the blinds up at home and go to work each morning.

I will do this, because Dad taught me to never give up. I will do this, because working is a way to swim against the current of my marriage, which I know is failing. I will do this, because I've met Matt's parents and they need someone to stand up for them, and for him.

Once again, I make it personal, putting a photograph of Atkins up above my desk. Taken from Facebook after his trial over Matt's murder, it shows him at a pool party, standing in swimwear with his arms around a group of other topless men. He's big, he must work out, although his muscles are turning to fat with age and his hair is receding. The men he's posing with are skinny, young and underdeveloped, as if they're barely out of their teens.

I silently compare the photo to the other faces I've pinned up in its place during other investigations. Anthony Perish has been up there. So's James Hide. Only, this time, something is different.

After my year away, I have a new perspective: I look at the photograph and realise it's not me and him. Atkins is not my enemy this time. Nor is James Hide. Nor, really, was Anthony Perish.

My enemy is the senior cops who won't devote enough resources to these cases. It's the court system that prevents juries from hearing all the available evidence, and the judges who hand down short sentences so killers can walk back into the community after only a few years inside. It's the lawyers and politicians who won't let the victims' families go to the appeal court and try to overturn not guilty verdicts. It's the media who, sometimes, just won't listen. It's everything I've been fighting against all my life, everything that prevents me from doing my job.

All this time I thought *the crooks* were my opponents, but now I can see properly.

Who am I fighting against? The whole fucking justice system.

Justice Comes in Different Ways

1 May 2014: 29 years in

Another motel room. Another comfortless bed, wardrobe, table and single chair, a bar fridge and a big television. In the bathroom, I'm lying in the motel bath, staring up at another motel ceiling.

I've spent all night getting in and out of this bath, or pacing up and down between the wardrobe and the bathroom door, trying to stay awake so I can memorise what I need to say later today, after the dawn, when I'll be the first witness called to give evidence at a new State parliamentary inquiry into the three Bowraville murders. The public hearing will be at the council chambers in Macksville, near where my motel is and just down the river from Bowraville itself.

This is my chance to make people listen. In my head, I run through the things I must remember to say when I give my opening statement: mistakes were made in this investigation; not all victims are treated as equals; I believe we already have the evidence to convict the serial killer responsible.

I can't stand up in front of the inquiry and read this out with my head bowed, looking down at a piece of paper. I want the Members of Parliament to look at me directly, which means speaking without notes. I need to hit this point, then that point: could these murders have been solved? Yes. Should they have been solved? Yes. I still think they can be.

I listen to the night-time silence, broken only by the electric hum of the bar fridge. For years now, it feels like the murdered children's families have been ignored, not just by the police force, who are content to let this triple murder case be run by myself, Jerry Bowden and Bianca Comina in what little time we can steal from other investigations, but also by the State Government, who have now turned down *three* requests to have the case sent to the appeal court, and by the media, who print articles listing notorious unsolved murders across New South Wales, with no mention of the Bowraville children.

Sinking back I let the bath water close over my face. Another eight years have passed now since 2006, when I rediscovered the Norco Corner evidence about an unconscious teenager lying on the road outside Bowraville and the white man standing over him. I think back to how, on the strength of that evidence, in 2007, we applied to the State Director of Public Prosecutions (DPP) to send the case to the appeal court. It was refused four months later.

In February 2010, using the lawyers who agreed to work for the Bowraville families without payment, we sent an application to the State's Attorney General, asking for the same thing. Eight months later, in the October, he refused to. Remembering how I felt back then, tension runs down my neck and into my shoulder muscles, unhelped by the hot water.

Eight months later, in June 2011, we tried again, after a different Attorney General was appointed. This time, it took him more than a year and a half to respond, during which time, the children's families had marched in protest outside the State Parliament, but no one seemed to notice. In February 2013, that Attorney General refused to send the case to the appeal court.

I hold my breath underwater, ignoring the discomfort.

In a letter to the families explaining his decision, the Attorney General said that 'although there is a reasonable argument that the "Norco Corner" evidence is compelling, it is not "fresh"'.

I didn't understand it. In 2007, the DPP said the evidence was 'fresh' but not 'compelling', and, in 2013, the Attorney General said the evidence was 'compelling' but not 'fresh'. In March 2013, the families marched outside State Parliament again, and then a third time, in November that year. I stood with them, mindful, as a cop, not to be seen in the front ranks of the protest, but making my presence felt.

This time, the politicians noticed. A Greens MP, David Shoebridge, invited the children's families into the State Parliament and they sat in the Legislative Council Chamber as David spoke about the murders. He also worked hard to get the parliamentary Standing Committee on Law and Justice to hold an inquiry into what happened, which was established on 26 November 2013, a week after the families' third protest.

As I saw it, anything that helped get them some attention could be useful and I drafted a submission for the inquiry while in the last few weeks of my time with Tracy in Perth, working through the night to get it finished. On the last page, I wrote, 'I have been asked so often by the families whether this matter would be handled the same way if it was three white children from a wealthy suburb in Sydney who were murdered. I cannot with a clear conscience say it would be.'

The police commissioner, Andrew Scipione, also wrote a letter of support, expressing his sympathies for the families. Having his endorsement of what we were saying was a victory, but I still doubted my bosses' commitment. A colleague showed me an old report of mine about the murders on which a senior officer had written: 'The views of Detective Inspector Jubelin are not necessarily the views of the New South Wales Police.'

Releasing my breath and rising back out of the water, I open my eyes and run a hand back from my temple over my close-cropped scalp. I don't have the same thick hair I used to when I joined the cops; I'm balding now, and shave my scalp down to the skin. Staring up at the ceiling, I go through my lines again ahead of the inquiry hearing.

Am I the only cop who's losing sleep over these murders? I've started saying to the Bowraville families, 'I work for you guys, not the police.'

Years ago, before the 2004 inquest into Colleen's and Evelyn's deaths, I sat down with Aunty Elaine, the woman who, when I first came to Bowraville, had asked me, 'Why should I trust you? You're a cop.' Sitting side by side at Nambucca, on the coast near Bowraville itself, she looked out at the horizon and told me I was here for a reason.

'What do you mean by that?' I asked her, but Aunty Elaine always seemed to speak in riddles.

'Justice comes in different ways,' she told me. 'It might surprise you. It might not come the way you think it's going to.'

It would be a long journey but I had to travel it with them, Aunty Elaine said, looking serious.

'I can't leave,' I joked, trying to lighten the mood. 'I'd be too afraid of getting in trouble with you, Aunty.'

She smiled. Over the years she'd guided me and the rest of the strike force, putting us in touch with different witnesses and convincing them to trust us. 'Don't you ever give up on us, whitefella,' she told me, looking back at the ocean.

Car headlights slash across the darkness outside my motel window, bringing me back into the present. I was right not to leave the cops when Tracy suggested that I do so. That would have been betraying Aunty Elaine.

Besides, everyone who leaves the cops regrets it. Jason Evers, who worked with me in Bowraville, has left. A couple of years after the disappointment of the not guilty verdict over Evelyn's murder, during which we'd begun to fix up our relationship, I'd called up the Ballina Police Station to speak to him and had been told he was off sick. Something about the way the person on the end of the phone said it told me he wasn't coming back.

I'd called Jason at home and he sounded embarrassed. He said the thing that got him in the end was being called to the scene of a shark attack where a 16-year-old boy had bled out on the sand. Jason said it was the only kind of death he hadn't already seen in the police and, all together, they'd taken too much from him.

I couldn't help but think that the pressure and the emotion of the Bowraville case had also contributed to his decision to leave the cops. Jason had lost his swagger. I told him it was the right call for him to leave when he did, and he had nothing to feel bad about. He should be proud of what he'd done in the police.

He said he still regretted not being able to help solve the children's murders.

Without Jason, I have Jerry Bowden working with me now. He's a smart, confident, no-nonsense Homicide detective with an easy smile, just like Jason's. In the sleepless moments which the case has brought me, like tonight, it is good to have Jerry, because when you're going up against everyone, it affects your confidence. We're telling two attorneys general and the DPP they've got it wrong, and sometimes I wonder, *What if they're* not *wrong?*

Then I will ask Jerry, 'Are we doing the right thing?', and he'll tell me, 'It's three children murdered. Fucking oath.'

I'm also lucky to have Bianca Comina, the analyst working with us on the strike force. Bianca's so good she's worth 10 people. She knows every line on every page in every folder full of evidence we've gathered, and she knows why this line or that line matters, because of what is said on *that* line in another document.

Unlike other analysts I've worked with, who can see their job as an abstract thing, looking for patterns of calls among phone records or mapping out a suspect's movements, Bianca cares. She's met the Bowraville families. She sees them as people. I couldn't do my work without her.

The bathwater is getting cold. I haul myself out and dry off, then wrap the towel around me and go back to pacing the bedroom, brought up short by the walls and furniture.

I find it difficult to concentrate on what I should be doing. Instead, my mind plays over what I hear other cops are saying about this investigation, which is now in its 24th year since the first of the children went missing, and 18th since I became involved.

'He should just give it up.'

'Too bad, too sad.'

'He's only doing it because he loves the blackfellas. He wants to be their saviour.'

'You know he even married one?'

The *Underbelly* series has only amplified those whispers.

Even Axeman, our hardarse informer on the Bowraville investigation, got jealous of the TV show. After its broadcast in August 2012, he and I met up at a café and he said, 'Mate, we did some jobs together, didn't we? They could make a TV series about us, you reckon?'

There is still only darkness outside the motel window. I sit at the table and go back through the points I need to hit when speaking to the politicians: the lack of cooperation from prosecution lawyers; how the State Government's own submission to the inquiry contains factual mistakes.

I pad up and down the carpet, repeating to myself what I will say tomorrow.

The hours pass.

***

The sun rises, turning the sky grey outside the motel curtains and softening the shadows cast by the lamp at my table. I get up, shower and put on my white shirt and black jacket, then make my way to the sprawling, white council building for the inquiry hearing.

Inside, Colleen's, Evelyn's and Clinton's families are waiting, looking nervous. We talk almost in whispers, hushed by the still air of the council chambers. They tell me I am speaking for them today, that this is the first time anyone has spoken up on their behalf, and not to let them down. I don't need the extra pressure.

The committee chair welcomes the watching children's families and acknowledges that this hearing is taking place on the country of the Gumbaynggirr people. He calls me to the stand and asks whether I want to make an opening statement, before they ask me questions.

I hit every point I stayed awake last night trying to remember.

The Homicide Squad commander, Mick Willing, listens from the front row of the public gallery. He has made the journey up from Sydney to support me, his presence reassuring the politicians that I am not just a rogue cop; that today I represent the views of the entire New South Wales Police Force.

I am grateful for that, it carries weight. It has taken a lot of arguments to get here but, slowly, it seems like the police hierarchy are more prepared to stand up and say that what's happened in this case is wrong.

The inquiry chair, David Clarke asks if the police are going to keep pursuing the children's killer.

'I can assure the families we will not forget about these crimes,' I say, turning to where the families are sitting. 'We will continue to do everything humanly possible to bring justice to the families. I am saying to the families: we have got the evidence, we just need to fight for it.'

After I've finished speaking, the families listening in the council chamber stand up and clap. My father is on his feet too; he has also driven up from Sydney to be here at the hearing. I don't want to look at him in case I start to well up. When the hearing is over, Dad tells me he is proud of me. Him saying that, feels like he is passing the baton over, from father to son. It is as if, for the first time, he understands what I do at work and why I think it matters.

***

Four months later, in early September, we bury Aunty Elaine in the Bowraville cemetery. I am devastated at the loss. We used to talk every fortnight, when either I would call to ask for her help or give her an update on the case, or she would call to check how I was going. We got so close that she'd say something and I'd laugh and she would say, 'I just wanted to hear your laughter.'

The funeral service is held in the Catholic school just outside the Mission, where her family are all wearing red bandannas. When I arrive, they give me one to wear, which leaves me humbled.

The funeral procession carries her coffin through the Mission to the graveyard, where the stone monuments to Bowraville's white population stand in neat rows on top of the hillside, and the graves of its black inhabitants are kept separate and beneath them, marked with wooden crosses or, sometimes, only piles of stones.

I'm standing back, trying to keep a respectful distance while Aunty Elaine's family lower her coffin into the ground when one of her sons walks up to me. He asks if I can help bury the coffin, saying that his mum would like that. I nod and take a shovel, helping to throw the soil down into the grave and knowing I could not have been given a higher honour.

Back in Sydney, I put the funeral notice with Aunty Elaine's photo on my fridge. It will remain one of the few photographs inside my apartment, and whenever I look at it, I'll remember her telling me that justice comes in different ways, and that it might surprise me. They are words I'll cling to in the years that follow.

What Other Options Have You Got?

12 September 2014: 29 years in

I hear about it on the news and think, *OK, a three-year-old is missing.*

The lost boy's face stares out of every news report: William Tyrrell is thin, with cute red cheeks and brown eyes so big and wide you could get lost in them. He's wearing a Spider-Man suit and has been caught in the act of roaring, or laughing, at the photographer, who is behind the camera. The photograph was taken less than an hour before William went missing.

Each year, tens of thousands of people are reported as missing to police but most are found, or return home, soon after. It's rarer still for a child to still be missing hours later and, even among those, few such cases attract this kind of attention. I don't know if it is William's skin colour – he's white – his age, the vulnerability on that little face in the photo, or the fact his family are from Sydney, where the newspapers and TV companies are based. Maybe it's all of those things together. Whatever the reason, this is a case where people are sitting up and taking notice.

The police response appears confused: it's not clear who's running the case – the local uniformed commander who's doing the press conferences, or the Homicide Squad, who are called in after almost a week when it seems likely William hasn't simply wandered off into the bush, but who never appear on television.

Homicide got the call after my old mentor, Paul Jacob, sent some of his detectives up to Kendall, the tiny town on the Mid North Coast of New South Wales where William went missing, to help out. At that time, the cops were treating it as a missing-persons case and a huge search of local bushland had been mounted, but the disappearance of a child inevitably raises fears of something darker and Jaco now works for the Sex Crimes Squad, who specialise in dealing with those kinds of tragedy.

Something about it didn't feel right, he later tells me. The house where William was last seen is on an isolated road with only a few houses on it. The bush surrounding the property is thick, too thick for a child to wander off into. Jaco says he telephoned the Homicide Squad and told them, 'I think you guys should be here.' The cops needed to get on top of this, and quickly, he says. It needed that level of expertise.

Weeks later, Hans, the Homicide cop leading the investigation, walks past my desk in the Homicide office in Parramatta, western Sydney. We chat briefly about the case, and he tells me William Tyrrell is a foster child. The house he disappeared from was his foster grandmother's, Hans says. And, get this, his biological parents had stolen William before. They tried to stop him being taken into care by going on the run together and hiding out for a few weeks in a relative's home, until the police found them.

I say it sounds like a good line of inquiry. Statistically, when a child is murdered or goes missing, the perpetrator is usually someone close to them.

Hans walks on, looking confident. An old-school cop and veteran of countless murders, he's coming to the end of more than 40 years in the police and is now only months away from retirement. The feeling around the office is that this should be a straightforward case for Hans to finish his career on.

***

Almost four months later, in early December, William is still missing. Homicide Squad commander Mick Willing calls me into his office.

By now, he says, there is no evidence suggesting either William's biological parents or his foster parents were involved in his disappearance. Hans has ruled them out. But there's little evidence suggesting anyone who could replace them, Mick says.

Mick wants me to return from the Unsolved Homicide Unit to the squad proper and take over Hans's team when he retires in February, which means taking over this case.

'Jubes, I need you to sort this out,' he tells me. 'It's all over the place.'

Back at my desk, I take a look at the e@gle.i computer system, and can see that Mick is right. It's obvious how much was missed in those first hours and days when the local cops treated it as a missing-persons case and before Homicide was called in. Neighbours' houses were not properly searched, cars came and left the street where William disappeared without being checked, and no crime scene was established.

Even since Hans's arrival, there is still work that needs to be completed. The e@gle.i system shows over 1000 items – reports, statements, investigators' notes – still waiting to be reviewed. Hans prides himself on being a shoe-leather cop, he likes to be out there, on the street, talking to people. As a younger detective, he spent a lot of time at the Armed Hold-Up Squad and still has their heads-down, keep-moving-forward approach, rather than standing back and taking a considered view at what's in front of him.

Going through the computer files, I can't even find a written investigation plan. There are only a few cops from Hans's team working with him on the case. It's not enough.

Reading through the files, it looks like, for two weeks following William's disappearance, the cops still clung to the idea that the three-year-old might have simply got lost, that he was still a missing person, meaning someone whose disappearance has not been classified as something worse. Hundreds of cops and volunteers scoured 18 square kilometres of bush, farmland and tangled lantana. They searched dams and drains, waterholes and sheds, caravans and cubbies.

Taking this over, it is important to keep my mind open, but even so, it looks almost certain William was not lost. If he were, the massive search effort would have found him.

If not, that means he might have been abducted. That kind of crime is rare, and when it happens, for the family not to be involved is almost unknown. It would be a once-in-a-decade crime within Australia, but it happens.

And if he was abducted, then whoever took him must be someone who was in the area that morning. We need to find out who was there. Most likely, the answer is already somewhere among the hundreds of reports and witness statements on e@gle.i.

The answer is always there, I think. *You just have to find it.*

But the failure to treat this at least as a potential abduction early on has made this work harder. Not least because the hundreds of people who helped with the search, thinking William was lost, were given free access to the road outside the house where he went missing, meaning they would have trampled over any forensic evidence. Nor do we have complete records of who took part in the search itself, among them SES volunteers, surf lifesavers and even a local pony club on their horses.

This won't be easy to take over. If Matt Leveson's unresolved disappearance had called me back into the dark waters of Homicide investigation, this case means taking the plunge completely. *I'm ready to do that now*, I think. After 29 years in the cops, I have the right skills, energy and experience. This will need a considered, determined approach. Instead, the confusion continues.

I'm told the strategy agreed on by our bosses is for Homicide to lead the investigation but to cooperate closely with the local cops, who will handle the media.

That way, it's explained to me, if William was abducted, whoever took him won't know who's really coming for them. But this plan isn't helping.

Ahead of his retirement, Hans takes me to meet William's foster parents, Jane Fiore and Tom Nevis (not their real names). On the drive to their home in Sydney's north, we hear Paul, the local police commander in Kendall talking about William on the radio. He says the case is 'actually baffling'.

I turn to Hans. 'I thought you were leading this.'

'Whatever that bloke says, it's got nothing to do with me.' He shrugs.

Hans and I knock on the foster parents' door and wait. They answer, looking at us in hope, as if we might be bringing them answers, with faces that are drawn and exhausted.

We're barely inside before Hans says it looks like William's been taken by a paedophile, and if he has been, statistics show the chances are he'll have been killed within a day of disappearing.

Jane and Tom are crying. I can't let myself feel anything for them, however. Instead, I watch them, thinking: *You were both with William that morning. That makes you my first suspects.*

Jane pushes some strands of hair behind her ear and looks back at me, as if guessing what I'm thinking. She's obviously intelligent. She's had a successful career before becoming a foster parent and there is a stillness to her as if, even in grief, she is still considered. She's asking Hans about the case; what has been done and what hasn't. Despite my suspicions, I get the sense she is genuine in her desperation to find out what happened to William.

Like Jane, Tom is smart and has been successful, but he seems the more emotional. Watching him, I can see his feelings welling up, his words are catching in his throat, as if they're threatening to choke him. If he's play-acting the part of a grieving father, then it's a good performance.

They tell us how William's five-year-old sister doesn't understand what's happened to her brother. They don't understand themselves. On the day before William went missing, they'd made a last-minute decision to head up a day early for a visit to Jane's mum, Anne (not her real name), in Kendall. They arrived late and, the next morning, Friday 12 September 2014, Jane and her mother played with the children on the back deck, while Tom went into town to find somewhere with decent reception in order to make a Skype call for work.

William was playing with dice and then, when he got bored with that, he started a new game pretending to be a tiger. Around 10.30am, he jumped down off the deck onto the grass, ran around the side of the house and gave a tiger roar. Then there was silence.

Jane went looking but couldn't find him. She says she heard a faint, high-pitched scream, as if a child were in pain. It seemed to come from some tall reeds, not far from where she was standing. She ran and looked all through them, but there was no sign of William.

'I was saying, "William, it's Mummy ... you need to talk to me ... it's Mummy ... You need to tell me where you are ... You've got to say something, William."'

She called 000 and the cops came. Soon the street was full of people, searching.

'It's not a little boy lost,' she says. William had asthma, which was brought on by stress. He'd not been known to wander off. The bush surrounding the road was so thick the people heading into it were coming out with ripped clothing.

Within moments of losing sight of him, Jane feared he'd been taken.

She's also sure she saw two cars, one white, one grey, parked on the road outside her mother's house that morning, before William vanished. That was strange, because it's such a quiet place – some distance from Kendall itself, which is only a small town, so small you stay there for any length of time and you'll recognise most of the people.

'You don't see strange cars parked on the road,' says Jane. Partly, that's because all the houses on it are on acre blocks with long driveways, so when people come to visit, they tend to park off the street. And it's practically a dead-end road, her mum's house is the second-to-last one before the bitumen turns into a gravel fire trail leading up into the forest. You wouldn't be there unless you're visiting somebody.

Jane says a third car also drove past the house that morning, while she was playing with the children. It was a dark green-grey sedan, she says, heading up the road, towards the fire trail, but then it stopped, turned into the neighbour's house and reversed out, heading back down the road past them. The driver stared at her directly.

'The guy held my eyes, he challenged me,' says Jane. Then he was gone.

I ask her about William. She describes how he adored his sister. How close he was to his foster dad. How he liked to wait outside the house when Tom was driving home from work to welcome him, so the couple had got into the habit of having Tom send a text just before he arrived, so she could get William ready.

As far as I can see, they are a decent couple, though I am not yet willing to rule them out. Still, when Hans and I leave, I try to reassure them. I don't want them to fixate on the idea that William was taken. Instead, I tell them that we don't know what happened to him yet, but we won't give up until we do. We'll do everything we can to find out where their boy is.

***

A phone call wakes me in the night. Elsewhere in the flat, my son, Jake, is sleeping. He arrived yesterday and will soon be heading overseas for a few months, so I'd been looking forward to seeing something of him. But, instead, the voice on the telephone says three people have been killed, and I am to run the crime scene.

I drive into Sydney's city centre through the early-morning darkness of 16 December 2014, remembering the images I saw on the TV news just a few hours before: of hostages standing helpless in the windows of the Lindt Chocolate Café; of the gunman with his black bandanna and heavy rucksack.

In Martin Place, blue lights are reflecting off the office buildings. Inside, the chocolates are still lined up on the shelves in their brightly coloured wrappers. The floor is littered with fallen chairs and smears of blood, as well as sharp fragments of shattered stone from where the bullets of the tactical police have hit the walls and marbled pillars.

Forensic officers in their blue body suits have started to pick their way around the bodies lying among the wreckage. The siege has led to the deaths of two hostages, Tori Johnson and Katrina Dawson, as well as that of the gunman. My role is to coordinate their work, as well as the ballistics analysis that will aim to track the route and impact of every shot fired within the café, to make sure all this and any other evidence is preserved, the physical exhibits bagged and secured, accurate records kept, and to report back to the officer leading the investigation, Angelo Memmolo.

Normally, managing the crime scene is one part of the lead detective's work when running an investigation, but this is no normal job. From what I saw on television, this was a terrorist attack in the heart of the city, and from what I am told on my arrival, one that ended when tactical police stormed the café, despite fears the hostage-taker was carrying a bomb.

It is as yet uncertain who fired the fatal shots and I can imagine Ange's responsibilities on this case are already vast. They will weigh him down for months to come as this investigation and the inevitable high-profile inquest follow. My job is to take at least a little of that load.

Normally, I tell myself: *Don't put life into the bodies.* Don't let yourself imagine them as living people, as it will distract you. While I think it's important to get close to their families, to offer them some comfort and to use their grief as rocket fuel to help propel you through the work ahead, at this point, when their death is at its rawest, it doesn't help to animate the victims. Don't think about the horror they experienced. Emotions are for later, when you've left the crime scene.

Just get in there and do your work. Only this time, it is harder. I saw the crime take place on television before I went to sleep. I saw the hostages when they were alive, pressed up against the café windows, the fear on their faces.

By the time the sun rises, people have started leaving tributes to the victims in Martin Place, outside the cordon of police tape. A few scattered blooms expands into a sea of flowers, so wide that we have to part them, clearing a path for the forensic team to get to the café door. I thought I'd seen everything at crime scenes, but I have never seen a whole city grieve before now.

That also makes the work harder to bear.

***

For days now, I've been telling Hans, 'Please don't do this.' It's too public.

He's been looking at Bill, a local white goods repairman, who visited Anne Fiore's house in Kendall a few days before William's disappearance, to look at her washing machine. Bill told her he needed to order an extra part and would come back when he'd got it. Hans is interested in this because, five days after William disappeared, a tip-off to Crime Stoppers revealed Bill was the subject of lurid child sex allegations decades ago, although he'd not been charged.

At about 9am on the morning William went missing, his foster mum, Jane, called Bill from her mother's house, to ask why he hadn't been back to fix the washing machine. William was last seen an hour and a half after that phone call.

Maybe Bill picked up the message, Hans thinks. Maybe he went back to the house. He can't have gone inside it, otherwise the family would have seen him, but maybe he was out there, on that isolated road.

So Hans wants to search Bill's home and business.

I say that, if we go in, we need to do so covertly, putting listening devices in place first to listen to Bill and his wife, Margaret's private conversations.

Going in like this is all or nothing. By now, William's disappearance is easily the most high-profile criminal investigation in the country. News of the raids will leak.

Sure, get it right and we might find William's body. But get it wrong, spook Bill before we have any real evidence against him, and we risk losing everything.

But Hans is not persuaded, and he is still running this show. I need to get the search stopped. With Mick Willing on leave, I go to Jason, the acting commander, and, when he won't call off the raids, ask him to call Mick at home and put the boss on speakerphone.

'Mick, stop this,' I say. I don't want these raids to happen. I also want to hold a press conference, announcing I am taking over the investigation from Hans. We need to make it clear who's running this.

Mick does not agree with me. 'Gary, Hans is retiring in two weeks' time,' he says. 'He's been in the job for 40 years, just let him retire in peace.'

'I don't want this.'

'Mate, it's not your problem at the moment. You worry about it when you take over.'

***

The raids on Bill's home and business go ahead on 20 January 2015. At the time, I'm in Perth with Tracy, trying to keep our marriage going, and also training with David Letizia, the local boxer who has now asked me to work his corner during his final fight, which will take place next month.

Dave's told me his greatest fear isn't losing but being embarrassed. I understand it. When you climb through the ropes into the boxing ring, you're on your own. There's no one looking after you.

In the world outside that ring, Dave has his family and reputation to fall back on if he needs them, but once he gets inside it he will be exposed.

Which is how I feel, sitting with Tracy, watching reports of the police search on the evening TV news. As I feared, the story leaked. The cameras caught everything.

We watch the cops take a cadaver dog inside Bill's house, trying to smell a body. We watch them rake over the garden. We watch them drain the septic tank.

I try to imagine the effect of these pictures on William's biological and foster parents but I cannot. It's too awful.

Afterwards, Bill is put through a six-hour interview, but isn't charged. When I get back to Sydney, the word is that they found nothing during the searches, but Bill's weird. He's got a strange, nasal voice and a sly way of answering your questions. You can't form a connection with him. But he denies having anything to do with William's disappearance.

One of the detective sergeants on Hans's team, Justin, led the interview with Bill. He asked why the call from Jane on that morning doesn't show up on his phone. Did he delete it?

No, Bill said. He didn't. Only much later will we learn this may have been because Bill was talking to someone else when Jane phoned him, so her call doesn't show up in his records.

After a full-scale search and six hours in the interview room with Justin, what have we got to show for it? Nothing. All that's changed is now Bill knows the cops are watching him.

I tell Tracy I have to sort this out, and shut myself away for two days solid to draw up a proper investigation plan. Tracy is supportive. By now, with all the media attention, everyone in Australia knows who William is, and that we need to find him. As the cop who's now facing that task, I need to salvage what I can from this chaos.

Given Hans has started working on Bill, I need to see it is done properly rather than drop it. For one thing, Bill's alibi has not been checked and we need to do that. For another, we should search the storage shed he owns in Wellington, a bush town six hours' drive inland where Bill used to run a business. We've received a report that his car was seen there the day after William disappeared.

We also need to go back to the start of the whole investigation and make sure there have been no missteps, which means ruling the biological and foster parents in or out to my own satisfaction, sorting out the mess on e@gle.i, where sometimes William's surname isn't even spelled correctly, and dealing with the media, who are crawling all over this and causing problems – like with the raids on Bill's house.

At the same time, we need to widen the investigation. We can't just follow Bill and see where he leads us, we need to also identify and pursue other persons of interest, meaning people who are not suspects but who the police want to talk to, including the large number of known sex offenders living in the area.

How has it come to this? I think, looking at the work in front of me. *Why has half of this work, at least, not already been done? A three-year-old has gone missing and we can't bring our A game?*

I fly back to Sydney, determined to correct that.

***

It's the silence I notice on Benaroon Drive, the wide road where William went missing. You can hear birds calling. You can hear insects in the forest. You can hear a car drive past, even from inside a house.

Before coming here, I looked at maps, as well as diagrams of the area drawn up during the investigation and showing who lives in each of the scattered houses, as well as the dates on which they each were interviewed. I also know the area around here personally, from coming up to nearby Port Macquarie for holidays when the children were little and for my wedding to Tracy, although it is a tougher country than the one I remember.

Drive inland, towards Kendall and away from the coast, and it becomes a place of twisted forests and black swamps, through which the roads and tiny country towns thread their way like thin ribbons of brightness. The road leading up towards the house where William went missing bends left, and because of the trees, it's only once you're close to it that you get a clear view of the house and the sloping lawn behind it, which leads down to the road itself.

If you were close enough, on the morning when William jumped off the deck, where his foster mum and grandmother were sitting, and ran away, making a roar like a tiger, you would have seen him appear around the corner of the house at the top of that slope, facing the road.

Was there enough time for somebody standing here to run up there and take him?

I have come here because Hans's retirement on 2 February means I am now in charge of the investigation, giving me the opportunity to run it my way, the way I was taught to. The strike force working on the case is called Rosann and based in Port Macquarie, in the same room from which Strike Force Tuno once investigated Terry Falconer's murder. The trial over Evelyn's death in Bowraville was also held in Port Macquarie. Since then, my parents have bought a house up here to go with their holiday property, which they are now renting out. I don't stay with them when I'm here, though, sleeping instead in the El Paso Motor Inn near the police station. To me, Port Macquarie is no longer a place I go for holidays. It is a place where I work on murders.

Looking up, I reckon it would have taken someone a couple of minutes to get up to the back of Anne Fiore's house, taken William and got back to their car. But they would have had to be waiting here at the moment the three-year-old appeared. Then they would have had to get William into the car, get in themselves and drive off. All of that would also have taken time.

According to his foster mother, Jane, William disappeared at around 10.30am. She called 000 at 10.57am. The first cop was on the scene at 11.06am. It is a small window of time for anything to happen.

Only Anne knew the family were coming to visit, and the CCTV of their journey here from Sydney shows no one was following them. So it cannot have been a targeted abduction. Looking up at the house in silence, I try to picture how a predator could have happened to be here at just the right moment.

Standing on this isolated road, I have to accept that Hans is right. To abduct William and get away, you would have to have a reason to be here. You don't end up in Benaroon Drive by chance. This is the thinking that led Hans to Bill.

Following Hans's thinking, I've also found what look at first like signposts pointing in the same direction. During the raids on Bill's property, a toy Spider-Man figure was found inside Bill's van. He said it belonged to a grandchild, but this hadn't been confirmed. I have it checked. Bill's telling the truth. A covert search of Bill's storage shed in Wellington also turns up a Spider-Man suit, and for a moment my heart seems to stop beating. We check: it is the wrong size to fit William.

Then a neighbour comes forward, saying he saw Bill's van the day after William went missing, driving up a bush track near Kendall, which the locals call the Ghost Road. We search it, sending a line of uniformed cops forcing their way through the bush, looking for any sign of William and provoking another media frenzy.

While the TV cameras are recording, Bill drives right past us, looking out his window.

We find nothing, though in this bushland, with the humidity and heat, a body would be skeletal within weeks and a child would have little bones, making them easier to hide, or to miss when you are searching.

Again, we check, though all of this takes time. It turns out Bill was at a function in his local club the afternoon his neighbour claims he saw him, so it couldn't have been his van driving up the Ghost Road.

Bill also says he has an alibi for the morning William vanished, although this proves more difficult to confirm. Both Bill and his wife, Margaret, say they were at a school assembly for one of the three boys who live with them. But that assembly was months ago now, and, while we speak to everyone who was there, their memories have faded. We can't find anyone who is certain they saw him.

It's frustrating; why wasn't this checked much sooner, before Hans raided Bill's house. We are playing catch-up.

I take Margaret to the school itself and get her to retrace her footsteps. She says she and Bill arranged to meet for coffee before the assembly and a receipt from the café opposite the school shows the couple were there, at 9.42am. And yet, it only takes 18 minutes to drive from there to Benaroon Drive – I know, because we timed it – so Bill could easily have left and been at Anne's place by 10.30am. Normally we'd be able to track Bill's movements using the signal from his mobile phone, only his was switched off.

Compiling everything we know about Bill so far, our analyst draws up a profile, which also reveals his first wife is the sister of Jeffrey Hillsley, whom I locked up in 2005 for child sexual assault and murder. I take a breath. What does it mean? Maybe nothing. This could be like all those other signposts that seemed to point us in a clear direction, but led to dead-ends when we followed them.

I talk about it with Dad. While I prefer not to stay over at my parents' house when I am working up here, I do go round for dinner, where he and I will sit on their deck, have a beer and look out at the Hastings River. He asks how the case is going.

I tell him about these different obstacles. I also tell him how the Department of Family and Community Services are refusing to allow either William's foster parents or his biological parents to do press conferences encouraging witnesses to come forward. They say it's to avoid revealing William is a foster kid, which they say comes with a stigma, but I think they're only covering themselves. I saw the same response when one-year-old Jayden March was killed by his foster mother. I think the department is terrified of scandal.

I blow up over their decision – a family appeal can really help – but the truth is we are not short of publicity. The front page of one newspaper announces we intend to track the movements of everyone who was within a kilometre of Benaroon Drive at the time William went missing.

'If you were in the area and did not come forward, we would have grave concerns and a certain amount of suspicion would be attached,' I'm quoted as saying. Under the headline 'You'd Better Come Forward', the paper runs a photograph of me standing on Benaroon Drive, showing that it's Homicide, not the local cops, who are now running this investigation.

I've also managed to increase the size of the strike force from two detectives to half a dozen, though that is still short of the numbers William deserves and I am still working this case as well as my other open investigations. Returning to the Homicide Squad also means I'm back to spending one week in every six on call.

Keep going, my dad says. Put your head down and work. You'll get there. We've grown closer as I've got older, and now speak a few times a week, at least. When I am working in Port Macquarie, I get up early to train, then go for breakfast at a café across the road from the El Paso Motor Inn, where I can sit and read the papers. One morning, the owner asks if I'm related to Kevin Jubelin. When I say yes, she says I look like him. He rides his bike out here, she says, and always sits in that same seat to read the papers. 'He does exactly the same thing as you,' she tells me.

I tell her he's more hot-headed than I am sometimes, but older and wiser. After my breakfast, I head to the police station, go up to the strike force room on the first floor and put my head down and work. Like dad says, we'll get there.

***

On 10 February 2015, I'm coming to the end of a week on call and due to fly over to Perth to see Tracy when we get a report of a category one critical incident – a police officer has killed another person.

A young woman, Courtney Topic, has been shot dead in the car park of a Hungry Jack's in Hoxton Park, southwest Sydney. The 22-year-old was carrying a knife and, according to the police radio reports before her death, was visibly distressed, hitting herself in the head and pointing the knife at her own body.

Courtney was shot within 41 seconds of police arriving in the car park. Afterwards, when we arrive at the local police station, all the regional police bosses seem to be there before us and are in a room together, watching video footage of the shooting captured by a Taser carried by one of the three cops who were present.

It shows Courtney walking towards the camera, a thickshake in one hand and the knife in her other. You can hear one of the cops call out 'Taser' and fire the weapon, but it doesn't work. Another cop tries pepper spray on Courtney, who stumbles but keeps walking. Then one of the cops shoots her.

Watching the tape, I see the bosses nodding at each other and one says, 'Well, nothing wrong with that shooting.'

I shake my head. Maybe he's right and those cops did follow the regulations, but, to me, it looked like the situation escalated too quickly.

As we investigate, it turns out Courtney was most likely suffering from undiagnosed schizophrenia and a severe episode of psychosis. Her parents say she was a gentle, loving woman, who had never before been aggressive. No one knew why Courtney had a knife with her that morning.

One Sunday, her grandfather calls me up. He's angry, saying the family hasn't heard from me, they don't know what is going on and that I've not had the decency to call them. I try saying that I gave Courtney's father my contact details, but it is not enough. I get in the car and drive round to Courtney's parents' house, then sit with them at their kitchen table.

They unleash. They've never had any contact with police before and now a cop has shot their daughter. They didn't think they were allowed to contact me. What right had they to contact a detective inspector?

Looking at them, I realise how the relationship between the police and the people we deal with is out of balance. We have all the power. Those on the receiving end of a police investigation have little control over what is happening to them. I thank Courtney's family, saying they have taught me to be a better cop, and promise to keep them informed from now on.

They're sceptical but I tell them we won't cover up anything. This will be an honest investigation.

Before the inquest that follows into Courtney's death, I'm called into the office of the Crown Solicitor and asked for my opinion of the shooting. I say my role as the critical incident investigator is to look at whether the operation was done within the parameters of police operations. I think it was. But, if you're asking me personally, was it the right decision to shoot her? No, I don't think so.

The counsel assisting the coroner, Gerard Craddock SC, does not call me to give evidence at the inquest. It's the first time I've been a senior critical incident investigator and not been put in the witness box, although, ultimately, it makes little difference. The Deputy State Coroner, Elizabeth Ryan, finds errors were made in the way police dealt with Courtney, and her death exposed a 'compelling need for change' in how the force treats mentally ill people.

Almost half of the people shot by police were suffering mental illness, the inquest hears. Sometimes, as with Ryan Pringle's death, I know the cops have no choice. In this case, the coroner says there had not been a breach of police procedure and that the cop who shot Courtney had a reasonable basis for believing his life was in danger

Afterwards, Courtney's mother, Leesa, tells the gathered reporters her daughter was a beautiful little girl. 'She is not a statistic.'

***

The bureaucrats' refusal to let both sets of William Tyrrell's parents be identified and talk about his disappearance in public means there's a void at the centre of this case, and rumours rush in to fill it. We see them spread on TV, in the newspapers and on social media. There are sightings of William by the hundreds: a boy in Queensland seen travelling with an older woman; a boy at Central Station in Sydney; a boy in a Spider-Man suit seen less than an hour from Kendall.

Online conspiracies sprout up, claiming we're hiding the real offender. The phone lines at Port Macquarie Police Station are infested by psychics calling up to offer their help. At 10 o'clock one Sunday night, I get a call saying William was seen among the passengers boarding a flight to New Zealand. The CCTV from the airport is inconclusive, so we arrange for local New Zealand police to meet the plane when it lands. It isn't William.

In April 2015, seven months after the three-year-old went missing, one of the local detectives on the strike force speaks to a 75-year-old Kendall man called Ronald. A retiree and judge at local flower shows, Ronald says that on the morning William disappeared, he was sitting at a table in the sunroom of his house, which is just two turns – one left, one right – from Benaroon Drive, when he saw an old, beige or fawn-coloured, four-wheel drive tear past, followed closely by an iridescent blue sedan, driving so fast it cut the corner.

Ronald says he got a glimpse of the driver of the first car, enough to see she was a blonde woman in her late twenties to late thirties. A small boy was standing up in the back, without a seatbelt, says Ronald. The boy was peering out, with his hands pressed against the window. He was wearing a Spider-Man suit.

Ronald says he didn't come forward at the time because he was waiting for police to come to him. They would knock on his door eventually, he thought. When they didn't, he went down to the Kendall Services & Citizens Club one Friday night, hoping to bump into the town's police officer, who he'd known since childhood. She wasn't there, so Ronald left a message with her sister-in-law, asking her to call him.

The message was not passed on and, eventually, we hear about Ronald's story second- or third-hand. As the weeks passed, he'd told other people, though often the details were different. Two relatives staying with him at the time William went missing say he never mentioned seeing the boy in the Spider-Man suit being driven past. When pressed, Ronald tells the local detective that maybe he only dreamed it.

But the detective says he's definitely talking about William, because he showed him a photograph.

'What photo did you show him?' I ask.

'I showed him a photo of William Tyrrell.'

That concerns me. It's just like what happened in Bowraville, when local cops were prompting people's memories by going round with photos of Evelyn and Clinton, asking if they'd seen them, rather than showing potential witnesses six photographs of different people and getting them to pick out the person they'd seen.

In Bowraville, most of these 'sightings' turned out to be false. They were memories that could not be trusted, but which hung around like bad spirits and jinxed the investigation.

Still, we follow up Ronald's evidence. It turns out his neighbours had their four-year-old grandson visiting on the morning William went missing.

This boy was wearing a Spider-Man suit. Just like William's.

***

On 23 April, Margaret screams, 'No!' as we tell her husband Bill he is under arrest and needs to come with us. Walking with him away from his house back to our unmarked car, I look at the long line of TV trucks and hire cars on the road beyond it and wonder: *What the fuck has happened? How do all these journalists, from every major outfit in the country, know that this was happening today?* I didn't tell them. God knows who in the police hierarchy did. I'm furious.

Margaret shouts at the photographers and cameramen crowding closer towards us: 'Get off the property! Right now!' They fall back, wide enough only for the car to move forward. Camera flashes fire at Bill through the windows.

This evening, I guess, Margaret will sit in her empty house and watch her husband's arrest on the television news. I hope she's shocked; the charges against him are shocking – the alleged sexual and physical assault of two girls, aged three and six, in 1987 – but I did not invent them.

It's taken months of careful work to get to where we are today. Unlike the first, rushed raids on Bill's home and business, this moment has been planned for, tested and carefully considered. I know the damage those television images will wreak in Margaret's home, as well as in the homes of William's foster parents and his biological family. That's why I wanted to avoid them. But once you take hold of a line of investigation, you have to follow where it leads and, from the moment I took over this investigation, Bill has been the main thread I was given.

The allegations that form the basis of these sexual assault charges are not connected to William. They come instead from the same Crime Stoppers tip-off that brought Bill into Hans's reckoning when he was running the case.

The alleged crimes date back decades. While Bill was not charged at the time, or after, once we received this report it was our responsibility to follow it up. I've spoken to both of the alleged victims. One of these women's medical records from the time also suggest an assault took place.

Even then, the decision to act on this evidence was not one I made alone. I spoke to my old team member, Nigel Warren, who worked on the Barbara Saunders and Terry Falconer murders and who now leads a team of his own in the Sex Crimes Squad, asking him to take a look at what we'd gathered. Nigel's work now regularly involves prosecuting historical child sex offences and I trust him. He'll always do the right thing for the right reasons.

He said we had the statements of the alleged victims, one of which seemed to be corroborated by the medical evidence. Nigel had seen cases prosecuted with less, he told me.

I also asked the advice of friends, without naming Bill but saying, 'I'm about to pull the trigger on a guy's life.' I knew that Bill's name had already been linked publicly to the investigation into William's disappearance. Charge him with these crimes and there was no way to hide it. Get it wrong and I destroy him. At the least, there would be public court hearings in which he would be accused of being a paedophile.

I told my friends we had the evidence of the alleged victims. 'What other options have you got?' they asked me.

The police's own lawyers also looked at the brief of evidence before any final decision was made. Their advice was that there was enough to go ahead. As a cop I can't ignore that.

As a cop, I wouldn't be doing my job if I did not also try to take advantage of the extra pressure this will put on Bill by seeing if I can gather evidence to rule him in or out of any role in William's disappearance.

Bill is silent during the drive to Port Macquarie Police Station. Once we arrive, a custody sergeant reads him his rights, his fingerprints are taken and he is shown into a jail cell ahead of tomorrow's court hearing. Anyone would find this frightening. If he is hiding something, maybe this will be enough to crack him open. Maybe it will be enough to make Margaret think about him differently.

In the evening, after Bill has been interviewed about the sexual assault allegations, which he denies, I speak to him about William. He must be feeling that the ground beneath his feet is now much more uncertain and I want him to know that we are waiting, should he stumble. A thin man, Bill looks back at me coldly. He denies having anything to do with William's disappearance.

Late into the night, the light from the strike force's room in the police station shines amid the darkness. Inside that room, I am working, still trying to find a missing three-year-old. Beneath it, in the cells, Bill must know his life has changed for ever.

***

Bill is not our only line of inquiry. So far, we've spoken to 18 known sex offenders who live among the acre blocks and rural properties that lie within a 30-kilometre radius of Benaroon Drive, and another 60 who live further beyond it. There seem to be so many such offenders on this stretch of the Mid North Coast. It's as if they've settled on this quiet, overlooked backwater like mosquitos.

One of them, Gavin (not his real name), is now Bill's cellmate at Cessnock Correctional Complex where the white goods repairman is waiting for his next bail hearing. We monitor their interaction. Both men live near each other in Kendall and both have past links to Wellington, yet it seems they have never met before.

While Bill is in the cell, I go back at him again. We launch a covert operation, the details of which are kept within our strike force and the bosses who authorise it.

It seems to work. Bill continues to insist he was nowhere near Benaroon Drive when William went missing.

That's it, I think. *He didn't do it.* On 8 June, I update the strike force's investigation plan, to say that, accepting on the balance of probabilities, Bill was not involved in William's abduction and we need to refocus our investigation.

I know Bill's reputation and his business have been ruined, the three kids who lived with him and Margaret have been taken away, and Margaret herself has suffered greatly. I must have made her doubt her husband. But this is a murder investigation. Justice is what matters here, not injury.

I needed to be certain. Yes, getting here was painful, but as the person leading the investigation, I had to weigh up the cost of charging Bill against the cost of doing nothing and found the scales did not balance. The cost of doing nothing was heavier.

All that's left is for the child sexual assault charges to play out in court.

***

In June, I drive southwest, through the sun-baked country inland from Sydney to the Army Recruit Training Centre at Kapooka where my son, Jake, is due to pass out after his basic training. Over the past three months, since saying goodbye to Jake when he climbed onto the bus that brought him here, I've known he was being yelled at, just like I was at the police academy. I've known that the instructors would be doing their best to break him, just as they did with me back then.

As his dad, I'd wanted to protect him but known that I couldn't. I just had to hope Jake would survive it. Watching them march out onto the parade ground, searching for his face among the ranks of stern-looking recruits in their khaki uniforms and slouch hats, there is a sense of pride, of course, but also sadness. He is no longer a child. He looks tougher now and more confident.

After the ceremony, I hug Jake and tell him I'm proud of him. Standing back, I can see that he is different now, he can survive in life without me. His military training was a test and he has passed it.

***

On 17 June, Bill's lawyer tells the Supreme Court he should be released on bail, arguing that someone else, a 'known paedophile', had access to the alleged victims of his assaults at the time they happened. That paedophile was his then brother-in-law, Jeffrey Hillsley. It's possible, the lawyer argues, *Hillsley* committed these offences, not Bill.

After eight weeks in prison, Bill is released on bail. The case moves slowly through the courts and, a year later, he is still fighting it, with no trial scheduled to take place until another year has passed, and which is then delayed again until 2018.

When finally it gets to the New South Wales District Court, Bill's lawyer argues that the allegations against him were made to Crime Stoppers by his ex-wife, following a bitter divorce. He argues that evidence has been lost and witnesses have died in the decades since the offences were allegedly committed. The presence of Hillsley in Bill's life at that time also means it cannot be proved who committed the offences, if any did take place.

The judge says he believes no jury could say for certain that Bill's guilty and, on 5 March 2018, throws out the charges against him.

Walking away from the court, I feel a deep sense of sympathy. Sympathy for the women who were the alleged victims and who told the police about the most awful alleged crimes being committed against them. Sympathy for Margaret, Bill's wife, who has been an innocent bystander in all of this. Sympathy for the scrutiny and sheer pressure that we put Bill under.

But it was the right thing to do to charge him. Going to court is usually a bruising experience and not every criminal charge results in a conviction, although it is rare to have your whole case thrown out like this one. I'd still rather take a case to court and lose than never go to court in the first place. Sometimes, like when I fought with Trevor as a schoolboy, you just have to take your lumps.

Bring Him Home

June 2015: 30 years in

In the strike force room at Port Macquarie Police Station, a poster fixed above my desk carries the words, 'Have you seen William?' Above it are three smaller photographs: William grinning at the camera, William in the driving seat of a fire truck, and the photo which has by now become famous from TV news reports and newspaper pages, taken in the hour before William disappeared and showing him in his Spider-Man costume, his open mouth revealing tiny white baby teeth, his eyes like two dark pools of deep, still water.

On whiteboards along the length of the room are a timeline, maps and aerial photographs. One map is coloured pink to show the area covered by foot during the search for William. Another shows the places searched by cadaver dogs. On one board, a photo shows the place where Jane thought she saw two cars parked on Benaroon Drive that morning. Another shows the one-kilometre radius from her mother's house, within which we've tracked every human movement. There were close to 200 people within that area at that time.

Beside the door, on top of five full filing cabinets, are stacked more than a dozen lever-arch files of documents. In front of them, a tangle of electrical cables spills from the office tables, on which sit the computers and laptops that hold over 3000 different items, from weeks' worth of listening device recordings to 50-page witness statements. The computers also hold details of the more than 1000 reported sightings of William we've so far received, some of which are ridiculous, like the claim a ball boy at a televised NRL match looked like William, but all of which add to the relentless flow of information pouring into the strike force room.

It is enough to drown in. Every single new sighting, tip-off, investigator's note or witness statement must be logged, triaged, examined, cross-referenced and finally acted on.

My desk sits on its own, against the far wall. As the investigation supervisor, I oversee everything that happens both within and outside this room, putting me in a powerful position, but one that is also isolated. My job is to guide the strike force, to navigate our way across the pool of information they're collecting, while it keeps getting deeper beneath us.

Those people arrive for work about 6.30am and stay as late as 8pm. I usually work later, by which time the strike force room is almost silent: just me tapping away on my laptop and the ticking of the clock on the office wall. Each time I leave, I know we will be here again tomorrow, and the next day, and the next day. Each day means going further into these dark waters.

To do this work, you have to be prepared to leave the shore behind you, swim out and hold onto the pieces of potential evidence that come to the surface. I grasp at one and then another, trying to remember everything Jim Williams and Paul Jacob taught me. My greatest fear is still that we'll miss something. The strike force is now bigger than when I took it over, but we're still short-handed.

Nine months after William went missing, there are still over 1600 files on the e@gle.i computer system that are yet to be properly reviewed. Any one of them could contain the sighting of a car, a name, or the few words in a witness statement that we need to grab hold of before it's lost amid the inflow of new evidence and sinks beneath the water again, unnoticed.

We have hundreds of hours of listening device recordings, but too few detectives to listen to them, so they are piling up, unheard.

I'm losing faith in the police force. Despite being a Homicide detective, I've been told to report to Paul, the local uniformed police commander, who is still giving interviews in which he's described as the man leading the investigation. We clash when I complain that this arrangement means the cops are giving out mixed messages. Later, Paul says his staff need to use the room in which my strike force are working for meetings. I say we can turn the whiteboards round, to hide the confidential information on them, and leave the room during these times but this compromise fails. We end up leasing a room instead on Port Macquarie's main street, at extra cost.

I don't have the energy to waste on these battles. In the evenings, alone in my motel room, I practise qigong and meditation. Both help me deal with the chaos and my anger, as well as the constant fear of being overwhelmed which laps at my mind.

In a few days it will be 26 June 2015, William's fourth birthday. I stay in contact with his foster parents constantly, by phone or in person. By now, I'm satisfied there is no evidence of their involvement in what happened, but they are still our most vital witnesses, because they were known people to see him before he disappeared.

It's heartbreaking, having to call them up and say that I have nothing new to tell them. They have a thousand questions, among them, 'Is it possible he's still alive?' All I can say is it's possible, but I know that with hope comes pain, and their thoughts, like mine, are often pulled beneath the surface.

What do you do with William's clothes? I wonder. *Do you pack his toys away? Do you convert his room to something else, or leave it in case he comes home?*

What about William's sister? How do you protect her? How do you go on with your life?

I also know there is no evidence that William's biological parents took him and sometimes, though less frequently, I visit them, or they call me.

Their lives are more chaotic. There's been some drinking and drug use. At times, his birth mother will shout or spit her anger at me. Sometimes we agree to meet but they don't turn up. *You can only do so much*, I tell myself.

I have to kick hard to stop all of this from dragging me under. I have to keep on searching, through the forests and the one-acre blocks, the homes of the people living around Kendall and the black waters of my own imagination, because the worst is not that we find William and I have to tell his parents he's been murdered, the worst is we *never* find him.

***

On 22 August, Tracy and I are in court, getting divorced. The last time I saw her was two months ago in Perth, when she was running the city's marathon. At the finish line Tracy ran straight past me and, when I caught up with her, she was talking to one of her friends. Back in Sydney, my calls to her went unanswered. Finally, she phoned me and asked me when we were going to talk.

'The talking's done. We're over,' I said. During the long silences I'd come to accept the distance between us for what it was – the width of the country. It felt like a simple choice: break up or have the strain of trying to bridge this gulf break me.

In court, I know enough from the criminal trials I've been involved with at work to guess at what this process will hold; the arguments, the delays, the lawyers' fees, the paperwork. In a way, going through it will bind Tracy and I to each other until it is over but I will never see her in person again.

***

On 12 September 2015, the anniversary of William's disappearance, thousands of people across Australia take part in 'Walk for William' events. They wear ribbons, T-shirts and Spider-Man costumes to show their support for his parents and for the effort to find him. It is a milestone nobody wants to reach.

The strike force is assigned another member: Laura, a recently promoted detective sergeant who comes recommended by my old team-mate Nigel Warren, who worked with her in the Sex Crimes Squad. I like the fact she represents another link in the chain between detectives that was once broken by the Wood Royal Commission; Paul Jacob was my sergeant, I was Nigel's sergeant, Nigel was Laura's sergeant. Now she is here to help guide the other detective constables.

Laura's been told she'll be with us for only eight weeks. She ends up staying for years.

At times, she steps in to cover for Craig, the officer-in-charge of the strike force, who reports directly to me as the investigation supervisor. Craig is a dedicated cop and a champion kickboxer. I like his intensity, but he can seem strangely silent. Like each of us, the job bears down on him and, as the next most senior detective, Laura often ends up becoming a bridge between him and the junior members of the strike force.

Craig also insists on reviewing the other detectives' work himself, until he has more than he can cope with, and often sends each report he receives back demanding more be done. In the monthly written progress reports I submit to my bosses, I record how much work each member of the strike force has outstanding. Many have dozens of tasks or items of potential evidence still to review. Some have hundreds. Craig, alone, has thousands.

We're one year in, and no closer to finishing this work.

***

Everywhere, William's face stares back at me. Driving on the freeway from Sydney to Port Macquarie, I pass billboards with the question 'Where's William?' and that same photograph of the three-year-old in his Spider-Man suit that hangs above my desk.

The same image is on posters, on beermats, all over Facebook. Across the country, kids are donating their pocket money to the official Where's William? Campaign, set up by a PR company working with the three-year-old's foster parents. The company also works with the New South Wales Police Minister, Troy Grant – a former cop – to organise a private event at Parliament House in Sydney on 17 September. Politicians are invited to come and meet William's foster parents in person. They try to reassure them by saying how lucky they are to get me; that if anyone is going to solve this, it's Gary; that they have the best cop in New South Wales leading the investigation.

It's well meant, but it's pressure. At one point during the event, a singer performs a solo of 'Bring Him Home' from the musical *Les Misérables*. His voice echoes from the stone walls of the parliament building. I can feel tears welling up. The State Premier, Mike Baird, is also crying. Afterwards, I give a speech, saying the case is solvable and we owe it to William to keep trying.

The premier introduces himself and says if there is anything we need, to let him know. Troy says the same thing, as does the Attorney General, Gabrielle Upton. The next morning, back in the Homicide Squad office, I tell my boss, Mick Willing, about this. I tell him that I told the politicians we were fine, that I had enough staff and resources were not an issue. Mick nods, saying nothing. Within a week, I get a call to say the strike force is being doubled in size, to 14 people.

With them, we now have an opportunity to properly investigate some of the paedophiles we've identified living along the stretch of the Mid North Coast where William disappeared.

There are dozens of known child offenders in the area, mostly living inland, among the small, overlooked towns where property is cheap and there are fewer eyes on them than in a city block. We've learned to navigate our way around this stretch of country by their crimes: there's Wauchope, where we find one child abuser; there's Logan's Crossing, where we find another; there's Dunbogan, where one abuser says he was on the day that William disappeared.

This offender, a retired priest, has been found guilty of indecently assaulting a boy in the late 1980s, and of possessing child abuse material 20 years later. Another is the founder of a local support group for grandparents caring for young children and has won an award for his volunteer work.

A second member of the same group is a heavy drinker with a long handlebar moustache, a white station wagon similar in appearance to one of the cars Jane remembers seeing before William went missing, and no one to vouch for where he was that morning. He says maybe he was out collecting scrap metal, which he sells to buy beer, while his wife says she only knows that he came home drunk at lunchtime.

Soon after we speak to him, he is arrested and jailed for assaulting a child.

Another name floats up. Frank Abbott is a heavy, bullying man who lives in a caravan near a sawmill, a few kilometres from Kendall. He has twice stood trial for the murder of a 17-year-old found buried near a timber cutters' road southwest of Sydney in

1968. The first jury failed to reach a verdict and the second found him not guilty.

All these men live so close together, yet when we ask, they say there is no connection between them. But still, there is something unhealthy about this place, something that lives in the black pools of water overshadowed by the forests. As we head into the second summer since William went missing, the heat and the humidity, the constant drilling sound of insects, are exhausting. Driving back to Sydney, after another few days trying to pursue this case, I turn up the air-con and try to blast myself clean of all these feelings.

William's eyes stare at me from the roadside billboards.

The Right to Silence

17 December 2015: 30 years in

Faye Leveson looks at me and tells me, 'No.'

I was expecting that reaction. Not just because of what I'm asking, but because Faye reminds me of myself sometimes in the way she often puts her fists up first and, only later lowers them.

This time, her arms are folded across her chest. Her face is set.

'Absolutely no way,' she repeats.

'Hold on, let's hear them out,' says Mark, her husband.

Unlike me, even when he's cranky, Mark is still a gentleman. He tries to see the best in people. I reckon he has every right to throw me out of this small room outside the court in which the inquest into their son's death is happening, but his decency prevents him.

The couple's two sons, Matt's brothers, do not try to hide their feelings. They look at me in angry silence.

Inside the court, after 10 days, the inquest into Matt's death has so far failed to provide any answers to their questions about what happened to him. His former boyfriend, Michael Atkins, is now due to give evidence. Only, the way the legal system works, he can decline to do so if his answers may incriminate him in a crime.

'Atkins is going to object to giving evidence,' I tell them. 'But when he does, there is an option available to the coroner to grant him a certificate under section 61 of the *Coroner's Act*.' The Levesons don't blink. They know this, as some of Matt's friends who've already given evidence about their social lives, including their drug use, have received the same protection.

I continue, saying that we could offer a certificate to Atkins. It means he is not able to refuse to answer any questions. It would also mean that, if he did confess to something, his evidence couldn't then be used to put him on trial.

The only crimes not covered by a section 61 certificate are perjury and contempt of court.

Faye shakes her head. I can see why she's angry: Atkins could confess to murder and never be punished. I know it doesn't sound like justice and, as far as I've been able to establish, no one has ever tried to do this in a possible murder case before.

But, as I've told Matt's family, I've been working on this case for almost two years now and I don't think I can take it any further with police work.

Since picking up the case again in early 2014, I've spent months following up the supposed Facebook confession from 'MikeyBoi Atkins', only for it to turn out to be false. That was a crushing blow, to me and Matt's parents. Working with local detectives from the Miranda local area command, which covered the area where Matt's car was discovered in 2007, we have made some advances. We've found new CCTV evidence showing that after the Levesons' son and Atkins left the ARQ nightclub together on the night before Matt's disappearance, the older man returned, alone, to complete a drug deal almost an hour later.

One of the Miranda cops, Detective Senior Sergeant Scott Craddock, is standing with me in the room with Matt's family. A tall, wiry, young bloke, Scott has impressed me; he's smart, much smarter than I am, with a real emotional intelligence.

Left with the not guilty verdict over Matt's death, Scott and I are in the same position that Jerry Bowden and I are now facing with the Bowraville murders – needing 'fresh and compelling' evidence in order to ask the appeal court to order a retrial. Despite our best efforts, we don't have this evidence. So I'd tried something that worked with the Bowraville case. I went to the new State Coroner, Michael Barnes, and told him Matt's family had put their faith in the court system and it had failed to give them any answers about what happened to their son.

This time, the situation was slightly different. Typically, no inquest is held after a murder trial, but I argued that this left Matt's family with no answers, only an acquittal, and the coroner had consulted his law books, finding there was nothing to actually prevent an inquest taking place. I'd also encouraged Matt's parents to petition the coroner in person, asking him to hold an inquest and, when he agreed, and a journalist at the *60 Minutes* TV program approached me saying she wanted to report on the case, I said I would cooperate.

The media attention would be useful, I thought, as I'd started to doubt my faith in the court system. Look at the decision during the trial over Matt's murder to prevent the jury from watching the footage of Atkins' police interview, or the way the Bowraville trials were separated, so each jury was only told that one child went missing. In both, the courts decided justice meant preventing evidence from being heard in public. Having *60 Minutes* sitting in the courtroom meant that, this time, the case would play out in the spotlight.

It risked provoking a confrontation with the coroner, or my boss, Mick Willing. Maybe later I'd regret that but, like Faye, I was putting my fists up and was prepared to slug it out because finding Matt was more important.

It also means there is now a huge weight of public attention on Matt's parents to make this decision. I tell them I don't want to pursue the section 61 certificate unless they agree.

'Let's break it down,' I tell them. 'What do you ideally want out of this inquest?'

'To prosecute Atkins and to find Matt's body,' Mark and Faye reply together.

I hesitate. 'What if you could only achieve *one* of those things? Which would you choose?'

'We want Matt's body back,' says Faye. Mark says he agrees.

'I can't make any promises,' I tell them. But this way, if Atkins gets immunity from prosecution, at least he might reveal the gravesite. They might get to hold a funeral.

***

When I tell Atkins' lawyers, they look at me as if I'm crazy.

'So you don't believe in the right to silence?' they ask.

'No,' I answer. The right to silence is about protecting the suspect, just like the double jeopardy rules that the Bowraville families overturned. But what about the victims? What about Matt's parents?

'Never have believed in it. Never will,' I tell Atkins' lawyers. I'm just trying to make the system work.

***

Over the coming months, Atkins will fight our attempt to compel him to give evidence all the way to the Supreme Court. On 12 October 2016, he loses.

On Monday 31 October, during his first day in the witness box, Atkins denies knowing that Matt was dead and says he told police the truth when he was interviewed in the days after Matt went missing.

Atkins returns to the witness box day after day, and his answers to the repeated questions start to stumble. On his fifth day, he admits that yes, he lied during the police interview when he said he hadn't bought a mattock and duct tape from Bunnings. Yes, he bought them, he finally confesses, but only to grow vegetables.

With this step forward, Atkins walks into a trap laid for him by the counsel assisting the coroner, who asks him, 'Your evidence was, you *did* tell the truth to police. That's your evidence here in this court?'

'Yes.'

'You agree that in your interview to police you told them lies, don't you?'

'Yes.'

'You've lied in your evidence in this court, haven't you, on Monday, when you said you told the police the truth. That's right isn't it?'

Atkins is silent for a moment. 'Yes.'

He's caught. Perjury – lying to a court – isn't covered by his immunity from prosecution.

But I don't want to prosecute him for perjury. I want to find Matt's body.

I go back to Matt's parents, then talk to the Attorney General. I ask both the same question: 'Will you allow us to make Atkins a second offer of immunity from prosecution – this time for perjury – in return for telling us where he buried Matt?'

This time, we can say to him, *If you don't tell the truth, you'll go to prison.*

I am certain he'll agree. The Atkins I've seen in the witness box is a coward. He'll be too frightened of what might happen to him inside to refuse this.

There's No Death That's a Good Death

January 2016: 31 years in

The deeper we wade into the lives of the people living around Kendall, where William Tyrrell went missing, the darker the water seems.

In the new year of 2016, we start looking at someone new: a fat, hairy gorilla of a man living in the area near William's foster grandmother's house, where the three-year-old was last seen.

He worries me. His name keeps coming up in conversation with locals. Without a clear suspect in William's disappearance, suspicion seems to be seeping through the area from its pools and rivers, pooling among the roots in the forest and poisoning the trees.

Up close, the man's house looks like the bush has grown right over it. Hanging in what remains of his garden are the bodies of dead animals, tied up with string. Walking inside, my worry deepens when we find what looks like a kind of shrine at the end of the man's bed made out of a photograph of William along with quotes of mine taken from newspapers, saying we'll never give up on trying to find him.

It's one of many disturbing things I've found, carried in the stream of trauma caused by William's disappearance. Talking to the man, however, I suspect he is more guilty of seeking attention than anything actually criminal. He seems lonely – when I go to his home, he doesn't want me to leave. But we put him under surveillance, to be certain.

I ask Greg, one of the junior detectives on the strike force, to look at whether we can install covert cameras in the forest to keep watch on this man. Greg's come over from the Robbery and Serious Crime Squad and doesn't have much experience of working homicides, if any. I've had him transcribing telephone intercepts for months because I was unsure about giving him anything demanding but I now tell Greg to drive out and take a look at where the cameras could be installed. Before he leaves, I remind him to walk through the bush to get there and not to park on Benaroon Drive. After all, this is a covert operation.

When Greg comes back he tells me he parked on Benaroon Drive, in full view of the neighbours, and walked straight through a big, open property to get to where we're thinking of setting up the cameras. The property's owner, an old bloke called Paul, who is in his 70s, approached him.

'G'day mate,' Greg said, introducing himself as a detective. Then, remembering the cameras were supposed to be a covert job, he tried to disguise what he was doing: 'I've been sent here because we have some concerns about the initial search for William Tyrrell and we believe it hasn't been searched on this side and I need to do an initial assessment before we do a search.'

Paul seemed interested. He hadn't been on his usual morning walk yet, so offered to go with Greg, who said he accepted.

Paul seemed to know his way around, Greg tells me. He seemed to be friendly. Listening, I wonder whether it occurred to Greg his new friend might be trying to ingratiate himself with the police.

After walking through the bush, the two of them returned to Paul's driveway, where they talked about the two cars Jane thought she saw parked on Benaroon Drive the morning William went missing. We'd just released these details to the media.

Paul said he didn't know why they were talking about two cars on the television.

'What do you mean?' Greg asked him.

'They weren't there on that day.'

'What day?'

'The day William went missing.'

'How do you know?'

'I walk every day. They weren't there on that day ... I saw those cars two days *before* William went missing.'

It is a strange conversation, and I ask Greg to make a written record of it. In the end, we wrap up our investigation into the hermit, calling him in for a formal interview during which time we search his house covertly, but find no evidence against him. We're just not making progress.

I think again about Greg's chance conversation with Paul and wonder if we've missed something. Paul lives opposite William's foster grandmother, Anne Fiore, and his front verandah looks out towards the back of her house, although the view is partially obscured by trees.

William was last seen running around from the front of Anne's house towards the back of her property. Yet no witness statement was taken from Paul until almost two weeks later and his house was not searched until three days after William disappeared.

I look at his witness statement, and another Paul gave almost a year after William went missing, when we re-interviewed everyone who lived near Anne's property on Benaroon Drive. He says that, on the day itself, he went for his daily walk in the State forest and returned home about 8.50am. He made some calls, then sat on his verandah having some tea and toast. About 10am, he heard children playing. That would make Paul only the third adult witness, apart from Jane and Anne, to have heard William and his sister shortly before the three-year-old went missing.

Paul's statements say his wife, Heather, left to drive to her regular bingo morning at about 10.30am, or a few minutes after – around the time William was last seen. Apart from sitting on the verandah, Paul himself was in and out of the house, packing to drive to Lismore, over four hours away, to pick up his brother from hospital. But he didn't see or hear any of the frantic search for William until he got a knock on the door from a neighbour saying the little boy was missing. After that, Paul cancelled the trip to Lismore and went out looking for him.

Leaving his house, Paul didn't go down the road to where everybody else was searching. Instead, according to his statements, Paul went in the other direction, alone, up the hill and along the same track he walks every morning. Having done so, he cut through the bush to the back of his property and went inside to have a cup of tea. At about 1pm or 1.30pm, just as he was about to go outside to search again, his brother- and sister-in-law arrived for a visit.

He doesn't have an alibi, I think. Heather's own witness statement, taken before her death, says that she spent the morning getting ready for bingo and left at 10.38am, but doesn't say what her husband was doing. No other witnesses confirm where Paul was between the time that neighbour knocked on his door and when his relatives arrived roughly two hours later.

My job as a detective means coming up with case theories, then testing them. That means asking questions: *Why would Paul go off into the bush and search alone? And why then come back to the house and go inside, without asking if William had been found yet?*

Which leads to another question: A couple of days later, Paul did make the journey to Lismore and back, to pick up his brother. Were the local police searching the cars going in or out of Benaroon Drive at that time? I check and find the answer is no.

But, so far, I have too few other answers, and the statements we have got from Paul so far are not detailed enough to provide them. There are also inconsistencies; in one statement, Paul says his brother- and sister-in-law's visit was scheduled, in the other he says that they just dropped in.

I ask Laura to visit Paul at home to take another statement from him on 16 March. He tells Laura the same story, although afterwards, she says he was difficult to interview, prickly and emotional. Whenever Laura tried to get into the nitty-gritty, she says he started to cry about his dead wife.

When Paul's name comes up at the next strike force briefing, other cops say yeah, he's odd. After his wife died last April he wore a photograph of her around his neck for a month. He also has an Apprehended Violence Order against him for harassing the local postwoman, and he's breached it. Someone says that Paul found one of the hidden surveillance cameras we'd been using to keep a watch on the hermit, and kept it for six weeks before finally handing it back to us. We'd known the camera was missing, but not who had taken it.

I look at the strike force. *Why have I not been told these things before?* And there are other questions: like why Paul told Laura that, once he found out William was missing, he went out the front of his house and spoke to Anne Fiore.

According to Anne, Paul didn't.

***

On a Sunday afternoon in April 2016, I am standing on an isolated clifftop on the Central Coast, looking down at a bag containing the body of a young, unidentified woman who has just been recovered from the blowhole beneath us. The longer I do this job, the more I learn what the dead can tell us. Are there defence wounds, usually scratches on the hands and arms, showing where a victim tried to fight off their attacker? Does this look like a crime of passion, where a killer has caved in their victim's skull, or was this a clinical killing, delivered with a bullet to the back of the head, leaving the skull around the entry hole relatively intact but the face through which it made its exit in fragments?

How has the body been disposed of? This, also, can tell you something. Did the killer panic? Was he practised?

Unzipping the bag lying on the clifftop, I look at her arms and see bright red defence wounds. A murder.

A day later, on 25 April, a Sydney couple report their niece missing. Mengmei Leng is a 25-year-old student from Chengdu in China. She'd been staying with her aunt and uncle but they say they haven't seen her for days.

Her uncle, Derek Barrett, says he last spoke to Mengmei by telephone on the morning of 22 April. A day later, he signs a police statement saying his niece recently started going out to parties and nightclubs, and drinking. He says his wife had gone away for a few days, leaving him and Mengmei alone in their apartment, then he woke up one day and the young woman was gone.

We talk to Mengmei's aunt, who says when she returned, she noticed how clean the place was, and that the bedsheets had been laundered.

But if the battered body recovered from the water is Mengmei, then what brought her here, to Snapper Point? It is over 100 kilometres from Sydney, where she was last seen.

Barrett has family in the area. His mobile phone pinged off a nearby tower in the early morning of 24 April.

We arrest him on 29 April, after DNA confirms the body is that of Mengmei. On his phone we find photographs of her, bound, naked and terrified, and also of the blowhole where he tried to hide her body.

Barrett will eventually be sentenced to 46 years in prison over the murder, with a non-parole period of 34 years and six months. We got justice and, once, I might have gone out on the beers after a result like this, but this time there's no joy in this. It is just an extremely sad case.

At least it's quick. At the same time, I'm also dealing with the Leveson inquest, trying to find a way to take the Bowraville murders back to the appeal court and searching for William Tyrrell. I'm wound tight as a metal spring. Most days, whether I am on call, leading a fresh investigation or in court, I wake up at three or four in the morning to start working, to ensure none of these other cases suffer.

***

Mum calls to say Dad has leukaemia. The news, coming soon after Barrett's arrest, forces its way through the crowd of deaths I'm wrestling with and demands my attention.

I knew Dad was having tests.

The doctor reckons he might have three years, but it could be only two, or one.

You tell yourself that you're OK receiving news like this, but there is a hollowness.

I visit him, when next in Port Macquarie working on William's disappearance, but Dad won't discuss his fears.

I say, 'Look, of course you're scared.'

'I'm not worried about dying. It's *how* I'm gonna die,' he tells me.

There's no death that's a good death. So, at what point do you let go? And what does it feel like when it happens?

What Do We Want?

5 May 2016: 31 years in

A young boy walking with his mother in the sunlight stops and stares into the shadows created by the overhanging fig trees. Advancing towards them through Hyde Park, in central Sydney, is a skinny, wild-haired woman, her raised hand and forearm painted with the same white ochre that decorates her face.

Behind her, carrying a huge black, red and yellow flag is a mob of hundreds more protestors. Their brown faces, and the Aboriginal flag they carry, are painted with the same white ochre as Dolly Jerome's fist.

'What do we want?' shouts Dolly, whose nephew Clinton was the third child to disappear in Bowraville.

'Justice!' the mob behind her answers, moving out from under the trees into the sunlight, heading towards Parliament House.

The young boy and his mother watch as they step into the road, forcing the city traffic to a standstill.

'What do we want?'

'Justice!'

'What have we got?'

'Fuck all!'

Other members of the children's families carry empty ring binders, representing the volumes of evidence about the killings sent to the Director of Public Prosecutions (DPP) and two attorneys general between 2007 and 2013, all of whom refused to send the murders back to court.

Just like the last time they protested, in November 2013, I am not a part of the crowd but not entirely separate from it either. My bosses told me not to come here, saying they don't want the police to appear politicised, but I've disobeyed them. I'm a detective chief inspector now, an automatic promotion after spending a decade as a detective inspector, and reckon I am senior enough to make my own decisions.

Today, I've swapped my black tie for one decorated with the pattern of a dot painting, given to me by the children's families. I've decided to stand with the mob from Bowraville.

The crowd is full of faces I recognise. There's Thomas Duroux, Clinton's father, his careworn face hidden in the shade of his baseball cap. He nods. Thomas is a man's man, just like my father is. He doesn't show a lot of emotion, but it would be a mistake to think that he isn't hurting. I've spent hours sitting with him on the Mission, seeing how his sorrow bows his shoulders forward and how his eyes still light up softly whenever he talks about his son.

Behind Thomas is Michelle Jarrett, standing tall and staring in defiance. Her niece Evelyn was the second child to go missing. Michelle has grown over the time I've known her, into a real leader. I wouldn't like to be on her wrong side – when she goes off she's terrifying – but, like Aunty Elaine used to, she will often now reach out to check I am OK when she sees me on the TV news, busy with another murder.

The protest forces its way north along Macquarie Street, up to the locked metal gates of the parliament building. Within it, Muriel Craig walks past me, surrounded by her surviving children. Even among the crowd, there's something in the way Muriel carries herself that makes her seem isolated. Her daughter, 16-year-old Colleen, was the first to go missing and, it is as if she has been stranded ever since by the grief of losing a daughter and never having even found her body.

She and I have often argued. I can't count the number of times Muriel has abused me, saying I'm not doing enough to convict her daughter's killer – and she's right. I feel I've let the families down: all these years, with no result. There's always something more to be done. If anything, her anger's made me more determined.

Sometimes, when I tell myself I can't do this anymore, I look at the children's families, who keep getting up after all the times they've been kicked in the guts, by the courts, by the DPP and the attorneys general. I watch Thomas, Michelle and Muriel join the angry knot of people outside the locked gates of Parliament House and think, *No, let's go. Let's keep fighting.*

The parliamentary inquiry into the murders was good – it made people listen – but it had no power to overturn the last Attorney General's refusal to send the case to the appeal court.

'What do we want?' shouts another voice from within the crowd, not Dolly's this time. A voice I do not recognise, amplified by a loudhailer.

'Justice!' the crowd shouts in anger. The loudhailer gets passed round and different voices start calling politicians cunts, or saying that they hate the cops.

'Except this bloke.' I look up. The man with the loudhailer points at me. It feels extraordinary to be singled out. After the protest dissipates, I walk away thinking, *Well, the police might not like me being here but at least I've got my convictions.* I took a stand.

And the protest is only the beginning.

For months now, I've been meeting with journalists, trying to get them interested in the case, knowing that could help put pressure on my bosses and the politicians.

Four reporters told me the story was old and cold, and going nowhere. A fifth seemed interested but made no promises. Then, months later, he called back.

This morning, 5 May, his article appeared in *The Australian* newspaper. It began:

> The investigation into a serial killer responsible for the unsolved murders of three children 25 years ago has been criticised by federal and state politicians, who say the result would have been different if the victims were white.

The article quotes the country's first Indigenous Member of the Federal House of Representatives, Ken Wyatt. 'If this had been three children in Sydney's Point Piper, then would there have been a different approach?' he is quoted as saying. 'The approach would have been tackled with a lot more rigour ... by police, by authorities. There would have been an outcry.'

That should make the State government take notice.

The next day, following the protest, the newspaper reports:

> NSW Police will present an 18-volume submission to the state's Attorney-General calling for a retrial of the man alleged to have carried out the unsolved murders of three children in Bowraville 25 years ago.
>
> The submission, drawn up in cooperation with lawyers acting for the victims' families, details similarities and links between the killings as well as evidence uncovered by police that has not been heard in court.

It's accurate, except for one detail – I haven't actually got all the signatures I need from my bosses to make the submission. But I will do.

The protest, these newspaper reports and the submission calling for a retrial have all been carefully coordinated. All we're asking for is the appeal court, not the politicians, to look at the murders and decide if there is a case to answer. If the not guilty verdicts are overturned, James Hide can be put on trial for all three of the murders together. Should that happen, a jury can hear all of the evidence against him for the first time, including the new information we have uncovered in the years since he was acquitted.

It's not traditional policing, to be cooperating with campaigners, lawyers and the media to push your government into making a decision, but it is an attempt to get justice. And, if not that, then what is police work for?

The Australian starts campaigning on the issue, running stories on the murders daily, often on the front page, creating the pressure I hoped for. After a fortnight, one of its journalists records an interview with James himself, who's never spoken about all three of the children's killings, and publishes this conversation in a podcast.

In it, James says he played no part in what happened to the children. When asked why he did not give evidence at his trial for Evelyn's murder, he says his barrister told him not to.

'Why didn't you want to give evidence? Why not clear it up?' the reporter asks.

'At that point it's not about clearing things up, it's about winning the case,' says James. His voice is dull, and without being able to see him across the interview room table, it's hard to judge what he is thinking.

Asked to explain how a pillowslip from his caravan was found with Clinton's corpse, James says maybe the teenager took it with him and went walking into the bush to collect some marijuana.

But he didn't have his shoes on, the reporter counters.

'It's not my explanation, it is a theory that's consistent with the evidence, and that's what they said in court,' says James. 'If you look at the law, and this is what the judge said in the trial, if there is a scenario that fits the evidence and is consistent with innocence, you have to find not guilty.'

He's right. The law protects the suspect.

Asked whether he would welcome an appeal court hearing, James says:

> … almost, if it wasn't for the strain it puts on the family, emotionally and financially, and all the other things that go along with it, the national celebrity that comes with it, I don't want none of that but then again, I want the actual evidence to be all heard and seen that it wasn't me.

The reporter follows this up, asking, 'But you're saying there's a part of you that would like to see this go to court?'

'A small part, we'll put it that way.'

The newspaper also prints his words, under the front-page headline: 'Trial would clear me: accused killer'. That can only make it easier for the current Attorney General, Gabrielle Upton, to make her decision. On 25 May, after the Police Commissioner finally signs off on our submission and after three weeks of unrelenting pressure from the families and the media, Gabrielle does what none of her predecessors would do and asks the appeal court to look at all three Bowraville murders. She asks them to assess whether the previous not guilty verdicts should be overturned and James put on trial again.

I picture Michelle talking to her sister Rebecca, Evelyn's mother. I picture Thomas celebrating with Leonie Duroux, who's spent hours on the phone with me over the years, working out how to push this campaign further. I picture Muriel hugging her remaining children.

We're in with a chance, I'm certain. It's always been about making people listen. After so many years, I feel such happiness that the families will be heard.

A Million Dollars

11 August 2016: 31 years in

The other members of the strike force, Jerry Bowden and Bianca Comina, stand with me on the Mission, watching the smoking ceremony before the Police Commissioner Andrew Scipione steps up to a wooden lectern facing the gathered families. The black faces watching him are guarded, unsure what to expect. Ash from the burning gum leaves settles on our shoulders as Andrew says he came here to pay his respects.

'I want to acknowledge that for 25 years you have been fighting for justice. A dignified and committed fight for the truth about what happened to your children,' he says. The crowd is silent, listening. There is still a great mistrust of the authorities among this community but I sense there is also something deeper in the silence, a willingness to hear what the policeman is saying.

'I want to publicly acknowledge that the New South Wales Police Force could have done more,' Andrew continues. 'We could have done more for your families when these crimes first occurred. We should have done more. I know this has added to your pain.'

He looks up from the words written in front of him, directly at the families. 'And can I say to you that I am sorry?' He repeats those words – 'I am sorry' – four times over.

Afterwards, he carries a wreath of flowers through the smoke, placing it at the base of a memorial to the three murdered children that now stands on the grass, opposite Thomas Duroux's house, close to the Tree of Knowledge.

The families surround Andrew and gently thank him for coming. I see relief on Michelle Jarrett's face. Muriel Craig is smiling.

Jerry, Bianca and I are also impressed. His words have helped repay the trust the Bowraville families put in us to correct what went wrong here. As Andrew walks away across the grass, Bianca watches him go with her head tilted to one side. She says the apology is welcome, but the truth is, the evidence we've gathered about this case has not changed in the past decade. All that's changed is the politics, she says. She's right, I know, but at least we got here.

I get embarrassed sometimes, comparing the staff and resources the police put into pursuing the Bowraville killer over the past three decades to what I've now been given to investigate

William's disappearance. Earlier this year, we set up a second strike force – Rosann 2 – in an attempt to find our way through the tangle of over 1000 different people we've nominated as persons of interest (PoIs), hoping to eliminate as many as we can in order to find suspects.

Rosann 1 has drawn up a list of around 400 PoIs and spent weeks drawing up background reports on each of them. These are then sent to the detectives in Rosann 2, drawn from different squads within State Crime Command, as well as local area commands to follow up. They report back. It is a huge commitment, with detectives travelling across the country to find people and strike them off our list, which means this investigation is being attempted on a scale I have never before seen in the police force.

But, as always on this case it seems, it's not enough. We need more staff, more resources. Whatever you throw at this, it eats it up. And right now, more than anything, I think we need more money.

One Friday night towards the end of August, I get a call on my mobile from the State Police Minister, Troy Grant. He asks about William's disappearance and if there's anything we need to solve it. We talk about announcing a reward for information. It would have to be substantial I say, as whoever out there knows something – and someone must – they've not come forward before now. We need enough money to turn heads, to make a wife inform on a husband, maybe, or make one paedophile betray another.

Enough to make someone believe they can change their life completely.

'What about a million dollars?' Troy asks.

That might do it.

Later the same idea comes up in conversation with William's foster parents. They ask what kind of reward a murder normally attracts and when I tell them that for Bowraville, it is $100,000 for all three children's killings, Tom says that it's not enough.

'What about a million dollars?' I say. I can't promise them that we will get it; no case in New South Wales has ever attracted such a reward, and once you set that kind of precedent for William, it would be hard to refuse any other murder victim's family that comes after. But, after speaking to Troy, I'm confident. With so much public attention on William's disappearance, the State Premier and Police Commissioner are also in favour.

There's just one catch. They want to first be absolutely certain neither William's biological nor foster parents were involved.

We've already established that his birth parents were nowhere near Kendall when William went missing, as CCTV, telephone records and shopping receipts put them both in Sydney. Nor have we found any evidence that someone else took William on their behalf over the years since. At first, I am reluctant to re-interview Tom and Jane, as we've grown close and I know how much they have already suffered, but I do it. This is my job. On 1 September, I sit down with each of them and go hard. Nothing either of them says makes me doubt them.

The reward is announced less than a fortnight later, on 12 September 2016, the second anniversary of William's disappearance. It makes the TV news and is shared thousands of times on Facebook. A special video is created for the Where's William? website: '$1 Million Reward, Make the Call!'

We sit by the phones and wait, but we get nothing. The silence makes me doubt myself at first, and then I realise we have at least learned something from it.

It makes me think we're looking for somebody who acted on their own.

***

I joke that my whole life is affidavits: the coroner keeps demanding more paperwork be completed as part of our offer of immunity from prosecution to Michael Atkins; so do the lawyers preparing to take the Bowraville murders to the appeal court; the Supreme Court wants affidavits written out each time Strike Force Rosann applies for a listening device or telephone intercept warrant, and each of these will only last so long before you have to go back to court, asking for it to be extended, carrying another affidavit.

At home, two weeks after the million-dollar reward is announced, my divorce from Tracy is listed in the Federal Circuit Court, which means dealing with more documents.

Legal letters seem to arrive every Friday at 5pm, ruining the weekend and forcing me to reckon up our assets – the apartment we bought together in Pyrmont, my super, my two motorbikes – and the costs of our relationship, including more than $21,000 I've spent on flights between Sydney and Perth.

We agree to sell the apartment and I move out as directed by the arbitrator we had engaged, only the money from the sale doesn't come through as expected, so I can't afford to buy a replacement. Facing my mounting legal costs, I sell my bikes. By chance, an apartment comes up for rent – next door to the one I shared with Tracy.

Each evening, I come home from work and walk past our old front door to get to my new apartment. I'd planned to retire at 55, but will no longer be able to afford that, so have to accept I'll work until 60. Police work is hard and already I am among only a handful of those who graduated with me from the police academy who are still serving. When I visit my parents, hoping to pour out my troubles, I can see Dad is getting sicker.

He lashes out at Mum sometimes, like he did when we were kids, and she tells me my divorce is worrying him more than anything. I mean to sit down with him and tell him not to worry, I'm OK, but instead, I get angry.

'Look, regardless of what you're going through, you can't treat Mum like that,' I tell him.

Maybe anger is one kind of defence. So is denial: *He's Dad, he's tough, never mind what the doctors say, he's going to get through this.* I'm overloaded with emotions, fear of losing him and guilt because I didn't spend more time with him before his illness, resentment of myself for not spending more time with him now because instead I am spending every weekend dealing with my divorce.

Anxiety about all my different cases. Worry that I might not solve them. When I'm in Port Macquarie working on William's disappearance, if work isn't going well, I find it difficult to visit Mum and Dad because their first question is always, 'What's going on with the investigation into little William?'

Sometimes I tell them I don't want to talk about it, and the question hangs in the air inside their house, unanswered.

Yet, at the same time, I'm doing some of my best police work. My attempts to answer the questions of what happened to Matt Leveson and the Bowraville children are setting legal precedents and overturning old, established obstacles like the right to silence and double jeopardy. The investigation into William's disappearance may be the biggest in the country.

When I think about how this period of blackness contains this single point of light, it reminds me of the yin-yang symbol. The black side, yin, contains a white circle. The white side, yang, contains a black one. If I accept that my life now is yin, and that there is no longer any balance, then maybe I can reach that point of yang within it. I might find Matt Leveson's body. I might jail the Bowraville killer. I might discover who took William.

Maybe I've been reaching towards this point all my life.

***

I keep taking on more work.

In October, I travel north, to the flat inland country near the New South Wales State border. The family of a murder victim, a 43-year-old mother of three called Theresa Binge, have contacted police because they've heard my name from Bowraville, and because Theresa is a cousin of Clinton Speedy-Duroux.

Theresa was last seen alive in July 2003, drinking in the grand Victoria Hotel on the high street in Goondiwindi, Queensland, just north of the State border. A local man had bought her half a dozen beers. He himself drank about a dozen heavy pots of XXXX. The two of them left the pub together at around midnight.

Theresa was part of a big family, one of 17 if you counted her half-brothers and -sisters. When she didn't turn up to a birthday party the following night on the nearby Toomelah Aboriginal Reserve, where she grew up, they started to worry about her.

Her family went out looking for Theresa on the Saturday, and reported her missing to police a day later. At first, her disappearance was treated as a missing-persons investigation, led by the Queensland police but, more than a week later, on Tuesday 29 July, her partially naked body was found lying beside a culvert running beneath the Boomi Road, which runs like an arrow through this empty country.

Theresa was on her back. Her silver tracksuit trousers were down around her right ankle and she had bruises around her neck, arms and thigh, as well as the right side of her face, suggesting she'd been punched and kicked.

There were drag marks in the gravel leading down from the road to where she was lying, along with an empty pack of Peter Jackson Virginia cigarettes. The culvert was on the south side of the State border, meaning the New South Wales police had taken over the investigation, without success.

Once again, it was worked by the local cops, with little help from the Homicide Squad. When I sat down with them in Toomelah, Theresa's family wanted to know why nothing had happened? Why had no one been jailed? Was it because Theresa was black, while the man she left the pub in Goondiwindi with was white? I listened as they vented all their raw frustration, suspicion and disappointment. It was like the first time I went to Bowraville, all over again.

The last thing I need right now, I tell my dad, is another murder. Especially one that is an eight-hour drive from Sydney. But there's talk of a new witness, and I go back with Scott Craddock, who I'm working with on the Matt Leveson case and who has now joined the Homicide Squad.

He and I spend days searching for people, being passed from one person to another, just like in Bowraville, before eventually running a witness to ground and finding there is nothing in what they were saying. We talk to the local cops, and work through the files of the original investigation.

It looks like the cops who worked it the first time went hard, but that they came up against a great, impenetrable silence. But I think we can break it.

'It's solvable, Dad, I'm sure of it,' I tell him when I next visit, looking out over the Hastings River. 'It just needs some commitment.'

I Thought I Would Get Blamed

9 November 2016: 31 years in

I look up when I hear the soft padding of the lawyer's heels on the thick carpet. She says that they're ready. It must be close to midnight.

Scott Craddock and I were already tired after a full day's work when we got to these plush offices at 4pm. Since then, we've been pacing up and down or sitting, listening to the sound of cleaners elsewhere in the building, while the lawyers argued.

Michael Atkins has finally agreed to talk about the death of his boyfriend, Matthew Leveson – but with conditions. His lawyers wanted to get it in writing that anything he says will not be used against him in a criminal trial, and that he will not be recalled to give evidence to the inquest. We, too, have one condition: Atkins only gets immunity from prosecution if we find Matt's body.

His lawyer leads us into a small conference room. I watch Atkins walk in. Scott opens up his laptop to type a record of the conversation.

Close up, Atkins is almost childlike. He sits, sagging, in his chair at the table. He's dyed his hair to look younger and built up his muscles to look bigger, but I get the sense that the real person is hiding. He looks at his lawyers, sitting on either side of him, as if asking for reassurance: 'Is this what I should do?'

I have to control my excitement. I've pursued this man for more than two years; I've staked him out, listened to our surveillance of his private conversations and worked with the police force's forensic psychologist to get inside his head. Following her advice, we have a plan for how Scott and I should approach this moment. We are not to judge Atkins or give him any reason to throw up his defences. Instead, we are to give him every opportunity to open up and reveal the truth.

I ask him, 'Can you tell me your knowledge as to what happened to Matthew Leveson?'

'Yes.' He takes a breath and exhales it. 'He had a drug overdose.'

I panic. My mind spins, thinking, *Fuck*.

Even his lawyers look stunned. Everyone in the room expected him to offer up a murder.

Atkins says he and Matt drove home from the nightclub, barely talking to each other. He fell asleep in front of the TV, and when he woke up in the morning, 'I went into the bedroom and saw that Matt was lying on the ground with his eyes open, and he was not breathing and he had a funny colour.'

Atkins says a vodka bottle full of a clear liquid was standing open on the kitchen counter. Inside it was GHB, the drug he had been dealing at the nightclub the evening before.

'Did you cause Matt's death?' I ask, trying to slow the pace of the interview and regain some control.

'No.'

'Why did you cover up Matt's death?'

'Because I thought I would get blamed.'

'Why would you think that?'

'Because we were dealing drugs, and everyone thought I was the more responsible one so I should be the one caring for him.'

'Who were you concerned about blaming you?'

'Everybody, I think. Matt's parents. I thought everybody as in society, I suppose.'

So, he didn't want people to blame him. To avoid it, he buried Matt's body. Do I believe him?

I hold his gaze, watching the way he looks at me or avoids me, listening to whether his answers flow or hesitate, using all the skills I've learned from Jim, from Jaco, and from three decades spent sitting in interview rooms like this one. Nothing tells me Atkins is lying.

'How did you think burying Matt's body would make it all better?' I ask him.

'I was not thinking very clearly. I thought people would think he has just gone away or is missing because he had done that before.'

'What would that achieve?'

'I thought the problem would all go away in some weird way.'

'To describe the death of someone as a "problem that would go away" is very unusual. Can you explain to me what you mean by that?'

He seems to flinch. 'I don't really understand what I was thinking at the time. I look back now and I don't understand it. I just don't know. I thought I was going to be blamed and be shamed. I've always thought of myself as a good person.'

'So you buried a person that you loved in an unmarked grave to protect your reputation. Is that correct?'

His voice is low, 'I think so. The whole thing about being blamed and the guilt. I did not want the drug thing to come out so I was trying to protect that, and I was worried about what my family would think of me. I was worried about what my mother would think of me … She didn't know I was gay.'

This is the tipping point. I believe him. I'm looking at a grown man who buried his boyfriend because he didn't want his mum to know about his sexuality.

Matt's parents, I know, may never accept this is what happened to their son, but it makes sense. It's too stupid a motive to make up.

Atkins looks at me, as if he is pleading, and I hold his gaze. His confession is not enough. If there's to be any kind of justice then we need to find Matt's body.

I get him to describe how he bought the duct tape and mattock. How, back at the apartment, he had covered Matt's body in a blanket or a donna cover – he can't remember which – then, went down to the garage beneath the apartment building at night and removed Matt's big stereo speaker from the boot of his car. How he went back upstairs and wrapped Matt's body fully. 'I can't remember if I used the tape, I think I did.'

How he waited until after midnight before carrying Matt down to the car.

Atkins says he drove Matt to the Royal National Park.

By now, it's two or three in the morning. We print out the statement Scott's typed up of Atkins' confessions and he signs it. I tell his lawyers: 'I want to take him down there. I want him to show us the location.'

The five of us, myself, Scott, Atkins and his lawyers, Sharon Ramsden and Claire Wasley, crowd into my car, and drive through the empty city to where the streetlights stop at the park's edge, then on into the darkness.

The road winds down between thick forest. Nobody talks, until Atkins says: 'Pull in here.'

***

Staring out at the forest in daylight more than a week later, I remember the look on Atkins' face at that moment. There was nothing noble in his expression. There was no remorse. There was relief.

I keep telling myself that as I stand with Mark and Faye Leveson, watching an excavator dig trenches in the soft, dark earth. The growl of its engine seems to infuriate the birds, which are wheeling and shrieking above us in the canopy of trees.

The forest is so thick here you cannot see the sky. Not that anyone is looking upward. Everyone is looking down, at where the excavator is digging. So far, we have not found Matt.

After driving Atkins into the park before dawn on 10 November, we stopped at a couple of different places beside the road snaking its way down into the forest. At each, he looked around and then dismissed them. One was too open, Atkins said. At another, the space for a car to pull up beside the road itself felt too small.

At the third, I watched Atkins edge his way out into the bush, ten, 20, 40 metres, talking to himself as he moved forward: 'I remember that tree', 'I remember that slope'. About 70 metres in, he stopped. It seemed a long way to carry Matt's body from the car, I thought, but he told us, this was it. We marked the spot and left two other detective constables, who had just arrived, carrying high-powered flashlights, to organise a police guard of the area.

After daybreak, Scott and I went back to the coroner's court to tell Mark and Faye Leveson what had happened. A day later, on Friday 11 November, Matt's family joined us to watch the bright yellow excavator roar into life, sending the outraged cockatoos soaring into the air.

After seven ugly days of searching, by Thursday 17 November this stretch of bush beside the road has been torn up like a battlefield, with rows of trenches dug 30 centimetres apart, and Faye looks as if her heart has been ripped open.

'He's lying,' Faye says of Atkins. 'Toying with us. Matty isn't here.'

Mark is more resolute, saying that they will still find their son. I say nothing but am beginning to doubt.

There's no good reason Atkins would be lying. He knows the deal: no body, no immunity. If we don't find Matt, he'll go to jail for perjury after lying to the inquest. I think again of that look of relief on his face.

So what are we missing? I ask Matt's parents if there's anywhere among the trenches they'd like us to search again. They walk out across the savaged, broken earth, planting white flags, and the excavator follows, digging beside each of these markers. Each time it finds nothing. Today is the last day of the search.

A line of TV cameras is filming the operation, crowded behind the crime scene tape. As the sun sinks, Faye walks up to them, carrying a card she'd hoped to leave on her son's grave.

'Matt, our beautiful son and brother, we made a promise to you nine years, one month and 24 days ago to find you and bring you home,' she reads, her breath ragged with sobbing. She breaks off, her body bent with pain. Behind her stands her husband. Nearby, a solitary, bright green cabbage palm still stands amid the destruction.

'We haven't fulfilled our promise to him yet,' Faye continues, looking up at the cameras. 'But I promise you, Matty, we will bring you home.'

***

I'm the one who has to find him. I drive away from the park, back to my rented flat next door to the home where I used to live with Tracy. Inside it is my gym equipment and a rack full of white shirts. My family photographs are still in boxes, meaning the only pictures on display are a promotional shot from the *Underbelly* series, a painting of Buddha I did on my meditational retreat in Nepal and Aunty Elaine Walker's funeral notice, stuck on the fridge door.

***

Also living with me in the flat in Pyrmont is Josie. As I open the door and walk inside, seeing her gentle smile makes the weight I've carried back with me from the park feel a little lighter.

I've known Josie for years, from the yoga and pilates classes she teaches at a nearby fitness studio. After moving back to Sydney from my year in Perth, I started taking her classes more often, and found they helped unwind some of the tension coiling inside me, caused by my separation from Tracy. Sometimes, we would chat after the class was over, but I never thought it would lead to anything. Once, when I'd been away for a couple of weeks with work, Josie asked where I had been. I told her I'd been hunting.

Things moved slowly. I was dealing with my second failed marriage while Josie had also recently come out of a long-term relationship. We went for coffee together and, sitting at the café table, I was struck by how relaxed she seemed. There was an innocence about her; a way of looking at life I'd not experienced before, neither concerned with the future nor the past, but instead living truly in the moment.

She was just what I needed. Shortly after we got together, Josie went back to her native Brazil for Carnival and, while she was away, I realised how much I missed her. When she got back, we moved in together in Pyrmont.

Josie taught me to take pleasure in simple things, like a picnic in the sun or drinks with her eclectic mix of friends from around the world.

At first, it frustrated me when I wanted to talk about work and she would change the subject, but slowly, I felt myself beginning to unwind. We found happiness together. In a way, I think she saved me.

After I arrive back from the Royal National Park, Josie cooks while I put on some meditation music and practise my qigong, concentrating on my breathing.

Later, I know I'll need to sit up late, preparing documents or dealing with multiple requisitions from Tracy's lawyers as part of our divorce. This process just keeps on getting harder, expanding to take up all my spare time outside of work. There are too many evenings like this one, which end with me sitting, sleepless, in a pool of light at the table, while Josie reads, or goes to bed without me.

The divorce also means court hearings on both sides of the country, which means legal fees and the cost of flights. Unable to afford a barrister in court, I represent myself, which doubles or trebles my workload and often leaves me struggling, like an animal caught in quicksand, to make sense of the complicated legal language the lawyers use. Eventually, it will get too much. I won't be able to pull myself out of this quagmire. Josie will need to get on with her life and I cannot save us both. We'll separate and move out of the flat in Pyrmont. With my finances in tatters from the legal process – I'm in my 50s, in a good job and do not own a home to live in – my younger sister, Michelle, and her partner, Jacqui, will offer me a room, living with them in Redfern.

I can see it coming. But, for now, I focus on my breathing, taking each breath deeply into my abdomen.

I've done qigong for more than 25 years now, longer than many of my cases. Longer than the lives of some of those people whose deaths I have dealt with at work. At first, as a raw qigong student, I was taught the movements dictate your breathing: raise your arms and breathe in, exhale as your hands return to the centre of your body. Later, I learned it is really the other way round: the breath dictates movement.

Standing in my apartment, feet shoulder-width apart, I think, *Breathe in.*

***

In December, Scott Craddock and I take Atkins back to the Royal National Park, driving the same route from his apartment that he took to dispose of Matt's body, looking again for the site where he buried his boyfriend.

As we drive, Atkins describes his thoughts and memories of that journey. He was panicking and felt he had to get into the park quickly. He turned into the park at the Waterfall railway station and followed the hill down. He pulled over onto gravel near a bend in the road, where there was space enough for a few cars.

He became disorientated when he left the car and walked into the bush. He stumbled, trying to carry Matt. When he stopped, there was enough moonlight breaking through the trees for him to dig.

Our hope is that something about this experience, some sight, some sound or smell in the forest, might trigger his memory. It doesn't work.

We leave and take him back again, after night has fallen. I wonder at how, in the darkness, everything seems different.

'It's really scary down here,' Atkins says. Scott looks at me in silence. He's worked this case harder than anyone, putting in hours of his off-duty time driving these roads.

We pull the car over and tell Atkins we have a surprise. Opening the boot, inside it is a life-sized mannequin for him to try dragging through the bush. He takes a step back but we insist. Maybe this will help him to recover those memories. With no prospect of a criminal trial, given our deal that Atkins will get immunity from prosecution, we're not bound by the same rules of evidence and I do not believe Atkins carried Matt's body as far into the bush as he claims.

The forest is silent except for the sound of Atkins struggling to drag the dummy away from the road on which we are standing. He says we're right, there is no way he took Matt 70 metres into the bush. We should be looking much closer to the road.

On 9 January 2017, we bring the excavator back to search a second site, which Atkins says might have been the one, although he isn't certain. We find nothing.

***

Breathe out. My divorce from Tracy is made final on 16 January 2017, although the legal arguments over how to divide up our private life together continue, which means more money, more court hearings, more expensive flights across the country trying to resolve it. As a result, when my daughter, Gemma, gets married, I feel ashamed that I cannot afford to help pay for her wedding.

***

Breathe in. We keep trying to find Matt's body. In February, Scott talks to an expert in human decomposition, asking what to expect if we do discover the gravesite. In March, we bring Atkins in for a 'cognitive interview' – a kind of hypnosis – meant to aid his memory of what happened. We give him Matt's car, the one he drove to the park that night, and let him head off in it into the park, alone.

Anything to find a way through the tangle of his memories. But he keeps coming back to the same turnoff near the railway station, the same bend in the road, the same gravel strip with room for a few cars, the stretch of bush we have already excavated.

***

Breathe out. On 10 March, after Atkins has spent three days driving round the Royal National Park in Matt's car, we meet with him and his lawyers. He's certain Matt is buried at the first site he took us to. I'm reluctant to go back, thinking maybe Faye was right and he's just playing with us, but his solicitor Sharon Ramsden argues that we have to. There are still the 30 centimetre gaps between the trenches that we dug there.

Sharon says we don't know what is in those gaps. She's right. In May, we send the excavator back in.

For 20 days, we dig that ground over, watched by Matt's family, who come down every day to sit beside the road and watch us. Every single square metre of dirt is dug, down to the depth of close to a metre, and checked. We find nothing. Wednesday 31 May is set as the last day of searching.

Around 2.30pm, with an hour or so left before we call the search off, the excavator rips up a bright green cabbage palm that has so far stood, untouched, among the devastation.

Scott calls 'Stop!' and raises his hand. He edges closer and looks down. He stiffens.

I'm standing with Matt's parents, but excuse myself and walk over. Following where he is looking, I can see something cream-white among the dark brown earth. Looking closer, I make out part of a pelvis. Leg bones. The top of a skull.

We walk back to Mark and Faye, who lets out a sob and collapses into my chest. I pull her in then put a hand on Mark's shoulder.

I ask them if they want to see their son.

They do. Their faces are numb. When Faye looks down, she howls. Lying in the ground beneath us is her nightmare.

This is a kind of justice, I think as Mark holds his wife tight. *At least you have your son back.* It is a point of light among the darkness. But nothing I can say will ease their pain.

White Spider

March 2017: 32 years in

As we search for William Tyrrell, I rely on the other detectives in the strike force to tell me what they've found when picking through the different threads of evidence. But the decision on where we look next is always mine.

This responsibility is worse than in other cases. It's worse because William Tyrrell is a child; because he might still be alive somewhere; because if he was abducted, that person could strike again; because this case is always in the newspapers, which means the politicians read about it then ask questions of our bosses, who expect us to give them answers; because society expects whoever did this to be brought to justice; because when each of us leaves work each evening, we'll know we were supposed to find William by now and we haven't.

During a briefing in March 2017, Laura says we should do more work on Paul, the neighbour who lives opposite the house where William went missing. There's no evidence he was involved, but nor do we have anything to rule him out. There are also odd, unexplained things about him. William's foster grandmother, Anne, says that he started turning up at her house unannounced after her husband's death in February 2014. One time, she saw Paul standing outside her glass sliding doors, watching her inside them. Anne spoke to Paul's wife, Heather, asking her to tell him to stay away. After Heather's death in 2015, the year after William went missing, Anne says he walked up to her in a café and tried to kiss her. She was scared.

She also thinks it was strange Paul did not come out of his house after William went missing, when her daughter was running up and down the road, shouting for him. Anne says she couldn't understand it. Paul was normally a stickybeak.

Other members of the strike force also agree with Laura. 'OK,' I say, 'let's look at him more closely. If we find nothing, great, we rule him out and then move on.'

Craig, the officer-in-charge of the strike force, has a different opinion. He wants to look at the local postwoman who took out an Apprehended Violence Order (AVO) against Paul, saying she, also, had a reason to be in Benaroon Drive that morning.

We bring the postwoman in for an interview in April 2017. She tells us her mail run to the street that day was unusually early, at around 8.45am, so she would have been gone long before William disappeared.

Although there's no CCTV on Benaroon Drive, we can follow her movements around Kendall on different cameras and see nothing to contradict her version of events. But Craig is insistent. He wants to search her financial and travel records, to find out the kind of mail she was delivering, what time she started work that day and how long it took her to complete her route.

It strikes me as a waste of time to be pursuing the postwoman and I tell the strike force not to do it. If anything, during her interview, I was more interested in the reasons why she sought the AVO against Paul.

She said he was erratic. He kept approaching her, making her feel uncomfortable. And, around the time William went missing, Paul was often outside, or watching the street, waiting for her arrival.

Paul says he was out for his morning walk at around 8.40am that morning. The two times, his walk and her post run, are so close together it's possible he might not have known she had been and gone, and still have been watching for her.

We've got nothing to suggest Paul's involvement with William, but he could be our best eyewitness, I think.

***

In May, we go to the Supreme Court and get warrants authorising us to install listening devices in Paul's home and car, and intercept his phone calls. The devices in his house record him listening to conservative shock jock Ray Hadley on the radio at full volume, talking to his dead wife, Heather, or ranting about the Greens, Aboriginal people and homosexuals. As we never know when he'll start talking to himself, every hour we record has to be listened to in real time, transcribed and logged. Throughout June and July, the work mounts up. The transcripts are also far from perfect as, too often, the quality of the recording is poor. When he talks to himself about the postwoman, the transcript reads: 'The AVO's a pack of bullshit, they gave me one day, one day, one day … I was advised by some idiot … he was the bloke, the receiver of the phone call … and I told her … and I went to court … that I tried to stop her with my car and I used to run around the post office … some fucking bullshit.'

At other times, the recording fails, just like it did in the Bob Ljubic and Terry Falconer murder investigations. When this happens, the transcript reads 'Inaudible' or 'File does not exist'. At one point it says simply, 'Gap in data – about three days of recordings. Reason is unknown.'

***

I want to stir Paul up, to provoke him to talk about William's disappearance, so we can listen to what he's saying. This strategy has been agreed upon with my bosses and our forensic psychologist, but it's my job to advance it.

On the morning of 14 June, we send in an undercover cop, posing as a freelance journalist. Thinking of Paul's reputation as a stickybeak, I tell her, 'Don't worry about how you approach him, he'll approach you.' It happens. She parks on Benaroon Drive, gets out of her car and Paul approaches, asking if she's lost.

She tells him she's writing an article about the impact of William's disappearance on the community in Kendall and they end up speaking for two hours. Paul tells her the only way he can see William being taken was if someone used the fire trail leading from where Benaroon Drive ends towards the town cemetery. That trail isn't used often he says, 'Only people like myself who go for a walk that way.'

On 5 July, the undercover cop goes back and talks to Paul again, both in his house and while they are walking through the bush around it. Paul tells her William might have been taken by someone who was hiding under his foster grandmother's house, who put something on the boy's face to quieten him and then drove off. He doesn't think it's worth police searching the area again.

After she leaves, the listening devices record Paul sobbing to himself inside his house: 'My angel. My love. My angel. I love you.' He sobs throughout the evening, mumbles to himself or shouts at the television. On the phone to his son, he talks about the freelance journalist's visit, repeating his theory that William's was a planned abduction by someone who left through the Kendall cemetery. When he goes to bed, alone, he is recorded saying, 'Love you darling. Good night, sweetheart.' We can only guess he's talking to his dead wife.

Later, in the silence, Paul says to Heather, 'I love you.'

***

I'm uncertain what to make of what we're hearing. On 26 July, I test Paul's reactions, not seeking to gather evidence this time, but rather to get some indication of whether we are justified in looking at him more closely.

We leave a child's Spider-Man suit beside the track where Paul takes his morning walk, having first buried it to make it look old, then dug it up. A surveillance team are hidden in the forest, watching.

Afterwards, their report reads: '[Paul] continued walking west along the dirt track, bent over and looked at a Spider-Man suit lying next to the dirt track. [Paul] stopped for approximately 12 seconds.' Paul does not report seeing the suit to the police.

That afternoon, we record him at home, mumbling, 'You know I love you angel' and 'I bloody screwed up, eh' while the radio continues in the background.

We leave the suit out again the next morning, and this time Paul stops, puts out his foot to touch it then walks home and calls the local police station. Asked whether he walked the trail the day before, he said he did but 'I never seen it yesterday'.

That afternoon, we record Paul saying, 'I never seen it before, maybe a dog's dragged it, from wherever. I don't know, it's no good asking that.' Later, while mowing his lawn, he says 'Oh shut up Paul.'

Two days after, we record Paul talking to himself again. It's indistinct, with parts where different detectives think they hear different words, but it sounds like, 'No, yeah, well I'm gunna run into your property too.' He continues: 'This is my place, you're in my place, you do what I want … don't want to take too much crap, hey, I'm not interested in your bullshit mate … you're a little boy, you're nobody. You're just a little boy, you're nobody. You don't tell me, I'll tell you, I did tell you.'

***

With more than one listening device operating in Paul's house day and night, the backlog of unlistened-to surveillance recordings grows into the hundreds, then thousands of hours. We haven't got the people to go through them.

As July ends, we record Paul saying, 'You haven't got anything to do with this, so it's ridiculous.' Minutes later, he continues, 'I don't know what's going on with the little bloke.' Some of the junior detectives who spend their days listening to these recordings tell me they believe him.

Craig also thinks Paul is innocent. I tell him that we have to prove it. Craig doesn't respond. He's often silent in our briefings, also. He is a kickboxer, and a good one, so sometimes the best exchanges he and I have with each other are when we put on boxing gloves and spar in the car park, going hard at each other until we're both exhausted.

Hoping to move forward, on 16 August, I ask Paul to come in for an interview. Laura, who interviewed Paul before, also sits at the table with us. The narrow, green-grey room feels so small the three of us barely fit inside it.

This has gone on too long, I think. *Not knowing what to make of Paul. Not knowing what to make of what he's saying.*

I want us to be able to rule him in or out. If I can press down hard enough in here, then he might break, or say something when he gets back home we can record on the listening devices. It won't be pretty but Paul's been read his rights by the custody sergeant, so he should know what is coming.

Paul sits with his shoulders slumped and arms crossed: a grey-haired 72-year-old with a wiry, Clint Eastwood body. We've barely begun talking when he starts to cry, talking about his childhood, how his parents separated and the children were broken up, leaving him to be moved between nine different families.

'Nobody wanted me,' he says. At one point, he stands up, saying that he's got a cramp, and tries to walk it off in tiny circles.

He denies having anything to do with William's disappearance. I ask him about that morning, when he was sitting on the verandah of his house and could hear the children playing.

'Did you see them?' I ask.

'Nuh.'

'You can see from your verandah, you can see up into the back of Anne's place.'

'No, I can't see into the back.'

I try to make it clear. From his house, you can see where the grass slope runs down from the back of Anne's place towards the road. The grass slope that William was last seen running towards, when he jumped off the front deck at Anne's house ran round the side of the building and disappeared.

'You can see it directly through there,' I say to Paul.

'Possibly, without the bush.'

'Well, there is no bush, there's trees.'

'Yeah, I can't remember now.'

'But the trees are high, the foliage is high,' I say. I can't believe we're stuck on this. He was sitting out the front of his house shortly before William was last seen. He could be our best witness. 'You could see that area.'

'Yeah, well, I most probably could. I don't know. I never studied it.'

'You've lived there for 15 years and never looked up there?'

'Oh, well, I might have looked up there, but I don't carry things like that around in me head because it's not important.'

'No? Well, it could be important.'

He tells me he didn't see William.

I drag him back and forth over the details of the AVO taken out against him for stalking his postwoman. He tells me it's a load of rubbish.

'You're lying,' I tell him.

'That's a load of crap.'

'What about the Spider-Man suit?' I ask him. Did he see anything the day *before* he reported seeing it lying in the forest?

'I didn't see anything, no.'

'So if I look you in the eye and say, "I know you're lying to me and I'm not even going to tell you why or how I know you're lying," what would you say to me?'

'Well, I'd say you're badly mistaken. I am telling you the truth.'

After Paul leaves, Laura tells me she believes him.

As Paul drives home, the listening device inside his car records him talking to Heather again: 'Make sure you don't tell anyone, love, they're right after me. Don't tell anyone love, please, they're right after me.'

***

The ambulance arrives for Dad. I've tried to steel myself, ready for this moment, but there's still a hollowness inside me when it happens.

Someone needs to make the journey to the hospital beside him. When I climb into the ambulance, he tells me, 'This will be where you are in three months.'

I frown, then he reminds me about the boxing match I've got coming up at the end of November.

We laugh. Nothing like your dad to build your confidence. As I sit beside him, driving to the hospital, I think that Dad taught me how to live and now he's teaching me how to die.

Do you give up yet?

Never.

Not giving up, no matter how much it hurts.

At the hospital, Mum's in a state of disbelief, as if she can't imagine life without him. I try to help her find acceptance, saying it is the right time. He's very sick. He wouldn't want to live this way for long.

I spend the night sitting alone with Dad in hospital.

'How you going, Dad?' I ask him.

'Good.'

'That's good, Dad,' I tell him.

That's me saying *I love you, Dad, and thank you for being my father.*

My dad, Kevin Jubelin, dies the next day, on 29 August 2017.

That afternoon, I call into the strike force room in Port Macquarie. One of the detectives asks me how my dad is.

'He died,' I say. She looks at me with wide, open eyes. We've both seen so much death. We both know what an effect it leaves on the living.

At the funeral, I help to carry Dad's coffin. Then I sit at the front, wearing a black suit, white shirt and black tie, with one arm around Mum. My sisters, Karen and Michelle, are there, as is my brother, Jason. My children, Jake and Gemma, are with us, surrounded by their cousins. Behind us, the service is crowded with other family, friends and even my old sergeant, Paul Jacob. I'm proud Dad had so many people who now want to pay their respects.

The celebrant begins the service she has written, saying:

> Kevin was part of the world's healing and not of its hurt. He valued his successes and what he had been able to achieve and believed you never say you can't do something you set your mind to. He had a mischief about him that meant he could be hard to read. A clown sometimes, a devil other times. He's also described as a man who was complex and contradictory, however, he was also a man of integrity who had a strong ethical code to do the right thing. He expected high standards, but he also held himself up to those high standards as well.

Afterwards, Jaco comes up to me and jokes, 'Well, now we know how you turned out the way you did.'

***

I don't take any time off. I'm angry at myself for not taking a moment to stop and breathe. I ask myself, *What's more important?* But I have so much work on.

***

The strike force stumbles forward. Detectives who were told they'd be working on this case for weeks now see it stretching out ahead of them for years. At different times, our covert cameras fail. We get a second set of listening devices for Paul's home, but they're worse than the first ones. The batteries inside the device recording in Paul's car run out and are not replaced. Some of the junior detectives tell me they now believe Paul when he says he didn't see the Spider-Man suit on the first morning.

I tell them I trust the surveillance team who were there on the day and said they saw Paul looking at the suit. Disobeying my direction to leave it alone, four of these junior detectives look more closely at the surveillance footage taken on that morning, and go out to the forest track where we left the suit itself. They don't take one of the surveillance team with them, to ask where they were located. They don't know precisely where the suit was left. They don't take a tape measure with them. Instead, they come up with a report that concludes, in bold capitals:

> It can not be determined what [Paul] was looking at for 12 seconds.
>
> It can not be excluded that he was not looking back towards the direction of the suit.

It's meaningless, a waste of time and energy, when we have little of either to spare. All they've found is that we can't exclude whether Paul was looking at the suit. It's ludicrous.

But it means the strike force is divided. In September, Laura films an interview with Paul at home, asking him to recreate his movements on the morning William vanished. Paul can't find the path he says he took through the bush while searching, but on her drive back, Laura calls me to say, 'I just don't think he was responsible.'

The next day, during a briefing in Port Macquarie, Craig argues with me publicly. He now wants to investigate the circumstances of the AVO taken out against Paul by the postwoman; he says he doesn't trust her. I ask Laura to do it. It takes her weeks. When she comes back, she says the witnesses back up the postwoman's account that Paul was following her around. But all of this takes time that could have been better spent working through the masses of unheard listening device material.

When we do get to the recordings, we hear Paul calling Laura a 'stupid girl' and me 'as low as the bastard who grabbed him'. He complains the door to the room in which I interviewed him was locked, and that the room itself was freezing. He seems to think this was deliberate: 'I wonder if that was to stop me thinking.'

One morning in September, Paul starts crying to himself at home, saying how sorry he is, 'I'm sorry, I shouldn't do it again.'

He turns the radio in his house back on. It plays at a fierce volume, but still we can hear him saying, 'Great, they're gunna find something Mum, don't dob on me OK ... OK Mum, oh, oh, oh, oh Mum, oh Mum, oh Mum, what do I do? What do I do? Hey? 'Cos everything he said to tell me is all lies, you know ... I'm sorry.'

***

On 5 October, I visit Paul at home. I tell him we know that he saw the Spider-Man suit on that first morning, despite his denials, because we had surveillance officers in place who saw him. Once again, he denies it.

Afterwards, we record him talking to his daughter: 'I didn't see the suit, from memory I just seen this white thing on the ground that was covered in dirt.' Later that day, Paul says to himself, 'Because it wasn't the suit, it wasn't the suit Gary, it was half the suit, I'm not sure, I think it was the top half of the suit ... from memory the white bit, the white top or whatever it is, with the spider.'

I think about the spider. The suit William Tyrrell was wearing when he disappeared had a white spider on the back, but not the front. The suit we left on the walking track was lying with the front upwards.

I wonder whether any image showing the spider on the back of the suit has been used in any TV reports, Facebook campaign posts or billboards over the past three years.

We need to be certain of that, I tell the strike force, but, looking around the briefing room, I see doubt on their faces. I know there are some good, dedicated cops in here, but others are sick of this job and want to get out. Some are talking behind my back, saying I've pushed Paul too far, and that he's starting to confuse his own recollections with the version of events I've put to him.

Without them, I am beginning to feel isolated. Every time I go on call, or focus on another job, when I get back it feels as if the strike force has lost direction. Craig and Laura are no longer talking to each other. Craig isn't talking to anyone, it seems. We've got 15,000 different items to manage on e@gle.i and are drowning in information.

When the intercept warrant for Paul's landline and his mobile phone expires, I let it go. With the backlog of unlistened-to material and too few staff to work through it, I can't justify an extension.

***

Late on Friday 3 November, I get the news: no image of the white spider on the back of William's suit has been used in the media.

We have to move, I think. Sometimes, in police work, you might advance a line of enquiry by only millimetres, but you have to take them. I promised William's parents I'd do everything I could. Not to explore this now because this case is hard, or it means staying late at the office would be a betrayal.

But I'm in Sydney, where I've spent the week working a different case, helping to lock up some bikies over the death of a 42-year-old, Clint Starkey, who was bashed at a service station. That means I can't travel up to interview Paul tonight, but I can still telephone him. The warrant covering our telephone intercepts has now expired, but the listening devices in Paul's house are covered by a separate court order, which still has a few days to run – another reason to act quickly.

For a moment, I feel doubt. What if the pressure is too great and Paul reacts? He's already accused me of locking him in a freezing room, what if he now says that I did worse? We've heard him sobbing late at night; what if he harms himself? I think of Bruce Matthews, the race-track owner who took his own life, knowing I was planning to interview him in prison. What backup do I have of what Paul and I will say to each other? The listening devices in his house will record his part of the conversation, but not what I say on the phone. And listening devices fail.

I call Craig into a room in the Homicide Squad offices, along with Greg, the junior detective who met Paul when he went to organise putting covert cameras near his property.

Looking at them, I realise my sense of isolation's grown. Even inside this meeting room, I feel alone.

I want to talk to Paul, but only if there is a record of what we say to each other.

I know the law. It says I can't record a private conversation without consent, unless I am protecting my 'lawful interests'.

Dialling Paul's number, I switch the call to speakerphone and tell Greg to get out his mobile phone.

'Record the conversation,' I tell him.

He looks at me. He looks at Craig. Craig looks down. Greg presses record.

What none of us can know is that this recording will one day be tendered in my own trial, when I will face criminal charges.

An old man's voice answers the phone, saying, 'Hello?'

'Hello, Paul,' I say to him.

Knock 'em Down, Bowra!

29 November 2017: 32 years in

The hearing date for the Bowraville murders approaches, 18 months after the Attorney General's decision to send the case to the appeal court.

It's difficult handing over 20 years of work to the lawyers at first and, when I go to meet them with Jerry Bowden, the other detective on the strike force, I am nervous. Their team, led by the fierce, austere barrister Wendy Abraham QC, sit in a crowded, cluttered office, which looks like it was somewhere a lot of work was done and ask us a lot of questions. My nerves begin to settle, I like their approach. When Wendy says she doesn't like to lose, I smile.

I also watch how heavily the lawyers come to rely on analyst Bianca Comina, the third member of our strike force. That makes me glad, as Bianca's knowledge of this case is matched only by her commitment. The three of us, Jerry, Bianca and myself, wonder how the lawyers are going to run the case, only they won't tell us. Then, four months out, I'm asked to take part in a charity boxing match, raising money for the families of dead police officers. I go to mark the date on my calendar and realise the fight would be on the night of the third day of the appeal court hearing.

I hide the fact that I'll be fighting from the lawyers, so they don't think I'm distracted. Preparing properly for court, or for a fight, is hard work; it should be all-consuming. I'm also worried about being called to give evidence in court. If that happens, I'll need to be at my best, and I've been in enough boxing rings to know that your brain gets rattled for a few days if you cop a bad beating.

***

The first day of the court hearing comes and row after row of weary black faces take their seats in the public gallery, opposite the three white judges. This is the Banco Court, the State's biggest, ceremonial courtroom. The judges wear red robes and white horsehair wigs. The Bowraville families wear brightly coloured footy shirts, printed with large photographs of their long-dead children, Colleen, Evelyn and Clinton.

On three sides, the high walls are hung with heavy, gilt-framed paintings of other, long-dead judges. I have a sick feeling in my stomach – I've been around courts my whole career and I'm still intimidated walking in here this morning – but I can't help feeling hopeful.

A court hearing is like tossing a coin, I've learned. You throw the facts up into the air, while the two sides, prosecution and defence, argue about which way they should land. There's really no predicting.

Wendy stands and outlines the argument for overturning the previous not guilty verdicts. She says there is so much evidence suggesting the same person must have murdered all three of the children. That is the first step in her argument. The second is trying to convince the judges that James Hide was that person. The families shift uncomfortably, frowning as they try to follow the bloodless legal argument, despite this case being about their children. At times, I also struggle to understand it.

To my surprise, the lawyers have decided not to rely on the Norco Corner evidence about a white man standing over the body of a black teenager on the morning that Clinton went missing. They say it doesn't pass the test of being 'fresh and compelling' because the police did know about it at the time of Clinton's trial, although they never followed it up. Instead, Wendy argues, the evidence we've gathered about Colleen's death was not used during the separate murder trials over the deaths of Evelyn and Clinton, which means it is still 'fresh'.

It is 'compelling' because of the similarities between all three of the murders.

I look up at Colleen's mum, Muriel Craig, who sits surrounded by her children. Near her sits Rebecca Stadhams, Evelyn's mum, who is watching the judges and twisting her greying hair around the fingers of one hand. Thomas Duroux, Clinton's father, sits in the front row, with his arms crossed, listening intently. When I first met each of them, their hair was darker, their faces less lined with time and sorrow. But working this case has changed *me* too.

Before going to Bowraville, I was a young cop caught up in the idea of catching crooks. I was naïve. I would say stupid things, like calling somebody an Abo, without thinking. That changed.

I also used to think my fellow cops and I were part of one team, but this case has made me realise I'm heading in a different direction. When I was starting out, I was taught not to connect with the families of crime victims, because it made it harder to do the job, but now I think you *have* to.

You have to take a murder on as if it happened to your family. You have to open yourself up and let some of the hurt in. Their pain might drive out your own feelings, but that only makes you tougher. It is your compassion for how the victims' and their families are feeling that makes you want to solve the crime.

I look back at the judges, while they and the opposing lawyers debate the meanings of 'fresh' and 'compelling'. How many of them know what it's like, I wonder, to sit down with a family whose child has just been murdered? Certainly, none of them has taken on the load of finding a loved one's killer. Nor have they carried the weight, as many other cops have, of taking part in an operation where somebody dies. In my case, I went through the door of an apartment where a man was shot while I was talking to him.

Without this real, direct experience of life and death, the judges' and the lawyers' words seem weightless. To me, at least, and to the children's families, this is real. This is their lives. In Bowraville, I've learned things that were simple, the people there taught me values: tolerance, humility, a refusal to give up and accept injustice. I've tried to teach the same things to my children.

In black law, if one man kills another he accepts there will be payback. In this court, such certainty seems to slip through our fingers and rise instead into the air, twisting around the different meanings of words, as quick and tricky to grab hold of as is the breath that carries them.

***

On Wednesday evening, after three days of court hearings, I make my way to the boxing match. Dave Letizia, the boxer I trained with in Perth, has flown over to work my corner with another fighter, Glenn McDougal, and I'm grateful. I can think of no one better. Craig, who I count as a friend despite our disagreements over the William Tyrrell investigation, is also here supporting me. Jake and Gemma are among the spectators. So are the Bowraville mob. As the announcer calls my name, I can hear the families cheering, calling me their 'Gumbaynggirr warrior' and shouting out, 'Knock 'em down, Bowra!'

How good would it be if Dad could see me here, like this? I ask myself. I owe him so much. He made me unbreakable.

Never give up.

It helps me find the confidence to win.

Is Everyone Happy?

February 2018: 32 years in

Forget anything else you're doing, I tell the strike force. Focus on Paul, either to finally eliminate him from the investigation or find solid evidence against him.

The start of February marks my third anniversary of leading the search for William Tyrrell and I don't want to see a fourth one. At the end of last year, the Homicide Squad also got a new boss, Scott, the detective superintendent. He doesn't want cases sitting on the books – I guess that, like all squad commanders, his life is ruled by statistics – and has brought in a rule saying all investigations should run for only six months before being reviewed to see whether they can be sent to the coroner.

'This case is still solvable,' I tell Scott. He doesn't seem convinced. We brief him on the plan to focus everything on Paul and he gives his commitment to support it, but others on the strike force overhear him talking on the phone, saying, 'It's a waste of time, we'll never get anyone for this.'

During my recorded phone call with Paul on 3 November, I asked him again about the Spider-Man suit we planted on the forest track where he was walking. He said he saw a white top or a white bit of cloth on his walk, but not the blue and red material of the suit itself. I don't know what to make of that. Like everything with Paul, it doesn't lead us further forward, nor does it give me a good reason to stop pursuing him.

Since then, we've kept on asking questions. We've approached his close friends and family but they didn't tell us anything. We've still not got any DNA, forensics or witnesses that tie Paul to William's disappearance, only an empty period of time, when he says he was on his own that morning.

The biggest absence is the lack of any forensic evidence from the morning William went missing. For months now, I've been submitting written reports suggesting an update to the police force's standard operating procedures regarding missing children, so a separate investigation team would be set up within hours, operating independently of any ongoing search. Had that happened, a crime scene might have been set up on Benaroon Drive, we might have gathered DNA, or fingerprints, perhaps a tyre track in the dirt. We'll never know what we are missing and I don't want to see this happen again, the next time a child disappears. But my suggestion goes unanswered.

In April, Scott holds a formal review of the investigation, saying he wants to send it to the coroner. The coroner's role is to finally establish how a person died. Once that is done, it is no longer an active investigation.

We have too few detectives, I tell Scott. Right now, Strike Force Rosann is three detectives from the Homicide Squad, including myself and Craig, who is also currently working on a second, high-profile investigation. We have one detective from the Unsolved Homicide Unit, who is on annual leave, two from the Sex Crimes Squad, one on loan from Robbery and Serious Crime and two local detectives from Port Macquarie. After the review, I'm told to send the local detectives back to their commander, while Sex Crimes say they also want Laura back working with them.

I formally protest, writing in my monthly progress report that the removal of these three detectives will have a significant and negative impact on the investigation. Despite this, I'm told all three are to leave the strike force.

We now have over 2500 hours of listening device material piled up. It would take the entire strike force, working full time, more than 10 weeks to go through it. I ask for four more cops to clear the backlog. I don't get them.

***

In the mid-afternoon of 2 May, I lean back on the bonnet of my car and look around me at the bushland outside the old, abandoned police station at Kew, near Kendall. This is to be our form-up point, where I'll brief the strike force on the operation ahead and where they'll wait, ready to respond if I need them, while I go into Paul's house, alone, to talk to him.

Again, I'm not going to collect evidence; I just want to provoke conversation, which we can then record on the listening devices inside his house. What we've heard so far on those tapes is contradictory and uncertain. We need to keep him talking.

So I am going to confront him. The plan, which my bosses have signed up to, is to go in alone because we want Paul to identify me as representing the police force. We want him to think that I, alone, can resolve this. So, if he decides to reach out, he will do so to me.

I'll tell him how we're planning a huge search of local bushland. No such search has been undertaken since William went missing and we need to do one before the inquest can begin, if only to be able to rule, with forensic certainty, that the three-year-old got lost in the bush.

It's also an opportunity to see how Paul reacts. A surveillance team is hidden in the bush behind his house, waiting to follow him if he leaves the property after my visit. At Kew, we get word they are in place and, also, Paul's daughter is in there with him.

That's good, I think. *I'd like him to have someone there.*

The low sun casts long shadows among the gathered detectives. 'Can you show me how to record on my phone?' I ask one. I'm planning to record this conversation with Paul on my mobile, just like I asked Greg to record our phone call in November, and for the same reasons. I'm wary of going to Paul's house alone like this. I don't enjoy putting anyone through this kind of experience and being there alone will be unusual for a police investigation. It means there will be no one there to defend me should I need it, or to back up my version of events.

She shows me.

'OK, got it,' I say, putting the phone back into my jacket pocket, and getting into my car. On the drive to Paul's house, my phone rings. It's a real estate agent, calling about an apartment I'm trying to buy in Sydney. The purchase is meant to be the last step in putting the divorce from Tracy behind me.

Fuck. Everything always happens at once. I pull over and take the call. The sale will continue.

Approaching Paul's house, I press record, narrating what I'm doing out of habit: 'Time is 5.20. I'm just going into Benaroon Drive to speak to Paul. It's the 2nd of May. Just pulling up now. Pulling in right behind his car.'

Again, I cannot know that the recordings of my conversations with Paul will end up being tendered in court, when I will be the person put on trial.

Inside, the house smells old and musty. The rooms inside it are cluttered. Paul leads me past a lounge room containing an old-fashioned sofa with curved wooden armrests and floral cushions. His kitchen fittings are timber and green Laminex. A tea towel is tucked over the handle of the upright stove. Through a glass door, I can see the verandah overlooking the road, where Paul sat with his tea and toast just before William went missing.

I take one of the chairs and put my phone down on top of a stack of paperwork on the kitchen table.

Paul watches me. Since I arrived, he's kept it very civil.

His daughter's sitting with him. My stomach twists. It made me feel dirty going through the niceties of 'G'day, Paul, how are ya?' at the front door, knowing what I am going to tell them.

I stumble over my words, 'Look guys, I, I don't know where to start with, start with this –'

'Yeah,' Paul interrupts.

'And, er, as I said, er, um … I'm not interested in the gathering of evidence or whether, um, you know, you've committed an offence.' I tell them I've got concerns about his erratic behaviour, and about some of the answers he has given us in the past, which we're not convinced are true.

'Such as?' Paul asks.

'Such as, from the time William disappeared –'

'Yeah?'

'– we don't know where you were for two hours.'

'Well, the main thing was I went looking for the boy.'

He and I keep cutting across each other, starting to say something but being interrupted. His daughter watches me in silence. I get to the point: 'How do you think we convict people?' I ask.

He says nothing.

'Do you think every murderer I have locked up has sat there and gone, "Yeah, I did it"?' I ask.

A television is playing elsewhere in the house, but not loudly enough to trouble the listening devices, so long as they are working.

'No,' I answer for him. 'We get witness statements. We get statements from people. We follow up phone records, we get CCTV footage.'

'Yeah,' Paul is cautious. I'm leading the conversation. There is a strategy in place here. Each word I say, the way I sit, the way I look at him, is meant to make him think I'm in charge here. *Look at me*, I'm saying to him. *I'm the person to reach out to.* It's like holding someone under water.

'We do stuff like the Spider-Man suit,' I say.

Three times Paul starts to interrupt, but falters.

'It's not on people's word,' I tell him. This is the biggest police investigation in the state, maybe in the whole country. We have over 15,000 pieces of information.

Time to let him take a breath. 'Paul, I'm seeing, I'm seeing decency in you, and I'm seeing some confusion in you, and I'm seeing some trouble, a troubled mind in you. That's genuinely what I'm seeing.'

'Well …'

'And I am really trying to get to the bottom of this, just so we can bring William home, for his family. But we're not getting that because I'm not getting to the bottom of what you're saying. I'm not getting the truth from you.'

'You *are* getting the truth.'

Back under the water. By now, I am committed. I feel no emotion.

'We have turned this town upside down,' I go on. 'I know things about this town, and people in this town, that you would have no idea about.'

His daughter laughs. The moment's lost. I have to hold him under the surface again.

'There's problems in this town but we have eliminated all those people. They weren't here; they were somewhere else. We can't eliminate you, Paul.'

I let him take a breath of air, talking about the interview at the police station in August last year, when he broke down in tears talking about his childhood. I tell him I felt sorry for him.

His daughter tries to interrupt us. I ignore her.

'And I honestly see, with a lot of people, when they're holding back secrets,' I say. 'Sometimes the start of working through it is to just own what's happened, and once they've owned what's happened, then they can start rebuilding their life.'

He looks at me.

'Could it have been a case of an accident with William?' I ask him. This is another case theory: William's foster father was due back from town at around the time the three-year-old went missing. Soon after, William's foster mother, Jane Fiore, told one of the first cops on the scene, 'William had had enough of sitting and started jumping off the deck and was being a tiger, he kept going around the side of the house to see if his father was coming.'

William's sister also said he was looking for 'Daddy's car' before he disappeared.

I put this theory to Paul: his neighbours said they heard a car's wheels on gravel around the time William went missing. Paul drove a silver four-wheel drive, similar to William's foster father's. Paul was packing the car that morning, ahead of driving to Lismore to pick up his brother from hospital.

'If he ran over here all excited, all excited to see his dad, thinking it's his dad's car,' I tell Paul. 'You're moving the car.'

Or, maybe it wasn't Paul who was driving. Maybe it was his wife, Heather.

'I'm not here to sit in judgment,' I tell Paul.

He looks at me. His skin is paper thin. He's an old man.

I tell him that, if William had come running over, all excited, thinking he saw his daddy's car, that's understandable. 'It's not something that you've got to carry with you.'

His daughter interrupts, but I keep talking. 'If that's what's happened, we can deal with that.'

'I know what you're saying,' Paul says. He looks down at the table.

We are both silent, for a moment.

Paul looks up. 'But there's no way in the world I would have done anything like that,' he tells me.

***

Late into the night, the listening devices record Paul talking to his daughter about the police investigation. I wonder: *Has she started to doubt her own father?* It's one of the cruellest things I've ever done, to sow suspicion among a family, but I have to. This isn't about me or her, or her emotions. It is my job to hold her father there, beneath the surface, until I know for sure whether we can exclude him.

The next day, Paul wakes up early.

I go back to his house that afternoon.

Again, I press record on my phone as I pull up outside. Music is playing somewhere inside the house.

I knock. He comes to the door.

'Hey, Paul. How are you?'

'Good, good.' Only, I am sure he isn't.

He tells me a solicitor has told him not to talk to me.

'That's interesting, Paul. It's the disappearance of a three-year-old and you don't want to help us?'

'I've helped you every way I can, and you come here and accuse me of doing it. And you say I'm not helping you? You're kidding.' He says I've lied to him about some of the evidence, like the neighbours who said they heard a car's wheels on gravel around the time William went missing. He didn't have a gravel driveway then, Paul says. His was a 'sand-based thing' instead.

'I've helped you all I could,' Paul says again. 'I've had youse go through my house. I've done everything I can to help youse, and all you want to do is put shit on me.'

'Put shit on you, Paul?

'Yes, you did. Last night.'

'I put shit on you last night?'

'Yes, you did.' He is grim-faced, insistent.

'How did I put shit on you?'

'By saying that you better plead guilty or else.'

I did not say that.

He's angry now. Standing in the doorway, pointing his finger at me. '"If you don't plead guilty, it will go on further." That's what you said.'

'I did not say that, Paul.'

'Well, it mightn't have been the exact words, but that's what you were saying, Gary. And I'm not talking anymore.'

He closes the door.

Back inside the car, I switch off the phone recording.

***

Through May and June, I have a number of meetings with the Deputy State Coroner, Harriet Grahame, about holding an inquest into William's disappearance. Like with Michael Atkins and Matt Leveson's disappearance, I think I've pushed Paul as far as I can with police work. Maybe, like with Matt's death, an inquest can help break this case open.

The coroner and I agree an inquest would allow us to formally establish William's disappearance was the result of human intervention. I say I'd like the hearings to focus on Paul as a priority; I know how long a court process can run and because of Paul's age, his evidence may suffer if we delay talking to him. I don't want to be working on this case in 10 years, wondering what we might have learned if we'd moved more quickly. The coroner seems receptive to the idea.

The counsel assisting the coroner is Gerard Craddock SC, who I last dealt with when he chose not to call me to give evidence at the inquest into the 2015 death of Courtney Topic, who was shot by police. I ask what they want to do with all the surveillance recordings we have of Paul. I'd like to bring him back in for interview and ask him to explain what he meant by some of them.

'No,' says Gerard. 'Don't do that. We'll do it at the inquest.'

***

On 21 June 2018, I get a call from my daughter, Gemma's husband, Matt. Their first son, my grandson, has just been born. His name is Zion. I'm not ready to be a grandpa. In my mind, I'm still 21. I also know that Gemma is part-way through a law degree and has been accepted to join the New South Wales Police Force. As a parent, I know being a mum will ask even more of her and there is little I can do to help.

All these thoughts disappear the moment I see Zion. He is perfect.

I see Debbie, Gemma's mum, at the hospital. We smile at each other and I tell her, 'We must have done something right to get such a beautiful grandchild'.

***

A little more than a month later, on 31 July 2018, I sit at the head of a long table in a briefing room in the Homicide Squad offices, looking at tired faces. The coroner has asked for a brief of evidence by the end of the year, laying out everything we know about William's disappearance, which means we now have a huge amount of work ahead.

In total, we've interviewed 263 local residents, collected CCTV from 12 businesses in Kendall and 169 cameras beyond it and received reports of over 2000 different sightings of William from around the planet.

We still don't know what happened. The last time William's foster parents came to meet us, I could see the pain of this not-knowing written on their faces, as well as those of every member of the strike force. Looking down the table now, I see the same crestfallen faces.

As usual, Craig doesn't say much during the briefing. More than most of us, perhaps, he is adrift amid the ocean of what we don't know about what happened to William, with over 3500 items on the e@gle.i computer system now waiting for him to review them.

Craig is a concrete thinker. He's set himself the task of working through those thousands of items, but it's going too slowly. They are becoming a prison. Now, the coroner wants to see all the evidence on Bill and Paul, and there's no way, with the staff we have available, that we can get through the thousands of hours of unreviewed listening device material on both of them by December.

I suggest that we give the coroner the entire transcript we have so far, including Paul's statements of his innocence, but with those sections that seem important highlighted.

'Is everyone happy with that?' I ask.

'No,' Craig answers.

'Well, why not, Craig? Why don't you agree?'

'That's misleading,' he says, sitting upright. 'He's denied it.'

'I know he's denied it, Craig. If the coroner wants to have a listen to something, it's all there. We're not hiding anything. It's not just selective evidence.'

Both of us are frustrated. Both of us are ready to take out our anger at not knowing what happened to William on each other.

'I strongly disagree,' Craig says.

I look around at the other, watching faces. 'How about everyone leaves? Craig and I have got to talk about this.'

They walk out and Craig goes from zero to 100, 'Right, we're gonna have it out.'

'Craig, what is your problem with this? You've gone on about the postwoman, and I wasted all that time on that. You can't move past that.'

'That's bullshit!'

Those outside the closed door can hear that we are yelling.

'Craig, you've been running this for three years. Your job is to come to me with people for us to investigate. Have you given me one person of interest? Because our role here is to find out what happened to William.'

He gets up, tears open the door and walks out into the main office, shouting, 'Fuck it, I'm out of here!'

I give him a couple of minutes, then follow him out. I can see him talking to another senior detective.

I approach them and ask, 'Craig, mate, can we discuss this?'

Before today, I would have said that he and I were friends. Just months ago, he stood with me at the boxing match. But now, he moves towards me.

'Come on, I'll fight you!' he shouts.

'I'm not fucking going anywhere.' Everyone in the office is watching.

I drop the folder I'm carrying, to show I am not backing down. Craig's hands are up. He's a kickboxer. I'm a boxer. Both of us know how to hurt the other. Other cops rush past me, grab Craig and pull us apart.

'I'll take you any time!' he's shouting. 'I'll take you on now!'

Craig's led away, shouting insults at me about the investigation; that I'm obsessed with Paul, that I've been illegally gathering evidence, that I falsified affidavits. Someone walks with him out of the building.

I turn back and try to get on with our work.

I Know Where William Tyrrell Is

August 2018: 33 years in

The investigation doesn't stop. It cannot.

I don't have the time to dwell on what happened with Craig. I see too much of myself in him, for one thing. He has an iron commitment to his training, which I recognise within myself. As well as his kickboxing, he runs marathons and if his training schedule tells him he needs to get 30 kilometres on any given day, he does it, even if it means getting up in time to pound them out before arriving for work at six in the morning.

I used to tell him to take it easy when I saw him heading for the office door at the end of a shift, ready to start running again when still stiff from yesterday's workout, but he didn't accept excuses.

The lack of flexibility became a problem. The two of us had fixed ideas and were looking in different directions. But I assume we'll patch up the damage, so decline to lodge a grievance over what happened.

In Homicide, however, we are always held to account, either by a judge, a coroner or the victims' families.

Within the squad, we're also closely monitored. When Craig returns to work in August, our commander, Scott, tells me to use the command management system, put in place to review those officers I directly supervise.

I don't think it will help. Already Craig's become more withdrawn from others on the strike force and, despite my hopes of reaching over the divide between us, the conversations between him and me are functional, but distant.

In September, I email another senior officer in the squad, asking if he can intervene. I tell him there's a lit of tension in the team, which is impacting on morale, and I don't want to inflame the situation if we can avoid it. But Scott doesn't change his mind and I'm forced to lay out my thoughts on Craig in writing.

Scott also emails us both, wanting an update on the investigation. He wants to know how many of the more than 1000 persons of interest identified to date have not yet been ruled out, and how many hours of listening device recordings from Paul's house are still outstanding. The answers are still in the hundreds and the thousands.

Craig takes extended leave. I am now filling both his position as officer-in-charge of the strike force and my own of investigation supervisor, while Laura has gone back to the Sex Crimes Squad. It is a move she had been pushing for but it means the loss of another driven, quietly determined detective.

Always, there is the nagging fear of something lurking in the darkness that we've missed, so I ask two other Homicide cops, Mark and Andrew, to go back and fish again through the black waters. They look at an old tip where the burned-out car of one of the paedophiles we uncovered living around Kendall was found lying upended in nearby bushland. The car's owner, Tony Jones, has also been seen with another person whose name surfaced during the investigation, Frank Abbott. Abbott is an old guy in his 70s who lived in a caravan near a local sawmill, who was previously found not guilty over the murder of a 17-year-old and has since been jailed for child abuse.

I ask Mark and Andrew to look at the two men and whether there is really a connection between them.

When they come back, they tell me Jones is a drinker, while Abbott looks like a silver-haired grandpa from Central Casting, but when he speaks, you can hear that he is cunning. It's hard to know if he is only lying for the sake of lying, but he's been telling people he knows where William is. People say he's told them about a place in the bush where he smelled a dead body. We are back in the swamp again with this investigation, picking our way between rumours and hearsay evidence, trying to take hold of something solid.

Abbott is also said to be friends with a third man, called Geoff. Witnesses say Abbott used to go up to local people saying, 'I know where William Tyrrell is, why don't you check Geoff's place?' Nobody believed him and, on its own, it is evidence of nothing, but when Geoff's name comes up during a briefing at Port Macquarie, someone mentions that he called Anne Fiore's house on the morning William disappeared.

Say that again?

Phone records show a call between Geoff's and Anne's place just before William went missing. The front deck – the one William and his sister were playing on – needed repairs and Geoff was going to do it. He'd already visited the property once.

Which means, after Bill, we have a *second* tradesman connected by a phone call to the house where William disappeared. Again, a phone call itself is evidence of nothing, but why did we go after Bill? Because of a phone call from the house that morning.

Why the fuck have I not heard about this call before?

We need to concentrate on Geoff, I say. The phone call connects him with the house and he is also connected with Abbott. I tell Mark and Andrew, OK, he's not a suspect, and there's no information to suggest he's directly involved in William's disappearance but we need to eliminate him. Concentrate on his friendship with Abbott, I tell them. Try to break it.

Maybe that will help lead us through the shadows in front of the strike force.

In contrast, my boss Scott wants this case done with. As the year marches towards a conclusion, I get a call from Ken Jurotte, manager of the cops' Aboriginal Coordination Team, set up to improve our relationship with Indigenous communities. Ken says he tried to nominate me for an Australian Police Medal for my work on the Bowraville investigation. He asked Scott to sign off on it but he declined, telling Ken the case had not been solved yet.

I don't have the time or attention to wonder about this, though it does not surprise me. Scott's also been questioning me in person, asking, 'Why are you so hands-on? Why are you all over the Tyrrell case? You're the investigation supervisor. You're supposed to *supervise* it. Why are you interviewing people?'

Because I have to, I think. Because we don't have the staff. Because I have the skills and experience to do it. Because it's what I promised William's family: that I'd do everything I could to find William. That I would work each line of inquiry to destruction.

This is what I do. It's what I am. This is how I catch killers.

The Pain and the Sorrow

13 September 2018: 33 years in

I stand alone in the emptying courtroom, feeling as if the life has also emptied out of me. Today is the twenty-eighth anniversary of 16-year-old Colleen Walker-Craig's disappearance from Bowraville, and the appeal court judges have just announced their decision.

They said the evidence surrounding Colleen's death is not 'fresh and compelling'. The Norco Corner evidence is not 'fresh and compelling'. None of the other evidence we've gathered over decades is 'fresh and compelling'. None of it is enough to overturn the previous not guilty verdicts and order James Hide to face trial again.

Outside, there is a hollowness among the children's families.

A meeting room has been set up, to give them a place to sit and try to comprehend what's happened. I make an effort to say the right things, to assure them that we will keep on fighting. We share the usual sandwiches and drinks. We take some photographs, in which they look like broken people.

Justice comes in different ways, Aunty Elaine told me. James himself didn't come to these court hearings. Instead, he sat and watched a live broadcast on a TV screen set up in a court building near his home, to save him being chased down the road each morning by TV cameras or out of fear, perhaps, of what the families might say to him.

He's spent a lifetime since the murders happened being chased, by me or by the media, or living in fear of what people might do to him if they found out what he'd been accused of. That life can't have always been a pleasant one. In that sense he has suffered.

But that is not enough, not yet. It doesn't feel like justice.

***

The Attorney General takes the case to the High Court, challenging the appeal court's decision. The hearing is on 22 March 2019, held in a blank-walled courtroom packed with people in the multi-storey Law Courts building in central Sydney. A fire alarm keeps sounding while the lawyers argue. It's like this case is jinxed.

The judges don't take long to come to their decision. The High Court will not overrule the appeal court's decision. When it is over, the families and I go into another, smaller, official room, this time in the State Parliament building. I face them and try to hide my tears.

I never cry. I try to joke that this is hayfever causing me to choke.

'I'm standing here, looking into your eyes, guys, and I just see the pain and the sorrow and I just don't know what to say,' I manage.

Through tears, I recognise so many different faces in the room, all wanting me to say: *Fuck this, we're not giving up. We're going to try something else.*

But I have nothing to offer them. Over three decades, through two police investigations, different inquests, two trials, the appeal court and now the High Court, we've failed to put their kids' killer in prison.

Looking at the roomful of desperate, saddened faces, I remember how the judges stood and walked out of the courtroom after announcing their decision, without a word to the families, without a backward glance.

There's no compassion in the court system, I think. *Just arrogance.*

Broken Beyond Repair

November 2018: 33 years in

Things move fast in the last few weeks of 2018, as we are also hurrying to complete our brief of evidence on William's disappearance, ready for the inquest next March.

In November, I get an email from an investigator working for the police force's insurance company. Craig, the officer who was in charge of the William Tyrrell case, has made a claim against the cops. The investigator's email says:

> The Claimant has alleged whilst working with yourself on SF Rosann, there had been a significant deterioration in the working relationship (between yourselves) as a result of proposed work practices (in respect to a person of interest to the Strike Force). The claimant has described some of these practices as illegal and unethical ... The Claimant stated the working relationship with yourself was broken beyond repair.

Reading it, I am offended. That wasn't what happened, or how I saw our relationship. I wonder what this might mean but, once again, am distracted by the work ahead.

Scott tells me not to worry, he's taken care of it.

***

On 4 December, a senior official in the Department of Justice emails about getting the coroner to grant a court order for us to search Paul's home and car. He seems supportive, saying 'you may wish to consider providing' the coroner with an application outlining how Paul lived so close to the house where William went missing; how 'there has been no forensic search of his house, car, garage or carport, caravan etc', to date and how, without one, 'should any person be charged in the future, such person could reasonably say that a necessary step to eliminate [Paul] from suspicion has not been taken'.

The coroner grants the order, while we keep working long hours trying to clear the backlog of unreviewed recordings from Paul's home, as well as trying to find out more about the two paedophiles, Tony Jones and Frank Abbott. Especially with Craig off sick, I just don't have enough resources to do everything. The interest in William's disappearance is waning, and with it the number of staff the police will commit to finding him. *Failing to properly resource a criminal investigation is also a crime*, I think. *But we can make this work. It's solvable.*

The inquest could give us the breakthrough we need.

***

On 20 December, I'm copied into an email from Scott about the investigation into the death of Theresa Binge, the cousin of Clinton Speedy-Duroux.

Since going up to Toomelah to meet Theresa's family, I've got to know the local cops and we've started looking at a person we think knows more than he's admitted. I've also started to suspect there might be someone else involved, if not in Theresa's killing then in disposing of her body or protecting the killer afterwards. I'm sure the case is solvable. It just needs time, commitment and resources. I've suggested that, along with the local cops, I keep pursuing it.

Scott's email says I've overstepped the mark; Theresa's unsolved murder has instead been sent for a review by someone else. When that comes back, it will be put through what he calls a quality control process and a committee will decide whether to investigate it further.

I feel gutted. What am I to tell Theresa's family? News like that will only cause them grief.

***

I'm at Mum's place in Port Macquarie for our first Christmas without Dad. There is an emptiness in the house without him. I drift about it, wishing I had spent more time here with him when I could. Mum seems distracted by the family and playing host – Jake is here, as well as Gemma with Matt and little Zion – but I know she is missing him deeply. After we're gone, the house will be too big and quiet for her to be here alone.

Paul calls me three days after Christmas. His car has been returned to him following the search covered in white fingerprint dust left by the forensics team. He wants me to sort it out.

This is an opportunity to talk to him again.

I borrow my mum's car, leaving my gun behind, and drive over to his house alone, arriving just after 10am. Once more, unsure what Paul might do or accuse me of doing after, I record the conversation on my mobile.

He's friendly, greeting me with an unguarded, 'How ya doin'?' We talk about our Christmases. He says the powder on his car seems to disappear when you wash it, but it comes back. I say I'll take some photos and we can arrange to get it cleaned, or recommend something he can use to do it.

We talk about the inquest coming up. I ask if he's got a solicitor. He says that he hasn't.

'As I've said, it's, you know, if you do want to talk ...' I say.

Paul says he's got nothing to talk about. He's told me the truth, he says again. 'I always tell the truth.'

I try again. Maybe it was an accident, that it wasn't him who hit William. Maybe it was his dead wife, Heather. If I can provoke some emotion, maybe he'll talk to me now.

'This is not the way I usually talk to people in investigations,' I say. 'I just can't help thinking it's a tragic set of circumstances that can be resolved without being painful for anyone. So that's all I'm saying.'

Paul insists he had nothing to do with William's disappearance. I try again, then leave it.

We're standing outside, on his bush block. It's a hot summer morning. The place reminds me of my parents' house in Dural when I was young, before joining the police.

'It's peaceful out here, isn't it?' I say.

'Oh, it's beautiful, yeah,' says Paul. It is beautiful country. It is a shame that so much death has ruined it.

We chat about the cricket, I say I'll get his car sorted. 'All right. Well you take care,' I tell him.

'Yeah.'

'OK.'

'All the best to you over the New Year,' says Paul.

***

A new year. If I was tough before, I resolve to be tougher. On 2 January, I email the team I lead in the Homicide Squad, telling them where their work over the past year impressed me, and what we need to do differently in 2019.

Working on Strike Force Rosann has broken many staff, I tell them, but I want to thank those who have hung on in there and understand the importance of solving a crime of this nature, regardless of whether our organisation fully understands or supports it.

I've also decided to act on my own sense of isolation, writing that it is detrimental to team harmony when decisions I've made are undermined, even after I've given everyone an opportunity to speak up on them.

It has also come to my attention that some people on the team might not want to be here, I write. If that's the case, and you don't wish to be part of this team, for whatever reason, then I will help you leave it.

***

On 19 January 2019, I head northwest, to Glen Innes, to investigate a critical incident, where two cops have been shot. Watching their bodycam recordings is terrifying. They pull up at a house, get out of their car and start talking to a man on the balcony. Then he shoots them. Both of them survive, but are badly injured.

A day later I go to Newcastle, on the coast, to help the local cops with a murder. We get some information into the local press and receive a tip-off in return. The suspect is arrested in a fast food joint opposite the police station.

On 22 January, the day after I get back to Sydney from Newcastle, I'm preparing to travel north again the next morning, to meet the legal team involved in the inquest into William Tyrrell's death in Kendall.

If Dad hadn't made me tough, this pace of work would break me, I think. *It would be great to sit on the deck right now and have a beer and tell him what I'm thinking.*

Just before 3.30pm, I'm told an inspector from the force's Professional Standards Command is here to see me. He is polite, professional, with greying hair and glasses.

He hands me a three-page document. The first sentence reads, 'You are a suspect in a criminal offence.'

There are five allegations: that I prepared false affidavits; that I misused my authority to influence others to prepare false affidavits; that I made a surreptitious recording of a phone call with Paul, the elderly neighbour, over a year ago, in November 2017; and that I made surreptitious recordings of my visits to his house on 2 and 3 May.

'As this is a criminal investigation, it is intended to caution you,' the document continues. 'You are directed not to interfere or compromise the integrity of this investigation in any way.' There is a long list of cops I am not allowed to talk to, including my own strike force.

I am also not to speak to William's family.

Why Are They Doing This to You?

January 2019: 33 years in

My mum is in tears on the telephone. She's only recently lost Dad and now her son's been accused of falsifying evidence.

'Why are they doing this to you?' she cries. 'I feel like telling someone. I feel like ringing the Prime Minister!'

'Mum, don't be stupid.' I try to reassure her. Jake and Gemma call, to ask if I'm alright. I don't know what to tell them.

On 23 January, Stuart, the boss of State Crime Command, emails every one of the hundreds of cops working under him, to tell them Professional Standards are looking at a case being worked by the Homicide Squad and 'I direct all of you not to discuss this investigation.'

The Homicide commander, Scott, also tells the entire squad I'm facing serious criminal charges and may not be coming back. Inevitably, news of the investigation leaks and I am front-page news.

I am assigned a 'Monitoring Officer', who I am to meet with on a fortnightly basis. I don't know if the choice is ironic or deliberate, but it's Linda – my old partner from Hornsby and, later, the Homicide Squad commander I argued with about the Bowraville investigation. On 24 January, I write to Stuart and Linda, asking that I be allowed to keep working on Strike Force Rosann. Pulling me off it now, after years of work and just as we are about to go to an inquest, risks damaging the case itself, I tell them. 'We will not get a second chance at this investigation.'

The Police Association, the cops' industrial body, also writes to Stuart, saying the force's handling of this 'will have an immediate dramatic negative effect on the investigation'. No one else has worked this case as long as I have. With the inquest two months away, why not allow me to keep working, even as an advisor? Put an independent inspector in place to supervise me if necessary, the letter says.

A week later, Stuart writes back, saying this will not be possible 'due to the complex investigation process underway and the potential of exposing either Gary or one of the team inadvertently to any further harm'. That use of 'further harm' makes me fear they have prejudged their own investigation. Stuart seems to think the harm I am accused of causing has already been done.

***

In February, I fly to Brisbane to watch Jake's passing out parade before being deployed to Afghanistan with the army. As his father, I'm thinking, *I'm meant to be the tough one, it's my job to protect you.*

Before he leaves, I tell him to be strong. That night, we're staying in a hotel with Mum, Gemma, her husband, Matt, and little Zion and my mum's fussing over Jake, telling him to be careful and how she's worried for him.

I tell her to stop it. 'Mum, we don't want him soft now. Let him be hard. He needs to be a soldier, he is going to war.' I think back to when I passed out of the police academy 34 years ago. Dad didn't say much at the time, but I reckon he would have been thinking something similar about me back then.

***

On the morning of 13 February 2019, the custody manager at Sydney's inner-city Redfern Police Station reads out the words of the standard police caution, which I have heard read or said myself to so many crooks before now: 'You do not have to say or do anything, but anything you say or do may be used in evidence. Do you understand that?'

'Yes.'

On his paperwork, under 'Name of vulnerable person', he writes 'Gary Jubelin'.

Not that vulnerable, I think. I made my own way here this morning. I know what's coming, and I'm ready for it.

I'm shown into the grey interview room, and this time it's me sitting at the far end of the table, facing the ERISP machine. Two detectives from Professional Standards are on either side of me, the desk between them crowded with documents and disposable cups.

I don't blink. Rooms like this used to be my happy place. I will stay calm and answer their questions. This is my chance to get out ahead of their investigation and have them understand exactly what I did and why I did it.

'These five allegations all relate to a person of interest, Paul,' says Darrin, the detective inspector who first served me with the paperwork notifying me I was facing investigation and who now leads the interview.

I tell him why we looked at Paul: the stalking of the postwoman, taking our covert camera, his strange outbursts on the listening devices, the confusion over when he saw the Spider-Man suit. The fact we could not account for his movements in the hours after William went missing.

Darrin sits in silence. He's smooth, well-dressed, with greying hair swept back from his forehead, which is set in a frown. His offsider, a jowly detective sergeant called Neale, sits in his chair, with his chin in one hand.

I explain we were trying to get Paul to talk, how our approach was documented and signed off by senior police. How, after I did a formal interview with Paul, he started saying I'd put him in a freezing room and not given him a drink.

I *did* record the conversations, I say. I did so to protect my lawful interests. I try to explain my thinking to the detectives: what if Paul made another allegation that I'd abused him? We'd had problems with the listening devices. I needed some protection.

Darrin mentions the affidavits used in court to request a warrant authorising our listening devices. He asks, 'Have you ever directed any officer of what material should or should not be included in that affidavit?'

'No.'

He hands me a copy of one affidavit I signed off on when working with the strike force.

I read through it and look up. 'I'm very comfortable and all the information there is reported accurately.'

'Are you aware of any misleading information contained in that affidavit?'

'No.'

'Are you aware of any false information contained in that –'

'No.' I cut him off. It's obvious they have nothing. I've been accused of falsifying evidence used in a court process on the basis of what? They haven't told me where the allegation came from and Darrin doesn't seem to have anything to back it up.

Darrin doesn't press the point. But I am seething. These allegations, which make me look like a corrupt cop, have already been leaked to the media. *I'll never get my reputation back from that*, I think.

I hand over a stack of paperwork I've pulled from the police computer system, including Strike Force Rosann progress reports and the minutes of meetings chaired by Scott and attended by inspectors from the surveillance and undercover branches. Despite not being allowed back into the Homicide Squad offices, I still have access to the computers and, if I am going to be investigated for going after Paul, I want it understood that I didn't do so without my bosses' agreement.

'In summary, a commitment was given from the various commanders to fully support the operation,' I tell the detectives. 'The strategy is not one person going off blindly, it's a considered strategy supported by the top level of State Crime Command.'

***

Five days later, I'm sitting in the small office the cops have put me in while I'm under investigation when David, a detective chief inspector, walks in and says Scott's told him to collect all the documents from the case, which I've been using for my defence. He's well-meaning, with an old man's white moustache and greying eyebrows, but just shrugs when I protest, saying he's only doing what he's been told to do.

David will now be running Strike Force Rosann. He piles up the documents and walks out of the office. Watching him go, I hope he's bringing a more positive attitude to the investigation into what happened to William.

My new office has a glass front wall facing onto the hallway, so anyone walking by can see in, which makes me feel like a zoo animal. Each day, the senior officers who put me here walk past on their way to or from another meeting.

I've been taken off my cases and given no work, so every day I turn up, take a seat and listen to whale song or meditation music, partly to relax and partly to show my bosses that if they're trying to stir me up, it isn't working. I imagine that they want me to snap, run out into the corridor and scream so they can suspend me. Instead, I prowl my tiny, glass-walled office, knowing full well that there is only one likely way out of here; the cops will put me on trial.

In March, another of my former Homicide commanders, Mick Willing, takes over as the Police Commissioner's assigned delegate, meaning it is he who will decide my future. I think back to how Mick and I got into a yelling match on more than one occasion. In fact, all the bosses who might have a say in whether I get out of here are people I've fallen out with. My relationship with Linda's never been the same since I blew up at her over the Bowraville murders. Scott and I weren't close when he started at the Homicide Squad, and drew further apart during his time there.

To him, I guess I was just another problem. He wanted cases dealt with quickly, while I was prepared to fight to keep working on them. That's who I am. I've fought everyone since Trevor challenged me in school, shouting, *Come on, come on, I'll fight you!*

I fight for my cases now, like every other detective should go in to scrap for theirs. That's what our victims' families are expecting. That's what I promise them, and I hold that commitment sacred – more so than loyalty to my bosses.

I don't regret this combat, though, looking back, I realise I am war-weary now as well as battle-hardened. The person I am now is so fucking different from when I joined the cops. That's because, in Homicide, every case is life and death. We bleed for them. They never leave us.

Each case I've worked has taken a piece out of me and added a piece. Until there's only pieces.

***

After telling me they are only looking for specific files, the cops decide to go through my phone again, downloading everything this time and finding two more recordings.

One is from February 2018, during one of the darkest days in my separation from Tracy. Representing myself in court against barristers dressed in braces and bow ties, trying to understand what was being decided about my private life and unable to afford a transcript, in desperation I'd recorded the conversation on my phone, to listen to it later. The second recording is from my last visit to Paul after Christmas.

Once again, I am cautioned and, on the morning of 5 April, sat down for another recorded interview with Darrin from Professional Standards.

The interview is brief – I tell them, yes, I did make the recordings. In court, I had been up all night working on the legal papers, and trying only to make sure I did not make a mistake in my written notes. There was no malicious purpose.

Darrin asks if I'm aware it is an offence to record any part of a trial or conference in court?

'No, I wasn't,' I say. Of course, I've seen the signs inside court buildings telling people not to use their phones during a hearing, but I wasn't thinking clearly. 'I'm aware in courts obviously you can't take photographs, but, ah, no, I wasn't aware.'

Eventually, the cops drop this.

Darrin moves on. What about the conversation with Paul?

Again, I say, that was to protect my lawful interests. When the interview is over, Darrin tells me the most serious charges, accusing me of falsifying affidavits, are being dropped.

I look at him. Am I supposed to be relieved? Does it even matter now? Everyone has read about those allegations in the paper. I've been taken off my cases.

We take the lift to the ground floor together and, once outside, Darrin looks around and says he's never seen so much interest in a case like this from the people above him.

It's out of control, he says. Some people are on your side. Other people want to crush you.

This feels like a witch-hunt.

A Decision Made in Anger

25 March 2019: 33 years in

The William Tyrrell inquest begins in Sydney. No one will explain the decision, but I haven't been called as a witness. Bill is on the list, as is Paul. In the years I spent running this case, I oversaw the investigation of both but my name is missing. William Tyrrell's foster parents, his birth parents and the lawyer representing Bill all ask that I be called to give evidence, but their requests are rejected.

I ask the cops if I can attend, not as a witness but just so I can be there, and am sent a written Commander's Direction from Linda saying no. She says she's concerned my attendance might compromise the integrity of the police force and any ongoing investigation.

Being shut out is offensive. I made a promise to William's foster parents, Tom and Jane, that I'd be there.

Fuck this, I think. *I made a promise and the cops are telling me to break it. I'll leave the force.*

I will retire.

It's a decision made in anger, by a man who feels abandoned.

***

On 8 April, I write to Mick Willing and Deputy Commissioner Dave Hudson, saying I no longer believe I have a future in the New South Wales Police Force. More details of the internal investigation have just come out in one of the Sunday papers, yet there was no mention that the most serious allegations, of falsifying evidence, will not be going any further.

I tell Mick and Dave how, after reading this online, my son, Jake, called me from Afghanistan, to ask if I was alright, when he should be concentrating on his own safety. My daughter, Gemma, is also now having second thoughts about joining the cops, because of the stigma that's been attached to her father.

I tell them I plan to retire in three months' time, around 12 July. Being taken off the investigation into William's disappearance has been soul-destroying, I write. I ask to be allowed to provide a handover of everything I know about the case before I leave the force.

My email says we owe it to William's family to do everything possible to find out what happened to him. I also need to de-brief with the Bowraville families before my retirement, and assure them their fight for justice will not be forgotten.

As Homicide commander, I would have expected Scott would have made sure that this happened.

I meet with Mick and Dave in April. Dave says he doesn't want to see me leave the cops. If I do leave, Mick says the internal investigation will not have any impact on me.

That won't help if you pursue criminal charges against me, I think. At home, I've started smoking in the evenings, two cigarettes a day, a self-destructive habit I thought I'd given up before joining the police. I tell myself I just need something to deal with the pressure. I write again to Mick and Dave at the end of April, asking to provide a handover on the investigation into William's disappearance.

In May, I write a third time, trying to convince them it's in everybody's interest for me to pass on what I know.

No handover takes place. On 13 May, I formally confirm my retirement, in writing.

***

Outside the cops, William Tyrrell's foster mum, Jane Fiore, calls me often, though both of us have been told not to talk to each other. She tells me the police are shitbagging me to her, saying that I'm a bad detective, that I have mental health problems.

I'm starting to lose faith in myself and those around me. I get a sense of what I've put people like Paul through. In June, I go on holidays to Portugal with Jake, while he's on two weeks' leave from Afghanistan. The plan is for both of us to find some quiet and go surfing, just like we did when he was little.

It's difficult to find the peace we're after. I can tell Jake's mind is still with his mates, on active deployment. It helps give me some perspective – I can't whinge to him about what I'm going through when he will soon be heading back to a war zone – but I am never far removed from my own conflict either. Waking up in the mornings, I receive barrages of texts and emails from the Bowraville families, talking about a new parliamentary inquiry being held in July, looking again at the laws around double jeopardy.

Once again, their hopes have been raised that this may finally clear the way for James Hide to have his acquittals overturned and face retrial. And, again, I'd been expecting to give evidence, but the families have now been told I cannot because of the allegations hanging over me.

They tell me they are lobbying the police force and politicians to allow me to attend. I send a text to Mick asking for his approval.

I like Mick, and I trust him. When he took over the Homicide Squad, he brought a good energy with him, he wanted to make a difference and respected his detectives. He stood with me at the first parliamentary inquiry into the Bowraville murders, back in 2014. Since then, he has risen through the police hierarchy, becoming an assistant commissioner.

On Thursday 13 June, he texts back saying: 'I understand the request and the issues you raise and am sympathetic to it. I will talk to the Deputy over the weekend and let you know.'

On Friday 14 June, the police create the paperwork to begin the process of charging me over the recorded conversations with Paul. I am to be treated like a criminal. I later learn that, as the commissioner's appointed delegate, this is Mick Willing's decision.

I arrive back from Portugal at 6am on 19 June and get a call from Darrin at 11am. He says I'm being charged under section 7(1)(b) of the *Surveillance Devices Act*. There are four separate charges, relating to the phone conversation with Paul that I asked Greg to record in the Homicide Squad offices and the three times I visited Paul's house, recording what we said to each other on my phone, while the listening devices were also recording.

Darrin asks if I will come and meet him, so he can serve me with the documents?

The cops didn't have to do this. They know that no one was harmed by those recordings, and I've explained why I made them. They don't have to explain their decision. Maybe their thinking is that they can't be seen *not* to charge one of their own; that failing to do so would be like going back to the bad old days before the Wood Royal Commission.

They are also already publicly committed. Having taken me off the investigation into William's disappearance, so close to the inquest, they have to have something to show for it.

It is an awful moment and sickness chases anger around my stomach, but I realise this confirmation of my worst fears also releases me from the responsibilities I have as a police officer.

I no longer have a duty to serve.

Like a runner crossing the finish line only to collapse, without carrying this burden, I have no reason to keep moving foward.

'How about you go and get fucked?' I tell Darrin. 'You're treating me like a crook, I'm going to act like a crook. You want me, come and find me.'

Nothing Here to Celebrate

20 June 2019: 34 years in

The worst part is the silence. After Darrin's phone call, I train for hours, trying to exhaust myself, but at midnight, I am lying awake in bed, staring up at the ceiling.

At 2am I get up and read through the *Surveillance Devices Act* again. It's all there: 'A person must not knowingly install, use or cause to be used or maintain a listening device to record a private conversation', unless the recording 'is reasonably necessary for the protection of the lawful interests' of that person. I did it to protect my lawful interests.

But at night, alone in my apartment, I have no way of explaining this in public. I have to wait until the cops charge me. Then I have to wait until it gets to court.

After day breaks, I speak to Margaret Cunneen SC, the barrister I have asked to represent me and who prosecuted the James Kelly killing in 2000, the first Homicide case I worked as a detective. She says the police have listed me as wanted, meaning every cop in New South Wales has the authority to arrest me. Feeling exposed, I call Darrin again and apologise for yesterday. He's treated me like a crook, just like I told him to.

Darrin says he wants to meet.

I tell him that I'll call him tomorrow morning. I want one more day of freedom.

***

The next day, before I ring Darrin, I call Mum to let her know what's coming. I don't call Jake, who is now back in Afghanistan and doesn't need the extra worry. I call Gemma; it's Zion's first birthday, and I try to make a joke of it: 'Happy birthday. Guess what your grandad's going to do today! He's getting charged!'

At 8.30am I call Darrin and we agree that he'll drive to my unit in an hour. At 8.50am, my phone lights up with a call from a TV journo. I don't answer. At 9.06am, the journo tweets: '@7NewsSydney understands former William Tyrrell lead investigator, Detective Insp. Gary Jubelin, will be charged today.' The news can only have got out so fast from the police force itself.

Darrin doesn't leak it. He listens to the same news being reported on 2GB radio as he drives to meet me. That means it came from somewhere higher, after he reported what was going on to his bosses. Around 9.30am, he and Neale park close to my apartment. I walk up, open the rear door and get in without warning. They jump. I tell them to relax. It's a show of confidence on my part; I won't let them know that I am broken.

Darrin hands me the Court Attendance Notice, giving me details of when and where to appear, and I take it back into my apartment, collapsing on the lounge to read through it.

I turn on the television and watch news of what's just happened breaking on every channel I switch to.

***

On 24 June, I drive to Bowraville again to meet the politicians on the parliamentary inquiry considering another possible change to the double jeopardy laws. They are, understandably, suspicious.

'I'm not Roger Rogerson,' I tell them and, slowly, convince them to trust me. We talk about the murders, the long history of inquests, trials, the appeal court and the High Court. We talk about how the final decision came down to the meaning of individual words in the legislation, not evidence.

In their report, published a few months later, these politicians will express their 'profound and sincere empathy with the families of Colleen, Evelyn and Clinton', and acknowledge that 'at the root of this unique injustice are the inadequacies of the police investigation that immediately followed each of the murders, borne from systemic discrimination'.

They will also say this is a complex area of law and they do not support a bill that's gone before the parliament in an attempt to change the double jeopardy legislation again.

That seems to be an end to the Bowraville families' hopes of challenging the courts' decision. It feels like only moments have passed since I was standing with them, celebrating victory in the boxing ring on the third day of an appeal court hearing in which we were feeling hopeful. And yet, since then, everthing is different.

***

On 6 July, I get ready to go into State Crime Command for the last time to pick up my few personal belongings. I start to put on my suit, but think, if they're treating me like a crook, I'm not going to turn up in my detective's costume. Instead, I wear jeans and a casual shirt. I catch the train in, just like I used to, and, when I arrive, am escorted back to the small glass-fronted office where I spent the past few months.

I pack up everything in a few boxes and walk out, leaving my badge lying on the empty table.

I hate the thought of being without it.

Paul Jacob, my first sergeant in Homicide, drives me home and helps carry the boxes into my unit. He was my mentor, my sifu, a tough, hard-driven cop from the generation who'd survived the royal commission and who cared about the victims more than his chances of promotion. He's everything I've always loved about being a detective but it now feels like he and I are two of the last gunslingers left standing, while the police force has changed around us.

Now I am gone.

Jaco invites me to lunch. Nodding at the boxes, I tell him, 'No, I'll deal with all this.'

'Are you sure?' he asks me.

'Yeah. There's nothing here to celebrate.'

Red Sun

13 July 2019: first day out

The first day after my retirement, I get up at 4am and work till 8am, pulling together an outline of all the work Strike Force Rosann did on Paul under my leadership, to send to the lawyers working on the inquest. Before I was pulled off the investigation, they'd seemed ready to focus on Paul. They talked about playing him the tapes of our listening devices in the court and asking him to explain what he meant in certain recordings. We'd talked about offering him immunity from prosecution, as I'd done before with Michael Atkins. But now I worry about a conversation I had with the counsel assisting the inquest, who called me after the news I was facing an internal investigation leaked, suggesting he and I meet up for a drink.

When we did so, Gerard seemed to now think Paul could be eliminated from the investigation. I email him, asking about this.

Gerard writes back, saying, 'I think you got the wrong impression about [Paul], or my views about him. I don't think he's even close to being a strong contender. The point is that he doesn't look like a strong contender BECAUSE of all the work that was done on him.'

William's foster parents also tell me the investigation into Paul has been shut down. They've been told there just isn't the evidence to keep going. That you have to make decisions based on facts, and there isn't any evidence against him.

'Why are the police stopping?' Jane asks me. She and her husband, Tom, are struggling to understand what's going on, except that the police are now looking at other people.

I am no longer a detective, meaning I am powerless to answer.

***

On 30 July, I go to the Downing Centre Local Court in central Sydney for the first time. It is a short, administrative hearing, but a chance for me to say publicy that I will fight the charges.

Standing beside me on the steps of the courthouse are Mark and Faye Leveson. Arms folded, looking out at the waiting TV cameras, they are just as decent and quietly determined as I remember from those long weeks of searching for Matt's grave. Only, this time, everything is reversed: they are here for me, not I for them; I am no longer a cop but an alleged criminal; I am no longer providing my strength to others but looking for support.

Mark reads a statement from the couple:

> We stand here today, with our support right behind Gary Jubelin. A former police officer who will work hard, push the boundaries, think outside the square and, very importantly, consider the victims of crime, always.
>
> … Gary was instrumental in gaining information that led to the location of our murdered son's remains during the course of our coronial inquest. We could not conceive what it would be like to lose our 'go to' person during the course of that inquest. This is exactly what has been done to the families of little William Tyrrell and that is bloody disgusting.

He says everything I wish I could say, but know I should not while the court process is in motion. Among the tattoos Mark's had etched into his skin since his son went missing is a portrait of the actor Charles Bronson, from the 1974 movie *Death Wish*, playing a man who becomes a vigilante. In the tattoo, Bronson is holding a pistol but, ask Mark about it, and he says it is not a symbol of vengeance, but of refusing to be beaten. Of peace, not violence.

I'm proud to be able to draw upon his courage today.

***

The days pass, though I have little influence over what they bring with them. Once I held the power to pursue a suspect, to arrest them and take away their freedom. Now I have nothing and nothing makes sense. On 5 August, Andrew Scipione's replacement as New South Wales Police Commissioner, Mick Fuller, is asked about me during a press conference at the opening of a new police station in western Sydney. 'If I saw him, I would certainly stop and shake his hand and thank him for what he did,' Mick says. What am I supposed to do with that? You thank me but you charge me?

I try to fill the empty time before my trial and go to Indonesia for a meditation retreat. It means doing it tough, forced to sit in an uncomfortable position for hours without distraction, fighting with my inner demons and my anger.

***

The inquest drags on and, in August, now that I'm retired, I am finally able to sit at the back of the courtroom. It is a strange experience, with months going by between short blocks of hearings, many of which are played out behind closed doors so none of the media, and even Tom and Jane, William's foster parents, don't know what's going on inside.

Sitting in the public gallery, it seems as if the two names that can't be mentioned are mine and Paul's. Last December, when I was still leading the strike force, I wrote out a long statement, explaining everything the police had done to find William and what we had learned over the years. I sent this to the inquest's legal team, but William's foster parents say they've never seen it – it was not in the brief of evidence they have received – nor have they heard it mentioned in court.

Despite my request to be called as a witness, the inquest calls Laura, who left the strike force in July 2018 – over a year ago, and before my time there ended. The ERISP recording of the interview she and I did with Paul is not played in public.

By now, Paul has a lawyer, Chris McGorey, who questions her about the interview, saying, 'There are assertions in there that are troubling to my client … perhaps Mr Jubelin has been careless in what he did.'

I sit there, listening in horror. The lawyer asks if I was right to question Paul over having a view to the back of the house opposite, where William went missing.

'You can't positively assert that [Paul] had a clear line of sight?' he asks Laura.

'Yes, I agree,' she says. I feel like I'm going crazy, watching. I'm in the room but no one asks me to explain if I was careless, or why we asked those questions, or plays the tape of the interview in the courtroom to establish what, exactly, I said.

Instead, I have to sit there and listen to my reputation being shredded. There is no consolation in the fact Laura seems to find it as uncomfortable an experience as I do. By the time she steps down from the witness box, it looks like she's crying.

***

The inquest plans to call Frank Abbott to give evidence. Another witness talks about how he made her uncomfortable, that she didn't want him near her children.

During breaks in the hearings, Gerard Craddock goes out to tell the waiting journalists to expect big things. It's clear the strike force is still working, and for a moment, I feel that same sense of fierce excitement I used to get when an investigation was making progress.

It's good to hear the cops are looking at Abbott. But, instead of the promised breakthrough, we hear about a dying man named Ray Porter, who apparently made a confession to a nurse at his aged-care home.

'I didn't do anything wrong,' he told her. 'All I did was give my best mate and a boy a lift.'

The nurse said Porter claimed he picked up his mate and the boy behind the primary school in Kendall and drove them 300 kilometres north. The nurse says she asked Porter if he thought the boy was William. She says he thought it was him.

Only, Porter himself is now dead, so this account cannot be tested. It's hearsay. Does Porter's dying confession mean anything? Porter was known to have two friends: 'Phil' and 'Frank', the inquest hears. Could 'Frank' have been Frank Abbott? We're left guessing.

Abbott himself is smart. He's also 78 years old now, and having been jailed for child sex offences, may well die in prison. The coroner's allowed him to represent himself by videolink from where he's being held, meaning Abbott gets to listen to other witnesses before giving evidence himself. He is also able to interrogate them in a mocking voice that echoes through the court's audio-visual equipment.

Surely, if you're interested in what Abbott can tell you, you'd put him in the witness box first, before the other witnesses, so he doesn't know what they say about him?

Abbott has also been given a copy of the brief of evidence, so knows everything the police have gathered about William.

When Tony Jones is called to give evidence, Abbott cross-examines him.

'You're full of shit,' Jones fires back at Abbott. I imagine him inside the prison, laughing.

Geoff, Abbott's friend, whose phone records show a call between him and the house from where William went missing, is not called as a witness. One day Jane says she saw him sitting in the waiting room outside the courtroom.

Some days, the inquest holds closed-door hearings at which even she, as William's foster mother, is not allowed to be present. Not knowing what is going on is driving her mad, she tells me.

Sitting in the public gallery, we are sometimes left guessing at what is going on, but it seems that Geoff is of interest because he may be a link between Abbott and the house itself, and he is not a suspect.

***

Throughout September, after the current block of inquest hearings end, I work my way through the brief of evidence the police have gathered against me. I have to keep working. With all this time alone, it is the only thing that stops me falling into a black depression. Each week has to have a purpose. Each Friday, I tell myself, I have to be able to look back and see that I've achieved something.

There is no evidence from Craig in the brief. Since he went on sick leave, I've not heard from him, nor was I ever told the details of what happened with his claim against the police force. But I can see who else on the strike force has given evidence against me, including Greg, the junior detective who recorded my phone call with Paul. His witness statement says I became 'fixated' on Paul and that 'the investigation was deviating away from the core issue', the disappearance of William.

The date on his statement, 8 January 2019, looks familiar. I check my records: that was four days after I called Greg at home, angrily demanding to know why he wasn't at work. He said he wasn't coming back and that he'd transferred to the Unsolved Homicide Unit. I was angry about the transfer and, afterwards, had tried to block the move, saying I needed staff on the strike force to prepare the brief for the coroner.

I also find the witness statement taken from Paul, saying he did not know I recorded our conversations. It's dated 5 September 2019: almost three months after the decision was made to charge me and after the details of these charges were made public.

That matters, because without knowing whether or not Paul had consented, the police could not have known that a crime was committed. This realisation – that they didn't check, they just went ahead with the prosecution – lights a spark inside me.

The year ends in an inferno as bushfires consume the State. Ash from the burning forests is carried on the wind until it falls like rain upon our shoulders. For days on end, a red sun boils through the choking smoke that settles over Sydney.

He Was a Boxer

3 February 2020: seven months out

I've told people I am looking forward to my day in court, but I don't really mean it.

Axeman, our prison witness at the inquest into Evelyn Greenup's murder in Bowraville, calls. He and I have stayed in contact since then and now he warns me about what to expect at trial.

'You can't win. Good guys come last, Gary,' he says.

Right now, I feel closer to him than I do to the police force. Walking to the Downing Centre courthouse on the morning of Monday 3 February 2020, the first day of my trial, I think how we were taught at the police academy that someone is to be considered innocent until they're proven guilty. It feels like a lie now. I've been treated like a guilty person since this started.

I'm also exhausted by the waiting. It's been eight months since I was charged, and more than a year since I was first put under investigation. Yet, I'm so certain the police will try to delay the trial longer, if only to frustrate me, that I woke up this morning at 3am, preparing a list of arguments Margaret can use if that happens.

I'm learning that the State has all the power in court, and the accused man has nothing. Jake's come to stay with me during the trial, and when he got up, he found me sitting at the kitchen table, working. After leaving the regular army, Jake joined the reserves and has just got back from a month in uniform, clearing up after the summer's bushfires. He, too, knows what it's like to face a tireless enemy. One night, he told me, they were pulled back and slept on a cricket oval as the fire advanced again, burning the already blackened ground.

In the end, though, Jake found satisfaction in the work. As we dress for court, Nick Kaldas, my Homicide commander in the early 2000s, sends me a text message: 'Go get them.' Michelle Jarrett, Evelyn's aunt, texts: 'You are our Gumbaynggirr warrior.' The parents of Courtney Topic, whose death in a police shooting I investigated in 2015, have also sent a good luck message. Terry Falconer's widow has done the same.

Jake's girlfriend, Vic, arrives and we leave the apartment together. The two of them have been together for months now and I like her. 'Have you got a spare set of keys in case I get locked up?' I joke.

We walk out, opening black umbrellas against the gentle rain. Both Jake and I are in dark suits. It feels like we're going to a funeral.

'Will Pam be there?' Jake asks. I nod.

'She's dad's ex-, ex-, ex-, ex-, ex-,' Jake explains to Vic, who smiles as if unsure what to make of our family.

'Thanks, Jake,' I say, smiling. The humour helps.

From Museum Station, we walk out the Liverpool Street exit, and look up to see the grand, old court building.

All at once it hits me: *I* am today's defendant. Everything I've been for more than 30 years has been upended. After a career built on bringing crooks to courts like this one, it's only now that I am the accused man that I can really understand what power we wield as cops when we charge someone. Walking with Jake, I'm powerless to know how hard the road ahead will be to demonstrate my innocence, or how long the journey to recover my reputation.

I wish I had my dad walking beside me now. I'd feel a foot taller if he was still alive.

The pack of TV cameras pick me up as I cross Elizabeth Street, just as I've seen them pick up dozens of defendants in cases where I was a prosecution witness. They catch me on the broad courthouse steps and circle round me. I walk up and they part.

Waiting inside are Leonie Duroux, from Bowraville, and her son, Marbuck, a nephew of Clinton Speedy-Duroux, the third child to be murdered. So are Mark and Faye Leveson. Ian Lynch and Angelo Memmolo, both former Homicide cops, are there as well. So are my mum, my sisters and my daughter, Gemma.

But there are no witnesses waiting outside our allotted courtroom. That means, as I suspected, the prosecution have no intention of going ahead with the proceedings today. Despite this, we are ushered in and take our seats. I sit at the front of the court, just behind Margaret and Lauren MacDougall, a fiercely intelligent solicitor, who is working on my defence and whose firm is better known for defending bikies than detectives.

The same ritual I've seen so many times before plays out; a knock on the court door, we stand, the magistrate walks in. We bow. We sit.

Today, the magistrate is Ross Hudson, who walks into the court in a black gown, with short, grey hair, designer glasses and an animal energy. He sits down, looks at us sitting facing him, and starts the trial by saying, 'Counsels, yes?'

It will be he who decides my guilt. Whatever you're accused of, in the local court your case is heard by a magistrate, sitting alone and without a jury. But the police are not ready. Their barrister says they need to get a signature to release some documents we've asked for. There are also many suppression orders in place, prohibiting the discussion of evidence that featured in the William Tyrrell inquest, which itself is currently in one of the months-long gaps between its public hearings.

The nature of these orders means even the magistrate cannot be told what's been suppressed, the police force's barrister is saying. To change that, the coroner will need to vary her orders, and unfortunately that can't happen until 4pm, although he does not explain why she is not now available, or why this has not happened before today.

The magistrate is angry; the delay is 'despicable', but he cannot prevent it. The police barrister also wants him to suppress the same evidence as the coroner, meaning my trial would be heard behind closed doors.

These are my worst fears made real: that I would come here to fight and they wouldn't let me; and that, even if the trial went ahead, it would be held behind closed doors, so nobody could see it. Innocent or guilty, that would mean the police never have to justify their actions against me. Margaret tries to argue but the magistrate says a decision will also have to wait until tomorrow.

Until then, I'm still silenced.

***

Walking out with Margaret and Lauren, a woman I don't recognise asks if she can talk to me. She says that she's come here to support me. Her brother was murdered 34 years ago tomorrow, and the case is still unsolved.

'He was a boxer,' she says.

I like to box, I tell her. 'Keep on fighting for him.'

I wish I could do more to help her.

***

When I get home, Gemma brings her son, Zion, who is now 19 months, round to play at my apartment. We teach him to balance on a sofa cushion, arms outstretched as if he's surfing. His little face is serious, while everyone around him is laughing. Looking at Gemma, I can see her mother, Debbie, in her.

My family don't judge me, I think as I watch them. *They know only too well how much I've given to the cops.*

Don't Cry

4 February 2020: seven months out

Tuesday. Magistrate Ross Hudson doesn't seem impressed by the police force. Inside the tiny, confined courtroom, its walls lined in pale wood like a cheap coffin, he dismisses their attempt to have the trial held in secret.

My mate Bill, who went through the police academy with me, nods to himself in the public gallery, as if saying, *Right decision*. Sue, my childhood friend, sits in the front row near my family and gives me a smile.

The prosecution agree to play the recording of the ERISP interview I did with Paul at Port Macquarie Police Station, which was not played at the inquest into William Tyrrell's disappearance.

After court, I work late, reviewing the hours of recorded material, working out which sections we should play in public. As night falls, Jake and his partner head off to dinner at my mum's place with Gemma and her family. When Jake gets back, I'm still sitting at my dining table, working, its surface swallowed up by stacks of court documents and white ring binders of evidence.

I get to sleep just before midnight and wake up at 3.30 to keep working.

***

Jane Fiore is at the Downing Centre courthouse when I arrive on Wednesday morning. She says she wants to see the interview with Paul. She wants to hear what he told me.

I nod. When I was charged, I told her that, if my case went to trial, it would be an opportunity to tell people what's happened: what Strike Force Rosann achieved; the evidence we gathered that hasn't been made public at the inquest; the mistakes made by police after William's disappearance as well as how the resources given to the investigation waxed and waned depending on the media and political interest.

I take my seat inside the court. Behind me there two rows of seats, both full, with other people sitting on the floor or standing against the walls. Jane sits in the back corner of the courtroom, hands folded in her lap, watching as my recorded interview with Paul plays on two television screens.

She leans forward when Paul says he went out looking for William alone, then came back and had some tea inside without talking to anyone.

'So you thought you'd just sit there and have a cup of tea?' I ask Paul in the interview.

'Well, whether, why I done it or even if I done it, I don't remember havin' it, but, uh, that's not the point,' his voice carries through the courtroom speakers. The only other sound is the reporters tapping on their laptops. Like Jane, they, too, have not heard any of this evidence before.

On the screen, I question Paul about whether he followed the postwoman in Kendall, whether he told her, 'We don't get enough time together.' He says that's crap, and that the postwoman told him that she loved him.

He looks old and thin and grey, on camera, sitting on his own in a police interview room.

'Do you think this could be slightly delusional?' In the back of the courtroom, Jane is still watching closely.

Paul says he left his house with his wife, Heather, at 10.38am on the day William went missing and nobody was then outside looking for the three-year-old. Jane stares, wide-eyed. *She* was out there. So were others.

'That's a lie,' I tell Paul on the television screen.

'That's not a lie,' he responds.

Watching it, I feel uncomfortable, as if I'm looking at someone other than myself on screen, and wondering, *Who is this guy beating up on this poor old man?*

But then I think, *That's what I was paid to do.* If I'm an attack dog on the ERISP recording, it is because the police trained me to become one. Then they put me in the Homicide Squad. They put me in charge of Strike Force Rosann because of what I was, a hunting detective.

What shits me about the cops now is how they don't want to take responsibility for what they unleashed.

***

Laura steps into the witness box. She seems nervous and frowns as she sits down. Her eyes, which are ringed with shadows, like mine are, as if *she* hasn't slept either, skitter across the faces in the courtroom. The prosecutor asks if I told her I was going to use my phone to record my conversation with Paul when I went to his house on 2 May 2018?

'Not that I can recall,' she murmurs, looking down.

Did I tell her I was going to use my phone to record when I went back a day later?

'Not that I can recall.' The same words, but in a whisper this time.

I realise these recordings will now be played in court – sooner than I expected. I lean forward and whisper urgently: 'Margaret, you've got to get me two minutes.'

Margaret asks the magistrate for a two-minute break, and I stand up and search the public gallery until I see Mark and Faye Leveson. I signal for them to join me outside the courtroom, then tell them that they are about to hear a recording in which I talk about their son, Matt. I tell them that I spoke to Paul about him, explaining how we'd been able to find out what happened to Matt and recover his body.

They're going to hear me talk about their son bluntly, calling him 'the gay guy', and saying that he died of a drug overdose, despite Faye's refusal to accept this happened. I tell them I'm sorry they are going to hear this. 'You of all people will understand I'm just trying to bring William back to his mum and dad.'

As they walk back into the courtroom, Mark says to Faye, 'Don't cry.'

The tape of my first conversation with Paul in his home is played. The courtroom listens as I tell Paul how Matt's boyfriend kept his secret for 10 years, but when he finally admitted what happened, you could see the weight of the world lifting from his shoulders. I tell him how Matt's parents made the decision to give him immunity from prosecution, despite believing their son had been murdered.

'He *has* been!' Faye whispers at the back of the tiny courtroom.

When I tell Paul that I believed her son had died of a drug overdose and Atkins panicked, Faye whispers: 'That's what *you* think, Gary.' A moment later she stands up and walks out of the door.

It's wounding to think I have inflicted more pain on her through my actions. I only hope she can accept I was just trying to give Paul a way out, like Atkins, should he choose to take it.

On the recording, you can hear me saying, 'He hasn't gone to jail; that was the deal I did with him. We just needed to get to the bottom of it for Matt's parents, and we got Matt's remains back.'

I'm asking him, *If you know where it is, just help us find William's body.*

A short time later, Faye walks back into the courtroom, and my mum reaches back from her seat in the front row to take her hand. Soon afterwards, the court adjourns. Outside it, I walk up to the Levesons again, holding my breath.

Faye reaches up to embrace me.

I let out a deep sigh of relief.

They Were His Words

6 February 2020: seven months out

On Thursday, I wake up happy from a dream then remember where I am and that I must go back to court today, and think, *I don't know if I can get through this.*

I put on shorts and a T-shirt, hoping to train for the first time this week before leaving, but then I get an email, containing two long witness statements served on my lawyers overnight by the prosecution.

My shoulders slump. I need to read these before doing anything else. I don't make it to the gym.

The only thing that gives me strength is the way the trial has become a kind of public inquiry into the William Tyrrell investigation, exactly as I hoped. In court, Laura is again called to the stand, followed by Greg. They give evidence about how our listening devices were poor quality and that they sometimes failed, about the dysfunction inside the strike force, about how there were thousands of pieces of information sitting on the e@gle.i computer system waiting to be processed and how the backlog of unlistened-to surveillance recordings grew and grew for having too few staff to hear them.

***

On Friday 7 February, the fifth day of the trial, the rains arrive, beating down like they did on Monday, but harder, and putting out the bushfires.

Inside the court, Greg is called back to the stand, and asked about recording my phone conversation with Paul on 3 November 2017. He says he worried the recording was illegal, but that, when he hesitated, I glared and told him, 'Just do it!'

'I was in fear,' he says.

'In fear of what?' the prosecutor asks him.

'Of my career in jeopardy, or being bullied, intimidated, all those things.'

'Bullied and intimidated by who?'

'Mr Jubelin.'

Watching Greg, I remember calling him into my office on the day he left the strike force for his transfer to Unsolved Homicide to thank him for investing almost three years into the investigation – God knows, it broke enough detectives. He'd looked at me in silence then. I thought maybe it was because of my anger when we'd spoken previously about his transfer. I didn't know how, only the day before, he'd signed his witness statement.

When Margaret Cunneen stands to cross-examine Greg, she asks him about his new job. 'That was your long-held dream and ambition, to get a job in that area of the Homicide Squad?'

'It wasn't long-held, but I was lucky enough to get a spot, yes.'

The magistrate picks up on the timing, that within a day of signing his statement, Greg landed his dream job, 'I think his credit is at issue,' he says. 'I am not running the case, but that's my reflection on how this is progressing.'

Other, smaller, consolations follow, when different cops from the strike force give evidence saying that, unlike Greg, they never saw me bully, belittle or intimidate.

***

Later on Friday, Paul is called to give evidence via audio-visual link from Port Macquarie Court House. His face is twice as large on the TV screen as in real life. When asked if he can see and hear what the lawyers are saying, he leans forward, licks his lips and answers, 'Yes.' Amplified through the court's speakers, his voice has a harsh, grating quality.

Paul says he didn't know I was recording the conversations. He says that when I went to his house on 2 May, I was giving him a hard time, saying how I knew he'd done it. 'He wound up saying, "I'll be back tomorrow to take you in", to arrest me,' Paul says.

'To take you in?' asks Margaret, standing at the bar table, looking up at the television screen.

'Yeah, arrest me.'

'I'd suggest to you he didn't say that, sir.'

'He said, "I will be out tomorrow to take you, to pick you up or take you in", something along those lines, because he'd been telling me how it was my fault, I had something to do with it.'

'But he didn't say he was going to arrest you the next day did he?' asks Margaret, choosing her words with care.

Paul insists, 'Yeah, he did. He said he was coming out to pick me up, he's coming out to get me. Those were his words. They were his words.'

I never said that. The recording of my visit has been played in court. I didn't threaten to arrest him. The conversation ended with me saying, 'All right, cheers Paul', and him saying, 'All the best.'

***

My old boss Scott has been promoted to assistant commissioner, which means the Homicide Squad has got a new commander, Daniel. I've never heard of him before, but hope things between us might be different. He's come to court today, so during a break, I ask to talk to him.

I tell him I'm not enjoying this process, that I'm not a rogue cop and that I've been backed into this corner.

There might be times in the future when I can help, I tell him. I'm thinking of other unsolved cases, not only William's disappearance but the murders of the Bowraville children and of Theresa Binge.

He looks at me without reaction and the conversation dies between us. With it goes my last surviving hope, of helping others to work on these cases in the future.

***

By every evening I'm exhausted.

The boundaries between work and home are breaking down. My family, the Levesons, Leonie and Marbuck Duroux and Jane Fiore all sit together in the same corner of the courtroom; they eat their lunch together; they hug each other hello in the morning and goodbye after the court hearings.

I tell myself that I am still unbroken, but it's Friday night and I'm drinking at home, alone. Jake and Vic are out together in the city. Like them, there must be hundreds of places in Sydney I could go to, only I don't want to face having another camera pushed towards me, or having someone ask me how the trial is going.

I don't know what to do, I am so angry. I haven't trained or meditated since the trial began. I haven't had the focus. Instead, I turn on the television and skip through the channels looking for a news program, worrying about what they're saying about today's court hearing.

I can't move on until this is done. Looking at my apartment, where the table is still covered in the white legal folders and a spill of court documents, it makes me think of other nights when I've sat up alone working on my cases.

I can't move on. I'm out of the cops, yet my flat is still covered in court papers.

***

The trial was supposed to last a week, but it drags into a second. On Monday 10 February, Darrin, who led the investigation on me, gives evidence. He confirms that he charged me months before checking whether Paul had consented to the recording of our conversations.

My interview with Darrin and his offsider, Neale, is played in court and it is strangely unfamiliar. The set-up, a narrow table with two detectives in shirtsleeves flanking the screen, is one I've seen so many times before, but never like this. This time, I am the figure sitting at the end of the table, staring into the ERISP machine camera.

Behind me, Mum leans over to my elder sister, Karen, and whispers, 'He looks just like Kevin.'

I've Been Waiting for a Year to Say That

12 February 2020: seven months out

The second Wednesday of the trial. I've been up since 2am, unable to sleep, seeking some distraction. Today, I'll take the witness stand and, leaving home, the shirt sticks to my back in the early-morning heat as I walk to the train station. It's cool inside the carriage, and now I'm moving, I can gather my thoughts. The train carries me underneath the city centre, turning back at Circular Quay, where I get a brief glimpse of the water and open sky hanging over Sydney Harbour before looping towards the city centre again, where I step out into the dark, underground warmth of Museum Station.

From here a short tunnel leads to the exit opposite the courthouse. It is a longer journey than I need to take to get there, but it means I don't arrive looking hot and sweaty. The worst part is the final stretch, crossing the road, being surrounded by the TV cameras, being outside, in public, exposed, before walking into the shadows of the courthouse.

In the lift to the fourth floor, I close my eyes and breathe in deeply before the doors open. In court, I take the affirmation, and Margaret, standing at the bar table, leads me through my career: from the day I joined the cops, 24 April 1985, back when detectives wore short-sleeve shirts with sports jackets and we still used unsigned statements to convict crooks, to my last day of active duty, 12 July 2019, when everything was different. How I've worked homicides since the late 1980s and led investigations into organised crime murders, serial killers, domestic murders and child murders, serving under eight different Homicide Squad commanders.

Margaret asks me about my last boss, Scott. Did I have a conversation with him about a photograph of William Tyrrell that was next to my desk?

'Yes,' I say. And I have since waited a long time to say this in public. If they are going to put me on trial, then I will tell the world what it was like to be the one left trying to find William.

Margaret waits for me to describe the conversation.

'He came over to my desk and … pointed at the picture of William Tyrrell and said to me, "No one cares about that little kid. Get him off the books. Get him to Unsolved Homicide."'

I hear Jane's sharp intake of breath and see her eyes well up across the courtroom. The journalists tap louder at their laptops.

I watch Darrin stand up and walk out of court, then come back a few minutes later and whisper to the lawyers representing the police force. Their barrister stands up and asks for a suppression order to be applied to the whole of my evidence.

The magistrate looks stunned. He refuses to grant it.

Later, the barrister says he would like to put it on the record that Scott denies ever having said that about William.

I wish I could get my denials put on the record as easily as that, I think. *Then we could do away with the whole trial.*

What was it Axeman told me, before this trial got started? *Good guys come last, Gary.*

***

My cross-examination by the prosecutor stretches across the afternoon and will continue into the next morning. He stands at the bar table and leans back, his belly sticking out, with one hand on the lectern, questioning me about my conduct as a detective.

'Your interview with [Paul] on 16 August went for something in the vicinity of four and a half hours?'

'That would be correct, yes.'

'Over 2000 questions.'

'Yes.'

He says I did not suggest Paul speak to a lawyer. That's true, although a custody sergeant had explained his rights to him before the interview had started.

My job isn't to give people reasons not to talk to me. Put yourself in my position. At every moment, working on this strike force, and in that interview room with Paul, there was the possibility that William was still alive. I needed Paul to talk. If we'd been able to establish that he was not involved, that itself would have been some progress.

I broke no laws. If Paul asked for a lawyer, he would have got one, but I wasn't going to suggest it.

The temperature rises in the courtroom. In the public gallery, people are fanning themselves as they watch us.

The prosecutor asks why I didn't caution Paul, telling him he had a right to say nothing. I say that Paul was not in custody.

He's getting more aggressive now, 'Is it possible that that was a deliberate decision on your part because you didn't want to disclose to him from the outset of the interview that you were going to accuse him?'

'I don't forewarn people if I'm going to ask them questions.'

'You put to him that he might have run over William?'

'Yes.'

'You put to him that Heather might have run over William?'

'Yes.'

I feel like I'm shadow boxing: I'm a suspect who's on trial and being questioned about my treatment of a suspect.

The day ends and I can't tell who has come out of the fight as the winner. I go home and change into my training gear, meaning to work the bag hanging in my yard, but I don't have it in me.

Again I can't sleep. By Thursday morning, the folders and stacks of documents spill off the table and along the corridor to my bedroom. But this time, walking through the tunnel from the station with Jake at my shoulder, the atmosphere feels different. The sound of our footsteps echoes off the tiled walls. It feels like we're about to walk into the Colosseum.

Inside, the hostilities resume. The prosecutor says the way I interviewed Paul crossed a line; I didn't warn him that I was going to accuse him, yet I told him more than once that he was lying.

'I suggest that the way you asked the questions, your demeanour, was designed to bully him?'

'It was designed to elicit honest answers from him.'

He says I could have extended the existing surveillance warrants to cover my recording of our telephone conversation.

I say we couldn't roll them over again by applying for another extension, as we didn't have the staff to listen to the recordings we already had, let alone another month's worth.

I also repeat what I've said from the beginning: I didn't trust our listening devices. And that telephone conversation with Paul wasn't recorded so I could use it as evidence, but for my own protection. Equally, I couldn't go to a judge and say I needed a warrant just to cover my back.

A grey-haired woman knitting in the back row of the public gallery drops a red ball of wool onto the floor. It rolls beneath the chair on which my mum is sitting and rests there.

'You also gave some evidence yesterday that Scott had said, from my notes, "No one cares about that little kid. Get him off the books. Get him to Unsolved Homicide",' the prosecutor says.

'I did.'

'You must have found that an outrageous comment?'

'I did find it an outrageous comment.'

He says I didn't make a note of it, or a complaint at the time. 'You are lying when you say that Scott said that.'

'I totally disagree.'

'Just like you are lying about believing that you made these recordings to protect a lawful interest.'

'I disagree.' I'm angry now. We are going toe to toe and I think I can take him. I've been in the witness box countless times over my career – going right back to my time in the Stick-Ups – when lawyers have been telling me I'm lying. Our voices rise.

'You're lying about believing that you were protecting your lawful interests, by making these recordings, in order to avoid the responsibility for your own illegal behaviour, aren't you?' he asks me.

'No, I'm not,' I snarl back.

Here I am, the attack dog. *You want to make me out like I am rough and tough, the kind of street-fighting detective who will do anything to bring a killer to justice? Fine, this is what a real detective looks like.*

The prosecutor smiles at me, then at the magistrate. He takes a seat. He thinks he's won. I step down from the witness box.

***

That afternoon, Margaret stands and says, 'I call Jane Fiore.'

For a moment, silence swells and fills the courtroom. Jane stands and takes quick, certain steps towards the witness box.

'Are you the foster mother of William Tyrrell?' Margaret asks her.

'Yes,' Jane says, and you can see the sadness in her.

'Did you attend the inquest hearings in relation to the disappearance of your son, William, in March of last year?'

'Yes, every day.' She is a calm, deliberate witness. I was reluctant to call her at first, knowing how much trauma she's been through, until she said that she *wanted* to give evidence.

'Did you have occasion to have a conversation with Scott at that inquest?' Margaret asks her.

'Yes.'

'Could you tell the court the circumstances of that, please?'

'We said hello, exchanged pleasantries.' Jane's face lifts as she talks, looking more confidently around her at the courtroom. 'After the pleasantries, Scott said to me, "You are not the only family of victims of crime." I stopped and looked at him and I thought, *No, but you are at the inquest of one of those victims.* He then proceeded to say, "William is not our only case." I then said to him, "William was three years old, he was taken from his grandmother's house. It was a street where there's probably 20 houses on it. We were sitting just around the corner and he's a child in care. I don't think you've got any other cases that can be described like that and I don't think you can just give up on him."'

'Did he make any reply?' asks Margaret, who knows enough to stand back and let her witness say everything she has to.

'No.' Jane starts to cry. 'I then asked him, "So, are you planning on taking William's case to cold cases?" He said, "Yes, it's going to Unsolved." ... I said to him, "You can't send it to Unsolved, you can't do it." He said, "It's going there." I said, "So, it's going to sit in a box and in six months' time you are going to pull it out again, lift up the box and go, 'Oh, nothing new,' close the box and put it away." And I'm saying that and he's looking at me and he's nodding and I'm thinking I can't believe you are saying this to us, here, at the inquest for this little boy. You're saying this to his parents.'

Margaret gently asks if anyone told Jane about a handover being done between myself and David, who took charge of the investigation after I was taken off it.

'I was really worried because I didn't know what was going on,' she says. 'I said specifically to Scott, "Who's doing the handover?" He told me Gary Jubelin was doing a handover with David.' Jane says she spoke to David, who told her there was no handover. That he was not allowed to talk to me.

'I was told by David ... "I don't need to have a handover,"' says Jane. She doesn't need to explain what that meant: All that knowledge gained in the years we'd spent trying to find William, who we had spoken to, what we had learned, where the different pieces fitted, where the cops could look next. None of it was passed between us.

'I am angry,' says Jane, her eyes now overflowing with tears.

The prosecutor doesn't try to challenge her. Jane steps down from the witness box, walks between the rows of seats, takes her handbag and leaves the court. Outside, after the trial is over, Jane sits against a wall, surrounded by a knot of women, including my sister Michelle and Faye Leveson.

Between them, Jane looks up, red-eyed and defiant.

'I've been waiting for a year to say that,' she says.

I Own It

6 April 2020: nine months out

The courtroom doesn't suit this moment. Right now, waiting to hear if the magistrate has found me guilty, I want to be somewhere dark, where I can hide. Instead, we are in one of the bigger, grander courts, where the walls are pastel-coloured, pink and blue and green, lit up by heavy, golden chandeliers suspended from the ceiling.

Magistrate Ross Hudson walks out and takes his seat above us. I close my eyes, running my fingers back over my shaved scalp and down the muscles of my neck, which are as taut as wire ropes.

He speaks fast, his words like machine-gun bullets. 'In terms of these matters, Mr Jubelin, the defendant, was charged with four sequences arising out of offending on 3 November 2017, 2 May 2018, 3 May 2018, and 28 December 2018 in regards to a number of recordings made of conversations between [Paul] and himself.'

I focus on my breathing. The magistrate fires out a short summary of the case, and of the legal precedent he has consulted. Looking down, he turns his sights towards me. 'I have to query this, what evidence?' he asks. Why did I pick out Paul as a person of interest, and why did I pursue him? 'There is no DNA, there are no fingerprints, there is no one necessarily who says, "I saw him go to the backyard where William Tyrrell was or could be." There are no leads, there is nothing.'

What does he expect? I think. *That with no DNA, no fingerprints, no eyewitnesses we just give up?* That's usually our starting point. If we have DNA and eyewitnesses available at the beginning, the Homicide Squad don't even get the call-out. A case like that would be left to the local cops.

As a detective, you can't ignore someone just because you can't find their fingerprints. Sometimes, it's only by eliminating people from an investigation that you can move forward.

I breathe out slowly, unable to say anything.

The magistrate continues: 'The inability to make concessions in his evidence about the way he went about the pursuit of [Paul] does impact upon the determination I'm about to make about Mr Jubelin's reliability and truthfulness as a witness.'

Breathe in.

The magistrate looks up and pauses, so that what he says next will ring out in the almost empty courtroom.

Breathe out.

He says my version of events is 'untenable' and 'unbelievable'.

He's calling me a liar.

I haven't lied. You've got the evidence in front of you. I've been as honest as I can be, to the point where it was painful.

He says my version of events failed to pass the test of cross-examination.

Instead, he says, I was pursuing a strategy at any cost. 'This was above and beyond legality. This was, "I am going after [Paul]."'

That was my job. I needed to be certain before ruling Paul out. Anything else would have been betraying William, and his parents.

The magistrate says he finds me guilty.

I have become a criminal, like all of those I spent a lifetime fighting against. I slump forward, weighed down by the burden of this judgment. It's one more load to put on the scales beside the loss of my career, my reputation and the promises I made to victims' families which got broken when I left the police force.

I told them I would not give up, and now I can't go on, not as a detective.

The scales are tipped against me. There is no place for people like me now in the New South Wales Police Force. The force has changed. During my trial, each of the three Bowraville families received a letter from the Police Commissioner saying, 'As you are aware, all applications, appeals and court proceedings are now currently exhausted.'

Instead, the children's murders will be 'subject to the new Unsolved Homicide Review Process' introduced by Scott. 'The review will be subject to quality control and ratified by the Unsolved Homicide Review Committee ... If a reinvestigation cannot be commenced, the matter will continue to be examined every six months.'

Like the family of Theresa Binge, whose murder was also taken off me by Scott and subject to the same process, the Bowraville mob no longer have the name or phone number of a detective they can call, day or night. William Tyrrell's foster parents, whose son's disappearance was once thought so important the State Premier promised every resource that I needed to solve it, have written to the Police Commissioner and made repeated phone calls to his office. He has not replied or returned their calls.

The magistrate stands. I stand. We bow. He leaves the court.

I shrug and try to smile at my legal team.

I'm still wearing the same black suit, white shirt, black tie I wore as a detective. It's now a crook's outfit.

Leaving the court, I think about what I've put my family through, during this trial, in recent years and, when I think of my children, throughout their whole lifetimes. I wonder if this verdict will change the way they see me.

It nearly breaks my heart to think about my kids. Apart from them, this job was the one thing I was proud of. The one thing I was good at.

Walking outside, I watch the TV cameras surge forward. Already, I am paying the price for what I've done. Yet, somehow, I look up, over the wall of microphones and lenses and realise that, really, I've been fortunate.

I've seen so many things. Seen death up close. Seen people at their weakest and at their strongest. It's all because I joined the cops – and it's all there for anyone who takes on the job, providing they want to push themselves and take some risks and experience some pressure.

If any of these reporters were to ask me what I've done in my career, I'd say I played a part, along with the Bowraville families, in overturning the double jeopardy protections, so that someone who's been found not guilty of a murder can now face trial again, if there is new evidence. I played a part in breaking down the right to silence, when we offered Michael Atkins a deal: immunity from prosecution if you tell us where you buried Matt Leveson. I played a part in raising the reward offered by the State of New South Wales for information about a murder to $1 million, hoping to find William. There are now a swag of other murder cases in New South Wales for which a $1 million reward is offered. I'm proud of that.

I hope some other cop will come forward and finish the jobs I started. But in my quiet moments, I will look back and think, *Fuck, yes, I made a difference.*

***

But if these reporters ask me, 'Do you wish you hadn't recorded those four conversations?' Then, yes, I do. At the time, it was the right decision, but looking at everything that's happened to me since, I wish I hadn't made it.

That's the burden you're given when you join the police force; the decisions you may make in a moment, carry consequences that can last for years, for the victims, the suspects, their families and for you, also.

I made that call. And I never made a secret of those recordings with Paul.

I did that. It's cost me everything, and that's the truth, the whole truth.

I own it.

***

The interview is over. The journalists turn off their cameras, pack away their microphones and start typing out what they will say on the evening news and in tomorrow's newspapers.

Later tonight, when I get home, Axeman will call me and say he's just had the word 'Dog' spray-painted on his door and his house shot up in a drive-by attack. He'll say he's tooling up and is going to go after them.

'Don't be stupid, keep your head down and call the cops,' I'll tell him. 'By the way, I've had a pretty shit day too.'

Yeah, he's seen that on the news and it's no good, Axeman will tell me, but if I end up being sentenced to prison he'll come in and look after me. I believe him. Right now, I do feel close to him and Rocco – my best, and worst, criminal informants.

In the eyes of the court, I have crossed the line between policeman and criminal. Both of them crossed a line when they agreed to cooperate with the police.

Later tonight, Axeman will tell me how, when he decided to become an informer during the Bowraville investigation, he went to see his criminal mates, sat down and put a pistol on the table, loaded with a parabellum round that explodes on impact. He challenged them, 'If you think I'm doing the wrong thing, then shoot me.' They didn't.

This was three children murdered. He'd done the right thing coming forward.

Or take Rocco. He's out of the bikie gangs and living life the right way now, working hard and paying taxes. He could have a hell of a lot more money if he lived the way he used to but he says his outlaw days are behind him. I trust him, so much so that I once said, in another life, he should have joined the cops.

With my days as a convicted criminal just beginning, Rocco sends me photos of his son, saying he hopes the boy will join the police when he's older.

***

Walking away from the court with my lawyers, we stop at the traffic lights, watching the cars roaring past us down Liverpool Street. A male voice yells, 'You're going to be fucked up when you go inside! The boys are waiting for you!'

I turn. He's two metres away from us, his finger raised, ready to throw another threat at me. He looks grubby and vicious, like a petty crook. *This is what being out of the cops means*, I think. I'm on my own and that makes me vulnerable.

There are plenty of people I have put in prison who are now out and living in this city, or who will be released in the coming years. Many would love to see me again, without an entire police force around me. The Perish brothers among them.

I know the TV cameras are still up on the top of the courthouse steps, ready to start shooting if I make a scene here, so I have to be careful.

The grubby bloke's still shouting, 'We're going to fucking do you!' He's expecting me to walk away, so I take a step towards him instead and he falls silent. We stare at each other, and I can feel the anger building inside me at everything that's happened.

The seconds pass.

I am not going anywhere.

He looks down at the footpath and retreats.

I turn back to the road, putting the courthouse behind me. The lights change. I take a step forward.

POSTSCRIPT

On 8 April 2020, Gary Jubelin was ordered to pay a $10,000 fine for recording his conversations with Paul. Gary appealed his conviction, but lost.

In June 2020, police searched an area of bush on the New South Wales Mid North Coast, near where Frank Abbott was living at the time of three-year-old William Tyrrell's disappearance.

In 2021, at the time of writing, it is more than two years since the opening of the inquest into William's death. Deputy State Coroner Harriet Grahame is yet to hand down her findings and no date for this has been set.

William would have been 10 this year.

Bill is taking legal action against the New South Wales Police Force, claiming malicious prosecution, false imprisonment, misfeasance in public office and collateral abuse of process.

To date, no one has been jailed for the Bowraville murders.

Gary's greatest regret on leaving the New South Wales Police Force is those cases where he has been unable to tell grieving families what happened to their loved ones. He is still in contact with many of the families he worked with.

ACKNOWLEDGMENTS

My story would not have been told without the support I've had throughout my life from my family and friends. Over the years, their generosity and sacrifice have allowed me to selfishly throw myself into my career, and given me the confidence to pursue my passions. They also helped to pick me up when I was down. To each and every one of them, I want to give my thanks.

Throughout my police career I have been humbled by the faith shown in me by the many victims' families who trusted me to investigate the deaths of their loved ones. Their resilience when confronted by tragedy has taught me so much about love, life and death. Their support has also given me the confidence to write about these experiences, and for all of this, I want to thank them.

I would also like to thank the dedicated police officers I was fortunate enough to work with, particularly those who taught me my trade and, later, those who trusted me to lead them when the pressure was on. My story is their story also. A special thanks to those serving and former cops who stood strong beside me when I was put under investigation and sent before the courts.

There are also other people in my life who shaped me and whom I would like to thank, many but not all of whom are mentioned in this book. It is as honest an account of what I've learned from each of them as possible. To achieve that, where possible all dialogue, particularly in the interviews with suspects and witnesses, is taken from police records, court documents or other contemporaneous reports. In places, these have been edited for clarity. Other dialogue is how I remember it.

My departure from the New South Wales Police Force was not what I hoped for, and afterwards many people felt an understandable degree of caution about dealing with an ex-cop who had been criminally charged. Amid all this, Helen Littleton, Claire Harvey and Kathy Lipari were three people who believed in me and, between them, helped me to find a way forward, which included writing this autobiography. They gave me my confidence back. I cannot explain how important that was.

It is a confronting experience telling your life story. At HarperCollins, Helen first reassured and encouraged me, then guided me. After more than three decades as a policeman, though, I could write a good set of fact sheets but still needed help turning my life into a book.

I'd known Dan Box for years as a crime reporter, particularly through his work on the Bowraville murders, and knew that his reputation was based on his integrity. The other thing I liked about Dan is that he would call me out if needed and challenge me to ensure the full story was told.

I am in awe of the professionalism Dan, Helen, editors Barbara McClenahan and Emma Dowden, Pam Dunne, Graeme Jones and the others working with HarperCollins have brought to this project. The generosity shown by News Corp Australia in allowing me to concentrate on the book is also greatly appreciated.

Thank you all for helping me tell my story.